# The Conservative Leadership
## 1832-1932

Each volume in the 'Problems in Focus' series is designed to make available to students important new work on key historical problems and periods that they encounter in their courses. Each volume is devoted to a central topic or theme, and the most important aspects of this are dealt with by specially commissioned essays from scholars in the relevant field. The editorial Introduction reviews the problem or period as a whole, and each essay provides an assessment of the particular aspect, pointing out the areas of development and controversy, and indicating where conclusions can be drawn or where further work is necessary. An annotated bibliography serves as a guide for further reading.

# PROBLEMS IN FOCUS SERIES

PUBLISHED

*Britain after the Glorious Revolution 1689–1714*
edited by Geoffrey Holmes

*Britain Pre-eminent: Studies of British World Influence in the Nineteenth Century*
edited by C. J. Bartlett

*Popular Movements c. 1830–1850*
edited by J. T. Ward

*The Republic and the Civil War in Spain*
edited by Raymond Carr

*Financing Development in Latin America*
edited by Keith Griffin

*The Hundred Years War*
edited by Kenneth Fowler

*The Interregnum: The Quest for Settlement 1646–1660*
edited by G. E. Aylmer

*The Origins of the English Civil War*
edited by Conrad Russell

*The Reign of James VI and I*
edited by Alan G. R. Smith

*Sweden's Age of Greatness 1632–1718*
edited by Michael M. Roberts

*Perspectives in English Urban History*
edited by Alan Everitt

*The Conservative Leadership 1832–1932*
edited by Donald Southgate

VOLUMES IN PREPARATION

*Industrial Revolutions*
edited by R. M. Hartwell

*The New Poor Law in the Nineteenth Century*
edited by Derek Fraser

# The Conservative Leadership 1832-1932

EDITED BY
DONALD SOUTHGATE

Macmillan

*First published 1974 by*
THE MACMILLAN PRESS LTD
*London and Basingstoke*
*Associated companies in New York Dublin*
*Melbourne Johannesburg and Madras*

SBN 333 11770 0 (hard cover)
333 11771 9 (paper cover)

*Printed in Great Britain by*
HAZELL WATSON AND VINEY LTD
*Aylesbury, Bucks*

For the *habitués* of the Sandy Park Inn

# Contents

*Preface*                                                          ix

*Introduction*                                                      1
   DONALD SOUTHGATE

1 Wellington and Peel 1832–1846                                    35
   NORMAN GASH

2 Derby and Disraeli                                               58
   J. T. WARD

3 The Salisbury Era 1881–1902                                     101
   DONALD SOUTHGATE

4 Balfour 1902–1911                                               151
   ALFRED M. GOLLIN

5 Between Balfour and Baldwin 1911–1923                           171
   J. H. GRAINGER

6 Baldwin 1923–1932                                               197
   DONALD SOUTHGATE

*Further Reading*                                                 247
*References*                                                      252
*Notes on Contributors*                                           255
*Index*                                                           257

# Preface

THIS volume presents a collection of essays based on published material, including recent writings, though we were fortunate to capture Professor Gash straight from his major work on Peel. References have been kept to a minimum and in many cases omitted altogether. The sources for each essay are, broadly, those listed in 'Further Reading' in each case. Dr Ward's long note on writings on Disraeli, though out of scale, was thought to be too useful to omit. I have commented in the latter part of the Introduction on fields of research which the preparation of this volume showed to have been inadequately tilled.

It had not been intended that I should loom so large in this volume. I wish to thank the other contributors for their patience and understanding while we waited in vain for a contracted essay on Baldwin and while, having despaired of receiving it, I wrote on Baldwin myself. I thank Professors Gash and Cornford for reading my essay on Salisbury and Professor D. F. Macdonald for his helpful comments on the drafts of both the Salisbury and Baldwin essays.

*Chagford, July 1973*                                         D. G. S.

# Introduction

PARTIES seek political power in order to install their leaders in office and in command of the patronage that goes with office, and to defend or advance the interests of groups especially associated with them. Both the acquisition and retention of power under a representative system require, however, a degree of reconciliation between those special interests and the wider interests of the nation as a whole. The leadership therefore often has to disappoint the party stalwarts both from a sense of public duty and of electoral interest (though these do not coincide when what the statesman must do is popular neither with those who usually and those who may conceivably vote for his party).

The Conservative party (from 1912 the Conservative and Unionist party) especially merits study, because it is fairly rare for an avowedly conservative party so to flourish that it can, over many generations, continue to provide (either by itself or with allies whose strength is comparatively minor, though sometimes marginally decisive) the government of a constitutional country, with some intervals as the official and loyal Opposition. The party which formed itself around Peel in the 1830s provides the government of the United Kingdom of Great Britain and Northern Ireland in the 1970s. So long and successful a record argues a continuing, if not wholly consistent, power of adaptation to changing economic, social and constitutional circumstances. It may be thought that the Conservative party has changed, as Winston Churchill put it in the early years of the twentieth century, from one 'of religious convictions and constitutional principles' to 'a new party, rich, material and secular', reflecting a change in the nature of electoral issues and a change in the role of government. Certainly, for all the conspicuous survivals in national and local leadership of members of the nobility and gentry, it is no longer enough for the Conservative party to be the party of agriculture and of the Church of England (which has been described as 'the Conservative party at prayer') and the licensed trade (to which Liberal leaders were over-keen to ascribe their defeats). Nor, indeed, though for two generations the majority of Conservative M.P.s came from the landed classes, and most Conservative Ministers for rather longer, was it ever enough. The party owed its formation to Peel's conviction that the conservative forces which could be mustered in a party, opposed to the Whigs with their large Liberal, Radical and Irish contingents, were wider than anyone else imagined. It lacked a majority for the long period 1846–74 partly because it had become too narrow and partly because from 1855 to 1865 Palmerston combined with great popularity a Whig conservatism in domestic affairs which inhibited the Conservative leaders from rallying their 'natural' strength. But from 1866 they began to gather to themselves not only the Whig minority of the landed interest but a minority, and soon a majority, of the business and professional classes, with a substantial section of the humbler classes in support.

The Conservative party has always combined among its adherents people holding three different attitudes to the Conservative function. Each may be summarised by a quotation from the writings of the marquess of Salisbury, who led the party from 1885 to 1902. As Lord Robert Cecil in 1859 he expressed the Diehard point of view – 'Hostility to Radicalism, incessant, implacable hostility, is the essential definition of Conservatism', and he added, in 1861: 'Once the dyke is breached by small concessions all will be lost'. But in 1863 he was less unyielding. 'We are compelled with heavy hearts to give up our aspirations after ideal churches and ideal commonwealths', he wrote, 'and content ourselves with patching a little here, and altering a bit there, in the hope that the systems under which we may live may at all events furnish us shelter for our time.' Here the purpose of the party is viewed in rigidly defensive terms, but scope is allowed for flexibility and reform, as Peel, Derby and Disraeli had already seen must be the case, though all were too opportunist for Cecil's taste. By 1883 a more constructive note appears. 'The object of our party is not and ought not to be simply to keep things as they are. In the first place, the enterprise is impossible. In the next place, there is much in our present mode of thought and action which it is highly undesirable to conserve. What we require is the administration of public affairs, whether in the executive or legislative department, in that spirit of the old constitution which held the nation together as a whole, and levelled its united force at objects of national import, instead of splitting it into a bundle of unfriendly and distrustful fragments.' Here Salisbury embraces the high purpose of Peel, the founder, and Disraeli, the re-founder, of the party, as a leader must if he wishes to be successful. It is at least arguable that Salisbury's nephew and successor, Balfour, failed as party leader for lack of that purpose.

After a Labour by-election victory in the Liberal stronghold of Jarrow in 1907, *The Times* suggested that the real political conflict of the future would lie between 'the two positive schools, represented on the one hand by Labour–Socialism, with its appeals to class jealousy and its impracticable panaceas and on the other hand by constructive Unionism, with its appeal to the instinct of national and Imperial cohesion, and its programme of practical material progress'. This editorial, which wrote off the Liberals prematurely, assumed an identification of the party under Balfour with a form of planned politics which was foreign to his nature. The real Balfour surely emerges in a speech he made at a Press Fund dinner shortly before the 1892 election. He said that the blindest must see that a change had come over the character of political controversy, speculation and aspiration, which were now concerned with the amelioration of the lot of the great classes of the community. And then he said, with his fatal air of detachment, that it would be 'interesting' to see 'how far the democratic constitution . . . is going to deal successfully with the social problems with which we are brought face to face'.

This collection of essays is not intended to be a history of the Conservative party during its first hundred years. It is not a competitor of Lord Blake's *The Conservative Party from Peel to Churchill*, though that work is naturally much concerned with the impact of the official leaders of the party and the present contributors have to take account of the official leaders' colleagues, especially of powerful ones like the meteoric young Randolph Churchill, the masterful Joseph Chamberlain and the latter's son Neville, who in 1930 so confidently expected to displace Baldwin at any moment. Nor is it concerned especially with Conservative 'philosophy' or attitudes; it is not a successor to, or commentary upon, the writings of Lord Hugh Cecil or Quintin Hogg. It is a study of the leadership of the party from 1832 to 1932. It is an historical study which, while not avoiding comparisons, seeks to avoid that kind of approach to leadership techniques which blur the distinction between one period and another. It is a study of the leaders and how they led. Each essay may be read independently, since the background of each leader is separately dealt with, in order that we may see what were his qualifications for the leadership and why he was chosen or, rather (in most cases), accepted by, the party. An assessment of the merits and demerits of each leader, *qua* leader, is made. This assessment may differ considerably from a rounded assessment of the man as politician or statesman. Though perhaps over-rated as a Foreign Secretary, Salisbury, for instance, was certainly far more impressive in that role than as a party leader. Balfour was far abler as a Minister than as a party leader; Baldwin more adept as a party leader than as Premier. An attempt is made to convey to the reader what sort of 'image' (to use a modern term which is really indispensable) each leader projected of himself and his party. The leader of the Conservative party is still formally the source of its official policy, whether he is Prime Minister or leads the Opposition, and no leader, in the nineteenth century certainly, would have considered holding the position on any other terms. Very much therefore has depended on the leader's image, and how appropriate it has been to the electoral needs of the party at any given time – needs themselves determined in the last resort by the effects of economic and social trends, fortuitous occurrences such as a good or bad harvest, a boom or slump in world trade, a rise or fall in the real cost of living, as well as the nature and effectiveness of the political challenge of a rival party or parties.

This is, by and large, a success story. Every leader either became or rejected the invitation to become prime minister.* Every one except Derby had at some time a majority in the House of Commons, though Balfour, inheriting one, failed first to hold and then, twice, to recover it. Every one except Balfour led the party through a major transformation of the electoral system, and every one but Derby lived to see it triumph under the new dispensation. At the end of the process (so far as the period with which we are dealing is concerned) the aged ex-leader, Balfour, explained in 1928 that he had favoured franchise extension and woman suffrage in 1883, both because there was no point in resisting what was in logic bound to come and because he believed that the more the responsibility was given to the whole community the more Tory would be the result – 'by Tory I mean averse to changes and inclined to continuity'. It is interesting to note that in 1883 Lord Randolph Churchill, who patented the phrase 'Trust the People' for use in his conflict with the party leadership group called 'the Old Identity', was inclined to *resist* giving the franchise to the rural labourer. And it is fair to note that, if Derby called the great franchise extension of 1867 a 'leap in the dark', he made it with his eyes open. *He*, if only in desperation, had decided to trust a wider 'people' than that which had the franchise since 1832. 'I determined that I would take such a course as would con-

---

*Early in 1922 Austen Chamberlain was invited by Lloyd George to replace him as head of the coalition government.

vert, if possible, an existing minority into a practical majority,' he said. The party had been formed in the aftermath of the electoral catastrophe of December 1832, which followed the Reform, which the Tories resisted, and had been managed with such effect that Professor Gash could entitle a book on the system of the 1830s and 1840s *Politics in the Age of Peel* – the very man who had led the resistance and then devoted himself to ensuring that the Reform should be 'final', as its Whig authors themselves intended.

The leaders we study were very diverse in personality and in their careers. One distinction may, however, be noted between the nineteenth-century leaders (excepting Disraeli, who was *sui generis*) and the twentieth-century ones. The former were academically eminent and, belonging to the recognised governing class (though the Peels were recent recruits) entered the House of Commons very young with the prospect of a lifetime in Parliament and an acknowledged eligibility for office and high promotion. Bonar Law and Baldwin (and Neville Chamberlain too) entered the House of Commons as middle-aged businessmen with no apparent prospect whatever of the leadership, which came to Law in 1911 when there was deadlock between the professional politicians Walter Long and Austen Chamberlain, and to Baldwin in 1923 because most of the recognised leaders of the party were temporarily estranged from the Conservative administration of the day. Neither could therefore expect to continue unimpaired the haughty attitude to colleagues and followers maintained by their predecessors. Peel and Salisbury had been haughty because they were shy. Peel, moreover, felt justified in treating the members of his party as 'the finest brute votes in Europe' because they were not, on the whole, politically intelligent and because, in his view, as Norman Gash notes, they had come to him only for the salvation he offered them. Derby was sociable enough, but he was a grandee who chose his own company, and was sometimes found to be incommunicado by agitated colleagues seeking guidance. On the other hand, he appreciated that as a peer he must meet the Tory M.P.s *en masse*, and held many 'party meetings' at his house or the Foreign Office to assuage discontents or explain policy. When Salisbury was leader, such meetings were exceedingly rare. According to his admiring daughter, he lived in intellectual isolation, was at sea in choosing men and 'had a difficulty amounting almost to an incapacity for working with others'. He was very much aware of the need for party organisation, but was personally one of those magnificoes of whom Disraeli had complained that they 'seem to despise all the modes and means of managing mankind'. Borthwick of the *Morning Post* complained to the Chief Whip of the party in 1892 that Salisbury did not understand 'the value of the House of Commons nor the feelings of the Constituencies'. That his leadership became secure although he despised the arts of leadership was due, firstly, to widespread distrust of Randolph Churchill, secondly to the skill and industry of W. H. Smith as Leader of the Commons and Captain Middleton at Central Office and, throughout, to the fact that public appearances and speeches (which he hated) were now the inescapable chore of a party leader. But a remoteness which was tolerable in a peer of great prestige was barely tolerable in Balfour, whose refusal to bother with the drudgery of parliamentary management or the cultivation of his followers is admitted by his admiring niece in the delicate statement that 'his influence may have been too seldom consciously exerted through contacts with the rank and file'. Bonar Law and Baldwin, lacking the prestige and self-confidence derivable from aristocratic connection, and lacking any impressive record before they were chosen, could not afford to be remote. The former was shy, morose and without small talk, and the latter secretive, though a good pipe-smoking listener to other men's chat (as distinct from Cabinet discussions). But they cultivated their followers, as Peel and Balfour had not, and as Austen Chamberlain and Neville Chamberlain did not. They mixed with back-benchers (including the 'mutton-headed' whom their predecessors had too obviously despised) and junior ministers.

Remote as many leaders were from most of their parliamentary followers, each rose to the leadership because he was, or had been, in one way or another, a consummate House of Commons man. Derby and Salisbury were peers when they became leaders, but the former, as Mr and then Lord, Stanley, had been 'the Rupert of Debate' and the latter, as Lord Robert Cecil and then as Lord Cranborne, had been a devastating critic of both front benches. If Peel 'played upon the House of Commons as on an old fiddle', Baldwin, in his day, was almost as proficient. Balfour's first year as Leader of the House (1891–2) was unsatisfactory, because of his nonchalance and lack of industry. His dialectics on Tariff Reform as Prime Minister (1903–5), cruelly terminated by his Liberal successor Campbell-Bannerman with the words 'Enough of this foolery!', were none the less brilliant. And his reputation had been made as Chief Secretary for Ireland 1887–91 as much by his cool effrontery and quick-wittedness in the House of Commons as by his ruthless efficiency in Ireland. After his defeat in 1906 he was never so proficient a House of Commons man and the change from him to Bonar Law in 1911 was a switch from an unpredictable *prima donna* to a sound and reliable debater who usually appeared, as Balfour often did not, to mean what he said and care about the subject under discussion. Law had a power of detailed exposition, without the aid of notes, which served equally in opposition and in office, and somewhat resembled Peel's. The next Conservative Prime Minister after Disraeli might have been Sir Stafford Northcote, who became Leader of the House of Commons in 1876 when the great man became earl of Beaconsfield, if Northcote's parliamentary style had not been more apt for a minister than an Opposition leader. But he lacked the power to inspire and the power, or perhaps the will, to hammer home an attack, and these deficiencies were exploited against him by more robust rivals, namely Salisbury and Randolph Churchill. The latter's House of Commons forays as an assailant of Gladstone, of Whig and Radical Ministers and of his own front bench gained so much from the contrast that Balfour said that if there had been no Northcote there would have been no Churchill.

It might equally have been said that if there had been no Peel, or if Peel had given Disraeli junior office when, though having no patent claim, he importuned it, there would have been no Disraeli. That eccentric's career is a conspicuous example of what, in the British system, can be achieved by sheer parliamentary talent. He lacked not only aristocratic but almost all respectable connections. A foppish Jew whose financial position was suspect, or worse; a man who delighted in his own cleverness and was 'a literary fella' peddling strange, exotic notions about that most pragmatic of institutions, the Church of England – he became the spokesman of the English squires. Though privately regarding them almost with despair, in public he romanticised them. He began his ascent of 'the greasy pole' with brilliant, savage indictments of Peel's progress towards Free Trade which the majority of Conservative M.P.s regarded as a wanton affront to those to whose votes Peel, as a party leader, owed his premiership. Disraeli rose as a House of Commons man upholding House and party against the executive despotism of the Minister–leader, and by 1849 all pretence that he was not the leader in the House of the Protectionist party (more and more reverting to the description 'Conservative'), had to be dropped. For, bereft of the leading men who had been Ministers, the two hundred and more inarticulate members had to give the brilliant debater, however unsavoury his origins, however bewildering his rich imagination, his due. In consequence they found themselves his prisoners. They might, perhaps, have turned into majorities the large minorities of the 1852 and 1859 elections if, by demoting Disraeli, they could have gained a Palmerston or regained a Gladstone. But a combination of their unwillingness to admit their inadequacy and the difficulty of displacing Disraeli from the position which he had won (which he usually, and astutely, professed his readiness to yield) with the reluctance, greater or lesser, of the important recruit to cross the floor, was decisive. And so Derby, who in 1852 had made Disraeli Leader of the House of Commons and Chancellor of the Exchequer although he was not a Privy Councillor and had held no office of any kind, when resigning the premiership early in 1868 recommended him to the queen as his successor. 'You have, fairly and most honourably, won your way to the highest round of the political ladder', he told him. Even so, Disraeli was not accepted whole-heartedly. There were those who complained, with the 1868 election lost after the extension of the franchise to the urban householder, that Derby and Disraeli had 'let the mob in' upon them. Perhaps only the fact that Derby's son and heir, the most frequently suggested alternative to Disraeli, was himself a liberal-conservative, and reckoned especially 'unsound' on the Church, prevented Disraeli being 'replaced' in 1869. As late as January 1872 the leading men of the party were said to have agreed that he had not the position in House or country 'to enable him to do what others might', but no one could be found willing to tell him this.

This episode is strange, because of the assumption that there was some means of 'replacing' the leader of the party when he was out of office. No such means were found when Disraeli, as earl of Beaconsfield, died, still leader, and once again in Opposition. There followed four years during which Northcote, who had succeeded Disraeli in the leadership of the Conservative M.P.s in 1876 and Salisbury, who succeeded him in the leadership of the Conservative peers, manœuvred for the leadership of the party, which would come to one or other in the form of a royal summons to assume the premiership when the Conservatives were able to take office again. Similarly, from 1911, when Balfour retired, his Commons' successor Law, and Lansdowne, who continued to lead in the Lords, were in a sense joint leaders of the party. If anyone made Law *the* Conservative leader it was Lloyd George, simply by treating him as such when and after he included him in his War Cabinet of five. Since he had resigned the lead in 1921 Law did not accept the king's commission to form a government in 1922 until he had been 'elected' at the sort of meeting that had voted no confidence in his successor, Austen Chamberlain. Subsequent practice was, however, modelled on 1923, when the king, on advice (*not* the advice of the outgoing prime minister, Law), chose Baldwin rather than Curzon as Premier and Baldwin subsequently went through the formality of 'election' – really 'recognition' – as party leader by M.P.s and peers.

Disraeli was the most imaginative, as well as the most picturesque, of the Conservative leaders studied here, and in a sense the most creative, in that it has been to him that Conservatives justifying their long-term record and, in successive generations seeking to formulate or reformulate a 'philosophy', and to deny that theirs is simply 'a class party', have recourse. If he does not loom so overwhelmingly in this volume as some might have expected, it is because, as Norman Gash remarked in *Solon* (January 1970), while the Conservative party's myth has been largely Disraelian, 'its practice has almost invariably been Peelite'.

From 1881, then, we are studying men acting generally in the spirit of 'the founder', Peel, even though they might quote Disraeli. Significantly, Disraeli's immediate successor, Salisbury, quoted him least and the last in our sequence, Baldwin, most. The Disraelian legend grew first on the back-benches and outside Parliament. It was cultivated, and in the Primrose League institutionalised, by that aspirant to power, Randolph Churchill, who in his own battles with the party establishment represented Disraeli as struggling all his days with aristocratic cliques in order to broaden the base and appeal of Conservatism (or Toryism, as Churchill, like Disraeli, preferred to call it) as represented by the party called 'Conservative'. What he was in fact saying was that Disraeli had dedicated himself to doing again what Peel had done, after Peel and his principal lieutenants had been sundered from the immobile Tory element in Parliament and country. The latter, under the Derby–Disraeli leadership, was difficult to move and difficult to recommend effectively to voters under the 1832–68 electoral regime. After the 1848 Chartist fiasco and the general acceptance of Free Trade (and during the fortuitous prosperity of agriculture) the Liberal party posed no threat to the Constitution or the social order such as Peel might with some colour detect in its predecessor of the 1830s. And Derby and Disraeli had no 'college' of able and professional lieutenants such as those Peel had trained – nor, for all Derby's acquaintance with the Turf, was either 'the Jockey or the Jew', 'the Derby or the Hoax', to be considered a trainer of ministerial talent in the same league as Peel. Perhaps with longer periods in office Gathorne Hardy (Lord Cranbrook) might have rivalled Cardwell, but Northcote was no Gladstone. Nor, surely, in the capacity here relevant, was Disraeli himself; his 1852 Budget was ingenious, but Gladstone's Budgets were 'businesslike'. Indeed it was the inability of the Conservatives under Derby and Disraeli to make Peel's claim that their party would provide more 'business-like' government that handicapped it until a long first Gladstone government reinstated the issue of Conservatism versus Radicalism which Peel had successfully exploited to win his 1841 victory. Only then did the drift of the middle classes from the Liberal to the Conservative party, predicted and predictable since the death of Palmerston in 1865, take effect, simultaneously with a rallying of working-class voters in certain urban areas, particularly Lancashire, but potentially also in London.

The Disraelian legend is absolutely dependent for its continued currency on the fact that Disraeli, under the new electoral regime of 1865–85, *won* in 1874, as Peel had won in 1841. He achieved what for more than a quarter of a century had seemed impossible; 1874 saw only the second Conservative victory since 1832. It was a tragedy that the victory came 'too late', when Disraeli was old and tired and devastated by the death of his beloved Mary-Anne. From 1876 all is anti-climax and ineffectiveness except for a flamboyance in foreign affairs which was probably popular, but which caused unease to Salisbury as it had caused alarm to his step-father and Foreign Office predecessor (Derby's heir), and was not exploited electorally. It mobilised and reunited the Liberals, and its by-products in Afghanistan and South Africa, coinciding with an appalling depression striking trade, industry, agriculture and Ireland, resulting in a major Tory defeat. But this severe national judgement on the first Conservative majority government for over thirty years did not ruin Disraeli's reputation in his party. There was some reliance, now, on the swing of the pendulum to reverse the verdict, especially if the rules of the electoral game were unaltered (and therefore the initial response of Churchill as well as Salisbury was to *prevent* the enfranchisment of the country householders). There was also admiration (if, in some, disgust) for Disraeli's part in writing those rules in the 1867–8 'leap in the dark' which Disraeli had called 'educating the party'. There was acknowledgement that only because it was 'educated' did the party now stand a chance; there was insistence by the young, by Balfour as well as Churchill, though in different ways, that the educational process should seem to continue. There was insistence by Salisbury, no less than Churchill and Gorst, that party organisation, which had played its part in the 1874 victory (with Gorst as Disraeli's Bonham) must be revived and be supplemented in the country seats more or less untouched by its newest forms. All of which amounted to the proposition that Disraeli's work must be done over again, without Disraeli, but with the aid of Disraeli's prestige and example.

Yet, as James Cornford has noted, Salisbury found in Disraeli, when he was an old man, one fixed political principle – that the party must on no account be broken up. This maxim, of course, explains the absence of Peel from the partisan pantheon. For 'the founder' of the Conservative party had, in the view of those who stayed with it after 1846, broken it up, had treated it as a thing of no, or comparatively little, account. Future leaders, for all Disraeli's memorable jibes about 'organised hypocrisy' and 'stealing the Whigs' clothes' (similar allegations of lack of principle were directed at Derby and Disraeli by Salisbury in his youth) would have to be 'pragmatic', opportunist, flexible and far more sophisticated than their followers. But they must never 'do a Peel'. Salisbury's resolve not to 'over-offend' the faithful, and especially to give no colour to the claim of his Chamberlainite Radical allies that his reforms were forced on him by them was, in plain terms of political necessity, superfluous, once he was the recognised bedrock on which Unionism stood. But it explains entirely why Gladstone's hope in 1885 that Salisbury's Cabinet would take up Home Rule was unrealistic. Balfour again and again asserted privately that *he* would never 'be a Peel'. This determination was of itself sufficient to render unrealistic Chamberlain's hope, from 1902, that he could carry the Conservative leader for whole-hearted Tariff Reform. The inheritance of the obligation to keep the party together explains why Bonar Law, a Tariff Reformer, both before and after the First World War, was willing to fight elections on a basis which would give him no mandate for a policy in which he firmly believed. Baldwin, when a novice leader, departed from the tradition of not risking the unity of the party.* Where Peel in 1846 had gone for Free Trade in the name of national economic and social necessity, Baldwin in 1923 went for the abrogation of Free Trade for the same reason. The electorate rejected the policy and so Baldwin did not find himself in Peel's position of carrying his policy in Cabinet but seeing it rejected in the party. It is not, of course, suggested that, if Baldwin had won, the *majority* of the party would have gone against him. His position was essentially dissimilar from Peel's in 1845–6 in that

---

*Baldwin's colleague, Lord Eustace Percy, thought, however, that the object of the 1923 election was to *reunify* the party by recovering the leading coalitionist Conservatives.

the majority of the party had been 'educated' by leading men, over a course of years, into supporting a policy not acceptable to the electorate, while Peel had the electorate and the Cabinet, but not the majority of the party, with him. Baldwin retreated, as Balfour and Law had done, not so much because of the opposition of a minority in the party, but because of the apparent uneducability of the electorate. But the cabinet which he formed in 1924 was one whose composition was unintelligible except on 'unity of the party' explanations; it was one that could never agree to undertake the task of educating the electorate to accept Tariff Reform. In Opposition, 1929–31, Baldwin faced the campaign of the Press Lords to bully the party into submission on this issue not merely as a leader beset, and resenting the besetting, but as one who would accept whatever tariff mix a combination of organised pressure and the force of world events and British trade and unemployment figures eventually dictated – as though he had himself no opinions or leanings. That this in 1932 enabled Neville Chamberlain to glory in the victory of his father's cause is, in the present context, almost irrelevant. The point is that Baldwin, having burned his fingers on Tariff Reform in 1923, adopted thereafter the standard Conservative leadership posture of 'unity of the party'.

The only official leader who, advisedly, risked the serious disruption of the Conservative party after 1846 was Austen Chamberlain in 1922 and he, an unsuccessful aspirant to the succession in 1911 fortuitously succeeding in 1921, appears in this book as a mere transient. His story is not simply that of a man of whom Winston Churchill said that he always played the game and always lost it, nor that he was merely a cut-out cardboard figure of his great father. He was the Conservative leader convinced that the Conservative party on its own could not prevail, and therefore repudiated by the followers, a majority of M.P.s, the ministerial cadets and the Chief Whip himself. Balfour had been deposed, after losing three elections in a row, because it was thought he could not carry the party to victory, or even continue it in unity, and because he was more than half willing to go. Austen Chamberlain was deposed for failing to share the party's faith in itself, its conviction, or at least its hope, that it could prevail if it dissociated itself from the false gods whose popularity had helped it in 1918 but hindered it now. In 1886 Conservatives had welcomed coalition because without it they evidently could not prevail. In 1918 they welcomed it as, in the very least, valuable reinsurance, and they did so again, though with less enthusiasm, in 1931. But in 1922 they regarded their official leader as the man who carried the ball and chain to send them drowning with Lloyd George and they therefore conscripted the retired leader, Bonar Law, as both more manly and astute, to lead them to a victory which is commemorated in the name of 'the 1922 Committee which the back-bench M.P.s have consistently refused to change. When the Conservatives are out of office, it is virtually the Conservative equivalent of the Parliamentary Labour Party. But its name recalls the rehabilitation of the Conservative party as an efficient competitor for political power, just as the Primrose League celebrated the man who, for a quarter of a century during the official Conservatives had been the political underdogs, personified the party's confidence that it ought to continue to exist and would in the end prevail. That, above all, had been Disraeli's contribution to Conservatism – and the role of Derby, willing to act as though the party might prevail, though he must have doubted any such prospect, should not be minimised.

Derby and Disraeli are treated in conjunction in this volume not merely because Derby was the official leader of the host which trekked through the wilderness, though he died before it reached the Promised Land, but because for twenty years Derby and Disraeli complemented one another in what was really a joint leadership in a time of adversity which lasted longer than any suffered by the Conservatives since. But for his attachment to Derby it is most improbable that Disraeli, so widely mistrusted inside and outside the House of Commons, would have remained in a position to be his undisputed successor and the harbinger of recovery of power. That Derby had been a Whig and then, almost to the bitter end, a Peelite, conscripted by the Protectionists to lend statesmanship to their leadership, is significant. Derby, not Disraeli, provided the element of continuity between the Conservative party of Peel and the Conservative party of Disraeli and Salisbury. He lacked, indeed, Peel's single-minded dedication to politics and his passion for 'business-like' administration, and was attacked as a none too scrupulous grandee and 'part-time' political leader. But his Wellingtonian patriotism, which combined the conviction that 'the Queen's government must be carried on' with the conviction, expressed in 1851, that his associates were not yet capable of carrying it on, and his highly counter-productive refusal to abandon until *after* the election of 1852 the Protectionist aspirations of the majority of his followers (even though by conceding what he knew in his own mind would have to be conceded he might have won), indicate, if not skilled leadership, at least a high integrity rivalling that of Peel himself. Peel, indeed, lost his party through serving his country, and thought it right so to do. Derby was conscripted to preserve the identity of the party, and did his duty by it without subordinating to it the interests of his country. The criticisms of his way of life, and of his political life, amount to no more than a complaint that he was not a full-time professional. But then nobody could have reasonably expected him to be other than he was, and his leadership was sought by the Protectionists with full knowledge of his outside interests and recollection that, had he been a mere opportunist, he would have remained in the Whig government in 1834 and become leader of the Whigs and Liberals.

So, Austen Chamberlain apart, every successor to Peel as party leader kept in his mind the prime objective of keeping the party together. This objective sometimes led to a lack of initiative in office and resistance to pressure from powerful colleagues – for example, Randolph Churchill and Joseph Chamberlain and, in Baldwin's time, the acolytes of the latter – though it did not prevent periodic, and sometimes successful, efforts to impel it forwards. Thus, for example, there was the 'leap in the dark' in 1867; the approval of an electoral system in principle democratic (1884); the advancement of democratic local government in Britain (1888–9) and Ireland (ten years later); the advancement of universal and free education and a merit educational ladder; the universalisation of the national insurance principle for the poorer working people; the acceptance of Home Rule for Ireland and of a larger, Dominion, status for twenty-six of its thirty-two countries; manhood and then adult suffrage. The adoption, when the party was in Opposition, of sharp and constructive alternatives to the policies of those in power was not common, the tendency being in such circumstances to exaggerate, by attacks on the governing party, the differences between ministers and alternative ministers by mainly destructive attacks.

Disraeli, indeed, during Gladstone's first administration produced a powerful distinguishing theme, but nothing like a programme. Bonar Law provided what he had been chosen to provide, an unyielding attitude of confrontation with Asquith which stained the party of loyalty, law and order with a streak of treason, the only justification for which is that it was required in order to elicit from ministers the admission (which they were unwilling to make even to themselves) that they were bluffing about the coercion of Ulster. But this is a wretched affair, which must embarrass anyone writing at all sympathetically about the Conservative party, for the idea of securing the exclusion of north-east Ulster from Dublin rule was strictly subsidiary to the real objective of preventing Home Rule *tout court*. It must be accepted that in the immediate pre-War years the Conservatives under Law, an Ulsterman allied with Ulster's adopted champion Carson, a Southern Irish Unionist, did not behave like a democratic party. When, by Irish votes, the Conservative House of Lords was stripped of its wrecking power, so that Home Rule became feasible, the party which insisted on the maintenance of the Union, and hence of the Irish votes in the House of Commons, treated any vote on Ireland which included those Irish votes as morally invalid and alleged that the majority of the House of Commons constituted a 'conspiracy' against the Constitution. Its leaders, the Ulsterman Law and the Southern Unionist landlord Lansdowne, even urged the king to dismiss the Liberal ministers and though the object was to secure a general election, this was a reactionary appeal to the royal prerogative which, if heeded, would have imperilled the monarchy. This was without doubt the most unscrupulous move ever made by the Conservative leadership, and one which was singularly inappropriate at a time when it was invoking 'law and order' principles against militant trade unionists and suffragettes. It justified the harshest strictures to the effect that it regarded itself as the 'natural' governing party and denied the right of any radical party returned by the electors to rule. The only extenuating circumstance was that at the same time it dallied with the idea of the referendum. This device for appealing to the sovereign electorate it considered, indeed, only as a means of returning to power irrespective of whether the electorate approved its tariff policy or not. It was patently a matter of a party suggesting a change in the constitutional rules, and one of a very radical kind, to suit its own convenience. In this, of course, the too belated conversion of the Liberals to proportional representation or, failing that, the alternative vote, and the timely conversion of the Labour party to the rejection of such devices show that the Conservative party is not unique.

One does not need to embrace any extreme doctrine of class motivation and conflict to find in the attitude of Conservative leadership to the lower classes – originally, in more definitively hierarchical days, 'the lower orders' – a question to be considered. It has been the strength of British Conservatism that those relations between classes which have political effects have been, particularly in England as distinct from Scotland and Wales, complex, not simple. Bagehot's emphasis on 'deference' is highly important, as is a tendency among the modestly successful, and, indeed, the unsuccessful, to admire, rather than to envy, those born to wealth and those who achieve it. The political history of

Lancashire, with its Conservative working-man's clubs in Peel's time, shows the existence of employee loyalty to Tory employers and hostility to Liberal ones (as well as many examples of the opposite) and political allegiances based often on religious affiliation rather than economic status. Given some degree of local paternalism and of paternalistic laws, working men, and more particularly Anglican or Anglican-influenced ones (and on occasion Roman Catholics too) would vote Tory. If the recently developed thesis that there was a switch at the end of the nine-teenth century, in Lancashire and London, and presumptively in other areas yet to be studied in depth, from 'communal', locally-centred, politics to the 'national' politics of class has force, the electoral statistics, even making the fullest allowance for the switch to the Tories of the upper and 'middle' classes, reveal a formidable Conservative strength among the working-class population (however narrowly conceived) which entitled Baldwin to regard his party as a more 'national' one – in the sense of one straddling the classes – than Labour or, in their decay, the Liberals. In 1931 a largely working-class electorate returned to the House of Commons M.P.s of whom a majority belonged to the Empire Industries Association. The electors, of course, personalised issues presented to them in grossly oversimplified terms, but many millions obviously voted as 'citizens' rather than members of a 'class'. The symbolism of Conservative meetings, which only a fraction of electors even in the headiest days of Randolph Churchill's eloquence attended – the Union Jack on the table and the singing of the National Anthem – symbolised not only a calculated Conservative appeal but one which evoked a notable response.

When it came to electoral argument, Conservative leaders did not necessarily show deference to particular demands or aspirations of working-class people. Peel made no concessions to northern dislike of the Whig Poor Law and defied the philanthropic Ashley on his Ten Hours Bills. No sharp lesson seems to have been drawn from Disraeli's victory in 1874 after he had explained that his party was devoted to the improvement of the condition of the people as compared with his defeats in 1868 and 1880 when he did not.* In any case, even in 1872-4, the social reform theme played third fiddle to the maintenance of the Constitution and the nationalist–imperialist themes. Later the talk was often mainly of tariffs, one way or the other according to the area and

---

* In 1868 Gathorne Hardy suggested that Disraeli add to his election address the words 'hope that time may be given for legal and social measures of improvement so long laid aside'.

its economic interests (especially in 1923). For the essential Conservative message is that the interest of the working class is best served by prosperity, to be achieved – so far as government can do anything about it one way or the other – by tariffs (as most said after 1903, but few in the fifty years before) or by low taxes and non-interference with enterprise and investment. The claim of the Conservative party is not that it particularly serves the working class, but that the interests of the working class are subsumed in the interests of men of property. It has no special relationship with working men (though it does, in effect, with men of property) but it argues the condition of working men will be worse if the destinies of the nation are entrusted to its political opponents, not least if those opponents in their misguided zeal seek to serve 'sectional' (which in this context means 'working class') interests at the expense of the 'national interest'. A number of opponents of Conservatism – often to their peril – do not understand that many a Conservative orator actually believes this to be true and is aggrieved by allegations of hypocrisy. It is not by any means simply a case of the ignorant herd being 'brain-washed' by evil-minded landlords and capitalists and their hirelings. It is a case of the leaders and the led sharing a common outlook which, for the majority of both, cannot be shaken by argument to the contrary however conclusive this may seem to those who do not share it. Explanatory analysis needs to operate at the level of the subconscious, not the rational. It is not surprising that we can put side by side one of Gash's verdicts on Peel – 'If Conservatism was to be a national party . . . it was necessary to have a policy which took all clauses of society into account' – and Baldwin's assertion that, despite the paucity of support from former Labour ministers and M.P.s, the 'National' Government of 1931 was properly so-called because of its obligations to, as well as its electoral support from, all sections of the people.

It is a fair question to ask, however, to what extent the Conservative leaders studied in this book knew of, and considered, the working classes as such. A certain factual knowledge, or at least impression, any literate man must no doubt have, and it would be deepened by railway travel. Yet, while Neville Chamberlain was wondering why his derelict Birmingham constituency continued to return him (in 1924 it nearly did not), Baldwin saw a real slum for the first time in his fifty odd years of life, when touring Dundee after receiving the Freedom – and confided to his diary that he felt like howling.

Peel's industrial contacts in the north were considerable and he was an avid student of trade statistics and Royal Commission Reports. Long experience in Ireland and at the Home Office made him apt to note, among the poor, revolutionary potential. His general belief in *laissez-faire* and his conversion to Free Trade offended both compassionate and protectionist members of his party; they were often the same people. That because of 'cheap bread' he was honoured in many a poverty-stricken home is only appropriate, since his objective was always not merely that of protecting the social order but 'making the country cheap for living' and he became convinced that Protectionists were both selfish and short-sighted, despite the paternalistic Colonel Sibthorp's assertion that the protection of land and the protection of labour went together.

Though author of *Coningsby* and *Sybil*, Disraeli had no close knowledge of social stress and distress, but he did inform the upper and middle classes that Britain was divided into 'two nations' and that public men had a duty as well as an interest in bringing these together in a common loyalty to Crown and Constitution. His language with regard to 'the improvement of the condition of the people' was more overtly paternalistic than Peel's or Salisbury's, and more suggestive of collectivist than liberationist legislation. That is his supreme importance for Conservative mythology, and this although if one turns from words to votes and proposals one can argue consistency only by placing out of focus some early votes and that social legislation of 1875–6 of which, Dr Ward thinks, recent scholars have perhaps been over-anxious to emphasise that Disraeli had little close knowledge. It is no doubt right to stress how much of this legislation was permissive rather than mandatory (that, to Salisbury, was its virtue) and the extent of continuity from earlier Liberal legislation – though with continuity there was development, and perhaps just enough to justify Baldwin's view that *since* Disraeli the Conservatives had not done as much as they ought in this field. Of course ameliorative legislation by Conservative governments became more common after Disraeli, but this was partly because Conservative governments were much more frequent and partly because 'the times' demanded it. The true comparison is not between what was achieved by Disraeli and what was achieved by his successors, but between the latter and what would have been feasible in terms of this particular Disraelian legend if Conservative leaders had been more dedicated to it. There seems little excuse for the failure to introduce in the 1890s Joseph Chamberlain's contributory pension scheme, ditched finally because of, or on the excuse of, the expense of the Boer War.

On balance Salisbury's leadership inhibited social reform. He felt so strongly all the prejudices and convictions which can make a generous man oppose it. There was a conviction that social progress is the product of economic prosperity and of the improvement of individuals rather than legislation (a conviction shared by Gladstone, who condemned Churchill and Chamberlain alike for helping discredit it). There were strong inhibitions about interference with private property. These were the natural heritage of a landed aristocrat, and were shared by the Whigs Palmerston and Hartington, but were confirmed in Salisbury by his deep knowledge of the French Revolution and by an intellectual conviction that 'confiscation', or the threat of it, impeded economic growth. From Salisbury's time there has been continuous Conservative harping upon increasing the size of the cake (either by letting well alone or by tariffs) to the detriment of concern for its division. This is not least because it has seemed to the property-owner, unless he is a successful speculator, that a 'more equitable division' (that is, one which taxes him more heavily than his father though possible) has been the tendency, ever since Joseph Chamberlain's 'unauthorised programme' of 1884–5 and certainly since Harcourt's introduction of death duties with the slogan 'We are all socialists now!', without Conservative leaders going out of their way to advance it. It is, of course, highly significant that Salisbury's leadership coincided with – and assisted – that harvesting of upper middle class support for the Conservative party of which it has only lately been noticed that Disraeli – if largely because he was the competitor of Gladstone – was the sower.

A further point must be made. Conservatives combine with an appeal to a 'Disraelian' interventionist legend a pejorative view of 'bureaucracy'. The latter has very old Tory roots, dating from those eighteenth-century days when the Whigs dominated Court and Cabinet and the Tories, where there was fair play, kept control of local quarter-sessions, and the growth from these roots flourished even in the days of *laissez-faire* because these were also the days of the 'tyrannical' Poor Law Commission, Public Health Commission and so on, both associated with the profoundly un-Tory personality of Chadwick. In the 1870s the Conservative Home Secretary, Cross, was willing enough to co-operate with Birmingham's mayor, Chamberlain, in ensuring that Birmingham received from Parliament the powers Chamberlain sought to institute 'municipal socialism', in which the Webbs saw the recipe for the nation-wide victory of Socialism. But there were the strongest doubts about compelling local authorities to do things even if they were admittedly desirable, for this involved the state policing the local authorities, and Salisbury wrote harsh words about the inspector with his red tape as the modern dictator.

The red tape advanced inexorably, despite the interesting experiment, when Goschen was Chancellor of the Exchequer under Salisbury, of devolving to the local authorities a portion of the national tax product ('the whiskey money') to be used, or not used, as they chose, for limited expenditure on technical education. Goschen, a Commercial Liberal, as well as the extremist Lord Wemyss, had been horrified by *Salisbury's* 'socialism' on the Royal Commission on the Housing of the Working Classes, which Salisbury secured while in opposition, and which had royal patronage in the shape of the queen's approval of the prince of Wales's membership of it. Itinerant inspectors multiplied, to make factory, public health and allied legislation, all at the time being consolidated and extended, effective. The supervisory role of government departments was accentuated as local authorities built up their services and accumulated large debts, to produce after nearly a decade of Liberal 'welfare' legislation, wartime interventionism and post-war expedients (some based on acknowledgement of enhanced public duty, some on zeal for economy, and many on an uneasy amalgam of the two) the complex agglomeration which it was so greatly to the taste of Neville Chamberlain (under Baldwin) to try to rationalise. Whether for good or ill (according to one's view of his relations with Hitler)*a Tory politician who had been unsuccessful in private business applied at the central level of public administration a business-like approach reminiscent of Peel.

Neville Chamberlain's predecessor as a Tory administrative reformer had been the very dissimilar Balfour. An aesthete, who seemed happiest at the rarified level of 'the Souls', he was as remote as a man could be from working-class experience, though his representation of Manchester imposed some awareness of harsh realities and, because Lancashire Tories at all levels of society tended more than was common to the Free Trade on which the industry and commerce of the area seemed so clearly based, this awareness fortified a natural scepticism of tariffs as a 'cure-all'. 'Social improvement' figured in his election address to the Cecil pocket borough of Hertford in 1874 as it had in his uncle's address to another Cecil pocket borough, Stamford, twenty years before. But it appeared in parenthesis, the form of words being – 'the party which while aiming at social improvement does not believe that that can be

---

*The reputation he gained as an administrator gave him the succession to Baldwin.

attained by the reckless subversion of existing institutions or the reckless destruction of existing interests'. This was a faithful repetition of
Peel's theme in 1833–5, the first rallying cry of the Conservative party.
In many of the reforms with which he was associated Balfour managed
simultaneously to serve Conservative interests as well as 'under-
privileged' people, and thus make a dual contribution to the Conservative cause. Land purchase in Ireland assisted landlords as well as
peasants, and Education Acts assisted the Church of England as well as
the bright children of parents not well-heeled. Both were *characteristically* Conservative reforms based on the principles of the Tamworth
Manifesto and Balfour's own Hertford election address; significantly,
Joseph Chamberlain did not like them.

That Balfour was a Tory root and branch is not to be doubted
simply because he co-operated in the First World War with Asquith
and Lloyd George, and after the war remained a coalitionist until after
the Carlton Club meeting of 1922. In 1915–24 he was concerned either
with immediate emergencies or with fighting off, by the in-gathering of
the naturally conservative elements including those which had previously professed Liberalism, the socialist threat (basically international in
origin), as Pitt in circumstances fundamentally similar had fought, by a
similar in-gathering, the French Revolutionary contagion on which
Salisbury must often have discoursed at Hatfield in his nephew's
presence. Balfour had been not merely the instrument but the personi-
fication of the policy of 'resolute government' in Ireland. He bears more
responsibility than any other man for that failure to reverse by legislation the Taff Vale judgement which, since the judges upset what
everybody had assumed to have been made the law under Disraeli, still
seems a betrayal of the Disraelian legend (if not, indeed, of the Disraelian
legacy) and certainly, taken together with the Balfour Education Act of
1902, provoked that electoral pact – for Conservatives sinister if, in the
long term, for Liberals lethal – between Herbert Gladstone, the Liberal
Chief Whip, and the Labour Representation Committee's secretary
Ramsay MacDonald, which in 1903 *preceded* the launching of the divisive
Tariff Reform campaign by Joseph Chamberlain. In 1906 the Conservative party, led by Balfour, would suffer, together with a run-off of
middle-class voters attached to Free Trade a possibly smaller, but
statistically significant, and permanent, loss of working-class Tory
voters, and this loss was deserved. Yet Balfour personified not only the
policy of 'resolute government' in Ireland, but also the policy of
'killing Home Rule by Kindness', which, if it did not succeed, was well-

conceived and well-contrived, and he carried through a Unionist Parliament the Irish local government measure which installed Catholic (and Home Rule) authorities in most of that land. His failure to contrive any similar strategy to forestall the growth of political Labour in Britain is conspicuous, though in fairness it should be added that his comment on the 1906 election result constituted a rapid acknowledgement of the error (*not* simply a relapse into the perennial pessimism of his uncle), and that the House of Lords (to which, in defeat, he looked for salvation, provoking Roy Jenkins to entitle a book *Mr Balfour's Poodle*) did not mangle Radical social legislation as it mangled educational and licensing legislation. This, no doubt, shows that Balfour was astute, rather than compassionate, but it shows that he was no Bourbon.

It may be argued that Balfour's sins of omission in matters relating to social and trade union legislation are the negative side of a coin whose positive side, though not electorally advantageous to the party he led, was statesmanlike. Balfour may have missed golden opportunities to wean working-class support from a divided Liberal party which lacked credibility with the electorate. He may have flouted, in 1902–3, the golden rule of political leadership – 'Divide and Rule'. He may have floundered, as Opposition leader, when confronted with the choice which had faced him as Premier, between inspiring the majority of its activists and maintaining its unity while affronting those activists. But, unlike his uncle, and like Joseph Chamberlain, he did believe in administrative reform. He saw the need to adjust Britain's international relationships to a changing pattern of world power. He saw the need to provide machinery for the planning of national defence. He saw the foreigners' technological and educational challenge to British supremacy and, consequently, to Britain's prospects of economic growth on which depended the avoidance of distress, agitation and social subversion. And so he changed British foreign policy, established the Committee of Imperial Defence, and did what he could to advance technical and secondary education. That he shied away from whole-hearted commitment to Tariff Reform by brilliant but inevitably damaging equivocation may be held to demonstrate not the peril of having an intellectual as a party leader but the terrible stress which afflicts a political party when its zealots descry 'a simple solution' to the nation's ills, and the leader, who knows that this solution will alienate an important, though minority, element in the party and its electoral supporters, has his own doubts as to whether there is any simple solution to anything. That Balfour was perhaps the most intellectual of the leaders of the Con-

servative party and that he often gave the impression of being a dilet-
tante should not obscure the fact that, at least from his uncle's succession
to the premiership in 1885, he was a very professional politician. As
such in 1903 he viewed the drift of his party with an alarm which seemed
to dictate dialectical gymnastics in an effort to maintain unity and, if
possible credibility. The gyrations of Labour leaders in their attitude
to the Common Market in 1971–3 and to particular nationalisation
proposals in 1973 may be described as 'Balfourian'.

In 1911 the Conservative party, seeking relief from both schism and
uncertain, unsuccessful leadership, turned from a cultured aristocrat to
a practical Scots-Irish businessman. Law seems, in retrospect, an appropriate choice for a party gathering into its fold the majority of the
business classes, which, in many parts of the country had one or two
generations earlier been not only Liberal but hostile to the Conservative
party of Derby and Disraeli as the political embodiment of aristocratic
and Anglican privilege, rooted in rural England and dedicated to social
relationships which were 'feudal' rather than contractual and competitive. He had recently shown both courage and flexibility when he
accepted the suggestion of Goulding of the Tariff Reform League that
he contest Manchester North-West, still a citadel of Free Trade, and
then attempted to 'eliminate Tariff Reform from the contest', which he
narrowly lost. It would be easy to suggest that, under Law, the Conservative party essentially deserted the cause of social reform for an
outlook wholly sympathetic to business interests and that this development reflected his character, managerial rather than compassionate,
calculating rather than sentimental, with a Glasgow employer's easy or
resigned acceptance of the detritus left by the Industrial Revolution
and the glaring injustices of the capitalist 'system' as facts of life. But
there was in Law much capacity for growth, and for learning from
experience. He assimilated, as some of his colleagues and many of his
followers did not, the inexorable implications of the impact of the First
World War on British society and policy. He committed the Conservative party, with little evidence that his reappraisal was agonising, to
immense extensions of social services, despite the heavy increase in the
annual burden of the National Debt. Many Conservatives later heard
with equanimity, and some with relish, the thud of the Geddes axe. The
party as a whole, staunchly committed to pre-Keynesian economic and
fiscal precepts, seemed unsympathetic to the more unfortunate members
of society at whose expense retrenchment was dictated by the principles
of budgetary and insurance accountancy. But Bonar Law had brought

it over a hump which, had the driving been less skilled, might have shattered both silencer and springs. There was no cant in him, and he was surprisingly widely respected and liked. The victory of 1922 was his due reward.

All the same, it was probably fortunate for the party that Law yielded rapidly to a softer-seeming leader, overtly critical of the 'hard-faced men' of business and of the party. Radiating a genuine belief in remedial attitudes, Baldwin refurbished the Disraelian theme of reconciling 'the two nations' which economic circumstances, war and, to a certain extent, alien political philosophy had once again forced apart. 'The young and progressive wing of his party had a special regard for him', writes Harold Macmillan in his autobiography; 'the fact that the Right Wing and especially the so-called Industrials had little love for him, confirmed our feelings. . . . [H]e made it possible, through his reputation for decency and fair-mindedness, to win the support of working men and women throughout the country.'

On behalf of 'the Industrials', who mocked 'the young and progressive wing' as 'the Young Men's Christian Association', the *Daily Mail* asserted in 1929 that 'it was the semi-Socialist policy that went down in the great defeat'. They hoped, because of the defeat, to be rid of a leader they thought pusillanimous, as Balfour and Austen Chamberlain had been got rid of. But Baldwin was indispensable to the electoral prospects of the party, other things being equal, precisely because he could edge it – when he chose to exert himself – towards the recognition of unpalatable facts and necessities such as the need to recognise, in principle, the claim of India to Dominion status. Not that India, probably, was very important electorally, but it was important as a test case for party leadership. Nothing would have been easier than to beat the still resonant Victorian drums of Empire to drown the whispers of statesmanship and obligation. But that was not the way of Baldwin, nor the proper way for the Conservative leader in the circumstances. Conservative leaders may occasionally be chosen as Diehards – as was Stanley in 1846 and perhaps Law in 1911 – but a conscientious consideration of their role guides even such, commonly, to the centre or left of it. Seen from the top, the Tory Right is a terrible thing, the clumsy deadweight cross the leader has to bear. He beholds it, and educates himself and then educates his party. Had this not normally been so, the party could not have survived. Because it has normally been so, the Conservative party has a record of continuous existence, and of frequent success, over nearly a century and a half of democratisation of the political processes – a record unique in the annals of constitutional government.

For a full understanding of the continued prosperity of the Conservative party, and a better assessment of the contribution of its leaders to it, much more research into organisation, and the relations of each leader to the party machine, is required. What we can say at present is that there has been a variation in the quality of the central organisation which seems rhythmical. This is not surprising. It is probably impossible to maintain indefinitely a very high pitch of organisation. In a field of political activity where so much depends on personal gifts and satisfactory personal relationships at the top and down the main lines of communication between the centre and the localities, it is difficult for a new man to take over from a brilliant predecessor. It would have been difficult to replace Bonham even had he not been lost to the party with Peel, and unlikely that any successor of Peel could have quite such happy relations with Bonham. Gorst, Middleton and Younger all made superlative contributions to electoral victory, but there were unhappy gaps between Gorst and Middleton and between Middleton and Younger when the machine did not function well. The papers of J. C. C. Davidson, edited by Robert Rhodes James, portray the difficulties of a newcomer, especially one bent on organisational reform. In this regard a special responsibility rests on the party leader. He must give the party managers as favourable a case as possible to put to the electorate. And he must leave no doubt of his confidence in the central management, changing it if he cannot feel such confidence. This responsibility is direct and inescapable, in view of the principle that the national party machinery and the task of co-ordinating its activities with those of the parliamentarians should be firmly under the leader's control. It was for this principle that Salisbury, carrying Northcote in tow, battled with Randolph Churchill and Gorst after Disraeli's death.

Because of this direct and inescapable responsibility, blame must fall upon Disraeli in his last years and upon Balfour throughout his period as leader for neglect of duty. It is not suggested that mere organisation could have achieved victory either in 1880 or 1906, but defeat was surely made more severe by a falling-off in organisational efficiency. It is not clear why Disraeli, who certainly owed part of his 1874 majority to Gorst, failed to give credit where credit was due and saw with apparent equanimity Gorst's disillusionment and resignation. If, on the strength of a freak by-election result which determined for him the date of the dissolution he was so out of touch with public opinion as to expect to win, his long experience of just falling short of a majority and his knowledge of the importance of Gorst's organisation in the boroughs in 1874 ought nevertheless to have told him that organisation could make the difference between an inconclusive result and a narrow win, or between a narrow win and a working majority. Yet he allowed party organisation to lapse in a way which made the inquest into the causes of defeat a bicker between active organisations in the country, championed by Gorst, and the Whips' Office, on which the leader had apparently fallen back. By the time of his death the party's situation was chaotic, with Gorst playing a dual role as an organisational assistant, without authority, and a parliamentary critic of the Commons leadership and the Whips. Salisbury and Northcote, rivals for the succession, agreed that Gorst should be ousted from party organisation, and thereby invited a confrontation between themselves on the one hand and on the other the party's principal platform asset, Lord Randolph Churchill, and the party's most expert electoral organiser, Gorst. This encounter was nominally to determine what place in the party's counsels should be accorded to the National Union gathered in 'party conference' – or, more strictly, its executive, the membership of which was in the crisis contested between a party leadership, secure in the confidence of the parliamentarians and the control of the Whips' Office, and its critics upon whose exertions in the country the party must depend for the winning of vital marginal, and especially urban, seats. Any objective verdict must hold Salisbury, Northcote, Churchill and Gorst to blame, and probably in that order, for a condition of disarray which augured ill for party prospects against Gladstone and Chamberlain at the next election. But Salisbury was engaged in a deep game from which he emerged as the eventual winner. The extravagances of Churchill, having played their part both in the discrediting of Northcote and in borough victories, proved his undoing – and of a sudden we behold Salisbury in command with an adept Chief Whip, Akers-Douglas, and a brilliant party manager, Middleton, wholly in his confidence. Together these three, in 1886, maximised the Conservative contribution to the Unionist victory won in alliance with the Whig Hartington and the Radical Chamberlain, who broke with Gladstone over Irish Home Rule, and laid the organisational foundation for the triumph of 1895.

The mere fact that Balfour, who inherited from his uncle, Salisbury the large majority reaped from 'Chamberlain's' khaki election in 1900, won none of the three elections he fought as leader does not necessarily condemn him. It may be that in the circumstances no one could have led the Conservative party to victory in January 1906 or January or December 1910. In terms of seats the 1906 result was an unparalleled disaster, but even then the party was, in terms of votes, stronger than it was to be in the 1920s even when it won a majority in the House of Commons. On the other hand the party's biggest defeats – in 1880, 1906 and 1945 – have all been incurred when the central party machinery was being very badly run after being previously very well run.

Balfour resigned the premiership soon after the National Union conference, like the Liberal Unionist organisation a year before, overwhelmingly preferred Chamberlain's policy to his own. In resolving that it was 'desirable to strengthen the central management of the business of the Conservative Party by the addition of a popular representative element . . .' the party activists were carpeting Balfour's principal agent Wells and condemning both Balfour's policy and his style of leadership. With an election imminent, Wells resigned, leaving the memory of an 'officious meddler' who had succeeded in 'pulverizing Middleton's organization'. A. K. Russell in *The Liberal Landslide* (1973) shows Herbert Gladstone perfecting Liberal organisation and Labour alliance while Unionists struggled with the combined effects of 'apathy, inexperience and division' amounting to 'the collapse of [the] electioneering machine'. As late as September 1905 Acland-Hood deprecated a dissolution because the machinery was so 'sadly in need of repair' that every month counted. Yet Professor Gollin opines in this present volume that even after the great electoral rout of January 1906 '[Balfour] and his friends of the Old Guard did all they could to fend off significant changes'. It appears that Balfour, in concert with his Chief Whip Acland-Hood, was more concerned with fighting off the 'increased democracy' demanded by Chamberlain (like Churchill and Gorst a quarter of a century before) than with increasing efficiency. Indeed, that decline in the independence of candidates and M.P.s which may be ascribed, basically, to the effective limitation of election expenditure on behalf of a particular candidate during an election (enacted in 1883 by significant concurrence of the two front benches) combined with the enlargement of the electorate, now became blatant. The lost seats in Lancashire tended to be fought by 'professional politicians' rather than persons of local eminence, and they were required by Central Office to toe the party (i.e. the leader's) line, Central Office being in effect controlled by the Whips, who were, or ought to have been, the instruments of Balfour as leader. The combination of officious and jealous control by the parliamentarians with limpness at Central Office, as in 1878-84, produced a poor impression. Mutual recrimination between the national and the local leaders after the defeats of 1910 resembled that of 1880. It was not possible for Balfour to maintain the combination of Acland-Hood and Percival Hughes, which had been as unsuccessful as Akers-Douglas and Middleton had been successful, though he shared their view that fault lay mainly with the National Union people – i.e. the provincial federations – who thought they knew their regional electorates better than London did. He had therefore to write from Cannes on 11 January 1911 to ask Akers-Douglas, the member of 'the Old Guard' who had been the peerless Whip of Salisbury's high noon, to conduct an inquiry into organisation with the aid of 'younger and more ardent' spirits. The inclusion among these of strong critics of Acland-Hood and Hughes, such as Steel-Maitland and Goulding, with Salvidge of Liverpool, doomed the incumbents, and Balfour's admission, in the letter to Akers-Douglas, that no 'single person [could] do the work demanded of a modern head Whip', must be read as an oblique criticism not only of Acland-Hood but of himself. It led to the appointment of Steel-Maitland as the first 'chairman of the Conservative party organisation' – an adjutant of the leader of the party placed, in avowed independence of the Whips, over the principal agent and in control of Central Office. Thus, out of the trials and tribulations of Balfour as party leader, was bequeathed to Bonar Law the system which, in essence, survives to this day. But it must be noted that the appointment of a superintendent of organisation, directly responsible to the leader of the party, did nothing in itself to solve the problem of relations between Central Office and the local parties and regional federations. Steel-Maitland's appointment of a chief agent for Lancashire without appropriate local consultation was an abrasive action in the tradition of Acland-Hood. The new system increased the leader's problems. He had now to secure appropriate liaison between a party chairman at Central Office and the Whips' Office, while the chairman was responsible to the leader for adequate liaison with the National Union and its constituent associations, which were served by agents appointed by them but supervised by chief agents appointed by the chairman. The Davidson Papers show us a chairman wholly in the confidence of the party leader, his close personal friend, and dedicated to the same objectives, criticised on the one side by the grandees of the National Union for 'interference' and by M.P.s for neglect of the parliamentarians' point of view. That he had to be sacrificed to save the leader himself merely indicates the particular discordances in the party after it lost the 1929 election, but his difficulties were due to the nature of his office and show how crucial is the leader's co-ordinating role.

Much of the information on which the above comments are based comes from Lancashire. More than once Balfour, Law and Baldwin waited in apprehension for news of what Lancashire Conservatives in conference had resolved. Lancashire plays a key role in the Tory story, and not merely because the seventeenth earl of Derby and the 'boss' of Protestant Liverpool, Archibald Salvidge, were so influential there and able to exert strong pressure on the leadership of the party. If the editing of this book has underlined the need for a much closer study of organisation after 1885, and of the relations between the leaders and their party managers (documented so far only as regards Baldwin and Davidson for the short period 1927–30), it has emphasised almost as much the need for a systematic study of the Conservative party in Lancashire since 1832. For though in its electoral behaviour Lancashire has not been typical, it has been an area in which, under every electoral system since 1832, a combination of influences has produced Conservative strength, showing that even at the outset the party was based on more than rural estates and close corporations, and that it has been able to appeal to all classes in society. Here, if anywhere, 'the Tory working man' is discovered, frequenting his clubs in the days of Peel; responding to the boast 'We've shortened the hours of labour, and lengthened the hours of drink'; voting in his thousands (e.g. at Oldham) as soon as admitted to the franchise; resisting school boards (the Churches of England and Rome having provided many voluntary schools); resisting, later, in by-elections, Lloyd George's insurance stamps. Here trade unionism and Conservatism were found compatible, the combination personified by James Mawdesley, who would have been elected in tandem with the young Winston Churchill for Oldham (a most appropriate example of the 'Tory Democracy' Lord Randolph had preached), had the Tory peak in the cotton constituencies not been reached in 1895 rather than 1899–1900. In the Lancashire manufacturers, Derby's heir had informed Disraeli as early as 1853 that he saw 'material for Conservative principles to work upon'. Liberals here in the birthplace of the Anti-Corn Law League had often been Palmerstonian, not Cobdenite (they had sent Bright away to Birmingham in 1857) and were therefore 'convertible' to a patriotic and jingoistic Toryism. So the Conservative party had first an edge and then a predominance.

The Conservative leadership was always conscious of the importance of Lancashire. The landed estates of the Peels, their public school and Oxford educations, their pocket borough purchases, were made possible by the family factories at Blackburn and Bury, started a bare generation before the birth of the second Sir Robert, who 'founded' the Conservative party as something wider than a mere 'country party'. The semi-regal Stanleys of Knowsley near Liverpool were more than the 'natural leaders' of the landed interests in South Lancashire; they had large interests and prestige in the boroughs, placed from the late 1830s (except for the period 1878–85 when the fifteenth earl of Derby apostasised) in the Tory scale. To Manchester came Disraeli in April 1872 to receive two hundred addresses and 'meet' not only the county but 'all the boroughs of Lancashire'. He was well briefed by Gorst. He vindicated the Throne, the Lords (independent and 'representative' because based upon property), the Church of England and religious education. He told the farmer that he could not afford to pay higher wages, but asserted that 'the first consideration of a minister should be the health of the people'. He avowed his belief that the people were proud to belong to 'an Imperial country'. This was the famous reformulation of the Conservative theme, better known from the crisper summary later given to the representatives of the Conservative workingmen's associations at the Crystal Palace. One of Disraeli's most significant appointments in 1874 was that of Lancashire's Richard Cross to the Home Office.

Ten years later Cross was distinctly *passé*, and Randolph Churchill was the hero of the platforms. Rejecting Lancashire offers, however, he decided that in 1885 he would assail Bright in Birmingham, and it was Salisbury's nephew Balfour who carried the flag in Manchester under the new electoral regime which proved at first so advantageous to the Tories. In the North-West, as defined by P. F. Clarke in *Lancashire and the New Liberalism*, there were now seventy parliamentary divisions. In 1886 the Unionists took fifty nine; in 1895, sixty; in 1900, fifty six, Even in 1892 they held forty five. Clarke stresses that 'under Salisbury the Unionists became definitively the party of wealth – and thereby gained a decisive advantage under an electoral system that was geared to the representation of the wealthy'. But he admits that in many Lancashire towns the local Liberals must have seemed the party of the rich and powerful against whom Tories came armed with a 'Chartist' tradition and potent Evangelical Anglicanism. This admission somewhat weakens his assertion – if it is meant to apply to electors rather than 'active party workers' – that we must not look to class for the key to party cleavage because the class composition of the two parties was so alike. We can, no doubt, in the main accept his conclusion that in the first decade of the twentieth century a sea-change came over Lancashire Liberalism, now in contact and competition, but often co-operation, with political Labour. It was no longer true that 'in Lancashire the working class was characterised by Conservative politics and aggressive Churchmanship; by a certain racial and religious intolerance; by acceptance of good Tory principles of hierarchy, loyalty, and a solid unquestioning patriotism which could slide into jingoism'. We must, however, remember that the shift of voters, though decisive, was purely marginal, and that Conservative disunion on so sensitive an issue as Tariff Reform was working in the same direction, to the advantage of the Liberal–Labour alliance formed in 1903. Though it was in Lancashire that Ecroyd had raised the cry of 'Fair Trade' in the 1880s, the 'Free Trade' canon must have been peculiarly powerful here, partly for traditional reasons, but mainly because of the pursuits of the people. Here the scale of the 1906 defeat was particularly disastrous and the winning back of Lancashire was the principal objective in 1910. The fact that this objective was not achieved led to mutual recriminations between the local and the national parliamentary leaderships, for the Chief Whip Acland-Hood denied Central Office approval and support to candidates, whatever their views, who would not stand on the programme approved by the party leader. But the party leader himself at the second election of 1910 went into reverse gear, and approved a referendum instead of a firm commitment to the Tariff Reform policy, and did so on urgent advice from Law in Manchester. There were similar tensions on food taxes in 1912–13 and in 1923; in the latter year the Liberals, by often narrow wins, were able to take a third of the seats, some industrial but many suburban-residential, for they were competing here as a rival conservative party. But in 1924 no Liberal was elected anywhere in the North-West against Conservative opposition, and the Tories found that in competition with Labour they could do well in Lancashire, if rarely so well as they had done in 1885–1900 against the Liberals.

If Tory and Unionist successes in Lancashire under Salisbury came as no surprise, those in London, once its deliberate under-representation was ended in 1885, were not only pleasant but surprising. For they were by no means confined to middle-class constituencies, although we are now told that politics in the metropolis were 'class-based' as early as 1885. Even with the comparatively limited information available about the London constituencies we can say that some of the special features of Lancashire were either inoperative there (such as a local Tory-Chartist tradition) or less significant (such as Anglican influence and 'nativist' resentment against immigrant labour, though this had its importance in the East End, where East European Jews mingled with Irish). Yet in 1895 *The Manchester Guardian* rightly linked London with Lancashire as the central Tory fortresses that the Liberals had somehow to breach, for in the general election of that year, if the Unionists took forty-nine of fifty-eight Lancashire seats, they took forty-five of London's fifty-three. There has been a tendency to assert that London politics were class-based, and then to explain *away* the results of four elections (1886, 1892, 1895 and 1900) in traditionalist and simplistic terms (London unskilled labourers being more xenophobic than skilled workers, and therefore more prone to lapse into Imperialism; London being full of clerks, and so on), and to square the circle by the conclusion that, as James Cornford writes, the Conservatism of the densely inhabited, poor and highly industrialised parts of London was not as reliable or enduring as that of the middle-class constituencies. This statement of fact, by Cornford, does not, however, really square with the initial assertion by Bealey and Pelling, accepted by Cornford and by Clarke, who dismisses rather cavalierly Paul Thompson's point that in 1910 there was a Liberal advance in middle-class constituencies and decline in working-class ones. What *does* seem clear is that the extension and *simplification* of the franchise in 1918 occasioned a more rapid erosion of Conservative strength in London than in the Chamberlain Midland bailiwick based on Birmingham (brought over to Unionism in 1886 and held for it for over forty years) and in Lancashire. In London the Conservatives under Law and Baldwin depended heavily on middle-class, female and plural voters; they had little grip on manual working men.

In the days of the pre-war Liberal administration, the House of Lords had done the Tories a yeoman service in resisting the abolition of plural voting by virtue of property qualifications. This enabled Law to be Prime Minister as member for the Central division of Glasgow, as it had enabled Balfour to be leader of the Opposition as member for the City of London. Apart from Birmingham and Lancashire, the Conservatives were normally able to count only on country districts, city centres, middle-class suburbs and growing 'commuter belts' outside them (especially in the Home Counties) and coastal resorts – and even in these a dying Liberalism gave several uncomfortable kicks in 1923. The plural voters were important. On the other hand the Conservatives had used the Lords to prevent Home Rule for Ireland, and it would have been difficult for the Conservative party after 1918 to have secured a majority in a House containing over eighty Irish Nationalists. The Home Rule members turned their backs on Westminster in 1918 and the vast majority of Irish constituencies promptly replaced them by Sinn Feiners committed to boycott the Imperial Parliament. The Irish, in pursuit of their own interests as they saw them, thereby made it possible, and, as it transpired, likely, that the British would live mainly under the governance of the Conservative and Unionist party. The major change in the electoral system wrought by the absence from the House of Commons of all representatives from Irish constituencies, except a baker's dozen in north-east Ulster (the six counties officially known since 1921 as 'Northern Ireland'), returning mainly Unionist allies was for the Tories a great, and indeed necessary, boon if they were to prosper in the second quarter of the twentieth century.

That the Conservatives did flourish so mightily, until the major set-back of 1945, was due to a combination of circumstances, luck, judgement and the errors of their opponents. They gained from the maintenance of the time-honoured first-past-the-post system, momentarily threatened in 1918 when the two Houses disagreed as between proportional representation and 'the alternative vote', and threatened again in 1931. Women voters, some enfranchised in 1918 and the rest as from 1929, proved more favourable to the Conservative party than the men. Plural voting, university representation, the Ulster seats all helped. Conservative organisation was, in the inter-war years, nearly always superior to that of the main opponent everywhere it mattered. Because the political habits of a local community or a family have a certain staying power, traditional allegiances remained influential even though the majority of post-war electors had not been pre-war electors. But the need to establish the habit of voting Conservative among new voters (especially the young) who had no settled partisanship and among voters whose habits or traditions had been Liberal was shown in 1922–3 to be acute. For each of three parties was then capable of polling about a third of the vote and in 1923 the Liberals won, though usually very narrowly, seats which had been Unionist even in 1906. After his tactical error in precipitating an election on Protection in that year, Baldwin clearly understood the need to attract, and certainly to avoid deterring, both uncommitted and former Liberal voters, relying on the fact that the Diehards who criticised him for being a 'socialist' had no alternative political home. He was much assisted, of course, by the divided condition of the Liberal party, and especially by the personal quarrel between Asquith and Lloyd George, at the time when Labour emerged as the second party in the State. The Conservative and Labour leaderships conspired to persuade the electors that the issue at each general election lay between their two parties. The Tory ability to remain the largest party either in the House (as in 1924) or in the country (as in 1929), even when not possessing a majority in the House, owed much to the essential liberality of Baldwin's own outlook and 'image'. And this made easy the wide anti-socialist coalition of 1931, which guaranteed Conservative predominance through a decade.

# 1 Wellington and Peel 1832-1846

## NORMAN GASH

### I

IN the history of the modern British party system, the great divide is the Reform crisis of 1831–2. It is seen even in the nomenclature of parties. Before that date the terms liberal and conservative, though in frequent use as neologisms borrowed from the continent of Europe, indicated only general attitudes. The terms Whig and Tory were the old and well understood party appellations even though many thought that those parties themselves were becoming obsolete. After that date the position was reversed. The borrowed words were within a few years applied to the actual parliamentary parties. The native epithets were used increasingly to denote attitudes and types or, in the case of the Whigs, a social element within a larger political grouping. It was proof of the regeneration of the party political system after 1832 that the general terms current in the post-Waterloo era transferred themselves to specific political parties; the party labels of the eighteenth century only survived as descriptive words for individuals and outlooks. It was in reality not so much a transfer of labels as a readjustment of parties to new concepts with which contemporary society was already growing familiar.

For the party which was to become known as the Conservative party the assumption of the new name came with great suddenness. Up to 1831 the conservative party in the state or, as Wellington sometimes phrased it, the *parti conservateur*, merely denoted those of whatever class or political affiliation who wished to preserve the basic institutions of the country. After 1831 it became the current term for the party in opposition to Lord Grey's Government. The article in the *Quarterly Review* of January 1831, claiming the new name for the old Tory party, popularised the idea. The introduction of the Reform Bill two months later gave it substance. By 1832 the name was being generally applied to the opposition party even though some of the politicians themselves were self-conscious in their use of it. The duke of Wellington was thus the first man who can properly be called a leader of the Conservative party, since until 1834 he was the only man whom the opposition party could

For Further Reading relevant to this chapter, see page 247.

be said to acknowledge as its head. In this there was a double paradox. In the first place he was the least political of any nineteenth-century party leader; there is a sense indeed in which Wellington was not a party politician at all. Secondly, when he became Prime Minister in 1828, his object had not been to create a Tory ministry or a party ministry of any sort but to recreate the Government of Lord Liverpool.

That government had been in spirit and structure if not chronologically the last of the eighteenth-century administrations. It was characteristic that it had continued for fifteen years, that it broke up only when its leader was forced to retire because of a paralytic stroke, and that during its lifetime the chief threat to its existence had come not from Parliament or the electorate but from the Crown. It contained many diverse views and personalities, but the one common bond was the Pittite tradition to which Liverpool, Castlereagh and Canning in their different ways all believed they were heirs. To define the legacy of Pitt, who, if he called himself anything, called himself a Whig, would be a task of some complexity. Pitt, dead and buried in Westminster Abbey, was a Protean figure, who changed shape with every man who looked back on him, and whose shape often seemed to resemble his latest observer. But he had been the king's minister for nearly twenty years and whatever else he stood for, his name was enshrined in the political pantheon as the Great Commoner who had led the national resistance to the French Revolution and Napoleon. In turn, Liverpool's administration, which had presided over the glorious termination of the war and the less glorious post-war era, had been primarily a National Government. For Wellington, who had served that ministry as general, diplomat and minister, the transition from the battle-field to a seat in the Cabinet had been singularly untrammelled by political considerations. As a professional soldier he was ready to respond with military discipline to any call made upon him by the king's ministers. As more and more tasks were laid upon him, he began to regard himself, in his own phrase, as the 'retained servant of the Sovereign' whose duty it was to do the business of the State in whatever sphere he was required to act. For politics as such he had little aptitude and less sympathy. 'To talk of my being Leader of a Party or anything but the Slave of a Party, or in other words the Person whom any other may *bore* with his Letters or his Visits upon publick Subjects, when he pleases,' he wrote emphatically in 1834, 'is just what I call *Stuff*'. Fundamentally he was an administrator. He believed in government, preferably good but axiomatically strong. He shared most of the prejudices of the landed aristocracy in which birth had given him a humble position and fate a conspicuous one; but he was not a political Tory pure and simple. His experience was too wide, his administrative sense too strong, his freedom from partisanship too great for his actions to be tied to a predictable political path. In his refusal to serve under Canning in 1827 he was moved by personal distrust rather than public policy. When he was summoned to form a ministry in 1828 – the fourth in less than a twelvemonth – it was because of his personal prestige and authority in a shattered political world. But though at the outset he reunited most of the broken elements of Liverpool's old administration, the union did not survive a single parliamentary session. The duke had neither the patience nor tact that was necessary to retain the touchy and suspicious followers of Canning. The departure of Huskisson and the other Canningites in 1828 left the administration shorn of many of its liberal elements and short in debating talent. For a government which had never possessed a cohesive majority in the House of Commons it was an ominous start.

After this apparent lurch to the right, Wellington outraged his ultra-Tory supporters the following year by forcing through Catholic Emancipation. For the duke, whose views on the Catholic question had always been more tolerant than the public suspected, the growth of the Catholic Association and O'Connell's election for county Clare made necessary an immediate administrative answer to a problem which had dogged every Parliament and divided every Cabinet since 1806. But the passage of the Catholic Relief Act fatally alienated many of his Tory Anglican followers. In these circumstances political expediency might have been expected to dictate an attempt to enlist moderate and liberal support. Yet the fitful negotiations with the Canningites in the latter part of 1830 do not suggest that Wellington was ever persuaded of the absolute necessity of recruiting in that quarter; nor did Palmerston after Huskisson's death show much zeal for returning to the duke's command. Tired and disgruntled by the complexities of political leadership, so alien to the hard simplicities of his own nature, Wellington even momentarily contemplated retiring on the death of George IV, and handing over his thankless office to Peel.

The general election of 1830 made little difference to the parliamentary situation, but it did display the growing mood of the country in favour of reform, particularly parliamentary reform. At the opening of the session it was made clear that the Canningites regarded a limited measure of parliamentary reform as a condition of coalition, failing which they would go into opposition. This, for Wellington, was the final straw. Opposed to any alliance with the Whigs, unhappy about any reunion with the Canningites, he made up his mind to stop the rot and rally his sulky Tory followers by a firm declaration of policy. The reverse occurred; for his famous and uncompromising statement in November 1830, that he would resist parliamentary reform of any kind and at all times, brought an immediate defeat in the Commons and the end of his premiership. With his position crumbling and his troops still mutinous, the duke had risked everything on one pitched battle; and had lost. The tactical skill which had made him a master of war was something almost wholly lacking to him in politics.

In less than eighteen months he was to give another demonstration of his essentially unpolitical nature. When his ministry left office, all the Cabinet ministers except the duke told the king that some sort of parliamentary reform was inevitable. It was a mark of the hesitancy in the Opposition that, despite their leader's views, the chief members of the party in the Commons agreed to wait until Grey had produced his measure before deciding whether to oppose. In the event the radical nature of the bill brought forward in March 1831 rallied the opposition in both Houses. The Government was forced first to procure a more manageable House of Commons by a fresh election in 1831, and next to take the unprecedented step of asking the king to create some fifty new peers to ensure a majority in the House of Lords. Before the bill went through to the statute-book, however, Wellington, in May 1832, staggered his supporters and alarmed the public by accepting the king's commission to form a government. It was a very curious commission. The new ministers were to satisfy the country by carrying a substantial measure of reform; but it was hoped that since it would be a Wellingtonian bill, the House of Lords would pass it without the coercion of fresh peerage creations. The duke's attitude was simple. Reform was inevitable and he was prepared to answer an appeal from his distraught monarch to save the Upper House from the indignity which threatened it. Political consistency was a consideration which hardly troubled him.

His simple loyalty was thwarted only by the refusal of nearly all his leading party colleagues, headed by Peel, to have any part in such a spectacular reversal of their previous position. They thought they had saved the duke from an immense blunder; he thought them timid and lacking in public spirit. Fundamentally it was the difference between a soldier and a politician. But the open breach between the duke and his second-in-command not only embittered their relations, but left the Opposition more divided and lacking in leadership than ever. It is

probable that after the inept termination of Wellington's ministry in
1830 Peel had made up his mind never to serve under the duke again.
The Days of May could only have confirmed his conviction of the in-
adequacies of the duke as Prime Minister and party leader. Yet for all
his political naivety, Wellington represented qualities which were to
remain enduring strands in Conservative philosophy: patriotism,
respect for tradition, a desire to preserve the great institutions of the
state, a strong sense of public duty and concern for national interests.
Miscast as a politician, the duke still remained a pillar of the party and
an indispensable member (in Peel's view at least) of any Conservative
administration that might conceivably be formed.

The prospect of such an event seemed remote in 1832. Notwith-
standing his many great qualities the duke had done his party a great
disservice. Popular prejudice against a general, the duke's laconic contempt for the mob, together with his own incautious utterances, ensured
that the Wellingtonian stamp given to Conservatism between 1828 and
1830 was, in the public mind, one of reactionary authoritarianism. The
Conservative party's opposition to the Reform Bill and the grotesque
radical portrayal of the Days of May as an abortive attempt at a military
dictatorship merely confirmed this impression. That the image hardly at
any point corresponded with fact was irrelevant. In the short term
appearances in politics are more important than realities. The day
would come when the old duke would once more become a hero to the
man in the street. But that day was not yet; and by the time it came
Wellington had turned his back for ever on party politics.


II


The long struggle against Reform in 1831–2 had to some extent brought
together the divided elements of the opposition; but it was a tendency
rather than an accomplishment. The struggle had been less effective
than it might have been, partly because of the divisions in the House of
Commons' party and Peel's reluctance to set himself up as the leader of
men with whom he had nothing in common except dislike of the Reform
Bill, and partly because of the divergences between Peel and his nominal
leader in the House of Lords. Apart from all other considerations, the
difference between the two men in their reaction to the bill was instruc-
tive. Wellington, though ready in 1832 to yield to tactical needs and pass
a measure of reform, was in his strategy negative and despondent. He

thought that the bill would inevitably destroy the old constitution. When it became law his dominant concern became, in the words of his famous question, 'How is the king's government to be carried on?' His instinct therefore was to support the government, any government, that had a chance of remaining in being. His pessimism about the future disabled him from any constructive approach to the problems of the present. Peel, tactically, had stood to the last for uncompromising opposition, even though after the 1831 election there was no chance that the Bill could be stopped. His object was to make its passage so painful and odious that the Whigs would never again attempt any inroads on the constitution. Once the bill was through, however, his strategy was to accept the new situation and, within the new context of politics, to rally all the scattered forces of conservatism in the country against radical demands for further organic changes in Church and State.

The first reformed House of Commons, marked by lack of discipline, a vast and amorphous 'Reform' majority, and the patent uneasiness of the Whigs in dealing with their Radical and Irish allies, provided him with an appropriate background for the enunciation of what he believed to be true Conservative principles. The fact that he was not the party leader, and that the party itself in the Commons was headless and decimated, gave him almost total freedom of action. Wellington and Grey between them had cleared away most of the difficulties and inhibitions which had brought him in 1831–2 to the lowest point of his political career; and he was too good a politician not to sense that a new start could now be made. His famous speech of February 1833, supporting the Government's Irish legislation, laid the groundwork for his whole future policy. On the one hand he refused to join in any factious harrying of the ministry to secure a mere partisan triumph; and he promised his support for all measures designed to strengthen the basic structure of society – law and order, the maintenance of the constitution, and the security of property. On the other hand he declared his unequivocal and ungrudging acceptance of the Reform Act, and his readiness to continue the work of rational reform, gradually, dispassionately and deliberately, for any institution that demonstrably required it. The lesson was clear. In an inexperienced and volatile legislature he held up the banner not of reaction but of firmness, moderation and practical good sense. It was the speech not of a party leader but of a leader round whom a party could gather. In the confused and restless political situation that had resulted from the passage of the Reform Act, the effect was prodigious. At one stroke he had established his claims to statesmanship. In the next two years, while Grey's divided and harassed Cabinet tried to work out a common policy on the problems confronting them, all that Peel did enhanced his parliamentary stature. The personal supremacy which Peel achieved in 1833 marked him out as the man of the future. But he was not yet the acknowledged party leader; nor could a Conservative party in any formal sense be said to exist. At the end of the following year, however, the implicit logic of the situation was made explicit by the personal act of William IV. He had been perturbed by the resignation from office first of the Stanley group and then of Grey himself, alarmed by the reforming propensities of the Melbourne administration, and stung by the proposed appointment of the radical Lord John Russell as Leader of the House of Commons. In November 1834 he dismissed the Whigs and called on Wellington to take over the government. For the last time a British sovereign had exercised his legal right of dismissing his ministers. It was an irony of history that the final use of this royal prerogative marked, as clearly as any one event could do, the emergence of the modern party system which was to render that prerogative obsolete. Had Peel been in England at the time, instead of holidaying in Italy, he himself would have received the king's commission. The events of 1832 had been more than enough to convince the king that it was vital to secure the services of the leading politician in the House of Commons. Wellington himself, taught by bitter experience, consented only to act as caretaker until Peel returned to put himself at the head of the new Government.

When over three weeks later the Prime Minister designate arrived back in London, two things were already clear to him; and a third was soon apparent. Premature as he considered the king's action to have been, he could not humiliate his monarch, abandon Wellington, and disappoint his expectant followers by refusing to take office. Equally certainly there would have to be a general election. The 150 nominal Conservatives in the Commons could in no circumstances maintain an administration in office. What was further borne home to Peel after his return was that in the country at large there was wide-spread distrust of the duke, whose singular role as the only minister so far appointed in the three-week old government served only to revive the prejudices of the 1830-2 period. With the Whigs resentful at their sudden ejection from power, Radicals and Dissenters ready to believe that the king had once more called in his military servant to stem the onward march of liberal reform, it was an unpropitious setting for Peel's first essay as

Prime Minister. The prompt refusal of Stanley and his followers to join the new ministry was due, more than anything else, to their hostility towards Wellington and the reactionary character which they felt had been put on the administration at its birth. The issue of the *Tamworth Manifesto* within ten days of Peel's return to London was therefore a deliberate attempt by Peel to efface the Wellingtonian image which the accident of his absence in Italy had contrived to perpetuate.

In itself the *Manifesto* was an unprecedented act on the part of a Prime Minister, or even of a party leader. In form an address to his constituents, in fact it was an appeal to the whole electorate; as such it created an enormous sensation. It was not an enunciation of Conservative philosophy; nor was it a general party programme; nor was it new. Nearly everything in it had already been said by Peel in the House of Commons. Primarily it was designed to aid his followers in the forthcoming elections by a statement of his attitude towards the main political issues of the moment and of the general spirit in which he proposed to conduct his administration. Nevertheless, the concept of moderate, rational, objective reform as a middle course between negative Tory reaction and the doctrinaire radicalism of the Left was a novelty that was at once both attractive and reassuring. What made its impact on the country was that he was saying it now not as an individual politician on the opposition benches but as the king's minister. In an age when party programmes were unknown and when statesmen reserved their political utterances for Parliament or for a few select audiences such as the Mansion House banquet, the *Tamworth Manifesto* was a remarkable piece of publicity. In the field of political propaganda it was not matched by any party leader until the generation of Gladstone and Disraeli after the Second Reform Act.

In its immediate purpose it failed. Though the Conservatives added a hundred seats to their previous strength in the Commons, they had neither the candidates nor the organisation to win an outright majority; and party loyalties were already too strong to allow Peel to detach, as he had hoped, a significant number from the ranks of the opposition. After two months of stubborn fighting, the ministry finally abandoned the unequal struggle against the hastily cemented majority of Whigs, Radicals and O'Connell's Irish. It was inevitable in these circumstances that all the planned legislation of the ministry went by the board. The one solid and permanent achievement was the Ecclesiastical Commission of 1835; and this was possible only because it could be created by the executive power of the Crown and did not need the legislative sanction of Parliament. Nevertheless, by providing the Church of England with both the stimulus and the machinery to reform itself, the Commission not only saved the Church from its Radical and Dissenting enemies, but provided the first example of Peelite progressivism in action. Despite the shipwreck of all his other measures, however, the long-term effect of the Hundred Days in 1834–5 was immense. Office, and the fugitive glimpse of power, closed the ranks of the Conservatives, raised their morale and stimulated them to their first serious effort at organisation in the constituencies. For Peel himself it was a personal triumph. The temper and skill which he exhibited in his difficult position earned him praise from friends and foe alike. He had raised his standing in the country enormously. More than that, the party had come to him; he had not had to court or compromise in order to win it over. With his followers, as with the public, the elevation to the office of Prime Minister marked a decisive stage in his career. If any one individual can be said to have made Peel leader of the Conservative party, it was the tired, harassed, elderly king. But in accepting Peel as leader, the party had also accepted his principles. Tamworth Conservatism was now, as much as anything could be, the official party doctrine.

During the next six years Peel's strategy followed the lines he had sketched out in the Commons in 1833 and announced to the country in 1834. He assisted the ministers against pressure from their radical allies for such further parliamentary reforms as the ballot; he co-operated in passing measures, such as the English Municipal Corporations Act of 1835, which seemed to him in principle if not in all their details just and necessary; he resisted proposals for the abolition of church rates in 1837, and for a more secular form of national education in 1839, which affected the rights and property of the Church. The one tactical mistake he made was to press in 1836 and 1837 for the transfer of the Irish boroughs to the local county government in place of the proposed reform of the Irish municipal corporations put forward by the Whigs. This in the end proved an untenable position, though the long battle from 1836 to 1839 enabled the Opposition to extract concessions over other Irish measures like tithe and poor law. The most notable triumph was the ultimate abandonment by the Whigs of the attempt to appropriate part of the revenues of the Irish Church for secular purposes, the issue which had been the proximate cause of Peel's resignation in 1835. As session followed session, with a dwindling Liberal majority in the Commons and a confident and powerful Conservative majority in the

Lords, the Whigs found themselves increasingly confined within the narrow area of action chalked out for them by the leader of the Opposition. As an indignant Radical M.P. observed in 1839, Mr O'Connell governed Ireland, Sir Robert Peel governed England; the leader of the Opposition was satisfied with power without place; the Whigs enjoyed place without power. This was an exaggeration but it cut too near the bone for comfort. One undoubted reason for the decline of the Whigs in the years immediately preceding the election of 1841 was the widespread impression that they had lost political initiative and were clinging to office after they had ceased to be able to exercise it effectively.

This situation also had its dangers and difficulties for Peel. One great weapon at the disposal of the Opposition was their standing majority in the House of Lords, which at times resembled an executioner's scaffold waiting to decapitate government bills as they came up from the Lower House. It was this which gave rise to the intensive agitation of 1834–7 for a curtailment of the powers of the Upper House. Peelite policy required a measure of discrimination in the use of the Lords' veto; and there were times when it took all Peel's patience and skill, not to speak of an occasional exhibition of downright anger, to induce the Tory peers not to abuse their power, discredit the party and drive the Whigs to premature resignation. This in turn resulted in a modification of his own tactics in the Commons. One of the motives which led him to the false step over Irish corporations had been his anxiety to keep Wellington and the peers in line with the Conservatives in the Lower House. 'Few people,' he wrote grimly about the internal party dissensions over the Irish municipal question in 1837, 'can judge of the difficulty there has frequently been of maintaining harmony between the various branches of the Conservative party – the great majority in the House of Lords and the minority in the House of Commons.' Without Wellington's assistance in fact the task would have been hopeless. Confusion and disagreements between Peel and Wellington sometimes arose; but in the end, and on every important issue, the duke's influence was always thrown behind the official party line. In this Wellington was following an inner logic of his own. Not only did his sense of discipline range him behind Peel, but his foreboding sense of the difficulties which any Conservative ministry would meet in attempting to govern the country made him reluctant to do anything which would make the Whigs resign.

In the House of Commons' party the task of maintaining unity was less arduous. Apart from occasional manifestations from the Irish

Conservatives, the High Church Anglicans and what one Conservative party manager disrespectfully styled the 'fanatick Agriculturalists', the back-bench M.P.s showed a general readiness to accept leadership and discipline. A party in opposition but confident of ultimate success has obvious incentives to avoid domestic bickering. The efficient party organisation built up after 1834 reinforced this natural tendency and provided an increasing guarantee that victory at the polls could not long be delayed. The Chief Whips whom Peel appointed – Sir George Clerk and Sir Thomas Fremantle – were a marked improvement on Holmes, Ross, and Planta who had served in the pre-1830 era; and a notable new development was the small but hard-working committee under Lord Granville Somerset set up to supervise elections, provide money and candidates, and collect information on the registration of voters in the provinces. In the indefatigable Bonham, an Oxonian, member of Lincoln's Inn and former M.P., the party had an electoral expert of perceptibly higher social standing than the two Radical solicitors out-side Parliament, Parkes and Coppock, who carried out comparable functions for the Liberals; and Bonham, in a special sense, was Peel's man. There was scarcely a ripple in the party which was not reported to Peel by his faithful watchdog in the Carlton. Though Peel had no personal liking for the tedious and sordid details of party management, the party under his leadership acquired a more professional and competent organisation at the centre than it had ever possessed before or was to possess again until the days of Spofforth and Gorst. On a higher political plane, Peel's patient courtship of Stanley and Graham, the two principal seceders from Grey's ministry in 1834, had its reward when in 1837 those two outstanding cross-bench figures joined the Conservative ranks. It was now only a matter of time before an outright victory placed them in office. The Bedchamber incident in 1839, though it revealed Victoria's partisan feelings and retained the Whigs in power for two more barren years, did nothing to halt the advance of the party in the constituencies. The problem for the party leader in this final phase of opposition was to hold in check his impatient followers, who were thirsting for one final onslaught on the enfeebled Whig administration which would yield into their eager hands the fruits of office and patronage.

In his handling of his parliamentary following in these years Peel showed increasing skill and authority. Strong-willed, and a trifle con-temptuous of the backwoodsmen of his party, he had no intention of allowing either his tactics or strategy to be dictated from below. Nevertheless, as head of an increasingly powerful opposition between 1835 and 1841, he had both leisure and incentive to evolve his own technique of party management: the regular pre-sessional gatherings of the inner ring of his immediate colleagues at his great country house at Drayton, the special meetings of the leading debaters and experts during session, the periodic conferences with Wellington and the more influential peers, and less frequently, the full assembly of the parliamentary party in the Commons. These, reinforced by his regular political dinners at Whitehall Gardens and occasional appearances at the Carlton Club, served to give both direction and control to a body of M.P.s who were still unused to the restraints of party discipline and against whom few sanctions could be employed. Peel is often accused of being out of touch with his followers and taking too little pains to conciliate them. In fact his leadership in opposition exhibited a high degree of tact, patience and assiduity in keeping his followers together without compromising his essential political principles. Only when office after 1841 robbed him of leisure, and the needs of national policy overrode in his mind the class and sectional views of his party, did his personal control begin to deteriorate.

But it was not only in his handling of the parliamentary party that he showed qualities of leadership. A feature of the years after 1834, and one without which the victory at the polls in 1841 could hardly have been possible, was his growing appeal to a wider public. The work begun with the *Tamworth Manifesto* in 1834 was carried on whenever the occasion presented itself (and by the political conventions of the day it came rarely) to preach the gospel of Peelite Conservatism outside the walls of Parliament. Though the main themes of his speeches, as of the party spokesmen in general, were the defence of the Church, the integrity of the House of Lords, and the preservation of the monarchical constitution, he gave an emphasis and flavour of his own to those time-honoured arguments. It was not only what he said, but the kind of audience to whom he said it. He addressed himself repeatedly to the professional, mercantile and industrial middle classes. He sought to convince them that, supporters of the Reform Act though they might have been, their duty was now to combine with the Conservative party in maintaining peace, order and the prosperous evolution of society; and that in turn the Conservative party stood for the defence not merely of the landed aristocracy but of the interests of the solid middle classes of early-Victorian Britain. Two favourite themes, seen for example in his city speech of 1835, the Glasgow civic banquet in 1837, and at the

Merchant Taylors Hall dinner of 1838, were the interdependence of industry, commerce and agriculture, and the continuity of British political life and institutions which had shaped the character of the British people. What he preached he practised. In his friendship with scientists and engineers, his interest in the arts, his patronage of scholars and literary men, his recruitment of able young lieutenants from middle-class families like Praed, Gladstone and Cardwell, he sought to strengthen the links between political Conservatism and the educated moneyed classes of society. He had recognised, more promptly and explicitly than the aristocratic Whigs, that in the post-Reform world only a composite and national party could hope to achieve and retain power. The son of a cotton-manufacturer himself, he tried to effect the political amalgam of classes and interests of which his own family was an example. The electoral successes in the urban constituencies which, added to the more predictable victories in the counties, provided the majority of 1841, were a practical reward for all that he had worked for in the previous decade.

III

Accession to power in 1841 worked an uncomfortable change in the Conservative party. Its leader was now subject to the demands and restrictions of office; and the tasks confronting him were not those for which the party had been prepared in Opposition. The mere fact that it was in office seemed proof that the danger to Church and Constitution from post-1832 Radicalism had passed away. For many of its ordinary members the object of the party had been achieved. But for Peel the work was just beginning. Office gave him the opportunity to apply Conservative principles on a new and sophisticated plane of politics; but it took the professionals and the more intelligent of his party to appreciate this. The rank and file watched, admiringly or uncomprehendingly, while the Prime Minister launched into the soaring flights of his last great ministry. They were quite unprepared for what he was going to do; though if they had cast their recollections back to the 1820s they ought not to have been surprised. Nobody who had studied Peel's career could have expected him to be other than an active and reforming head of government. Governmental activity, however, is often as disturbing to its supporters as to its opponents. As long as Peel achieved triumphs in areas which did not touch the basic interests and instincts of the party, its members were content to share in his glory. It was a different matter when his policies affected them personally. Wellington had once observed to Peel that their supporters cared for nothing except their own property and the Church. It was a text for which the years 1841–6 provided an ample sermon.

In 1841 Peel came to power with a free hand to deal with the new problems of the new decade. Overshadowing everything else was the depression in trade and industry which had started in 1837 and which was getting steadily worse. Economic and social issues now filled the public stage. The emergence of the two greatest extra-parliamentary movements of the century – Chartism and the Anti-Corn Law League – marked the turn in the tide of national affairs. Early Victorian elections do not lend themselves to ready analysis, but there was a general feeling in 1841 that Peel and his colleagues would be more competent than Melbourne's Cabinet in solving the mounting difficulties at home. It was a confidence in men rather than measures. To a remarkable extent Peel had kept himself free from promises and commitments. Trust in the new men and disillusionment with their predecessors was the basis of the great Conservative victory at the polls. But what Peel had said, repeatedly and emphatically both before and after the general election, was that he would govern according to his own sense of national needs, and by that alone.

Proof that Peel meant the warning to be taken seriously came in the very first session. The great Budget of 1842 which laid the foundation for his whole economic policy was in three parts: a revival of the wartime income tax, a drastic revision of the tariff, and a new Corn Law giving a considerably lower rate of protection. It was over the last that the chief difficulty with the party was expected. Though protection for Britain's largest industry had never yet been a party issue, the agitation against the Corn Laws in the late 1830s had seen the Whigs slowly recede to the compromise of a low fixed duty. The Conservative Opposition, which even before 1841 included most of the representatives of the English agricultural constituencies, had increasingly been thrust into the position of chief parliamentary champions of a principle which had until recently been common ground between the two aristocratic parties. In the counties and rural boroughs it was clear that the Conservatives had reaped a handsome profit from the unpopularity of the Whig proposals on corn. Though the question was hardly raised in 1841, since it was never seriously in doubt, most Conservative candidates would have pledged themselves without a qualm to the maintenance of agricultural protection. Peel himself, though careful not to tie himself to the details of the existing Act, had always defended on practical grounds the continuation of a tariff on foreign corn.

On the other hand the 1828 Corn Law was unsatisfactory and it was generally assumed that it would be amended. Peel's revised bill proved in practice the most workmanlike of the four Corn Laws passed between 1815 and 1845. He had taken care to consult agricultural opinion in the party and the protection he offered was more generous than he privately thought was strictly necessary. As an additional precaution he brought the bill forward before the other two great budgetary measures and summoned a general meeting of the party to explain it on the opening day of the debate. His tactics succeeded perfectly and the Corn Bill went through more smoothly than anyone in the Cabinet had expected. Only later did the anticipated difficulties with his party emerge. When the details of the revised general tariff were revealed, it dawned on the agricultural members that the Government was pursuing a deliberate free trade policy over a wider front than corn alone. Protectionists by instinct and representing Protectionist constituencies, they grew increasingly distrustful of the principles on which their leader was acting. The flattering compliments paid to ministerial policy by Whigs and Radicals only deepened their distrust. The income tax did not disturb them; the extension of liberal principles to imported food did. On the import of live cattle in fact more than eighty of them went into the lobby against their leader. But there was no danger that the Government would be defeated; and probably many of the rebels were merely casting a vote to please their constituents with no expectation or even desire that it would have any effect.

It was an age when the independence exercised by leaders as ministers of the Crown was matched by the independence claimed by private M.P.s. General loyalty to a party, a genuine wish to maintain in office a particular set of men, did not by the conventions of the day preclude an individual politician from occasionally taking a line of his own when his personal convictions or the interests of his constituents were concerned. The extreme agriculturalist wing of the party numbered no more than the intellectual Peelites, less if the official men were thrown into the balance. As long as the Prime Minister could hold the party centre, he had little to fear. The general free-trade majority in the Commons would always be a safeguard against the 'agricultural Fanaticks'. Nevertheless the events of 1842 cast a shadow, even if at the time it seemed a transient one, over the relations between Peel and his party. Beneath the surface there was a separation of minds between the Prime Minister and many of his followers which widened steadily as time passed. For the Protectionists the measures of 1842 could be swallowed as a dose of unpalatable medicine which need never be repeated. For Peel the experience of office, especially the harrowing task of governing England in 1842, the worst year through which the country passed during the century, only hardened his conviction that what Carlyle had already christened the 'Condition of England Question' must be the major concern of national policy. If unemployment, distress and rioting were not sufficient, Chartism and the Anti-Corn-Law League were there to remind him that an aristocratic land-owning Parliament could ignore social problems only at the risk of weakening the whole political authority of the State. Protestations of general loyalty in those circumstances were of little use if they did not result in the steady voting support necessary to pass the Government's deliberate policy decisions into law.

The difference of approach was sharply illustrated in 1844 over two apparently disconnected questions of government legislation: the sugar tariff and a new Factory Bill. On both issues the Government was defeated as the result of amendments moved by Conservative M.P.s and supported by many members of the party in alliance with sections of the Opposition. Part of the Conservative support for Ashley's attempt at a further limitation of factory hours was inspired by genuine humanitarianism; but part was certainly due to a more unprincipled animosity against industrial manufacturers who were the backbone of the Anti-Corn-Law League. On sugar there was what looked suspiciously like a deliberate alliance from completely discordant motives between Conservative Protectionists and Liberal Free-Traders. Peel was understandably incensed. At a time when industry was just emerging from the great depression of 1837–43, it seemed to him that the House of Commons was trying to impose fresh burdens on the manufacturers. On sugar the Government's proposals were part of a careful transitional plan designed to loosen the monopoly of British West Indian planters without having recourse to slave-grown sugar from South America. What particularly angered the Prime Minister was that the policy of the Government was being obstructed by groups of his own supporters in combination with his official opponents. On both occasions he used the full weight of his personal authority, including the open threat of resignation, to force the House of Commons to rescind its decision. His action on the sugar amendment, coming only a month after the reversal of the vote on the Factory Bill, was particularly disastrous. A party meeting beforehand completely failed to reach agreement; and in the renewed debate Peel made a harsh and resentful speech which gave much offence. He believed in fact that he was going to be defeated a second time and warned the queen that this would probably mean his resignation. In the event he secured a majority and had his way; but in the process he destroyed much of the party's personal loyalty to him. To many Conservatives this second reversal of votes at the bidding of the Prime Minister seemed to verge on executive despotism. Whatever his justification, it could hardly be denied that Peel had handled the whole affair as badly as any in his long parliamentary career.

The tension in the party was clearly seen the following session. The great Budget of 1845, based on the solid foundation of the surplus created by the renewed income tax, effected an even more sweeping reduction in the tariff system. It imposed no new sacrifices on agriculture but on the other hand it made no concessions to it. While the public basked in the return of prosperity and acclaimed the financial mastery of the Prime Minister, all that the silent country gentry saw was yet another long stride along the path of economic liberalism. Alone among the great interests of the country they were to receive no compensation, not even a word of praise or encouragement, for the continued burden of the income tax. It was in this ominous atmosphere that Disraeli began his bitter guerrilla attacks on the Prime Minister, and the Government ran into fresh party difficulties over their Irish legislation.

The suppression of O'Connell's repeal movement in 1843 had opened the way in Peel's view for a policy of conciliation in Ireland. The most controversial part of the Government's programme was the proposal in 1845 to give a greatly increased subsidy to the Catholic seminary at Maynooth. This not only evoked the passionate opposition of the English Dissenters, but led to a complete cross-party division in the House of Commons. Liberal Conservatives, Whigs and Irish combined in support of the bill against High Anglicans, ultra-Protestants and Radicals. The bitter debate laid bare the roots of British political life and in the course of it the Prime Minister's whole career, including the leading role he had played in Catholic Emancipation, came up for searching and hostile examination. On the third reading of the bill the Conservatives split by a majority of one, 149 to 148, against the measure. Only the weight of the Liberal vote carried the bill through the Commons. It is possible that some at least of the Conservative opposition to the bill derived not from religious motives but from hidden resentments over protection and free trade. But the effect on the party as a whole was profound. After the strains of the previous session, this open desertion by half the party finally destroyed what remained of Conservative morale. Once more Peel had his way; but of all his actions as Prime Minister the Maynooth Bill had come closest to a repudiation of the classic Church and State principles on which the party had been built up in the years after the Reform Act. To many observers, not unsympathetic to Peel, it seemed a repetition of Catholic Emancipation and likely to have similar consequences.

Nevertheless, though the rock of party support was splintering beneath him, the tall figure of the Prime Minister still dominated the political world, unrivalled, irremoveable and irreplaceable. In the Cabinet his intellectual supremacy, demonstrated in the remorseless logic of his superb Irish memoranda, had completely convinced his colleagues. The only ministerial loss over Maynooth of any consequence was Gladstone; and that for peculiarly Gladstonian reasons. In the Commons Peel had shown not only all his customary tactical and forensic skill but a remarkable degree of conciliatoriness and forbearance. In private however he was filled with the same grim determination to enforce the Government's policy which he had exhibited the previous year. The success of his hard line tactics in 1844, and the ease with which he had passed his budget in 1845, had only strengthened his conviction that determination was one of the secrets of government. 'The fact is,' he wrote to a friend during the session, 'people like a certain degree of obstinacy and presumption in a minister. They abuse him for dictation and arrogance, but they like being governed.' It was a doctrine that had its dangers; but by the summer of 1845 Peel was in a stubborn mood. The strains and responsibilities of office and of continuous over-work caused in part by his minute supervision of all the departments of his administration were resulting in occasional periods of weariness and depression. His physical resilience was declining and with it his political resilience. Never a flexible man, Peel was becoming more inflexible than ever. The shock of the potato failure in Ireland in the autumn of 1845 fell therefore on a party and a leader already psychologically estranged.

The key to the Irish situation was that the majority of peasants lived on a subsistence economy. If their own food was destroyed, they had no money to obtain it elsewhere. It was clear that money would have to be provided by the Government, either to buy food for free distribution or to give to the peasantry directly through poor relief and indirectly through public works and loans in the form of wages. But could the Government ask the British tax-payer for millions of pounds for famine relief and still retain tariffs on imported food, at a time when the mass of educated British opinion had come to accept the arguments of the Anti-Corn-Law League and when that organisation was mounting a massive electoral campaign for the repeal of the Corn Laws? Peel, and, after an interval, Lord John Russell, judged not. The Irish disaster necessitated therefore a review of the Corn Laws. But to what end? Peel's view, guided by the remarkable success of his tariff-reduction policy since 1842 and sharpened by his acute sensitivity to the social problem in England, was that there was no middle course between his law of 1842 and complete repeal. What was crucial to his action in 1845-6, however, was the fact that he had come to this conclusion as early as the summer of 1843. All that the Irish famine meant was that he had been overtaken by events. There is no reason to doubt his subsequent statement to Prince Albert that he had intended to announce his change of view to the party before the next election and seek a mandate to repeal the Corn Laws in the new Parliament. The coming of the potato disease in the cold wet summer of 1845 did not therefore cause him to seek a solution to the Corn Law issue; it merely revealed a decision already implicit in his mind. The only problem was to secure the consent of his Cabinet. Given his elevated view of the responsibility resting on the executive, the question of personal consistency and party interest was one he deliberately put aside. It was insoluble; and to Peel largely irrelevant.

For most of his Cabinet, however, it was the principal reason for their reluctance in November and December to accept Peel's proposals. The delay was critical. It allowed Russell to come forward publicly as the parliamentary champion of total repeal; and it gave time for the agricultural feeling in the provinces to organise. Russell had his chance to form a ministry at the end of the year, and failed. His failure brought Peel back again with a united Cabinet (barring the loss of Stanley) and a mandate to repeal the Corn Laws – a mandate which derived not so much from Parliament and the electorate as from the Crown and the whole political situation in which the country found itself. But his inability the previous November to take the initiative by calling Parliament together in emergency session and putting forward his policy while the agricultural protectionists were unprepared, destroyed the last slender chance of keeping the party together. The decisive factor was not the subsequent emergence of Lord George Bentinck as the unexpected and aggressive leader of the Tory malcontents, but the pressure brought to bear on the representatives of the agricultural constituencies in the winter of 1845–6.

It was a paradox of the complicated politics of the forties that the activities of the Anti-Corn-Law League actually imperilled Peel's chances of repealing the Corn Laws. The League's brutal and unscrupulous propaganda against farmers and landlords had in the previous years provoked a natural reaction among the classes they so savagely attacked. It was first seen in the duke of Buckingham's Society for the Protection of Agriculture, formed in 1840. Then, following the intensive activity of the League in the English rural areas, came a new and improved Central Agricultural Society under the presidency of the duke of Richmond, which acted as a national focus for the numerous country protection societies already in existence. The League in fact engendered an Anti-League. Many of the leading Protectionist M.P.s were members of the central body; others were subject to the pressure from its affiliated branches in their own constituencies. The annual meeting of the Society in London in December 1845, when public speculation was raging about the intentions of the Government, took up the challenge offered by the intensified activities of the League and Russell's *Edinburgh Letter*. In the early weeks of 1846, before Parliament met and before Peel's plans were disclosed, meetings of local protection societies were held all over England to promote petitions and demand pledges from their parliamentary representatives. For the first time Peel's control of his party was threatened not merely by a dissident group in the Commons but by a powerful outside organisation able to exert pressure on Conservative M.P.s through the sensitive medium of their constituents. It was this external force, acting on the already strained fabric of the parliamentary party, which finally broke the great Conservative party which had been returned to power in 1841.

Whether in these circumstances internal party discussions would have made any difference is doubtful. But in fact no party meeting was held. Peel thought it worse than useless to call one; his mind was made up and preliminary talks would merely put weapons into the hands of the Protectionists. When the first decisive trial of strength came in February, two thirds of the Conservative party in the Commons voted against their leader. It was a repudiation on one issue only, though one which concerned the party's greatest social and economic interest. It did not prevent Peel, with the aid of the Liberal opposition, from carrying through all his 1846 fiscal measures intact. The failure to stop the Prime Minister, however, created in Bentinck's violent and ruthless mind a determination that, even if the Corn Laws were repealed, the renegade leader of the party should be expelled from office. On the Irish Protection of Life bill, a security measure which the Conservatives traditionally upheld, and which Bentinck himself had supported earlier in the session, he led a reduced band of less than a third of the Protectionists to join the Whigs, Liberals and Irish in overthrowing the Government.

The events of 1846 signified the most spectacular party disruption in British political history; and its effects were long-lasting. The brains and experience of the party went one way; the rank and file the other. 'Conservative reunion' was a subject frequently canvassed by politicians during the next decade. But the personal bitterness created by the split, as well as intellectual disagreement on policy, made it impossible for the leading Peelites to reunite with the Protectionists even after the deaths of Bentinck and Peel. It was the Victorian Liberal party which was in the end to receive this uncovenanted bonus from their opponents. Peel himself, weary of office, disillusioned with party, and bitterly resentful at the Protectionists' condonation of the gross personal attacks made on him by Bentinck and Disraeli, made it his sole object in the last four years of his life to sustain Russell and the Whigs in office as the only possible government of the country and the only effective guardian of his own achievements. Though he had in his own epoch-making years of power acted increasingly as minister for the nation rather than for a party, he never wavered in his conviction that what he had done had served the deepest interests of the party he led. The repeal of the Corn Laws was in his view the most conservative act of his life. The future of British agriculture depended not on the dead hand of legislative protection but on expanding consumption and the use of more scientific techniques. The attempt to maintain the Corn Laws had merely compromised the position of the aristocracy, evoked class conflict and damaged the cause of good government. The survival of the mixed and balanced constitution depended on the will and ability of the aristocratic parties to rule in accordance with national needs. The narrow electoral system, which left the mass of the people still unenfranchised, made it even more imperative to subordinate sectional interests to the fundamental requirements of a growing industrial nation. On those terms only could the historic political parties retain the confidence of the nation.

Peel's attitude to the party which he had not only led but in a sense created, remained hard and unforgiving. He always thought it had deserted him, not that he had betrayed it. 'In any part which I may have taken in laying the foundations of the Conservative party', he told Prince Albert in 1847, 'I cannot reproach myself with having gained its confidence on false pretences.' In his more perverse moments he was inclined to regret, not that he had paid too little attention to party opinion, but that he had paid too much. He remembered the many instances, long before Maynooth and the Corn Laws, when he had encountered the utmost difficulty in getting his views accepted without an open rupture. What angered him above all was that the achievements of his ministry apparently counted for nothing. Peace had been secured abroad, prosperity and contentment at home; Chartism had been extinguished; the national finances placed on a sound footing; trade and industry were flourishing; the Church was safe; the cry for more parliamentary reform silenced. But all this was forgotten by his angry followers because he had tried to pacify Ireland and had saved the landed aristocracy from the consequences of their own folly. Looking back on the years since 1832, he was half-persuaded that the disruption of 1846 had been inevitable from the start; that though the party had been reconstructed after the Reform Act the seeds of discord had always been there. In opposition the party had gathered strength and obtained the confidence of the country because of the sense and moderation with which it had acted. But during its years of power it had gradually forgotten the real sources of its influence in the country. It had ignored the new conditions created by the Reform Act; and in reverting, both in politics and religion, to its primitive past, it had forfeited its title to govern.

This was an incomplete analysis since it took no account of Peel's own deficiencies as a party leader: his temperamental shyness which often gave the appearance of coldness, his stubborn will, his contempt for the amateur country squires, his distaste for the petty arts of managing men, his resentment of attacks on his integrity and his impatience with criticism from those whose support he thought he had a right to expect. Bred in the older tradition of ministerial power, Peel had never come to terms with the new party system. Recognising that party must after 1832 be the basis of government, he still acted at times as though the constitutional principle of responsibility to Crown and Parliament was the only condition of ministerial action. Party for him was the servant, not the master of the executive. This is a constant dilemma of representative government to which there is no simple answer. In Peel's time there was the additional complication that the party system was still in its infancy. Both Conservatives and Liberals after 1832 found difficulty in working out a new framework of reference. The party rank and file, as well as their leaders, had much to learn before they adapted successfully to the changing conditions of political life. In a sense the great Conservative party of 1841 was a personal *tour de force*. But though Peel had driven his party too far and too fast, the road he had taken had been the right one. The man who was the real founder of modern Conservatism had read the signs of the times better than most of his followers. The public realised this; in the last four years of his life, as Greville observed, Peel would have swept the country in any popular election. In turning against him in 1846 the party had turned against its own future. Not for a generation did the Conservative party sufficiently recover its credibility to be given a working majority by the Victorian electorate.

# 2 Derby and Disraeli

## J. T. WARD

THERE were few similarities between the two men who preserved Toryism as a viable and meaningful creed in the years after 1846. In different ways they helped to save British Conservatism from the fate of much of the European Right and to create Britain's major political party of the future. They shared the unenviable task of leading a party against which the 'march of progress' appeared to be moving and which itself sometimes seemed to have a collective death wish – a body recently described as 'the backward and unpopular party, the party of bucolic obstruction and inertia, largely cut off from the new urban and industrial Britain, and lacking any point of *rapport* with its advancing social forces' and as 'a ragged, discordant phalanx which was reluctantly coming to accept Free Trade and its own seemingly ineluctable minority status'.[1] But they regularly disagreed over tactics, strategy and such philosophy as was possible in the circumstances.

Both men were, in a sense, converts to Toryism: Edward George Geoffrey Smith Stanley, the heir to Knowsley, from his family's traditional Whiggism, and Benjamin Disraeli, the son of a Jacobitical Jewish bibliophile, from a youthful radicalism. Both became earls: the one, educated at Eton and Christ Church, as fourteenth Lord Derby in 1851; the other, the product of forgotten establishments in Islington, Blackheath and Epping Forest, as first Lord Beaconsfield in 1876. As was proper for leaders of the 'Country' party, both became landowners: Derby as hereditary lord of almost 69,000 acres in five counties, which paid his son £163,273 in 1879, and Disraeli as purchaser (for £34,950, largely borrowed from the Bentincks) of 1004 Buckinghamshire acres, rented at £1494 in 1873.[2] Both made curious marriages: Derby to the dull Emma Caroline Bootle-Wilbraham – than whom, asserted Disraeli, 'no one had more splendid horses and equipages . . . [Derby] looked after this'; Disraeli to the doting, devoted widow Mary Anne Lewis, whose little fortune allowed him to continue to play the 'great game'.

For Further Reading relevant to this chapter, see page 247; for References, see page 252.

Vast social and 'caste' differences divided an uncrowned 'king of Lancashire' (whose son could refuse the actual crown of Greece in 1862) and 'that Jew', who so disgusted pious, snobbish, Liberal Mrs Gladstone as late as 1874. Fashionably, both men had debts; but Derby's (about £500,000) was inherited from a father eccentrically devoted to expensive zoological collections, while Disraeli's (something over £40,000) was inevitably 'self-earned'. A Stanley was eminently endowed for a smooth political career in both Houses of Parliament, via family borough and family peerage. A rather raffish Semite faced much more difficult problems. Stanley ancestors had earned English land from the Conqueror and had been men of mark in Plantaganet England, when d'Israeli forebears (despite the illustrious lineage dreamed up by their most famous descendant) were lost in Levantine ghettoes. It was not until 1853 that Disraeli was invited to Knowsley, which he found 'a wretched house'. The earl of Derby never found time to call at Hughenden.[3]

I

As a man who combined the inheritance of an authentic silver spoon with widely-acknowledged personal talents, Derby had a distinguished but sometimes disappointing political career. Despite an innate consistency, he was never a real 'party man'; whatever else the ultimate inheritance of broad acres might do to individuals, it rarely encouraged hacks. Born in 1799, Derby entered the Commons at twenty-one. The welcome young recruit to the Whig benches took nearly four years to steel himself for the ordeal of his maiden speech (on gas-lighting), but thereafter earned a parliamentary reputation. At twenty-eight he followed Lord Lansdowne into Canning's Government, as a Lord of the Treasury, and into Goderich's ministry, as Under-Secretary for the Colonies. It was not unreasonable for a 'progressive' Whig to make such an alliance with 'progressive' Tories. By July 1828 Sir James Graham, another Canningite-tinged Whig, saw Stanley as the potential leader of a new grouping – 'a party in the H. of Commons [formed] on some broad and intelligible principle, without any reference to leaders in the H. of Lords and without any direct compact with Brougham . . .'. Thereafter, young Stanley was regularly seen as a future premier: to many he seemed (in the words of a *Times* obituarist in 1869) the most 'brilliant eldest son produced by the British peerage for a hundred years'. To Creevey's amusement, Huskisson's reported view of Stanley as 'quite the Hope of the Nation' was read out at Knowsley in 1829. In a Britain still largely ruled by an hereditary peerage, an able scion of the house of Stanley inevitably set out on a political career with enormous advantages.

Following Wellington's fall in November 1830 Lansdowne, Carlisle, Graham, Stanley and their kind reverted to a more orthodox Whiggism. Stanley joined Grey's ministry as Chief Secretary for Ireland and soon earned golden opinions as a strong and capable minister: 'Grey was very loud to me in praise of Edward Stanley . . .' Creevey wrote in February 1831. 'He is quite ready for battle with O'Connell, and the greatest confidence is entertained that Edward will be too much for him.' The great maintainer of a strictly conservative line was rewarded by promotion to the Cabinet in June 1831 and became Secretary for War and Colonies in March 1833. But conservative principles could not be over-stretched. Parliamentary Reform was acceptable as a truly conservative measure. Secular spoliation of ecclesiastical property was another matter – especially, perhaps, if the Erastian operation was to be performed on the Church of Ireland for the delight of the loathsome O'Connell. When, in May 1834, Lord John Russell maintained tradition by assailing that 'Establishment' of which his family were highly privileged members by 'upsetting the Coach' over disendowment of the Irish Church, Stanley led a ministerial secession (of Richmond, Graham and Ripon). Within weeks, Irish problems drove Althorp and Grey himself from office.[4]

While both Melbourne (Grey's successor) and Peel made soundings, Stanley and Graham acted coolly. By November 1834 they had resolved that it was too early to accept any invitation from the Conservatives, and personal contacts were maintained with Melbourne. Early in 1835 there followed the attempt to create a new, transitional English party, the liberal–conservative 'Derby Dilly' with its 'Knowsley Creed'. Alignment with a Whiggism increasingly dependent upon O'Connellite and Radical votes was impossible. Consequently, despite inherited suspicion of Tory motives, Whiggish feelings of social superiority over Peel as a cotton master's son and reluctance to break with old friends, the dwindling group of Stanleyites gradually moved over to Conservatism. In June 1835 the group took seats on the Opposition benches, and in December 1837 Stanley formalised his support – because, as he declared in May 1838, of 'the strongest motives which could act on private feelings, or influence public conduct – . . . a sense of danger, a conviction of common interest'. The 'hope' of the Canningites and the splendid Whig minister thus became Peel's aide-de-camp. From 1834, after the death of his disapproving Whiggish grandfather, Stanley held the courtesy title of Viscount Stanley. Ten years later (at his own request) he was created Lord Stanley of Bickerstaffe. In 1841 he joined Peel's Cabinet as Secretary for War and Colonies, resigning in December 1845 as the only senior minister still unwilling to accept Corn Law repeal. As the hard-won Conservative alliance disintegrated during the classic debates of the spring of 1846, Peel was followed by his *alter ego*, Graham, and, with varying degrees of enthusiasm, by Wellington, Aberdeen, Gladstone, Herbert and Lincoln. Surveying his own host after the holocaust, Stanley must have wondered whether he had not protested too much once too often. The apparent talent in the party had been largely hived-off into the Peelite echelon; and while Stanley himself could always hold his own in the Lords, strange new leaders were emerging from the long-mute but now aroused and angered squires in the Commons. The Protectionist camp had a better case than was ever recognised by a liberal Britain about to become 'the workshop of the world' – and, indeed, by many subsequent writers. But its acceptable spokesmen were not numerous and its philosophy (in so far as it was ever adumbrated) held little attraction for the 'political classes'.

The future offered three possibilities: an alliance with another conservative group; the creation of an entirely new, non-Peelite, Conservative party; or the acceptance of a purely rearguard role in perpetual opposition, as an ever-diminishing group of 'ultras'. All three choices had attractions to different sections of this largest of Stanleyite groups. One could maintain conservative principles by rejoining old Peelite friends, if one could forgive superior attitudes, did not care too much about Protection and could follow the mistrusted and ambivalent Peel. One might favour a popular, paternalist (and often Protestant) new party, maintaining the traditions of radical Toryism already established in the north by Sadler, Oastler and Ferrand and their kind. Or one might simply say, with Colonel Sibthorp, that far too much had already been conceded and that, at whatever ultimate risk, one should oppose 'the march of progress' whether represented by Whig, Tory or Radical. Stanley had something in common with the first section – he had originally not intended even to speak, let alone lead, against Repeal, though he could not endorse it, and he did not plan the defeat of Peel's government over Irish coercion. He had much in common with the

third section, in that he always envisaged the party of which he became
the reluctant leader as the main bulwark against Radicalism, though one
who had served with Canning and Peel could never be a pure reactionary. The second section he at least understood, being a *northern* land-
owner with urban interests. But it did not seem sensible to risk splitting
a minority party by forcing the issue.

The Protectionists remained divided. Even in the vengeful division
on coercion, by Mr Robert Stewart's computation Lord George
Bentinck was supported by only 69 followers, while 105 backed Peel
and 74 did not vote. Like Stanley (from July the apparent leader),
many hoped to reunite Conservatism. But Stanley wished to postpone
the junction until after an election. His strategy was uncertain and his
relations with the leader and the Whip in the Commons were unsatisfactory, for if he deplored, with the ex-Canningite Bentinck, the
anti-popery stance of Beresford, he also deplored Bentinck's indulgence
in vitriolic personal attacks; both made the prospect of Conservative
reunion more remote. He noted the electoral effects of railway booms
and currently high food prices; while Bentinck talked of small fixed corn
duties and repeal of the malt tax, Stanley preferred to wait and see. By
January 1847 Stanley and Bentinck were as divided as their followers.
And reunion remained doubtful. Peelites and Protectionists could unite
to defeat a Bill (supported by Bentinck) to repeal penal provisions on
Roman Catholics; but Protectionists, with Whig support, carried the
Ten Hours Bill against Liberal and Peelite opposition.

Inevitably, the election of July and August 1847 was fought in low-
key. Few Protectionists opposed Peelites; even the fiery Busfeild Ferrand
deserted Knaresborough to W. S. Lascelles. And few campaigned for
restoration of the Corn Laws, though several adopted an anti-papal cry.
Government increased its strength at the expense of the assorted Conservatives. Free trade thus appeared to have been accepted, and the way
was open for Stanley to negotiate a reunion, based on acceptance of a
*fait accompli*. But within months the situation was completely changed,
as industrial slump, agricultural price falls, financial crisis and rising
unemployment raised Protectionist hopes. Stanley postponed approaches
to the Peelites; in any case, the Peelites themselves were disturbed by
Radical threats against a premature Tory government. Consequently,
to Bentinck's chagrin, a policy of indecision continued. Periodic
Peelite hints kept alive the hope of reunion; but to staunch Protectionists and ambitious young Tories alike the party appeared to be
collapsing.

A Protectionist revival set in from late 1848, as farmers and others flocked to G. F. Young's National Association for the Protection of British Industry, the electorate returned Protectionists at by-elections and Ferrand and Richard Oastler again roused the north. When, against all odds, Protectionism was rising again Stanley felt he could not weaken the cause. Yet his party still had no policy, little organisation and few propaganda outlets. And there was little proof of a Peelite return to the fold, despite hostility to Palmerstonian bellicosity and enlarged freedom after Peel's death in June 1850. Aberdeen and Stanley might consult together; but in October Cardinal Wiseman's 'papal aggression' in establishing a Roman Catholic hierarchy underlined differences between Peelite 'tolerance' and Protectionist 'anti-popery' (which Stanley could no longer honestly contain) – despite leaders' attempts to prevent militant Protestants from adding to Russell's denunciation. Conservative reunion became impossible. When the Whigs collapsed on 22 February 1851 Stanley confessed (in Buckle's words) 'his lack of available statesmen' and advised the queen to promote a Whig–Peelite coalition. The Peelites rejected Russell's advances, and Stanley was again invited to form a ministry on the twenty-fourth, but was refused a dissolution. The time of humiliation had arrived: on the twenty-seventh he had to give up the attempt, because (as Disraeli observed): 'One thing was established – that every public man of experience and influence, however slight, had declined to act under Lord Derby unless the principle of Protection were unequivocally renounced.'

It was with unpromising and untried material that Stanley had to work as party leader. None of his three ministries of 1852, 1858–9 and 1866–8 had a Commons majority. The 'Who, Who?' cabinet of February 1852 was an inauspicious start to the series of minority governments. There were splendid names – the duke of Northumberland, the marquess of Salisbury, the earls of Lonsdale, Malmesbury and Hardwicke and Lord John Manners – which guaranteed social distinction; there was Lord St Leonards as Lord Chancellor; there were the doubtfully competent J. C. Herries, J. W. Henley and Sir John Pakington (a 'disinterred Sir Roger de Coverley' to George Smythe); and there were the competent but inexperienced Spencer Walpole and Benjamin Disraeli. Lord Blake has fairly compared the 'Country party's' first ministry with the first Socialist administration of 1924. Contemporary observers could imagine no parallel. 'The new Government is treated with great contempt, and many of the appointments are pitiable', wrote the Whiggish Charles Greville, on 26 March:

But, while it is the fashion to exalt Derby himself, and treat with great scorn almost all his colleagues, I think Derby himself is quite as unfit for the post of Prime Minister as any of them can be for those they occupy. His extreme levity and incapacity for taking grave and serious views, though these defects may be partially remedied by the immensity of his responsibility, will ever weigh upon his character, and are too deeply rooted in it to be eradicated.[5]

Greville further denied any 'high-minded and chivalrous' nature to Derby, because of his 'transactions on the turf'. Six years later Greville admitted that Derby was 'of all men the one to whom I have felt the greatest political and personal repugnance'.

Greville was unfair, as he often was, especially to Tories. But there was some justification for his criticisms. Derby was light-hearted and easy-going. His own son told Disraeli in 1853 that 'the Captain does not care for office but wishes to keep things as they are and impede "progress" '. Disraeli's 'despatches from Knowsley' consisted only of venison; and when he visited Derby in December things were little better: Derby (recorded Malmesbury) 'seemed much bored because he was obliged to talk politics with him'. When Disraeli had doubted his qualifications for the Exchequer in 1852, Derby insisted 'You know as much as Mr Canning did. They give you the figures'. By 1854 Disraeli himself complained to Lady Londonderry that

There are a thousand things which ought to be done which are elements of power, and which I am obliged to decline doing or to do at great sacrifice. Whether it be influence with the Press, or organisation throughout the country, everyone comes to me, and everything is expected from me. Tho' so many notables and magnificoes belong to the party there was never an aggregation of human beings who exercised less social influence. They seem to despise all the modes and means of managing mankind.

As for our chief we never see him. His house is always closed, he subscribes to nothing tho' his fortune is very large; and expects nevertheless everything to be done. . . .[6]

At a time 'when Europe, nay the world was in the throes of immense changes and all the elements of power at home in a state of dissolution', Disraeli resented having 'a confederate always at Newmarket and Doncaster'.

Derby's principal political decisions (despite his activities as a steward of the Jockey Club) cannot be ascribed to any thought of personal advancement. Earls of Derby simply could not advance much further in the social hierarchy. And 'the Rupert of debate' was, in general, a courteous man. If principle periodically led him to rout his enemies with a slashing over-charge, he fully expected return fire from the mutilated. Derby, indeed, cherished and defended more principles than were recognised by allegedly 'consistent' partisans. A conservative Whig entering the governments of 1827 was breaking no trust. If the nature of Wellington's government drove honest Whigs out of office, the nature of Grey's ministry of 1830 inevitably attracted them – and others. But conservative Whigs must draw limits: radical assaults on national institutions – whether emanating from O'Connell or from Russell – were unacceptable. Peel's Tamworth Manifesto announced their kind of conservatism. It was logical that they should ultimately link themselves with a Conservatism apparently dropping its ultra-Toryism, to form a bastion against radical change. Such feelings brought the amiable patrician Stanley and the energetic administrator Graham into Peel's fold. Once enclosed, the two friends were soon to be divided.

II

Tory writers have always been fond of asserting what R. J. White summarised as 'the secondary importance of politics'. Politics is subordinate to religion. 'The championship of religion is ... the most important of the functions of Conservatism'; the 'defence [of the church] is the special function of conservatism'. For 'Conservatism sees Religion as an eternal necessity of human nature'. Indeed, 'this dualism, this belief in a civitas dei distinct from the political State, is the essential strength of Toryism'. And 'if Conservatives do not believe politics to be the most important thing in life, the great majority of them believe man to be a religious animal even before he is a political animal'. In fact, 'the man who puts politics first is not fit to be called a civilised being, let alone a Christian'.

This civilised doctrine embodies a Tory respect for Burke's view of 'man [as] a religious animal' and of 'religion [as] the basis of civil society'. But politics is also subordinate to pleasurable instincts. The Cavalier, Jacobite, Newmanite, romantic notion that 'Toryism is enjoyment' has had a long vogue, reaching down to the innuendoes of hostile satirists. Instead of 'painful lectures [and] dreary tracts' to propagate 'a wholesome Conservatism', advised Walter Bagehot, 'try a little pleasure. . . . So long as this world is this world, will a buoyant life be the proper source of an animated Conservatism.' 'To the great majority of Conservatives', commented Lord Hailsham, 'religion, art, study, family, country, friends, music, fun, duty, all the joys and riches of existence of which the poor no less than the rich are the indefeasible freeholders, all these are higher in the scale than their handmaiden, the political struggle.'[7] Loving God and enjoying oneself, is no doubt, a counsel of perfection, of which the latter part is the easier. But if such religious and hedonistic tests are valid criteria for at least one form of Toryism the fourteenth Lord Derby became a good Tory. He defended the Church, from a moderately 'High' position: Evangelical or Tractarian enthusiasm held no attractions for him. And he enjoyed life to the full, being (as George Lennox once complained to Disraeli) 'devoted to whist, billiards, racing, betting'; he also translated Homer.

Through uniquely long years of party leadership Derby faced almost unique difficulties. The generality of his supporters – those broadacred, armorially-guaranteed gentlemen from the shires – were better men than Bagehot allowed in talking of 'the finest brute-vote in creation'. But few were 'cabinet material'. The experience of 1852, periodic illhealth, and general agreement with Liberal ministries' domestic conservatism made Derby reluctant to solicit office. He reluctantly allowed Disraeli to support Roebuck's attack on the Aberdeen Coalition's conduct of the Crimean War in January 1855; but when the motion succeeded he refused to form a ministry unless Palmerston would join it. Not unnaturally, the experienced Palmerston preferred to select his own government. Disraeli might fulminate that 'our chief has again bolted'; but Derby could reasonably argue that only further humiliation would result from an acceptance of office. Disraeli's circle continually complained of the earl's seeming lethargy. But Derby was confident, as he told the prince consort in 1852, that 'Mr Disraeli knew that he [Lord Derby] possessed the confidence of three hundred of his supporters whilst Mr Disraeli, if he separated himself from him, would very likely not carry five with him'.[8] Even in 1858 he doubted Disraeli's wisdom in voting against the second reading of Palmerston's bill to restrain foreign revolutionaries. Many Tory M.P.s shared his feelings, but when the Government collapsed Derby knew that 'if he refused [office] the Conservative party would be broken up for ever'. However, his Cabinet was little better than that of 1852. The result was much the same: the Government was defeated by a Liberal alliance against its

Reform Bill and a spring election (permitted only reluctantly by the queen), while increasing Conservative representation, did not produce a majority.

Derby made his last approach to Gladstone and Disraeli invited Palmerston to lead the party, explaining that only 'a point of honour' kept Derby at his post – a feeling that 'he could never desert the Conservative party while it was in a minority, and while there was no member of it to succeed him'. But appeals to Whigs, Peelites, Liberals and Irishmen alike failed. Furthermore, at a famous meeting in Willis's Rooms on 6 June 1859 a new liberal alliance was forged, bringing together Russell and Palmerston, Whig, Peelite, Liberal and Radical, in favour of Italian nationalism against the Government's allegedly pro-Habsburg attitude. Despite Gladstone's support (a sign of the final disintegration of the Peelite hegemony) the Government was defeated and Derby resigned. The sprightly old Palmerston again took office.

The opposition within the party was now growing. Derby's position was to some extent challenged by the 'ultras', who could never understand that country squires – often good, benevolent men, devoting much unrewarded time to county business and a few months annually to Parliament and the London social 'season' – simply could not rule the workshop of the world. The rejection of a return to Protection, the rumoured negotiations with past compromisers and the ill-planned toying with notions of further parliamentary reform inevitably upset the party purist. ⌊Back-bench Protectionist unease, distress and occasional bitterness against the Tory leadership in the years following 1846 (and long before) is at least understandable. The watering-down of impracticable party writ is easily condemned as 'treason' by those of its votaries who are not called upon to render it practicable; and subsequent electoral defeat 'confirms' their prejudices. But party leadership involves greater duties than carrying out 'mandates'. It must maintain that alliance of interests and individuals which constitutes a party; it must seek a consensus of opinion but avoid domination by it; it must create opportunities for its followers to win elections. It is concerned with the actuality of political power, and must therefore propound viable policies and offer credible candidates. Derby's principal difficulty from 1846 was that there were too few 'names he could put before the Queen'. We now know that he envisaged this trouble from the start.⌉

### III

Throughout the Palmerston years Derby was largely content to 'keep the cripples on their legs'. Palmerstonian rule, whatever its *penchant* for foreign involvements, was domestically thoroughly and soundly conservative. Disraeli and other activists might sometimes dislike this policy, but there was little they could do. According to Greville, Derby was 'violently discontented' with his lieutenant; and if this was a Whiggish exaggeration, it is certainly that *rapport* between the leaders was rarely close. But, in fact, Disraeli seems to have generally agreed with Derby's strategy, while sometimes disagreeing over immediate tactics: 'as you well know', he told his friend Mrs Brydges Willyams in 1862, 'I had no desire whatever to disturb Lord Palmerston, but you cannot keep a large army in order without letting them sometimes smell gunpowder.' Derby's attitude was summarised in his speech to the Lords explaining his refusal to accept office after Aberdeen's fall:

> to hold that high and responsible situation dependent for support from day to day upon precarious and uncertain majorities, compelled to cut down this measure and to pare off that; to consider with regard to each measure not what was for the real welfare of the country but what would conciliate some half-dozen men here, or obviate the objections of some half-dozen there; to regard it as a great triumph of parliamentary skill and ministerial strength to scramble through the session of Parliament and boast of having met with few and insignificant defeats: I say this is a state of things which cannot be satisfactory to any minister and which cannot be of advantage to the Crown or to the people of the country.

Indeed, 'to carry on with a minority was an intolerable and galling servitude as no man of honour or character would expose himself to'. Disraeli considered that in 1855 Russell and Derby 'both made great mistakes in the course they took, the latter almost a ruinous one', as both believed that 'Ld. Palmerston could not form a government'; Gladstone later thought that Derby had made a 'palpable and even gross error'. One hesitates to disagree with both Disraeli and Gladstone. But Derby's attitude was justifiable; in the Lords he could only periodically rely on a majority, in the Commons never.

Derby's policy had the virtue of consistency to principle. To a natural reluctance to act precipitately was added an innate honesty. 'I will never consent to weaken an Administration to which I am opposed by increasing their difficulties in carrying the country through what has become an inevitable war', he told Disraeli in October 1855. 'If the Conservative party cannot be kept together on any other grounds it is time that it should fall to pieces.' 'I *never* was *ambitious* of office, and am not likely to become more so as I get older,' he told Malmesbury in December 1856: 'but I am now, as I have been, ready to accept the responsibility for it if I see a chance, not only of taking but of keeping it.' He pursued a dream of Conservative reunion and made considerable progress with Gladstone: the stumbling block was Graham and his group, who could never forgive the desertion of Peel or accept the Commons leadership of Disraeli. But the dream might well have become reality, bringing with it a considerably greater parliamentary reputation. The policy was not without difficulty, however, inside the party, and in February 1857 Derby bluntly declared that 'should any member of the Conservative connection attempt to dictate to him the course he should pursue with regard to any political personages whatever, he would regard it as an insult and no longer recognise that member as attached to his party'. Such firmness was the prelude to the Palmerston years: after the 1857 election Derby thought (as he told Disraeli in April) that the party was in a state of 'suspended animation'.

In 1858 Derby broke his self-imposed rules. But the circumstances were strange: to refuse the queen's offer would involve acceptance of a permanent minority and opposition status. This, indeed, was the future forecast by John Bright, when trying to dissuade Gladstone from joining the government. 'If you join Lord Derby,' he wrote, 'you link your fortunes with a constant minority, and with a party in the Country which is every day lessening in numbers and in power.' Furthermore, there were regular divisions even within the higher echelons of the party. Derby's task was to devise a viable Conservatism generally acceptable to his ministerial colleagues but also attractive to the electorate. Inevitably, the declaration (made in the Lords on 1 March) was 'Peelite' in tone. 'There can be no greater mistake', Derby told the House,

than to suppose that a Conservative ministry necessarily means a stationary ministry. We live in an age of constant progress, moral, social and political. . . . In politics, as in everything else, the same course must be pursued: constant progress, improving upon the old system, adapting our institutions to the altered purposes they are intended to serve and by judicious changes meeting the demands of society.

This was a refrain to be improved upon by Disraeli.

The refrain was not universally appreciated. From the Right Henry Drummond complained that Derby and Disraeli had 'led the Conservative party to adopt every measure which they opposed as Radical ten years ago . . . I do not think it creditable to the intelligence or to the honor of the country gentlemen of England to vote black to be white or white to be black at their bidding.'

Derby was 'saved by dissensions of the Liberals, by truckling to Bright and by courting the Radicals', asserted Lord Campbell. The Whigs were 'the only true conservatives. The Tories as a body are still staunch and sincere, but the Tory leaders are ready to sacrifice the monarchy that they make keep their places.' From the Tory shrine at Hatfield, much the same message was announced by Lord Robert Cecil, in *Bentley's Review* and the *Quarterly Review*: 'to crush the Whigs by combining with the Radicals was the first and last maxim of Mr Disraeli's [and, by implication, Derby's] parliamentary tactics'. And from the cross-benches, Shaftesbury, the custodian of the Evangelical conscience, wondered 'How are they, in any sense, Conservative? They accept every proposition and make every concession. They refuse no committees and grant all enquiries. . . . In what sense and of what are they Conservatives?'[9]

Shaftesbury's queries arise under any Conservative administration. The complaints of Whigs and Peelites were nullified by their own refusal to unite with the major defender of 'the conservative cause'. And 'ultra' views remained largely impracticable. Derby's conservatism was always (except on a few subjects, such as Ireland or the Church) empirical, pragmatic and practical. The 'finality' of 1832 was no more obligatory to him than it turned out to be for the pledger of 'finality', Russell. Throughout the fifties further parliamentary reform was not a major political issue and the Tory task was simply to support the general feeling against 'extensive change'. That change would come and that ultimately it would be 'extensive' was undoubted – except at the Hatfields and Chatsworths of the two traditional parties. In April 1857 Derby warned Disraeli against assailing the ministry on the subject. 'We must, after all, look to our own adherents,' he wrote: 'and I do not think it would please them to see us apparently anxious to take up the Question.' In other words, Tories did not need to initiate change; but when change was reasonably proposed and widely demanded, Tories should be prepared to make the change efficiently, moderately and conservatively.

IV

The death of Palmerston in October 1865 opened a new political age. With Russell as premier a further dose of Reform was inevitable. Derby, as usual, initially preferred a moderate measure – 'one of a very mild character', as he told Malmesbury. Thus the Tories might continue their custom of supporting cautious Liberal reform. But the measure proposed by Gladstone on 12 March 1866, while limited in scope, was unsatisfactory in its county redistribution provisions for the Conservatives. Derby had warned that his support of a Bill was highly conditional: 'if we disapprove of it and think it is imperfect, inadequate, or dangerous, and above all, if we think it one leading to future agitations within a brief period of a perilous character, then with whatever means we may possess we shall do our best to throw it out by fair debate and honourable opposition.'

Now he was determinedly hostile. He ordered Disraeli to tell the party that 'we cannot accept, and intend to resist to the uttermost, the Government Bill, reserving only for consideration the best mode of doing so effectively'. The best mode quickly appeared to be to act with Lowe's Adullamites in the Commons. Through long, bitterly-argued debates the Whig–Tory alliance fought every stage. On 18 June they finally defeated the ministry and Russell resigned on the twenty-sixth. Derby received the Queen's invitation next day.

The Whig 'Cave' had provided forty-eight votes to overturn Russell. But its members had not broken with Liberalism in order to prop up a Tory ministry. They were as demanding as Aberdeen's Peelites had been in 1852. Many wanted Clarendon as Premier, with Stanley leading the Commons: to serve under Disraeli was unthinkable – and Derby was only little less unacceptable. What they appeared to be planning was a take-over of the Tory party, excluding its long-established leaders. Disraeli insisted that such a plan was 'not consistent with the honour of the Conservative party'. Furthermore, he saw another danger. The Adullamites had proposed 'a long matured intrigue'. They hoped that Derby would decline office: 'What is counted on and intended (not by the Court) is that you should refuse; that a member of the late

Government shall then be sent for, and then that an application should be made to a section of your party to join the Administration; which application will be successful, for all will be broken up.' To Disraeli, indeed, there was only one possible course. 'You *must* take the Government; the honour of your house and the necessity of the country alike require it,' he told Derby. '. . . There is only one course with the Queen: to kiss hands. And the effect will be this: in twenty-four hours, all . . . will be at your feet.'

Derby consulted twenty-two prominent Tories on 28 June. It was agreed to form a government, with or without the Adullamites, only the marquess of Bath opposing the possibility of a purely Conservative ministry. This confirmed Derby's own view. He could not honourably drop Disraeli and was unwilling to hand over his own position to Stanley. He knew that there was as yet little chance of the Whigs joining a 'great Conservative party'. For the third time the earl, now gout-ridden and ageing, formed a Conservative minority ministry.

Derby's third government was his most impressive, though he muffed the arrangements for several (mainly minor) posts; 'he is awkward in these matters and there is no denying it', observed Northcote. But the result was a good mixture of now experienced ex-ministers and able newcomers. From the start, the ministers had to face the question of Reform. In his first ministerial speech on 9 July Derby shocked some followers by declaring that 'nothing, certainly, would give me greater pleasure than to see a very considerable portion of the class now excluded admitted to the franchise'. While he would not propose legislation impossible to carry, he stood by the notion of 'a monarchy limited, an aristocracy tempered, a House of Commons not altogether democratic'. These were not sentiments to be cheered at Hatfield or the *Quarterly* office – or, for that matter, in the 'Cave' or at Hawarden.

V

Undoubtedly the greatest of Derby's and Disraeli's legislative achievements was the second Reform Act of 1867. 'Shooting Niagara' by the 'leap in the dark' opened the way to ultimate democracy. 'We have inaugurated a new era in English politics this session . . . ,' Lowe despairingly exclaimed in May: 'This session we have not had what we before possessed – a party of attack and a party of resistance. We have instead two parties of competition who, like Cleon and the Sausage-seller of

Aristophanes, are both bidding for the support of Demos.' Furthermore, a right-wing party had, as its critics claimed, carried a major constitutional change without any compulsive necessity. Groups of *bourgeois* Radicals and Liberal craft unionists might campaign for suffrage extensions; but the finest club in Europe was not accustomed to taking orders from Reform Leagues and Unions. The alleged influence of the Hyde Park riots of July 1866 is a myth. Governments do not tremble before crowds dislodging a few railings. Certainly Derby and Disraeli took little notice of them. Men who had lived through the Chartist era were unlikely to be unduly impressed by a three-day riot in part of a London park. On the other hand, a sustained, cogently-argued and widely-supported campaign, as mounted by Bright, inevitably commanded attention.

The Reform Act had a long ancestry. Through the fifties and sixties there had been several proposals – including the Tory Bill of 1859, with its 'fancy franchises'. But Parliament had yawned away such measures. Palmerston had yawned more effectively than anyone. His death opened the way to Reform. 'The truce of parties is over,' Disraeli then told Lord Lonsdale. 'I foresee tempestuous times and great vicissitudes in public life.' In July 1866 Disraeli thought (probably rightly) that the matter could be settled by modifying Gladstone's bill. But by mid-September Derby was 'coming reluctantly to the conclusion that they should have to deal with the question of Reform'. The queen was 'most anxious to see it settled', and by late September Derby was 'not in favour of resisting all Reform, for which he believed that there was a genuine demand *now*, however it might have been excited, but in favour of the acceptance of a moderate and Conservative measure'.[10]

Once converted, Disraeli threw the whole of his energy and political cunning into the Tory initiative. Here was an exciting new chapter in 'the great game'. But Derby intended no ultra-radical measure. 'I wish you would consider whether, after all the failures which have taken place,' he told Disraeli, 'we might not deal with the question in the shape of Resolutions, to form the basis of a future Bill. We *need* not make the adoption of any of the Resolutions a vital question, while, if we should be beaten on some great leading principle, we should have a definite issue on which to go to the country. . . .'

No doubt Disraeli's doubts arose from his fears of the reaction of some cabinet colleagues. He was right to be worried. The Tory leadership was – at last – reasonably well informed on the probable effects of Reform. Dudley Baxter and many professional Conservative agents had produced statistical information which seemed to show that the Tories should not fear an extension of the suffrage. Of course, much depended on the extent of the extension: in general, expert advice showed that minor alterations of the 1832 Act would augment Liberal strength, while wider extensions would aid the Tories. But that Tory proletarian host of 'angels in marble' – later to be explained away by talk of Lancastrian tradition or serfish deference – was as yet, an unquantifiable commodity. Certainly, a Tory–Radical 'attitude' had been maintained since the days of Richard Oastler's factory agitation; but its strength was doubtful. Working-class Tories had joined Operative Conservative Societies in the 1830s and were now flocking to Working Men's Conservative Associations and clubs. But Disraeli must have wondered how representative they were. In any case, the 'education' of the Tory party involved greater and more immediate hazards. Within the Cabinet itself there were potentially serious disagreements. 'To bring forward any measure affecting the representation of the people in the presence of adverse forces strong enough to engraft democratic amendments on it', warned the *Quarterly Review* in 1866, 'would be to throw away all the advantages which the labours of this session have secured.'

The queen's offer to arrange talks with the Liberals was rejected as (in Disraeli's words) 'a mere phantom'. Instead, the Tories would proceed with thirteen resolutions, drawn up by Derby. The lead was thus taken from the Liberals, without any need for undue haste. Plural voting, fancy franchises, household suffrage and a Royal Commission on boundaries seemed likely to delay matters, so legislation was planned only for 1868. During leisurely winter discussions, Disraeli noticed that General Peel's 'eye lit up with insanity' at the mention of household suffrage, which was promptly dropped. But on 12 February 1867, despite the lack of preparation, Disraeli assured Lord Robert Montagu that the government would introduce a Bill rather than resolutions. Cranborne and Carnarvon were appalled: 'up to the delivery of the Queen's Speech, no proposition for immediate legislation had even been mentioned in Cabinet'. On 24 February Cranborne, Carnarvon and General Peel almost resigned – a threat which Derby saw as 'utter ruin' and Disraeli as 'treachery'. There followed a succession of *ad hoc*, constantly changing decisions. On 25 February, following a cabinet decision ten minutes earlier, Derby offered the party a Bill based on a rating franchise of £6 in the boroughs and £20 in the counties and a variety of fancy franchises. Disraeli unenthusiastically explained the measure to the House on the same day. Next day he dropped the resolutions and on the twenty-seventh and twenty-eighth Tory back-benchers declared for household suffrage. Matters were moving in the direction undoubtedly desired by Derby and Disraeli – especially the latter. But when the cabinet adopted the original measure on 2 March, Cranborne, Carnarvon and Peel resigned. Derby was aghast: 'this was the end of the Conservative party'.[11] However the dukes of Marlborough and Richmond and Henry Corry replaced the dissidents, and Disraeli promised a new Bill to the Commons on the fourth. With great difficulty the measure was prepared.

Despite the wide and detailed researches of many distinguished historians, it is still easier to determine what did not promote this major measure than to decide what actually did promote it. As Professor Asa Briggs has written, 'it was neither external pressure nor unlimited opportunism . . . which lay at the root of [Disraeli's] and Derby's desire to introduce a reform bill'. Both men had noted the extra-parliamentary agitation; inevitably, they were interested in party advantage, in 'dishing the Whigs'. But above all Conservatives wanted to end the long debate and to shape the redistribution of seats. From the party point of view, the immediate future lay in success within *bourgeois* suburban areas; but Tories need not fear suffrage extension to the workers – particularly, as they thought, outside the largest industrial cities. Derby's original plan was modest, while the ultimate Act went further than many Radicals had dreamed possible. 'The transformation of the Bill is explicable only by the determination of Derby and Disraeli to avoid a repetition of the humiliation imposed on them by Russell in 1859,' writes Lord Blake, 'and therefore to stay in office and pass a Bill of *some* sort, come what might.'[12] Consequently, amendments were acceptable from almost anyone but Gladstone. And amendments flowed in through the spring – including Grosvenor Hodgkinson's celebrated proposal, which led to the enfranchisement of occupiers who did not personally pay local rates.

At the end of the day, Tory leaders naturally claimed that their original secret plans had succeeded. There was more truth in this view than has often been admitted. However, an Act introducing almost complete household suffrage in English and Welsh boroughs and granting third seats to four large cities still (as Derby told the Lords in August) amounted to 'a leap in the dark'. But, in making the 'great experiment', Derby 'had the greatest confidence in the sound sense of his fellow-countrymen'. He hoped that the Act 'would tend to increase the loyalty and contentment of a great portion of her Majesty's subjects'.

Liberal politicians (ranging in attitude from Lowe through Gladstone to Bright) had mesmerised themselves with notions that only Liberals could appropriately deal with Reform. They had been proved wrong.

Derby had also acted, as he told the Tory peers in July, 'so as to place the Tory party permanently in power and not to place them in a position to be beaten as soon as they had served the purpose of the Opposition'. In the Lords he bluntly declared that 'I did not intend for a third time to be made a mere stop-gap until it would suit the convenience of the Liberal party to forget their dissensions and bring forward a measure which would oust us . . . and I determined that I would take such a course as would convert, if possible, an existing minority into a practical majority.' Delay over Reform was holding up 'every measure of practical improvement and practical legislation', and Derby therefore felt it vital 'despite of any opposition, to endeavour towards the close of his political career, to settle one great and important question of vital importance to the interests of the country'.

Reaction to the Act was varied. Whigs naturally hated being 'dished'; having themselves stoked the democratic fire (as they thought, carefully) for so long, they were furious to find Derby and Disraeli bellowing-up the furnace. It was all so unfair to 'liberal' defenders of conservatism, who for so long had enjoyed the best of all worlds, to find their 'liberalism' undermined by radicalism on the Right. Simultaneously, however, part of the Right – never large nor energetic enough to form its own 'Cave' – made its own protest. 'That ['the Derby–Disraelites'] go on calling themselves Conservatives after what has recently taken place', declared *Fraser's Magazine*, 'is one of the most extraordinary facts connected with them.' And another Tory who had not yet learned to live with the times made a more serious statement. Writing in the *Quarterly Review*, Cranborne insisted that 'It is true, as the Duke of Argyll observed, that Lord Derby, in his determination not to become a stop-gap, has become a weather-cock.' The furious Cranborne had a reasonable and reasoned case. During the shifting history of the Bill Derby and Disraeli did not always act with entire frankness even to cabinet colleagues. Nor, it should be added, did Cranborne act altogether honestly with his leaders. Cranborne believed the leaders' later claims of consistency and roundly attacked them for misleading supporters and keeping 'their counsel . . . from their colleagues in opposition . . . [and] their colleagues in office'. Except in the most general sense, he was wrong to assume that Derby and Disraeli had hatched deep-laid Tory–Radical franchise plans. While much less reluctant to accept and adapt change than Cranborne would wish, the leadership had in fact followed a policy of immediacy. Furthermore, Derby preserved his party; and Cranborne remained within it. And if Whigs could argue that the 1832 Act was a conservative measure, Tories could eventually claim similarly preservative virtues in 1867. If 1832 in a sense marked the end of the breakdown of party in the old style, 1867 helped to end party anarchy and to create new party images.

VI

The second Reform Act was Derby's last major political interest. But despite excruciating gout he contrived to play an active part in cabinet discussions and Lords' arguments with Russell, though colleagues knew that such activities could not long continue. By January 1868 he regarded himself as 'everything that a prime minister ought not to be'. He was sick, tired and old, but reluctant to let down a party of which he was by far the most distinguished doyen. However, his medical advisers strongly urged him to retire. He finally followed their advice on 25 February. His last actions were to secure peerages for several faithful followers and the succession for Disraeli. 'I cannot accept for you the position which you are willing to accept for yourself, of being considered as my deputy,' he wrote. 'You have fairly and most honourably won your way to the highest round of the political ladder, and long may you continue to retain your position!'

After resigning Derby was still active in the Lords, particularly during the bitter summer debates on Gladstone's proposals to disendow the Church of Ireland. Again Derby defended the Church and the peers threw out the suspensory Bill by ninety-five votes. There was pleasure to be had in taunting Russell and in seeing Lancashire (though few other areas) turn massively Tory at the 1868 election ('the proletariat had discredited itself terribly,' Engels told Marx). The battle was joined again in 1869, when Derby, though conscious of the dangers of opposing the Commons, led a staunch opposition to disendowment and disestablishment 'In Ireland and in Ireland alone,' he declared, 'we find the Roman Catholics joining in the cry for religious equality, which, if they had the upper hand, they would not for a moment countenance.' The Bill was 'a measure of which . . . the political folly was only equalled by its moral injustice'. When even Derby's moving peroration failed to move the majority, he helped to pass sixty-two amendments (of which thirty-five were adopted by the Commons) and made a last, dignified protest against the principle of despoiling the Church. Thereafter he lived quietly at Knowsley until his death on 23 October.

Derby had been an active and (as far as parliamentary conditions allowed) powerful Prime Minister. He was, as the queen once noticed, 'entirely master' of the Cabinet. And, despite colleagues' periodic complaints of his lethargy in Opposition, he took an interest not only in a variety of departments but also in party organisation. Indeed, he inaugurated several new practices. When Derby revealed his draft Bill in 1867 to a party meeting before the Commons, Gladstone protested at such an 'entirely novel' proceeding. And the 'king of Lancashire' was popular with his 'subjects'. It was never forgotten that during the 'cotton famine' Derby presided over the central executive of the relief fund, which aided many thousands of unemployed operatives. 'Lord Derby holds a position in the Empire hardly second to that of any other subject of the Crown,' wrote the Radical R. A. Arnold. 'He is a great lord in Lancashire by right of lineage and property, but neither the splendid annals nor the wide domains of his House would have won for him the position he holds by the higher rights of personal genius and character.' And Derby reciprocated this admiration, praising the 'noble manner, a manner beyond all praise in which this destitution had been borne by the population of this great county'. Although his family possessed great political influence in the boroughs and rural areas of Lancashire, Derby did not exercise it with a heavy hand.

'The great earl of Derby' led the Tory party through its most difficult years. His greatest achievement was to save it from the fate of other diminishing groups and preserve it as a great party. It was inevitable that this was only accomplished against the hostility of 'hard-line', high-and-dry representatives of the old school. In 1868 the duke of Northumberland told Lord Hylton:

> I don't feel interested in the elections. If the present government obtain a majority, it will be only an incentive to the Whigs to plunge further into revolution, and between Lord Derby and Disraeli they have let the mob in upon us, and will of course give way whenever they find themselves hard pressed. I would rather see the Whigs in power, and trust to their quarrelling with the Radicals than to the resolution of the present government.[13]

Upper-crust Tories were naturally annoyed that one of their own order should open the floodgates to democracy. After 1867 party politics was

never the same. The 1868 election reunited the assorted Liberals to
defeat the minority government. From 1874, however, elections were to
be fought by increasingly organised parties with increasingly planned
policies: the parties were back in business. To deal with this situation,
Derby handed over to Disraeli a changed party. Russell might consider
that Disraeli was 'only the heir of triumphant worry'. But in fact
Disraeli inherited a Toryism enormously altered since 1846. Here was
a party which still included a handful of great aristocrats and many
squires, but which also incorporated enthusiastic working men's associations, provincial businessmen's clubs and the embryo of the continuing Tory organisational dualism of the Central Office and the National
Union of Conservative Associations. In this change Derby had played a
considerable part.

Despite high intellectual ability, Derby was no great party philoso-
pher. But he always defended his own conception of Conservatism.
'My notions may perhaps be old-fashioned and contrary to the en-
lightenment of the day, but they are the opinions to which I have
steadfastly adhered through no inconsiderable period of my life, and I
cannot change them now,' he told the Lords in March 1857. 'I intend
to maintain inviolate the great institutions of the country. I intend to
support . . . the prerogatives of the Crown, the independence and
hereditary character of your Lordships' House and the rights of the
people. I intend to support the doctrines and rights of property of that
Established Church of which I have always been an attached member.
. . .' Throughout his life, the defence of the Church was paramount. In
Disraeli's words, Derby 'abolished slavery, educated Ireland and reformed Parliament'. He also played a major part in conserving
Conservatism.

## VII

The new Premier in 1868 was a very different man. Born in London in
1804 to a family of affluent Sephardi Jews, Disraeli was brought up as
a Christian. In 1821 he was articled to a solicitor and spent over two
dreary years in a London office. There followed a period at home,
reading in his father's library, writing unpublished essays, and amassing
debts by stock exchange speculation and adding to them by founding a
newspaper (the *Representative*) in partnership with John Murray.
Having failed as a lawyer, a speculator and a journalistic tycoon,

Disraeli achieved his first success in 1826 with the publication of his anonymous novel *Vivian Grey* – a youthful work which brought much criticism but considerable fame. Further attempts at 'high society' novels followed, and *The Young Duke* was published in 1831. 'What does Ben know of dukes?' his father, Isaac d'Israeli, wondered. Ben was then touring the Mediterranean and Middle East, playing the dandy before mysterious and fascinating audiences. On his return late in 1831 he was involved in his first, unpleasant connection with Edward Stanley, who apparently blamed him for his brother Henry's indiscreet behaviour in a London 'Hell'.[14] He resumed a raffish, flamboyant life among the minor literary and political figures of London society and developed a supercilious arrogance, probably as a defence against the latent and sometimes explicit anti-semitism which he regularly met. And through the Reform debates, he nurtured rising political interests.

Disraeli's early career, 'bohemian', amoral and financially rash, gave no indication of the qualities of the later statesman. There was no Oxonian prize, no theological commitment, no hereditary *entrée* to that high society imaginatively (and with many gaffes) described in a succession of novels, no family link with the great political dynasties. But there was courage, determination and ambition. He contested High Wycombe, near his father's house at Bradenham, in June 1832 (losing by twenty votes to twelve) and in December (losing, on the enlarged franchise, with 119 votes to the Whigs' 179 and 140), as a Radical (though already a Tory-accented one). He subsequently issued addresses to other constituencies and crowned their variations with a pamphlet, *What is He?*, supporting a Tory–Radical alliance in 'a National Party'. 'A Tory and a Radical I understand,' he wrote: 'a Whig – a democratic aristocrat – I cannot comprehend.' On a similar policy he again fought Wycombe in January 1835, and Taunton, as a Tory, in April. And he published his *Vindication of the English Constitution*, verbosely and not altogether clearly defending the House of Lords, following it up with articles in the *Morning Post* and *The Times*. Meanwhile, debts mounted and were only partially covered by the sales of *Contarini Fleming* (1832), *The Wondrous Tale of Alroy* (1833), *The Revolutionary Epick* (1834), *The Letters of Runnymede* (1836), *Henrietta Temple* (1837) and *Venetia* (1837).

Political reward came in July 1837, when Disraeli was elected junior Member for Maidstone. In December he delivered his maiden speech, on Irish elections, provoking uproar. 'I will sit down now,' he roared, 'but the time will come when you will hear me.' Later speeches were quietly received; and marriage to his late colleague's widow eased Disraeli's financial embarrassments. But politics was hard. There were shouts of 'Shylock' even in corrupt Maidstone. And the radicalism inherent in Disraeli's attitude to the Poor Law and Chartist prosecutions scarcely commended him to many fellow Tories. He remained ambitious, hopeful, optimistic, determined to make his mark. But he was immensely disappointed by what he considered 'an intolerable humiliation' when Peel (quite reasonably) gave him no office in 1841, when he was elected at Shrewsbury.

Disraeli thus began the 1841 Parliament as a disgruntled backbencher. Initially he acted quietly, but during 1842 he gradually assumed the leadership of 'a party chiefly of the youth and new members' – a group which, he told King Louis Philippe, 'must exercise an irresistible control over the tone of the Minister'. 'Young England' in fact never expanded beyond a little coterie of old friends – Lord John Manners, George Smythe, Alexander Baillie-Cochrane – aided by such allies as Henry Hope, Henry Baillie, John Walter and Busfeild Ferrand. 'Gothic' and 'medieval' in its attitudes, usually catholic and traditionalist in its philosophy and generous in its social views, it made its mark in Parliament by witty, sarcastic attacks on Peel's ministry. Youthful 'prancing, capering and snorting' seemed temporary to the Home Secretary, Graham. 'Disraeli alone is mischievous,' he told Croker, 'and with him I have no desire to keep terms. It would be better for the party if he were driven into the ranks of our open enemies.'[15] Despite temporary reconciliations, Disraeli's relations with the Conservative party generally deteriorated. By 1845 he was regularly attacking Peel: on 17 March, indeed, he announced his 'belief that a Conservative Government is an Organised Hypocrisy'. 'Young England' was by then breaking up after a brief career; 'feudal' paternalism did not cause the split.

As important as parliamentary speeches to Disraeli's break with Peel were the novels *Coningsby* (1844) and *Sybil* (1845), with their recognisable political characters and traditionalist Tory 'history'. The celebrated phrases rolled out in condemnation:

> The Tamworth Manifesto of 1834 was an attempt to construct a party without principles. . . . Conservatism discards Prescription, shrinks from Principle, disavows Progress; having rejected all respect for Antiquity, it offers no redress for the Present, and makes no preparation for the Future.

But there was a message of hope:

> . . . Toryism will yet arise from the tomb over which Bolingbroke shed his last tear, to bring back strength to the Crown, liberty to the subject, and to announce that power has only one duty: to secure the social welfare of the PEOPLE.

There was the clarion call to youth 'to believe in their own energies and dare to be great'; there was the description of 'the two nations between whom there is no intercourse and no sympathy . . . THE RICH AND THE POOR'; there was Mr Taper's definition of 'a sound Conservative government' as amounting to 'Tory men and Whig measures'; there was the insistence that 'it is the past alone that can explain the present, and it is youth that can alone mould the remedial future'.

VIII

The climax to Disraeli's long Tory-Radical campaign against the doctrines of Tamworth came with Peel's resolve, in December 1845, to repeal the Corn Law. Now the mute squires who had long suspected the implicit liberalism of the ministry, Churchmen still outraged by Roman Catholic Emancipation in 1829 or the Maynooth proposals of 1845, traditionalists (apart from Smythe) and angry Tory industrial reformers like Ferrand could join in opposition. But they lacked leaders. Stanley and the militant Protectionist dukes were in the Lords. It was Disraeli's opportunity to rescue something from Toryism, when almost all the Conservative leaders were (with whatever motive and conviction) deserting their pledges to the agricultural community. 'Let men stand by the principle by which they rise, right or wrong,' he declared in January 1846, as the great debate opened, '. . . for it is only by maintaining the independence of party that you can maintain the integrity of public men and the power and influence of Parliament itself.' In alliance with the surprisingly energetic and bitter Lord George Bentinck – hitherto known primarily as the arbiter of the turf but who could not 'bear being *sold*' – Disraeli rallied the shocked and largely unorganised Protectionist ranks. They made a stronger fight for their principles than anyone had expected. Peel had forbidden back-bench barking once too often, and now the hounds were loose. The 'intellectuals' might follow Peel (and some had the grace to contest their seats again); but the great roll-call of county families, those ancient territorial dynasties which the cotton master's son had been proud to lead, now followed – often, no doubt, to their own surprise, and certainly *faute de mieux* – the son of a Semitic antiquary. The youthful voluptuary, the *outré* dandy, the shady financier, the author of clever novels, the middle-aged Jew with his sartorial eccentricities and contrived kiss-curls – here was no natural leader for 'the gentlemen of England'. Bucolic squires might applaud the man who could splendidly phrase their inarticulate sentiments, and Tory Churchmen and the not inconsiderable number of Tory industrialists might agree. But, in addition to the 'social' problem, many must have asked the question which Manners put to himself, in 1843: 'could I only satisfy myself that D'Israeli believed all he said, I should be more happy: his historical views are quite mine, but does he believe them?' To mark his front-bench status, Disraeli was returned for Buckinghamshire at the 1847 election. 'The Jockey and the Jew' performed well together.

Among the new Members was the Liberal Baron Lionel de Rothschild. Disraeli had recently announced his curious views on Christianity as a continuation of Judaism in his novel *Tancred* (1847), and both he and Bentinck supported Russell's proposal to remove Jewish disabilities. It was a courageous act; Stanley and the Protectionist majority strongly opposed this further weakening of Anglican privilege and further extension of non-Anglicans' right to interfere in Church affairs. Both suffered: Bentinck resigned as leader in December and Disraeli was passed over as his successor. Manners' elder brother, the marquess of Granby, held the post for twenty-two days until 4 March 1848; thereafter the Whips, William Beresford (who hated both Bentinck and Disraeli) and C. N. Newdegate, managed the Commons party under Stanley's commission. Relationships remained strained and the leadership question was further complicated on 21 September, when Bentinck died. Disraeli had by now made some advance in the party hierarchy. But old scandals over finances, discarded mistresses, politics and personal morality combined with suspicions of a man 'too clever by half'. 'I have been warned repeatedly not to trust Disraeli' the puzzled Newdegate told Stanley. 'I can scarcely help believing there must be some foundation for so general an opinion as I have alluded to, and it makes me very uneasy.' Similar concern led Stanley to propose Herries as nominal leader, with Disraeli doing the work. Disraeli refused. Stanley then suggested a triumvirate of Herries, Granby and Disraeli. Disraeli refused, but did the work. The suspect Jew had reached the top of the pole, not by universal acclaim but by reluctant acceptance (speeded-up by his regretful hints that he might leave the party). Few could take Herries or Granby very seriously: from early 1849 Disraeli was effectively the leader in the Commons, and he led a new party.

It was a difficult task to lead a party when one was loathed by former allies, who might yet reunite with one's present followers. It was still more difficult when one was suspected by the Court (where the Peelite efficiency of Prince Albert was dominant), by the free-trading *bourgeoisie* (despite a sizeable Tory element) and, above all, by considerable sections of one's own party. The task was made even harder while the party was lumbered with strict Protectionist doctrine, the viewpoint of those hoary 'ultras' who had been the first to sniff at Peel's 'treason'. Protection was, as Disraeli knew, a 'hopeless question'; indeed, it was 'not only dead but damned'. His difficulty arose from having to persuade Stanley and the squires that 'the Country party', though defeated on this issue (itself not an entrenched part of Tory principle), could still fight again over ultimately more important causes – in other words, that Toryism, sensibly refurbished, could remain a major tradition. The playing-down of Protectionism in his biography *Lord George Bentinck* (1851) indicated this policy.

There were various differences between Derby and Disraeli, particularly over parliamentary tactics in Opposition. But Disraeli was too important to be ignored in the formation of governments. And the party was coming round to his views; after the 1857 election he told Mrs Brydges Willyams 'We shall now have a House of Commons with two parties and with definite opinions. All the sections, all the conceited individuals who were what they styled themselves 'independent', have been swept away, erased, obliterated, expunged. The state of affairs will be much more wholesome and more agreeable.' Yet his leadership in the Commons still did not command universal assent. Of about 260 Tory Members only 146 voted against Palmerston on the Orsini bomb affair in 1858. And in 1859 many Tories, led by Walpole and Henley (who both resigned), were doubtful about Disraeli's unsuccessful Reform Bill. On the other hand, the election raised the party to 290 Members – one result of which was the June meeting in Willis's Rooms which virtually founded the Liberal party of Whigs, Radicals and Peelites.

The hostility within the party was best represented by Cecil's article in the *Quarterly Review* of April 1860. Disraeli, asserted Cecil,

had never led the Conservatives to victory as Sir Robert Peel had led them to victory. He had never procured the triumphant assertion of any Conservative principle or shielded from imminent ruin any ancient institution. But he had been a successful leader to this extent, that he had made any government while he was in opposition next to an impossibility. His tactics were so various, so flexible, so shameless – the net by which his combinations were gathered in was so wide – he had so admirable a knack of enticing into the same lobby a happy family of proud old Tories and foaming Radicals, martial squires jealous of their country's honour, and manufacturers who had written it off their books as an unmarketable commodity – that so long as his party backed him, no government was strong enough to hold out against his attacks.

Cecil told his father that he had 'merely put into print what all the country gentlemen were saying in private'. Disraeli was, indeed, never forgiven at Hatfield. 'He was quite as much a man of theory as he was a practical tactician', wrote Lord Hugh Cecil, in 1912:

> The error of 1867 was not that he was blind to the nature of the movement towards democracy nor that he pressed resistance to it too obstinately, but on the contrary that in defiance of the previous attitude and old traditions of his party, he hurried forward an extension of the franchise before public opinion required it and to the scandal of Conservative sentiment. He was too quick where Peel had been too slow. He foresaw the ultimate establishment of a democratic system: he rated too low the moral disaster that was involved in Conservatives outrunning reformers and 'dishing the Whigs'.

In June 1860 Disraeli suggested to Sir William Miles that he should resign, on the grounds that 'fourteen years of unqualified devotion had not reconciled the party'.[16] Leading M.P.s talked him out of the idea. Disraeli's task in the sixties was two-fold: he must gain personal acceptance at Windsor and in London political society; and he must explore every avenue by which Conservatism might be extended and strengthened, without offending too many existing supporters. 'If Scotland and the Metropolitan districts are to be entirely and continuously arrayed against the Conservative cause,' he told Derby after the 1865 election, 'the pull of the table will be too great and no Conservative government, unless the basis be extended, will be possible.' But his own position remained somewhat precarious. Stanley, General Peel and Cranborne were suggested as possible Tory leaders of a 'conservative' alliance with the heads of aristocratic Whiggism. But it was Disraeli's tactical intuition and strategic tuition which led to the fall of the last Whig ministry in June 1866.

As an actual or potential Chancellor of the Exchequer, Disraeli was always in favour of economy. Military – and especially naval – expenditure seemed too high and much too lightly audited. 'These wretched Colonies will all be independent, too, in a few years, and are a millstone round our necks,' he told Malmesbury in August 1852. 'It can never be our pretence or our policy to defend the Canadian frontier . . .,' he wrote to Derby in October 1866. 'Power and influence we should exercise in Asia; consequently in Eastern Europe, consequently also in Western Europe; but what is the use of these colonial deadweights which *we do not govern?*' Withdrawal from Canada and West Africa would permit 'a saving which would at the same time enable us to build ships and have a good budget'. In these views he fairly expressed the sentiment of rural Tories who regarded Imperialism as a radical aberration. And in 1867 he carried almost the whole party into his reforming camp. Inevitably the majority did not include Cranborne, who thought the Reform Bill was 'a political betrayal which has no parallel in our parliamentary annals'. Equally inevitably, Disraeli claimed that the enfranchisement of the urban working class was perfectly consistent with Tory tradition. 'In a progressive country change is constant,' he declared in a celebrated speech at Edinburgh,

> and the great question is not whether you should resist change which is inevitable, but whether that change should be carried out in deference to the manners, the customs, the laws and the traditions of a people, or whether it should be carried out in deference to abstract principles and arbitrary and general doctrines. . . .

IX

Disraeli became Premier in February 1868. Malmesbury, Stanley, Manners and the earl of Mayo (the former Naas) retained Cabinet posts originally given by Derby. Lord Cairns was Lord Chancellor, the duke of Marlborough Lord President, the duke of Buckingham Colonial Secretary, the duke of Richmond President of the Board of Trade; Ben now knew his dukes. From the Commons came Gathorne Hardy (Home Secretary), Pakington (War Secretary), Northcote (Indian Secretary), Ward Hunt (Chancellor of the Exchequer), Henry Corry (First Lord of the Admiralty). The new Premier instantly started to charm the queen. Irish and Scottish Reform Bills were introduced, public executions were abolished, a Royal Commission on the Sanitary Laws was established and the Corrupt Practices Act was passed. But Cabinet and party were divided over Gladstone's resolutions on the disestablishment and disendowment of the Irish Church; even Derby and Stanley disagreed. When Stanley proposed the Government's vague amendment, Cranborne (shortly to become third marquess of Salisbury) was furious. On being invited to rejoin the Cabinet, Cranborne had told Northcote that 'he had the greatest respect for every member of the Government except one – but that he did not think his honour was safe in the hands of that one'. Now he assailed the 'ambiguous phrases and dilatory pleas' of an amendment 'too clever by half'. He confessed to Lord Carnarvon that 'pure "squire" Conservatism was played out'. But he could not trust Disraeli and told a Hertfordshire Tory 'If I had a firm confidence in his principles or his honesty, or even if he were identified by birth or property with the Conservative classes in the country – I might in the absence of any definite professions work to maintain him in power. But he is an adventurer: & as I have good reason to know, he is without principles and honesty.'[17] The fact was that Disraeli understood every British institution except, as Lord Blake suggests, the Church. To be 'on the side of the angels' against Darwin in 1863 was not enough; to pass the 1874 Bill against Anglican ritualists was to be unforgivable to many devout Churchmen.

The immediate return to an active, reforming Tory ministry was disappointing. At the election of November 1868 Disraeli was soundly trounced. The Liberal alliance rose from 364 to 384 seats, while the Tories dropped from 294 to 274. The defence of the Irish Church was no longer a telling electoral point, especially since many Tories no longer believed in it; and a Tory party which included Cranborne, now marquess of Salisbury and a numerically-unknown 'Cave' was not united enough to earn its reward for its recent 'radicalism'. Disraeli set a modern precedent by resigning without meeting the new House. And he made a novel, grateful gesture to his ageing and dying wife – that 'most severe of critics but – a perfect Wife!' to whom *Sybil* was dedicated; that generous lady who felt that 'Dizzy married me for my money but, if he had the chance again, he would marry me for love'; that loyal, devoted woman whose pie and champagne he preferred to a Carlton Club dinner on the night when he defeated Gladstone on 13 April 1867; that greatest supporter who was 'more like a mistress than a wife'. To the queen's embarrassment, he solicited the title of Viscountess Beaconsfield for his cancer-stricken Mary Anne. There have been many less-deserved 'dissolution' honours.

Having rewarded his wife, Disraeli returned to lead the Tories in their apparently normal Opposition role. He could easily have taken a peerage himself, leaving some younger man to restore gentility and obsolescence to a declining Right. Instead, he chose to fight. It was a brave decision. The old party establishment continued to support Salisbury (who still regarded Disraeli as a 'mere political gamester'); and the new 'democratic' strands in the party organisation generally 'knew their place' – and long continued to know it. Disraeli, in a considerable minority in the Commons, could not hope to defeat Gladstone's radical measures. In similar circumstances after 1945 Winston Churchill painted pictures in Morocco: now Disraeli wrote his strange but lucrative novel *Lothair* (1870). By 1872, when many Tories were again becoming restive, he determined to return to the political fray, instead of leaving Gladstone to make his mistakes without comment and allowing Derby to take the leadership without opposition.

Gladstone's errors had certainly had their effect: at the February thanksgiving in St Paul's for the prince of Wales's recovery, it was Disraeli who was cheered by the crowd. And now Disraeli went into action. At Manchester on 3 April he told the Lancashire loyalists that 'the programme of the Conservative party was to maintain the constitution of the country' – against plans 'to despoil churches and plunder landlords' and at a time 'when the banner of Republicanism was unfurled'. Toryism existed to defend the Monarchy, an hereditary, territorial House of Lords, a free Commons and an established Church (which 'to be national must be comprehensive'). 'But, after all, the test of political institutions was the condition of the country whose fortunes they regulated. . . . In political institutions were the embodied experiences of a race.' Toryism must therefore care for the condition of the people: indeed, on the punning principle of '*sanitas sanitatum, omnia sanitas*', 'the first consideration of a minister should be the health of the people'. Against Gladstone's ministerial 'range of exhausted volcanoes', Disraeli called up 'that unbroken spirit . . . which he believed was never prouder of the imperial country to which [Englishmen] belonged'.

On 24 June Disraeli addressed a Crystal Palace rally, telling the party of its previous errors and its future path. 'The Tory party, unless it is a national party, is nothing. It is not a confederacy of nobles, it is not a democratic multitude; it is a party formed from all the numerous classes in the realm – classes alike and equal before the law, but whose different conditions and different aims give vigour and variety to our national life.' Liberalism had 'endeavoured to substitute cosmopolitan for national principles'. Toryism, on the other hand, had three great objects: 'to maintain the institutions of the country . . . to uphold the Empire of England . . . [and] the elevation of the condition of the people'. Disraeli now appealed to an enfranchised working class to support ancient institutions, Imperialism and social reform. In changing his mind on the 'wretched Colonies', Disraeli of course was adopting a newly-popular course rather than pioneering a novel notion; 'so far from creating the sentiment, [he] merely recognised it and sought to exploit it'.[18] But again he touched a sympathetic chord among patriotic working men.

Gladstonian policies and Disraelian speeches together swung the pendulum back to Toryism. But the grief-stricken leader tended his wife until her death in December. And when a Tory–Irish vote defeated Gladstone's strange proposals for a new Dublin university (by three votes) in March 1873 Disraeli refused the queen's invitation to form a government. Tories had had enough of minority rule and Liberal blackmail. Furthermore, the by-election tide was running in their favour, and further Liberal ineptitude might well augment the flow. Disraeli was right on all counts. Because the Tories had defeated the Government with the aid of Irish Roman Catholics (who would certainly not support a Tory ministry) there was no reason why Tories should masochistically form another minority administration until such time as the Liberal alliance could put its house in order. Toryism was at last regaining its strength. It had reforming leaders with social backgrounds previously scarcely known in Tory (or other) Cabinets; it had a unique national and constituency organisation; it had at last an opportunity of regaining its stature. Disraeli was sixty-eight, a saddened, periodically ailing and often-traduced widower, a man whose personal ambitions had been only briefly realised. For the sake of his party, he was prepared to wait. He heard of Gladstone's decision to dissolve in his lonely London hotel suite in January 1874. But he acted instantly, as did John Gorst, the chief agent, and Charles Keith-Falconer, the Central Office organiser, who jointly ran the National Union of local associations. At the polls the Tories gained 350 seats, the Liberals 245 and the Irish Home Rulers 57. Gladstone reluctantly resigned, and Disraeli announced the first majority Tory Cabinet for twenty-eight years in February.

X

In the smallest Cabinet for forty-two years, Cairns, Malmesbury and Derby returned to the Woolsack, the keepership of the Privy Seal and the Foreign Office. Richmond became Lord President, Carnarvon took the Colonies and Salisbury took India. Richard Cross became Home Secretary; Hardy moved to the War Office, Northcote to the Exchequer, Hunt to the Admiralty and Manners to the Post Office. The triumphs were the inclusion of Salisbury (reluctant as he was to follow 'D. as dictator': he told his wife that 'the prospect of having to serve with this man again is like a nightmare. But except intense personal dislike, I have no justification for refusing') and the unknown but active Cross.

At last the Tories had produced not only a majority but also a talented and energetic government. The new party image was in a sense a measure of the success of Derby and Disraeli through the long years of Opposition. However, the party remained a coalition and consequently had some difficulty in framing a legislative programme. '. . . I had quite expected that [Disraeli's] mind was full of legislative schemes, but such did not prove to be the case,' complained Cross. Disraeli's mind envisaged broad traditionalist themes – the defence of an ancient monarchy, the maintenance of the landed classes. 'The office of leader of the Conservative party in the H. of C.', he told Derby in 1848, '. . . is to uphold the aristocratic settlement of this country.' But his social sympathies were sincerely generous. The man who had seen and movingly described the real poverty of many northern workers in the 1840s never forgot the broad aim of social reform. Supporting the Ten Hours Act in 1847 was 'one of the most satisfactory incidents' of his career, he told Glasgow industrial reformers in 1873. Four years later the 'Promoters of Factory Legislation of Great Britain and Ireland' sent congratulations on his peerage and proletarian thanks for past services.

Disraeli never hesitated to remind audiences that 'many years ago the Tory party believed that . . . you might elevate the condition of the people by the reduction of their toil and the mitigation of their labour, and at the same time inflict no injury on the wealth of the nation' and how bitterly Liberals had opposed the notion. 'The health of the people was the most important question for a statesman,' he had told the Crystal Palace audience:

> It is a large subject. It has many branches. It involves the state of the dwellings of the people, the moral consequences of which are not

less considerable than the physical. It involves their enjoyment of some of the chief elements of nature – air, light and water. It involves the regulation of their industry, the inspection of their toil. It involves the purity of their provisions, and it touches upon all the means by which you may wean them from habits of excess and of brutality. . . . It may be the 'policy of sewage' to a Liberal member of Parliament. But to one of the labouring multitude of England, who has found fever always to be one of the inmates of his household – who has, year after year, see stricken down the children of his loins, on whose sympathy and material support he has looked with hope and confidence, it is not a 'policy of sewage' but a question of life and death. And . . . the policy of the Tory party – the hereditary, the traditionary policy of the Tory party, that would improve the condition of the people – is more appreciated by the people than the ineffable mysteries and all the pains and penalties of the Ballot Bill.

Carnarvon, so often unfair to Disraeli, correctly observed that 'he detested details'.[19] Disraeli could fairly retort that having educated his party and the electorate by announcing broad guide-lines of policy he had done a massive share of the Tory task.

Recent historians have often been tempted by (and sometimes succumbed to) the idea that Disraeli was merely an expert in expediency, the greatest Victorian exponent of political 'pragmatism'. Inevitably, Disraeli, like any Tory, was an empiricist. Like any politician, he made mistakes. He had his fair share of original and other sins. Tory hagiographies trying to prove an innate consistency in every thought, word and deed of the most complicated of all Tory statesmen are unconvincing. But the views of writers ancient and modern whose only consensus is that there is something improper in Tory reform are equally suspect. Times have changed since T. P. O'Connor (a Nationalist M.P.) could describe (through eight editions of an anti-semitic 'biography' of Disraeli) the Treaty of Berlin as 'the triumph of Judaea, a Jewish policy, a Jew'. They have not altered sufficiently to prevent some latter-day opponents from continuing to regard Disraeli as simply as a clever opportunist and from explaining 'unnatural' Tory reform as either forced by external pressure or engineered dishonestly.

More important is the consideration of Disraeli's place in Tory history and legend. 'Many Conservative leaders have had a hankering for Disraeli's precept,' writes Lord Blake, 'but they have usually followed Peel's practice – and so did Disraeli.' Professor Gash makes a similar point: 'a curious feature of the Conservative party is that though its practice has almost invariably been Peelite, its myth has been largely Disraelian.' This is undoubtedly true. Peel demonstrated that Conservatism could accommodate itself to a *bourgeois* ethos and a middle-class electorate. Disraeli taught it to preserve a patrician presence and simultaneously to expand in suburbia and to welcome and solicit proletarian support. The party was generally more successful in the first two aims than in the last. Nevertheless, Tory radicalism, as reaffirmed in Disraeli's concept of Tory reformism, has had an honourable and periodically influential history.[20]

While it is true that Disraeli's major contribution to British politics lay in propounding Right-wing ideas rather than in spelling out legislative clauses, his legislative successes were impressive. Prime ministers do not need to be personally involved in every Act of their ministers. But they set the tone of and take the ultimate responsibility for their governments. And the tone of Disraeli's ministry in 1874 and 1875 was such as to make it the major social reforming government of the century. The Ten Hours Act, which had been mutilated in 1850, was restored in 1874, and factory legislation was consolidated in 1878. In that *annus mirabilis* of social legislation, 1875, the inequities of Master and Servant legislation were remedied by the Employers and Workmen Act; collective bargaining and the right to strike were finally recognised by the Conspiricy and Protection of Property Act; local authorities were authorised to commence slum clearance schemes under the Artisans Dwellings Act; the Friendly Societies Act improved safeguards for small savers; adulteration was proscribed by the Sale of Food and Drugs Act; and the Public Health Act codified health legislation. During the same year a new imperialistic note was sounded with the purchase of the Khedive of Egypt's Suez Canal shares and the 'elevation' of the queen to the style of empress of India. But, inevitably, the splendid start – backed by Court favour and enhanced by Gladstonian sulks – could not be maintained. The old Right did not like the ministry's attitude to the Church, while liberals like Derby wished to weaken or end Toryism's 'Church and State' image. In 1876 Lord Sandon's Education Act improved Gladstone's measure of 1870; the controversial Merchant Shipping Act enforced greater safety; co-operative societies and trade unions were given greater protection. But back-benchers complained that long toil was producing small measures. Certainly, Disraeli was old and tired. He toyed with the idea of resigning the premiership to Derby.

Finally he decided to retain office from the Lords. On 12 August he was created earl of Beaconsfield.

XI

When Disraeli moved to the Upper House he chose Northcote to lead the Commons It was an honest and decent choice – Disraeli was always loyal to friends – and Northcote was an honest and decent man. But, as events were to prove, it was a mistaken one. The kindly baronet was no match for the Liberal leaders or, later, for the Tory 'Fourth party'. Gathorne Hardy, brought up in hard-headed Bradford, or Richard Cross, the energetic Lancastrian banker, might have been better choices.

While enhancing the Tory record of opposition to *laissez-faire* liberalism and embracing an imperial vision, Disraeli's ministry also sought to follow an independent British foreign policy. A British voice would again be heard in European affairs. So, at least, Disraeli determined; but Derby largely disagreed. The differences between Conservative and Liberal foreign policies, or even between the policies of Lords Beaconsfield and Derby, continue to provoke controversy. In a sense, the debate presaged and represented the dichotomy between 'practical' men, who see the job of British ministers as involving the defence of British interests, and 'theoretical' men, who attune their policies to contemporary views of 'morality'. The contrast is exaggerated: the practical men have often been men of the greatest integrity, while strident purveyors of 'morality' sometimes proved to be hypocritical humbugs. Disraeli was a 'practical' man.

Disraeli increasingly devoted himself to foreign affairs and in particular to 'the Eastern Question'. His personal predilections and long Tory connections with Urquhartite doctrines led him to prefer the Turks to either their European subjects or those subjects' proclaimed defenders in the *Dreikaiserbund*. These concerns led him to doubt, or even deny, the *Daily News* report of Turkish barbarities committed against Bulgarian revolutionaries in 1876. It was not that Disraeli was fanatically Turcophil; his principal aim was to assert Britain's importance in Europe: 'what our duty was at that critical moment was to maintain the empire of England.' He had reckoned without Gladstone's sudden interest in *The Bulgarian Horrors* and the enormous success of his pamphlet on the question, with its call that the Turks, 'one and all, bag and baggage should . . . clear out from the province they had desolated and profaned'. Gladstone knew how to play on and with the conscience of what remained of Christian England and how to turn it against 'that Jew'. The publication enormously increased political asperity and bitterly divided British political opinion. To Disraeli, Gladstone was now an 'unprincipled maniac' with an 'extraordinary mixture of envy, vindictiveness, hypocrisy and superstition'. But the Premier also had to face the criticism of Salisbury, Carnarvon and Derby (the unforgivable Brutus of the trio). He made one notable appointment: on Ward Hunt's death in 1877 Disraeli replaced him with the bookstall king W. H. Smith, a proven success as Secretary of the Treasury.

Derby's leakages of information to the Russian ambassador, Count Shuvalov, remained infuriating, and his suspicions of Disraeli's willingness to fight over Turkey were extended to the point of disloyalty. In January 1878 Disraeli carried his policy of negotiating with the Emperors, while secretly authorising a vote of credit and sending naval units through the Dardanelles. Derby and Carnarvon resigned in protest, but when the naval plan was dropped the former briefly returned. In February a squadron anchored off Constantinople, but when in March the Cabinet resolved to send Indian troops to the Mediterranean and to call up the reserves Derby resigned again; two years later he left the party. However, at least partly through Disraeli's firmness, the Russo-Turkish war ended. And as Foreign Secretary Salisbury proved equally resolute in opposition to a 'big Bulgaria' and Russian claims under the Treaty of San Stefano. Preliminary negotiations with the Russians and the Turks prepared the way for the Congress of Berlin in June and July, a meeting of contemporary giants – Count Julius Andrassy, Shuvalov, Disraeli and Bismarck. Disraeli, though ill, enjoyed playing a role on the 'world' stage. He returned to an enhanced reputation, 'peace with honour', the Garter (and an offered dukedom), cheering crowds, a bitter Gladstone. *Der alte Jude, das war der Mann* at Berlin.

Success thereafter ceased. In Afghanistan, Turkey, Ireland and Zululand matters went seriously wrong. At home the so-called 'great depression' (including a very real agricultural depression) was developing from about 1873. Scandals in high society (which Disraeli enjoyed solving) were not helpful. Gladstone's stage-managed Midlothian campaigns, with their 'moral' indictment of Tory policies, added to Tory troubles – particularly as the ailing Premier preferred to ignore them. On the other hand, by-election results augured well, and Edward Clarke's victory at Southwark early in 1880 led the Cabinet to dissolve in March. It was Disraeli's last great error. He had ignored Gorst's warnings that the new party organisation was again failing. Unpopular proposals to buy out London's water companies, an allegedly unfair Corrupt Practices Bill allowing borough candidates to pay for electoral conveyances (as allowed in the counties), Northcote's Budget and Derby's desertion (to some extent balanced by Frederick Stanley's appointment as War Secretary) added to the burden.

The election resulted in a great Liberal victory. Liberal M.P.s rose to 353, Home Rulers to 61; and Conservatives fell to 238. It was a heartbreaking end to a campaign fought (however weakly, because many of the party's most talented men were peers) by the first Tory majority administration since 1846. Dizzy bore the reverse bravely, though privately feeling (as he told the countess of Bradford) 'discomfited, defeated, and, if not disgraced, prostrate'. He rewarded his friends, as always, by (no doubt enjoyably) 'making peers, creating baronets and showering places and pensions on a rapacious crew'. But his respect for the aristocracy in fact made him more reluctant than many ministries of the 'Left', then or subsequently, to confer titles. A major exception to his rule was the elevation of his devoted secretary, Monty Corry, as Baron Rowton. Less pleasant was the duty of suggesting his successor to the queen: he fairly mentioned the marquess of Hartington, the Liberal leader in the Commons, and himself resigned on 21 April. But neither Hartington nor Earl Granville could ignore Gladstone – whose premiership the queen was reluctantly forced to accept. Disraeli could have retired with dignity (and a dukedom). Instead, he accepted the enthusiastic acclaim of Tory peers and M.P.s on 19 May. 'The policy of the Conservative party,' he told them, 'is to maintain the Empire and preserve the Constitution.' And, to face the Liberals' new radicalism, he determined to continue to lead the Tories.

XII

In the Lords Disraeli could command the Tories – and, on some measures, many Whigs. But in the Commons poor Northcote faced many difficulties. Not only was he outgunned by Gladstone, but he was also subjected to sniping by the disrespectful Fourth Party. Like 'Young England', the Fourth Party was small, consisting of Sir Henry Drummond Wolff, John Gorst, Lord Randolph Churchill and Arthur Balfour; it was aristocratic; it was radical; it had no Whip and no rules.

Disraeli could scarcely refrain from sympathising with such a joyous, active, erastian group of younger politicians. 'He scouted the idea of Northcote thinking of coalition or being inclined to Derby', Gorst told Churchill, after visiting Hughenden in November:

> . . . We need not consult Northcote when Parliament is not sitting. . . . We should always courteously inform N., through the Whip, of any step we are about to take in the House of Commons, and listen with respect and attention to anything he may say about it; his remarks, even when we disagree with him, will be well worth attention. But just at present *we need not be too scrupulous about obeying our leader*. An open rupture between us would, however, be most disastrous; but Lord B. thinks if we are courteous and firm Northcote will make no open rupture and will not throw us over. . . .

To Drummond Wolff Disraeli declared that he had only left the Commons because of Gladstone's 'withdrawal from public life':

> I thought that when he was gone Northcote would be able to cope with anyone likely to assume the lead on the other side, and I wanted rest. I now much regret having retired from the House of Commons, as Mr Gladstone, contrary to my firm persuasion, returned. I fully appreciate your feelings and those of your friends; but you must stick to Northcote. He represents the respectability of the party. I wholly sympathise with you all, because I never was respectable myself. . . . Don't on any account break with Northcote; but defer to him as often as you can. Whenever it becomes too difficult you can come to me and I will try to arrange matters. Meanwhile I will speak to him.

Dizzy, in fact, seems to have tried to encourage the Fourth Party to revitalise a demoralised Toryism, but at the same time not to desert the party and Northcote. 'I approve of the light cavalry and all they have done,' he told Drummond Wolff in July. But talk of an alliance with Home Rulers would 'sever from our ranks some of our most respectable friends'; and Whigs, already 'for the first time, really alarmed since 1834', must not be put off by Tory ambition. 'Prudence is as much required at this moment as enterprise,' insisted Disraeli. 'You may help the development, but you must not precipitate it. . . .'[21] Meanwhile, Dizzy calmed the natural perturbation of his official lieutenants in the Commons.

Disraeli continued to surprise. In November he published *Endymion*, a three-volume novel, full of the usual romantic and political commentary. Indeed, he commenced another novel, evidently caricaturing the loathsome Gladstone – that 'Arch Villain' of his letters. And as society returned to London in 1881, the sick, drugged old man played his role at the dinner tables and in the Lords. But in March he was stricken by bronchitis and after a bravely-endured illness he died on 21 April. Many Britons sincerely regretted the passing of the most unusual of their premiers. Gladstone offered the pomp and ceremony of a State funeral at Westminster Abbey. But Dizzy won his last argument with the G.O.M.: his will specifically requested a simple burial next to Mary Anne, in Hughenden churchyard. Inevitably, it was a funeral such as few villages had ever seen, as princes of the blood, great noblemen and distinguished politicians paid their last respects to the most unlikely of squires. Gladstone did not attend. But the queen later travelled to Buckinghamshire to honour the Minister whom she had most highly regarded and who had revived the notion of a popular monarchy. And further honours followed. There were monuments and statues. There was the Primrose League of 1883, with Disraeli's call for *Imperium et Libertas* at the head of its lists of a provincial 'feudal' freemasonry. There was what O'Connor found 'a curious spectacle' on 19 April 1884, when half of London seemed to be sporting memorial primroses: 'the testimony of London to the dead Minister was sincere, enthusiastic, universal.' And there were already two Disraelian traditions.

For many years opponents in all parties had regarded the *maestro* with suspicion. At its lowest level, such hostility arose from mere anti-semitism. But it was backed by charges of Machiavellian inconsistency. 'He was potent and terrible because he revered nothing, he respected nothing,' asserted O'Connor. After Disraeli's death Gladstone curtly commented that he was 'all display without reality or genuineness'. Years earlier Greville had considered him 'a perfect will-o'-the-wisp, flitting about from one opinion to another'. The Peelites, never forgiving the insults to their master, had been particularly scathing. 'There was a day when conduct of [Disraeli's] kind would have been scouted as intolerable with unanimous scorn; but the House of Commons had never consented to be led by a Jew Adventurer,' maintained Graham – himself a party chameleon. And Sidney Herbert thought that 'the rogue was capable of anything for a party or personal object'.[22] Some modern writers have continued this tradition.

Not all Conservatives would disagree with the 'opportunist' view of

Disraeli, though few would accept it as the sole explanation of a distinguished leader. From the practical, organisational point of view, Disraeli's contribution to Toryism was seminal and vital. The cynical observer of the old *ad hoc* arrangements of the Tadpoles and Tapers in the Carlton was always conscious of the importance of professional organisation. The Peelite professionals, headed by Francis Bonham, had largely followed Peel in 1846. Consequently, the new Tories initially operated an amateur machine: William Beresford was an unimpressive Whip and a nonentity as organiser of the 1852 election. Disraeli divided the parliamentary and constituency tasks. Sir William Jolliffe was an excellent Whip; and Disraeli's personal solicitor, Philip Rose (the trusted executor, rewarded with a baronetcy in 1874) was an able manager of a new network of constituency agents and interviewer of prospective candidates. Rose's work was undertaken in 1859 by his legal partner, Markham Spofforth, who was assisted by Dudley Baxter. This arrangement was less satisfactory, and Disraeli changed it. The National Union of Conservative and Constitutional Associations – described by Lord Blake as 'the first centralised mass organisation to be formed by a British political party' – was established on 12 November 1867. Lord Nevill, from 1868 aided by a committee, supervised and integrated various party efforts. In 1870 John Gorst became principal agent and vigorously promoted working men's and other constituency associations, clubs and registration societies. And in the same year the Conservative Central Office commenced its work, under Gorst's able friend C. J. Keith-Falconer. Organisational troubles and personal differences lay ahead and were to harm the party in 1880; the relationships between the National Union, Central Office, the Whips, the parliamentary party and metropolitan and provincial groups required more diplomatic handling than was always available. Few political organisations had satisfactorily solved such problems even a century later.[23] Under Disraeli's patronage, the Tories were the first to face the issue – and they were certainly the first to find an acceptable solution.

Disraeli's practical contribution to Tory history did not end with his own career or with his influence on party organisation. Tory opinion has generally accepted that 'audacious paradox' discerned by G. M. Young: that Disraeli taught Tories that 'they were the party of the people: their true representatives and defenders both against those who would destroy the institutions, whether in Church or State, which were their self-appointed way of life, and those who would manipulate them to their own exorbitant advantage.' And Tories have largely accepted

Young's view that: 'the vitality and influence of the Tory party ever since have always been in exact proportion to the confidence with which it has accepted the paradox as its creed.' Such attitudes have received regular support from leading practical Tories. Colonel Walter Elliot maintained that

> Disraeli's fundamental strength was, that like Karl Marx, . . . he had grasped, though from the opposite end, the fact of the colossal and growing economic divergence between the masses and the classes. . . . There rings in his sentences the conviction that political freedom is not enough, that economic improvement must be secured, and speedily. . . . It was his insistence on domestic reform, his straddle from the eighteenth into the nineteenth century, that altered the whole course of political development in Britain. For it re-made the Tory party as a broadly-based national force, a position which it never again lost.

Disraeli himself stressed this theme more strongly than some recent writers have admitted. At Edinburgh in October 1867 he observed that thirty-two measures on the 'condition of the people' had been passed in three decades, that he had supported all of them and that the party had opposed none. Lord Boyle considered that 'the founder of Tory Democracy . . . on his death in 1881 had achieved only part of his vision of the Young England period, but had established a tradition of Conservatism that is still the inspiration of our own day. Disraelian conservatism stretches through Lord Randolph Churchill to be still vital. . . .' And Lord Butler, after recalling that Disraeli had been 'described as a product of a derisive post-war era', declared '. . . there is more behind Disraeli's mocking spirit than the accidents of birth and upbringing. That something, if we look deep enough, is the very philosophy of Conservatism itself.'[24]

The testimony of practitioners of Disraeli's craft surely merits at least equality of esteem with the conclusions of less 'involved' writers resting varied arguments upon theoretical premises. Disraeli's restoration of romance and imagination to politics is an intangible factor more easily appreciated by platform orators and their audiences than by political theorists and their readers.

Disraeli was the most unlikely and most controversial of Tory leaders. The great defender of aristocratic principles was initially almost desperate in his search for an *entrée* to high society and was grateful to early friends. Consequently, in 1861 he spoke at Durham of Lord Londonderry as 'a man of very enlightened mind, a man who thoroughly understood the characteristics and necessities and wants of his age, and a man who truly understood that in a commercial country like England the aristocracy of the country should place themselves at the head of that great commercial interest . . .'. But, late in life, he was profoundly conscious that many great houses had never really accepted him – indeed, some were still too grand entirely to accept the House of Hanover. 'It is a very difficult country to move', he warned the eccentric Imperialist and pioneer Socialist H. M. Hyndman, in 1881.[25]

Disraeli had tried, in different ways, to 'move' Britain. He had taught a party of haughty patricians and apoplectic squires to face unpleasant realities. He had regularly demonstrated that the defence of ancient institutions could be allied with 'radical' social policies: he had shown that Toryism need not fear an extension of the suffrage beyond the dreams of Radicals; that Toryism cared about health, industrial labour and urban housing; that Toryism would correct the unfairnesses of Gladstone's trade union legislation. But he also taught his party that politics was conditioned by possibility and that conservation involved knowing precisely what was most worth conserving at any period. He followed Palmerston in encouraging Britons to believe in an imperial mission and in their importance in European affairs. He largely invented that combination of respect for ancient things, British (or, from his viewpoint, English) nationalism and a reaction against the harshness of *laissez-faire* which restored his party to major status. And despite many vicissitudes and many alternative formulae, the Disraelian ethic still survives. It may well be true that Tory cabinets tend to be Peelite; but Tory supporters remain largely Disraelian.

# 3 The Salisbury Era 1881-1902

## DONALD SOUTHGATE

BEACONSFIELD's privately designated successor was Robert Arthur Talbot Gascoyne Cecil (1830–1903), third marquess of Salisbury. That statesman had indicated his willingness to place himself at the disposal of the party provided the feelings of Sir Stafford Northcote were respected. But there was no machinery for appointing or electing 'the leader of the Conservative Party' when that party was not in office, and it was only in the leadership of the Conservative peers that Salisbury succeeded Disraeli. Northcote, for all his ineffectiveness – he was 'no more a match for Mr. Gladstone than a wooden three-decker would be for a Dreadnought', Balfour recalled – and his chronic heart disease, was persistently ambitious. The fact that the Fourth Party was 'thoroughly in Salisbury's favour as opposed to the Goat' (Churchill's nickname for Northcote) was no asset to Salisbury. Sir Stafford could hardly be subordinated in an ostentatious way when he was being savaged by Churchill. Moreover, Salisbury, who had sat in the House of Commons as Lord Robert Cecil from 1853 to 1865 and thereafter as Viscount Cranborne, had gone – not willingly – to the Lords as long ago as April 1868. The Commons ex-ministers in 1881 pointed out that 'it is in the House of Commons that the great battle will have to be fought, and there that the policy of the party will from time to time have to be announced and asserted'.

This was a sensible argument, and behind it perhaps lay the feeling that Salisbury was more remote than the mere fact of his peerage absolutely required. It was, indeed, something of a miracle that he was in the leadership stakes at all, the miracle-worker being his wife, a lady of strong and sociable character, who 'managed and made happy one of the shyest and most sensitive men in the world' and was ambitious for him. He had had a miserable childhood and his Oxford career was curtailed by mental ill-health culminating in a breakdown mended by a voyage round the world. He was always afraid of going mad, and only the consolation of the Catholic faith in its Anglican variety and a blissful domestic partnership prevented his disorder becoming chronic or even

For Further Reading relevant to this chapter, see page 249.

catastrophic. He was known as 'the Ishmael of the House of Commons' as much for his unsociability as for the vehemence of his attacks on the leaders of the opposite party and of his own. Throughout his life he eschewed society, except when it was brought under his own roof. Remoteness was part of his nature, and he made no effort to overcome it. His greatest handicap as party leader was that all he knew of the House of Commons after 1868 was learned at second-hand. He never once went back to survey from the peers' gallery the scene of his philippics against his leaders and the spirit of the age. 'To most of the members of the House the late Prime Minister was personally unknown' said the leader of the Liberal Party on Salisbury's death. It was not on account of his physical myopia that Salisbury failed to recognise many of the non-cabinet ministers whom he appointed on the advice, successively, of W. H. Smith and Balfour. He had never seen them in action or even met them socially. He confined his contacts with colleagues to official business and, except for the occasional speech in the country and sojourns in France, moved solely between Hatfield (where he did nearly all his work and had his science laboratory), the Foreign Office, the House of Lords and Conservative Central Office. Anything more calculated to invite the development of a convention that the Prime Minister must sit in the House of Commons it would be difficult to imagine.

There was a further reason for legitimate doubt as to Salisbury's suitability for party leadership. If Northcote was insufficiently combative and prone to Peelite trimming, there was much in Salisbury's record to brand him over-vehement and too diehard. This aristocratic intellectual had been both in speech and journalism the most articulate assailant of the Disraelian approach to politics and of 'Mr d'Israeli' personally as an immoral opportunist. He left the Government in 1867 and moved the rejection of the third reading of the Reform Bill denouncing a betrayal of the mutual confidence which was the soul of party government. In a *Quarterly Review* article entitled 'The Conservative Surrender' he complained that parties were becoming nothing but 'joint stock companies for the attainment and preservation of place', that Conservative tactics had stripped political conduct of all that was inspiring or ennobling, that public life was degraded. His very last speech in the House of Commons gave great offence to his former colleagues, being (on the Irish Church) as Gathorne Hardy recorded 'sneering as regards us all, venomous and remorseless against Disraeli'. The latter did not harbour rancour (he could never afford to do so) and no doubt marked a similarity between the speeches of Lord Cranborne and those attacks on Peel by which he himself had made his own name. 'My Noble Friend is a great master of jibes and flouts and jeers' he told the Commons in 1874. Disraeli was pleased that Salisbury had consented to join his new government and that he did not feel bound to resign over the Public Worship Regulation Bill. Salisbury had viewed the prospect of serving under Disraeli again 'with intense repulsion', but his attitude mellowed especially when, from 1878, he was at the Foreign Office 'picking up the china that Derby had broken'. At the last meeting of the Cabinet, after electoral defeat, on 21 April 1880, Salisbury went out of his way to say that there had never been a cloud between him and Beaconsfield throughout all his arduous work. The sincerity of their reconciliation is not in doubt. It was confirmed by the fact that Beaconsfield's appeal to the people did not mention Tory Democracy, or even the reforms of 1875–6, for Salisbury was deeply prejudiced against anything which smacked of bid and counter-bid between parties seeking electoral favour. It was symbolised by Beaconsfield staying at Hatfield with Balfour (Salisbury being abroad, ill) as the election results came in. But the avowal of solidarity at the ultimate Cabinet was shrewd, for the old maestro was already passing into legend and his successor must be acceptable to his admirers. There seems no doubt that Salisbury (with Balfour, his nephew, behind him) sought the Conservative leadership, if only because he trusted neither Northcote nor Cairns to sustain the Conservative cause.

Salisbury's attitude to public life was one of basic pessimism. 'The flood of evils wells up ceaselessly: and it requires no small philosophy to labour on, baling it out little by little, with the certainty that no exertions that we can make will ever materially abate its flow,' he wrote in 1863. In 1867 he was near to despair. 'My opinions belong to the past,' he said. But this man who often voiced the feelings of obscurantists was not obscurantist in his cast of mind. Convinced that the country was going to the dogs, he blamed the 'comfortable classes', whose apathy and cowardice were the real cause of a calamity of which the politicians who raised surrender into a principle were only symptoms. He must try to muster them, for it was 'idle for the Conservative classes to think that the innovating force can be held under salutary control without labour or risk on their part'. Of the evils of democracy – akin to the evils of tyranny – he had a hard intellectual conviction based upon a study of the French Revolution, the experiments of 1848–9 and American political practice. He could not share the happy Whig illusion that Britain was insulated by prosperity, the character of her people and the clever concessions of 1832 and 1846–7 from Continental infections such as Communism, which would strike not only at property and inequality but family and religion. He was as sure as Robert Lowe (and John Bright) that democracy would be dangerous to liberty and property and fatal to economy and to that confidence on which increasing prosperity must depend. If he was to strike any distinctive note of Conservative apologetics it would be that the statesman should concentrate on preserving the conditions of inequality which would enable the national wealth to grow to the ultimate benefit of all and be very chary of any redistribution of wealth by confiscation (including confiscation disguised as taxation) which would deter the *entrepreneur*. This thesis is developed at length in his son Hugh's *Conservatism*, published in the Home University Library series in 1912, where the right to accumulate riches and keep them is defended on the moral as well as utilitarian grounds which had been so often discussed at Hatfield in the author's youth, the moral ground being libertarian. The lord of Hatfield did not romanticise the past and was saved from an unworthy – but all too common – contempt for the mass of the people by a strong historical sense. When had a dominant class ever taxed itself fairly? The lower classes differed from the higher only in that their experience had been not of plenty and privilege but of want. They were no worse than their 'betters' because this experience induced jealousy and, being uneducated, they were the natural prey of unscrupulous demagogues urging the plunder of the rich. But hideous danger arose from the fact that the State had become a joint stock company with 'this monstrous and unheard-of peculiarity, that it is a joint stock company in which the shareholders vote, not by shares, but by heads'. Salisbury had an ideal of a healthy community. It would look to men of wealth, intellectual power and culture and, in some countries, birth, who would be motivated by patriotism and a high code of honour, but, checked already by the opinion of the people among whom they lived, would need also to be checked by constitutional forms and watched by an active public opinion lest their rightful pre-eminence degenerate into mere class domination. The healthy British community, in other words, would be one governed by high-minded Cecils! The head of the Cecils was not confident that such a regime was possible after the 'betrayal' of 1867, but the Conservative classes must do their best, even if it meant going to the brink of revolution, as in 1832. They should 'make up their minds what is worth struggling for, and then not be afraid to struggle for it'.

Here, in a sentence, is the key to Salisbury's politics. It is not surprising that concessionary Conservatives, seeking electoral victory and office, required proof that Salisbury would not fight for lost causes or prove too unyielding. Could they prosper under a man who had written that once a dyke was breached by small concessions all was lost, and had shown no sign that if made the trustee for the Right he would seek to occupy that middle ground whose possession marks the difference between victory and defeat? He had, indeed, expressed the conviction, in 1869, after Gladstone's previous triumph, that the army of so-called reform at every stage converted a detachment of its forces into opponents until at last a political equilibrium was restored. But might this development not be better induced by the less vehement Northcote, resting his hopes on Whig disenchantment with Gladstone, the Radicals and the Irish, than by the combative Salisbury? None could foresee that Salisbury, to his great good fortune, would occupy the middle ground for many years because the Liberals, under Gladstone's leadership, wilfully abandoned it and that the least flexible of Tory leaders would, in consequence, hold the premiership for longer than anyone since Lord Liverpool. *Some* flexibility, of course, there must be, or he could never become the acknowledged party leader. In his last piece of anonymous journalism, the article called 'Disintegration' in the *Quarterly Review* of October 1883 (he was comically outraged that anonymity did not conceal its authorship), he showed that he had learned the Peelite lesson. He wrote as follows:

> The object of our party is not and ought not to be simply to keep things as they are. In the first place, the enterprise is impossible. In the next place there is much in our present mode of thought and action which it is highly undesirable to conserve. What we require is the administration of public affairs . . . in that spirit of the old constitution which held the nation together as a whole, and levelled its united force at objects of national import, instead of splitting it into a bundle of unfriendly and distrustful fragments.

This is the authentic note of Conservative leadership. Salisbury had achieved his own equilibrium between mere 'hostility to Radicalism, incessant, implacable hostility [as] the essential definition of Conservatism' which he had proclaimed in his first political speech (to the electors of Stamford in 1853) and the unprincipled bribery of a mass electorate to which he would have scorned to lend himself. He had equipped himself to face the future.

II

In his drive to the top Salisbury had to dispose of Northcote and use Churchill until it was safe to subordinate or discard him. For Salisbury agreed with Balfour (who was playing, in the interests of his uncle and himself, an equivocal role as a member of the Fourth Party) that Lord Randolph intended to reach the top of the political ladder in one step or two. At some stage he must be thwarted, for, even apart from personal ambition, neither believed this unbalanced and unpredictable man at all suitable to lead the Conservative party. But, meantime, there was no way of preventing him from having his head, and no harm need come of this – *except to Northcote*. In the great conflict about (ostensibly) the relationship between the National Union of Conservative and Constitutional Associations and the party leadership, which raged for a year from the spring of 1883, Churchill, on behalf of the National Union, addressed Salisbury in outrageous terms, and received an ultimatum (probably drafted by Balfour) giving the National Union notice to quit the premises of the Central Committee, which was dominated by the Whips on behalf of the parliamentary leaders. This ultimatum was an error of judgement and had to be retracted. But the nub of the matter is that Churchill always addressed Salisbury as though he were the undoubted (though misguided) leader of the party and that Salisbury, though he associated Northcote with him to the extent that decency demanded, kept the skeins firmly in his own hands. When the battle ended, as, predictably, it had to, in a compromise, Northcote was simply informed by Salisbury of the terms of the transaction. Both Salisbury and Churchill emerged with enhanced prestige. The loser was Northcote. Only the Northcote family was surprised when, in mid-1885, a minority Conservative Government being required, the queen sent for Salisbury as though this was a matter of course. Northcote's butler told importunate journalists that his master had been offered the private secretaryship to Lord Randolph Churchill. That remarkable young man had established himself as the champion of urban Toryism, and Salisbury had become the leader of the party by agreement with him.

Salisbury and Balfour understood in 1881 that it was valuable to have in Churchill a parliamentary *frondeur* who was expert at getting Gladstone to follow false scents and even to have a demagogue to keep alive the idea of Tory Democracy, whatever that might mean. Electorally, at least in Lancashire, it seemed to mean something, though

perhaps Lancashire was unique – with its strong and widespread
Evangelical Anglicanism and its numerous voluntary schools; the impact
of Irish immigration on the native population; a Tory–Chartist tradition; the attractions of iconoclasm in the very temple of Free Trade.
But Tory Democracy was rarely defined in such acceptable terms as
when Churchill, addressing a vast crowd in Manchester in the 1885
election, said it was 'a democracy that has embraced the principles of
the Tory party' and which therefore regarded hereditary monarchy and
the Lords as fortifications of democratic freedom. Too often in those
torrential orations in the great centres of the Midlands and the North,
by which Lord Randolph sought to force himself on the Tory M.P.s as
their leader, he held up to scorn not only Gladstone and Whig noblemen
but 'the old men crooning over the fires at the Carlton'. But in politics
the will to win, and the conviction that one can win, count for much.
Churchill had both and accused the official Opposition under Northcote
of a secret conviction that the party had nothing to look forward to but
endless opposition, perhaps occasionally chequered by glimpses of
minority government. He himself would play hard, and even play foul,
to win – and for Salisbury the business was too serious to be thought of
as a game.

In reply to a Manchester delegation asking him to stand for their
constituency Lord Randolph declared that it was the duty of an Opposition to oppose but 'this function during the three sessions of this
Parliament has either been systematically neglected or defectively
carried out'. Salisbury knew how true this charge was. There had been
a *débâcle* over the Arrears Bill. When the Land Act of 1881 failed to end
terrorism in Ireland, Gladstone made Tory noises about 'the resources
of civilisation' not being exhausted, and interned Parnell as ultimately
responsible both for parliamentary obstruction and terrorism. But in a
matter of months he could not keep his Liberal government together
without releasing Parnell from Kilmainham Gaol. His 'treaty' with his
political prisoner provided that the campaign against general recourse to
the new rent-tribunals would be called off if a bill dealing with arrears
of rent was introduced. The 'treaty' – which angered Balfour into
making his first effective parliamentary speech – became very unpopular
when the political and civil service heads of the Irish government were
murdered in Phoenix Park. The former was a much-loved M.P.,
brother of the Whig minister Hartington and nephew by marriage of
Mrs Gladstone; his widow's sister had been Balfour's one true love. The
Conservative peers were induced to allow the second reading of the

Arrears Bill only by the positive assurance of Salisbury, given them at his house on 21 July 1882, that wrecking amendments would be persevered with to the end. But when they met there again on 10 August in the knowledge that 'the end' might be a Liberal appeal, in an election, to 'the people against the peers', a majority opted for running away. Salisbury was aghast, and would have staked his position on the issue but for the risk of leaving the party at the mercy of Cairns and Northcote. He told the House frankly that if he had had the power he would have wrecked the bill, but that in the circumstances he would not divide. At least this made the Conservative peers look (and feel) 'like a pack of whipped hounds' and they never rebelled again. But the incident gives point to Churchill's declaration in *The Times* of 2 April 1883 that electors in a negative frame of mind might accept Northcote, in a cautious frame of mind might shelter under Cairns, but in an *English* frame of mind would rally round Salisbury. This challenge to Northcote produced a demonstration of support when he entered the Commons and a memorial from Tory M.P.s, which Balfour derived perverse pleasure from signing. But Churchill wrote again to say that the party must be led by 'a statesman who fears not to meet and who knows how to sway immense masses of the working classes and who either by his genius or his eloquence, or by all the varied influences of an ancient name, can "move the hearts of households" ' – i.e., by Salisbury, failing whom – Churchill.

The reference was clearly to the new custom of public speaking. The queen, deprecating this deference to the masses, concurred with the Tory leaders in blaming it on Gladstone's 'pilgrimage of passion' against Beaconsfield's foreign policy. Gladstone blamed it on *them*, but it was the natural result of the extension of the franchise in 1867, the development of communications and the spread of reading. From it Salisbury benefited more than most. Debarred by law from the Commons and by constitutional convention from participating in elections, he was afforded a means of projecting himself to the nation.

As a public speaker Salisbury cultivated no image; he was always himself. His speeches lacked excitement and, normally, memorable phrases (though there was the occasional gaffe). They were philosophical, thoughtful, anxious, responsible; in manner conversational, not oratorical. The jibes and taunts and jeers were left to Churchill now. In the flesh Salisbury was a bearded figure of six foot four, made majestic by growing rotundity despite a modicum of assiduous exercise, latterly on a tricycle. He owed much of the respect which he won to his habit of talking to persons and crowds alike on a footing of respect and equality which in fact emphasised his natural superiority. His horror of fortuitous public recognition and of casual contacts was a function of his shyness, a survival of the painful insecurity of his youth; it did not denote *hauteur* or disdain. Far more people, of course, read what he said than heard him or ever saw him. Churchill effectively ridiculed Gladstone's custom of showing himself at railway stations *en passant*, as well as his tree-felling habits. Salisbury, in contrast, travelled like a criminal on the run. Yet this nervous intellectual nobleman, who distrusted democracy and had no real confidence in the long-term survival of what he defended, contrived through his public speeches to earn public esteem and trust by his appeals on grounds of reason to conservative instincts as well as interests. Attacking 'wild teachers' he strove to inculcate 'a calm common-sense view of extravagant theories'. 'A party whose mission it is to live entirely upon the discovery of grievances are apt to manufacture the element upon which they subsist,' he complained. Extolling national unity, he sought to counter the attraction of dividing the property of the rich among the poor by arguing that to workman and shopkeeper alike 'confidence' among the investing and employing classes was of all things important. There were strict limits to what central authority could usefully do or should be asked to do. Civil servants were too prone to believe that *they* were the people who knew the right decisions to take. 'The great modern dictator' was the inspector, 'an image made of wood and clothed in red tape'.

Salisbury's practice was to be less negative than his precepts. In his very first speech at Stamford, in 1853, he had supported 'measures tending to social and sanitary improvements and the amelioration of the conditions of the labouring classes'. The same theme is found in the *Quarterly* article in 1883 and on 22 February 1884 he moved for a Royal Commission on the housing of the working classes. At its meetings, and apropos of its report, he was denounced as 'a socialist'. To such charges from the *laissez-faire* extremists he would reply with acerbity that 'if it is convinced that a measure is likely to answer Parliament never troubles itself about the school of thought from which the measure is drawn'. Indeed, for all the general gist of his speeches, he was a man of essentially utilitarian judgements, apologetically approving measures of great beneficence which mutton-headed squires and businessmen had not the wit to bless. This must be borne in mind when we adopt A. L. Kennedy's dictum that Salisbury frankly gave first place to the protective and defensive aspects of Conservatism. But his central theme was certainly the defence of liberty and property. Salisbury tapped many of the springs of traditional Toryism. At the same time he appealed to the *bourgeois* recruits who, ostentatiously in the metropolis, but throughout England and Scotland too, in the business centres, the suburbs and the market towns, moved, in the last third of the nineteenth century from the Liberal to the Conservative side either directly or, after 1886, via Liberal Unionism. It was a time when new-style Radicals talked the language of collectivism and redistributive taxation (and of Henry George's 'single tax') and when that rather old-fashioned Radical Whig Sir William Harcourt justified his 1894 death duties with the remark 'We are all socialists now'. In Salisbury was to be found a leader who defended liberty and property, and each in the name of the other; who championed acquisition and wealth-creation against the egalitarians; who preached that gospel of the interdependence of all classes in society which is so comforting to the possessing classes and enables them to blame the less fortunate for the divisiveness of class war. Salisbury's horror of 'spoliation' was patently sincere. It seemed the fruit of erudition. It sounded high-minded, and it was simple-minded. It placed the heir of the Cecils in harmony with W. H. Smith, who as a boy had risen at dawn to load his father's news-papers, and was now a conspicuous example of self-aggrandisement by honest Anglican business acumen and endeavour – and known, not wholly ironically, as 'Old Morality'. Mr Smith's election for West-minster in 1868 betokened, in the hour of defeat, prospects of middle-class reinforcement as important to the Conservative party as its mass vote at Oldham. On 3 February 1889 Smith, Leader of the House of Commons, wrote to Salisbury of his bewilderment that 'men who are strictly honest in their transactions with their neighbours have come to regard Parliament as an instrument by which a transfer of rights and property may equitably be made from the few to the many'. The Prime Minister replied: 'We are in a state of bloodless civil war. . . . To loot somebody of something is the common object, under a thick varnish of pious phrases. So that our lines are not cast in pleasant places.'

To those open to persuasion Salisbury was convincing because he was convinced, and he won a moral authority second only to Gladstone's. But whereas Gladstone overstrained that authority, and broke his party, Salisbury is open to the criticism that he did not use his very great authority to force upon his followers social reforms quite compat-ible with a general adhesion to *laissez-faire* notions yet more consonant with Tory than Cobdenite or Gladstonian Liberal tradition. Just before the final breach between them Randolph Churchill, as Leader of the House of Commons, wrote in November 1886: '... it is an idle schoolboy's dream to suppose that Tories can legislate ... in a democratic constitution ... I certainly have not the courage to go on struggling against cliques, as poor Dizzy did all his life.' Back came the devastatingly honest answer: '... we have so to conduct our legislation that we shall give some satisfaction to both classes and masses. But all legislation is rather unwelcome to the classes.' And as 'the classes and dependents of class' were the strongest elements in the composition of the Tory party it was 'evident ... that we must work at less speed and at a lower temperature than our opponents ...'. From this posture Salisbury was not to be shaken by all the arguments of Joseph Chamberlain when Home Rule had made that midland Radical first his ally and then his colleague. In 1892, the election having been lost, Chamberlain urged the production of a forward-looking Queen's Speech; though certain to be defeated in the new Parliament, this 'progressive Tory' programme would pre-empt ground and embarrass the prospective Liberal Government with its prime commitment to Irish Home Rule and its semi-commitment to a rag-bag of reforms attractive to various minorities (the Newcastle Programme) but offer little or nothing (except parish councils) to 'the masses' as such. A policy of social legislation, wrote Chamberlain, was as much or more in harmony with Conservative traditions than Liberal ones – 'We, the Unionist Party, can do it, which the other side cannot.' Salisbury replied that to suggest to Parliament measures which had not even been sketched would be dishonest. He told Balfour that the phrases which would 'please Joe' would 'alarm a good many people who have always been with us'. Here was a leader who, mindful of his criticism of his predecessors for pursuing electoral advantage at the cost of affronting the faithful, recognised a duty to those he led. With a pessimism which boded ill for the Conservative cause he added: 'I fear these social questions are destined to break up our Party, but why incur the danger before the necessity has arrived – and while the Party may still be useful to avert Home Rule?'

Many a Conservative will find this conclusion unforgivable, and see in this 'après moi, le déluge' attitude a kind of vanity. But we must judge Salisbury in the light of his firm conviction that in the competition of rival demagogues for mass votes lay the road to ruin. In practice Conservatives would have to do or support things because they were politically inevitable or even because they were just, but it was neither their duty nor their interest to force up the bidding. And so to the

rhetoric of Churchill and the 'unauthorised programmes' propounded by
Chamberlain as opponent or ally Salisbury opposed a reasoned moderation and caution which brand him as more of a diehard than he really was.

Certainly the worst starting-point for a fair judgement of Salisbury
is to take at its face value the rhetoric of Churchill. In all but noble
birth and youthful political vehemence Lord Randolph was Salisbury's
antithesis. He would take up anything he thought would serve, like Fair
Trade, and as quickly drop it. Who, reading that scathing attack on 'the
lords of suburban villas, owners of vineries and pineries' which was
provoked by W. H. Smith's objection to giving votes to Irish peasants
dwelling in mud cabins, would gather that Lord Randolph at Edinburgh
had opposed all franchise extension; had been repudiated by Balfour
from the platform; had then switched to the advocacy of extensive
electoral reform under pressure from the representatives of urban
Toryism? Lord Randolph dealt in the language of class war for the
delectation of mass audiences and the winning of seats – but also to
discredit Northcote and make himself at least joint leader of the Conservative party. Emulating and competing with Chamberlain, the
spokesman of the Radical wing of the Liberal party, he excelled him in
vulgarity and added a dimension of aristocratic snobbery in attacks
on the employing class which the Birmingham champion could not
match. But Churchill never developed a coherent social programme.
Only confusion can arise from taking his rhetoric literally, and confusion will be worse confounded if one gathers – as from his language
one might – that the elected executive of the National Union, which for
some months from October 1883 he controlled, represented the Tory
working man, and that the issue, for him, against 'dependence upon, and
servility to, certain irresponsible persons' who found favour in Salisbury's eyes, was one of democratic control or at least participation in
policy-making.

The people who went to National Union conferences, though in some
cases concerned with winning working-class seats, and in most cases
with winning urban seats, were neither in general working-class nor,
with important exceptions, 'Tory socialists', and they did not aspire to
dictate a policy, 'socialist' or otherwise, to party leaders. They were
middle-class people, for whom Gorst spoke, and upon whose discontents Churchill seized as a way of forcing himself on a largely
hostile parliamentary party. Gorst had told them that their exertions,
co-ordinated by him, had contributed significantly to the victory of
1874, but had received, like Gorst, inadequate recognition; that the old-

fashioned and incompetent Whips' Office which had mismanaged matters in 1880 must be prevented from leading the party to another defeat; that the Central Committee, under first Smith and then Stanhope, had changed from a committee of inquiry into the cause of the catastrophe into a standing committee to hold the constituency associations in subservience to a parliamentary leadership both aristocratic and inept. Gorst's somewhat ambiguous reinstatement as principal agent – which marched ill with his membership of the anti-leadership Fourth party – had not been a success and he was pursuing abrasively his vendetta against the Whips' Office. It was not difficult to persuade the delegates to the National Union conference at Birmingham in 1883 that 'something must be done' if Conservatism was to prosper outside the country seats and small boroughs. The circulation to them of a 'slate' of candidates for election to the executive by Lord Randolph Churchill, the principal platform asset of the party, in harness with Gorst, seemed to herald the breakthrough they had sought for years. Of course they cheered when Churchill demanded for their elect a large and real, instead of a sham, share in the party's counsels, 'the legitimate influence' of a 'popular body' confronting a 'close corporation'. They would cheer whatever Lord Randolph said about 'the great Tory Democracy, which Lord Beaconsfield's party constructed', applaud his attack on a narrow landowning class who half feared and half despised the common people, and raise the roof when he told them 'the Conservative party will never exercise power until it has gained the confidence of the working classes'. But they were perfectly ready to behave as Salisbury wished, and 'act in harmony with and under the guidance of the leaders, conforming [themselves] to any opinions of the leaders duly intimated' – if only the leaders gave the impression that they knew their business and would facilitate the organisation needed to win urban seats. They cheered Churchill – but usually, one suspects, it was the head rather than the heart which responded to the appeal to 'go with the people, and by the people . . . [to] organise and guide the masses and not treat them like scum as the Tories have so often done'. For were not the natural representatives of the delegates at the National Union jamborees W. H. Smith and Richard Cross, whom Churchill scorned as 'Marshall and Snelgrove'? Salisbury himself grasped the need to organise 'villa Toryism' before ever Churchill decided to exploit the National Union machinery. The ultimate scheme of hierarchical organisation in the country, based, it seems, on a Balfour draft, may have owed only delay to the Churchill–Salisbury conflict.

Elijah's mantle, Churchill complained, had been 'rent in twain'. Obviously nothing was to be gained by the rival heirs continuing to tear up the bits. The party could not afford to have *The Times* supporting Churchill and the *Standard* Salisbury, urban deputations acclaiming Lord Randolph and county members lauding Sir Stafford. A compromise was reached, enhancing the status of both Churchill and Salisbury. The Central Council disappeared. Churchill ceased to be chairman of the executive of the National Union. His agreed successor was Sir Michael Hicks Beach, the ex-cabinet minister most friendly to Churchill. The flanking vice-chairmen were to be Balfour, representing Salisbury's interests, the youthful Akers-Douglas from the Whips' Office and, it was hoped, Gorst – but that unhappy man denounced Churchill's surrender while lacking the financial means to continue in politics without office, which he must rely on Randolph to get him.

In 1883 the sporting of floral buttonholes to commemorate Disraeli's birthday suggested to Sir Henry Drummond Wolff a conception which Churchill institutionalised as the Primrose League. When he received the draft rules from Lord Randolph in December Salisbury doubted anything coming of it. His wife knew better and soon the marquess 'saw no objection' to himself and Northcote becoming patrons – or should they be called 'vavasours', he asked, with a scientist's contempt for flummery and neo-mediaeval romanticism. The Primrose League proved no laughing matter. By 1891 it had a million members. It provided opportunities for national and local gatherings of the faithful and the intermingling of Tories of different classes – especially the landed and the moneyed, the upper and the middle – in a common profession of intent to transmit to future generations some sort of Disraelian legend.

### III

A principal reason for *détente* between Churchill and the official leaders in 1884 was the need for unity in face of the Liberal Government's bill to confer household suffrage in county constituencies. With experience of farmers' revolts against landlords in the 1880 election rural Tories shivered at the thought of the labourers' revolt which Chamberlain and Jesse Collings proclaimed. They hoped that the Lords would defeat the bill so that an election could be held under the old system. Salisbury tended to agree with them, but too many colleagues thought that, though in other circumstances they would win, they would not win against the cry of 'the people versus the peers'. At the other extreme was a minority, including Balfour, which saw general household suffrage as inevitable and not worth contesting and regarded female suffrage as 'the trump Conservative card which Lord Beaconsfield kept in his hand'. What all Conservatives agreed was that Gladstone's bill could not be allowed to pass without a drastic redistribution of seats, for that would mean an election with the cards stacked and redistribution left to a large Liberal majority in a new parliament. Fortunately the leading Whig minister, Lord Hartington, also felt strongly about this, not wishing the Liberal party to fall utterly into the hands of the Radicals on the departure from politics of the ailing Gladstone. And the queen, who loathed Gladstone and feared the Radicals, sought accommodation between the two Houses. Gladstone was induced to promise redistribution before an election.

But what kind of redistribution? That was the question as the Lords defeated the Franchise Bill and Chamberlain launched his campaign against the peers, in the course of which he stigmatised Salisbury as the representative of a class that neither toiled nor spun and was therefore morally obliged to pay 'ransom' to the community for the privilege of enjoying its property. Hicks Beach put to ministers a drastic plan for the abolition of the separate representation not only of small but of medium-sized boroughs and for major surgery which involved carving up cities and counties into broadly equal electoral divisions, each returning one member, the boundaries being delimited with regard to 'the pursuits of the population'. This delighted the Radicals and horrified Gladstone and Hartington. The terms which they and the Radical minister Dilke eventually agreed with Salisbury and Northcote over tea at 10 Downing Street were somewhat less dramatic, but based on those principles. Under these rules the electoral system operated till 1918 and the Conservatives certainly had no ground to complain of them. Salisbury's particular contribution took the form of an insistence which almost wrecked the chances of agreement. In his youth Salisbury had aspired to represent Oxford University, then represented by Gladstone, who described his defeat there as a Liberal in 1865 as an 'unmuzzling'. In 1885 Salisbury insisted on the retention of the University seats. Gladstone conceded it as the result of a private visit from his fellow High Anglican, Lady Salisbury, who told him that on this her husband was inflexible.

Within a few months of the compromise on franchise and redistribution, and before an election under the new arrangements was possible, Salisbury became Prime Minister. It is thought that, with the Liberal Cabinet breaking up because Whigs and Radicals could not agree on what basis Ireland was to be governed after the three years of strenuous coercion which followed the Phoenix Park murders, the Liberal Whips connived at their own defeat, on 8 June 1885, on Hicks Beach's amendment to the Budget. Probably they thought that the Conservatives would not, or would not willingly, enter upon a period of minority government with a hostile House. But as Tories and Irishmen (who objected to liquor tax increases) marched together through the lobbies there existed some sort of compact between the Irish and Churchill which would make a Tory caretaker government possible and a Tory–Nationalist electoral alliance feasible. Salisbury knew no details, and perhaps there were no details to be known. Certainly the defeat and resignation of the second Gladstone Government took him by surprise. But he accepted office on the basis that the harsh Crimes Act of 1882 would not be renewed; that his old friend Carnarvon would take over Ireland at least till after the elections; that electoral utterances on Ireland would be delphic.

For Salisbury, Churchill and the party, the importance of this unexpected development was that Salisbury was sent for by the queen as though he were the undoubted head of the party, which he therefore became. Northcote was set down. If he could not be Premier, he expected to be Leader of the House and Chancellor of the Exchequer, as under Beaconsfield. Salisbury proposed to make him Leader of the House with the titular office of First Lord of the Treasury, which Salisbury did not want for himself as he was taking the Foreign Office in order to restore Britain's diplomatic prestige. But Churchill and Hicks Beach objected to Northcote leading the House, and Salisbury contrived, rather disingenuously, to remove him to the Lords as earl of Iddesleigh, in the Government but without office. Beach secured the position Northcote had claimed as his right. These dispositions were generally regarded as a triumph for Churchill, and Chamberlain, having privately congratulated him, told a public meeting that 'Goliath hath succumbed to David, and Lord Randolph Churchill has his foot on Lord Salisbury's neck'. Churchill found these tributes premature and feared he had overplayed his hand. Salisbury, he said, could form a government out of waiters at the Carlton. There was a week's wait between the summons to Salisbury and the amicable meeting at which Churchill accepted the India Office. But there was always Balfour to

remind his uncle that Churchill was indispensable until after the elections. The battle for the English borough seats would be fierce and
decisive, and everything would count – Churchill's appeal to the masses
and the provincial notables, the aid of the Catholic priests (on the
schools' question), the calculated benevolence of Parnell who issued a
declaration of war against all Liberals who did not support Home Rule
for Ireland. This, however, did not loom large in the election, as most
candidates opposed Home Rule, most Liberals did not go out of their
way to advocate coercion and the Tories had been tipped the wink not
to do so. Instead the Tories found (in Salisbury's words) that Gladstone
had wakened the slumbering genius of Imperialism. Exploiting the
recent tragedy at Khartoum, they added 'Remember Gordon' to the cry
'Remember Majuba' (the South African skirmish which had caused
Gladstone in 1881 to give up the coercion of the Transvaal). They
profited in the boroughs from the drift of the middle classes away from
Radicalism and the lack of 'an urban cow' to attract the working class
voter as Jesse Collings's allotments policy ('three acres and a cow') was
thought to attract the cottager. Churchill, a host in himself, seriously
threatened John Bright in Birmingham Central. In the English boroughs
the Tories won 49·5 per cent of the votes and half the seats. In the
English counties they won, with 46 per cent of the votes, only 40 per
cent of the seats, but the devotion of some of the labourers (and farmers)
to Liberalism was to prove transient.

The Tory successes in the English boroughs gave Parnell, by the
narrowest of margins, what he had sought – the balance of power. He
was now open to competitive bids from Gladstone and Churchill.
Gladstone maintained silence, hoping the Conservatives would take up
Home Rule as they had taken up Catholic Emancipation, Corn Law
Repeal and Household Suffrage. He indicated as much to Balfour at
Eaton Hall in Cheshire and his disappointment when Salisbury was
unresponsive and when he soon ran up a bright Unionist flag has been
made the basis of an attack on Salisbury's integrity.

The wish being father to the thought, Gladstone had convinced himself that there was a chance of the Tory leaders becoming Home Rulers.
This conviction is the only possible justification for the fact that he
assiduously concealed from the electors, the Liberal candidates and
such colleagues as were willing to be hoodwinked by sophistry, his own
conversion to Home Rule, prematurely revealed by his son in December
1885. What he found he had to do in 1886 was to try to convert colleagues
and M.P.s immediately after an election to a policy which few had

favoured in the election and which many, including the Whig Hartington and the Radical Chamberlain, had explicitly condemned to their constituents. He had hoped to have the easier task of inducing them to support the Conservative leaders in getting the Irish question out of the way. On the strength of Churchill's mysterious dealings with Irishmen, the wobbling and indiscretions of Carnarvon and the calculated ambiguity of Salisbury's keynote speech at Newport, he waited hopefully for Salisbury to renege. In vain was the net spread in sight of the bird. Gladstone was 'the Grand Old Man' to his admirers, but to Tories he was Disraeli's 'Arch-Villain'. Basic instincts of self-preservation dictated Tory union and Liberal division rather than the reverse, and forbade a *volte-face* which at best would leave Gladstone and Chamberlain, and soon Chamberlain alone, in possession of the political kingdom, and which at worst would rend the Conservative party asunder as in 1846. Balfour repeatedly declared that he could never emulate Peel, who had twice betrayed his party. The Peel of 1846 was Gladstone's mentor, not Salisbury's.

The Tory–Irish compact was a mutually profitable business deal for the 1885 election only. None of the backstage intriguers, Tory, Irish or Radical, seriously expected the Conservative party, or Salisbury, or even Churchill, to come out for Home Rule. Gladstone's misjudgement of Salisbury is as strange as it was profound. Salisbury was the last man likely to lead his party via apostasy to the wilderness. His record sparkled with condemnations of Peel and Derby and Disraeli for unprincipled opportunism. He had not changed the view he expressed in the *Quarterly Review* of April 1865 that a leader was in clear breach of the understanding to which he owed his position if he used it not to give effect to the political opinions of his followers but to promote opinions to which they were opposed. When the Unionist convictions of Hartington and Chamberlain were unshaken by Parnell's success in the Irish elections (which they expected, and discounted, in advance) and Gladstone's conversion, why should Salisbury's crumble? In the last day's debate on Gladstone's Home Rule Bill in 1886 Parnell declared that a Tory minister had offered him Home Rule. Salisbury explained the matter to the queen with equanimity rather than exasperation. He had known, the previous summer, of the secret meeting in an empty house in London between Carnarvon, then Lord Lieutenant of Ireland, and Parnell. He had deprecated, but not forbidden, what he took to be a probing mission and had not imagined that his colleague would see Parnell without Lord Ashbourne as a witness. It was difficult to judge exactly what had passed at the interview, though it was evident that 'Lord Carnarvon took singularly little precaution to protect either himself or his colleagues from misunderstanding'. By the publication of his correspondence with Carnarvon he, Salisbury, would gain, for 'if all I said was known, no one could suggest that I coquetted with Home Rule'. But he preferred to let his reputation stand the strain of the Parnellite smear. Liberal revolt had defeated Gladstone's bill by 341 to 311 in the House of Commons and the electors were about to endorse the verdict of the House. Salisbury became for the second time Prime Minister, representing, as he wrote on 25 July 1886, 'more than anything else the mandate of the country to resist Home Rule'.

Salisbury held that Ireland, like India, must in the British national interest be governed, by consent if possible, by force if necessary. In that anonymous article of October 1883 he had spelled out a case against a national assembly and responsible executive in Dublin which to his dying day he thought unanswerable and which appealed to the deepest instincts of Conservatism, not least now that Conservatism was tinged with Imperialism. He had written that there must be

a courageous maintenance of the rights of the Empire and a patient struggle with the resistance, however stubborn it may be, however long it may last. . . . One issue there is which, in the judgement not only of the Conservative party, but in that of the great majority of Englishmen, is absolutely closed. The highest interests of the Empire, as well as the most sacred obligations of honour, forbid us to solve this question by conceding . . . any licence to the majority in that country to govern the rest of Irishmen as they please. . . . All that is Protestant – nay, all that is loyal – all who have land or money to lose . . . would be at the mercy of the adventurers who have led the Land League, if not of the darker councillors by whom the Invincibles have been inspired. . . . It would be an act of political bankruptcy, an avowal that we were unable to satisfy even the most sacred obligations, and that all claims to protect or govern anyone beyond our own narrow island were at an end.

In the presence of such considerations we hardly care to speak of the strategical objections. But . . . the coast of Ireland, in unfriendly hands, would be something more than a pistol held to the mouths of the Clyde and the Mersey and the Severn. . . . We shall speedily have to choose between [this] and the reconquest of Ireland if once Home Rule be granted. Any political power conceded to an Irish assembly will be made the fulcrum by which more will be exacted, until complete independence is secured. . . . We may have the resolution to refuse Home Rule as a whole. Have we the resolution to refuse it in instalments? Or will our bargaining politicians when votes grow scarce open the market once more for a final clearance sale of all that remains of English rule in Ireland?

It would have been difficult to put the case more strongly, very difficult for any Conservative leader to repudiate what was so patently the general view of his party, and quite impossible for Salisbury to eat these words.

We should not be misled, because there were differences of opinion as to tactics, into thinking that the adoption of a Unionist strategy was ever seriously in dispute. As soon as the 1885 election was over, Salisbury was 'feverishly anxious to get out' of an office which he described to his son as of infinite worry but very little power. All he asked was that his ministry end with dignity. This was denied him because the two most important Commons ministers, Hicks Beach and Churchill, were unwilling to include the banning of the Irish National League in the Queen's Speech. They hoped that, if the Government remained delphic over Ireland, Gladstone would be forced to unveil his widely known but imprecise intentions. When it became clear that he was not to be drawn, and that ministers would be turned out on a 'three acres and a cow' amendment to the Address, there was an unseemly scramble to remedy the omission.

Salisbury took an understandable pleasure in warning Churchill that the Tories must be careful not to be branded 'the timid party'. 'The time is coming on us when people will long for government,' he said. His refusal to follow Gladstone – or, as Gladstone wished, to *precede* Gladstone, in public announcement – and recognise Irish nationalism as respectable, let alone as morally compelling, led on to the speech at the Unionist rally in St James's Hall on 15 May 1886 in which, because he categorised the peoples unfitted for self-government, he was alleged to have compared Irishmen with Hottentots. 'My alternative policy,' he said, 'is that Parliament should enable the Government of England to govern Ireland. Apply that remedy honestly, consistently and resolutely for twenty years and at the end of that time you will find that Ireland will be fit to accept any gifts in the way of local government or repeal of coercion laws that you may wish to give her. What she wants is government . . . that does not flinch, that does not vary; government that she cannot hope to beat down by agitations at Westminster. . . .'

Consideration of the twentieth-century tragedies of Ireland must not distort historical perspective. The majority of the *British* people, *whenever consulted*, except in 1910, endorsed the Unionist view. Salisbury's Unionist arguments from 1883 onwards appealed to his followers not least by virtue of their clarity. It is easy to affirm that Home Rule could never be 'killed with kindness' under 'resolute government' from London, but impossible, because Home Rule was withheld, to say whether Gladstonian Home Rule (which meant taxation without representation) would have become, as Salisbury firmly believed, the springboard for Separation, so that Home Rule was not really the issue at all. It is easy to question whether so confirmed a pessimist as Salisbury can really have hoped, once the Radicals were committed to Home Rule, for twenty years grace in which to experiment with 'resolute government'. But in the year (1903) when Salisbury died, when George Wyndham's great Land Act – which was to excise landlordism from the Irish Question – became law, there were many who thought that Salisbury's recipe was succeeding. When the Lords, mustered by Salisbury, killed the Home Rule Bill narrowly passed by the Commons in 1893, Gladstone, recognising that there was no majority in the country for Home Rule, even if linked to the cry of 'the people versus the peers', did not seek a dissolution. With Gladstone out of the way after 1894 the Liberals played down Home Rule, and virtually abandoned any commitment to it; this cause was their cross, not their crown. In the days of their greatest majority, 1906–9, they made no move towards it. Its relevance revived only when, as a result of the dramatic Liberal setback in the General Election of January 1910, caused by the Lords' rejection of 'the people's Budget', the Irish gained the balance in the Commons and held Asquith to ransom. And in the ensuing years the Ulster card which Randolph Churchill decided to play in 1886 proved a trump.

Gladstone's effort of 1886 was courageous, but quite hopeless. His indignation, when his political opponents refused to play into his hands by changing their opinions overnight simply because *he* had (at last) seen the light, was sincere. But it is hardly the aptest test by which to judge Conservative leaders. No political party, appealed to on grounds of higher statesmanship which it specifically repudiates, can be expected to turn its back on a policy in which it believes and which makes it popular, simply because later generations may say it was wrong. Exceptionally, in a constitutional system, a party may condemn itself to the wilderness on account of some doctrine, policy or quirk in which it believes, but which does not appeal to the electorate. No party can be expected to ruin itself at the behest of the leader of its opponents on behalf of a policy in which it does *not* believe.

IV

As Victoria, with Albert, had once worked for a coalition of Whigs and Peelites, so she looked in the 1880s to a coalition of Whigs and Tories. In 1867 Salisbury thought the Conservative party could flourish only if Whigs came over to lead it, but could see no role congenial to himself under such a regime. By October 1885, on the eve of the first election under general household suffrage, when most Liberal candidates supported 'the unauthorised programme' of the Radical Chamberlain, the Whig leader Hartington confided to a colleague that there seemed nothing for those who thought with *him* to do but turn Tory or disappear, and he thought he should do the latter. The strained relations between the Whig and Radical members of Gladstone's 1880–5 Cabinet, due to policy differences, had made an anti-Radical alliance of Whigs and Tories seem more than ever logical and likely. In the way stood tradition, habit and the distasteful vulgarities of Lord Randolph Churchill, between whom and Hartington there had been talk of a duel after public exchanges of abuse. Churchill offered to leave the Conservative Cabinet of 1885 to facilitate a coalition between Salisbury and Hartington, which would prevent Gladstone returning to office. 'They hate me as much as they hate you,' Salisbury replied, 'and if retirements are required for the sake of repose and Whig combinations, I shall claim to retire with you in both respects.'

The question was as yet academic, for although Hartington voted with the Tory Government against the Collings motion on which it was turned out in January 1886 and declined to join Gladstone's third administration on the basis of 'examining' Home Rule, he continued to repudiate coalition with the Conservatives. But Salisbury, as well as everybody else, anticipated coalition sooner or later, for he told Churchill that the 'extra tinge of Liberalism in our policy', which Lord Randolph wished to announce as an incentive, should be held back to be part of a bargain when it came to be struck. But it was Churchill who christened the coming alliance in advance. Having informed W. H. Smith that he had never thought 'Conservative' an attractive designation, and did not use it himself, he called at Manchester on 2 March

1886 for 'a Unionist Party' which would 'combine all that [was] best in the politics of Tory, Liberal and Whig'. 'Unionist' was the designation adopted by those Liberals who refused in and after 1886 to accept Home Rule. In Scotland it altogether ousted 'Conservative'.

Determined to use the House of Lords, when necessary, to thwart Liberal governments, Salisbury desired reform of its composition in order to strengthen it in its obstructive role. But in 1886 it was obviously desirable to contrive, if possible, that the Home Rule Bill be defeated in the Commons, so that the issue of the Union versus Home Rule in an election should not be confused by the cry of 'the people versus the peers'. Parnell said of Chamberlain: "There goes the man who killed Home Rule' because it could not have been killed *in the Commons* if Chamberlain had not taken his Radical M.P.s into the Opposition lobby with Hartington's Whigs. So the affinity and easy relations between Churchill and Chamberlain, who in their attitudes to their respective leaders (and one another's) and their exploitation of party organisation and mass meetings were kindred spirits, were useful. The secrets of the third Gladstone Cabinet were conveyed to Churchill until Chamberlain and Trevelyan walked out of it. Lord Randolph paved the way for Balfour to meet Chamberlain on 22 March 1886. Balfour reported to his uncle Robert, who was at Monte Carlo (and barred from the casino for his shabby appearance!), that they would find in Chamberlain 'a very different kind of ally from the lukewarm and slippery Whig, whom it is so difficult to differ from, and so impossible to act with'. Summoned home by his colleagues, Salisbury met Chamberlain (at the Turf Club!) just before the Radical leader delivered his Unionist speech to the Commons which spelt doom to Gladstone. If, Salisbury said, Gladstone when defeated, resigned (instead of appealing to the electorate) there would have to be a dissentient Liberal government. But he was bound to say that his support for an administration including Chamberlain must be a very conditional one. In this there was no guile.

For Hartington to co-operate with Churchill, or Salisbury with Chamberlain, required conscious effort and acts of oblivion. It is too easily assumed that to Salisbury and Hartington co-operation came naturally. Had they not lineage, class and substantial identity of views, and even age and length of political experience to unite them? No two men with all this in common had less affinity than the chancellors of the universities of Oxford and of Cambridge. Robert Cecil lived for science, diplomacy and politics. He was essentially a scholar whose complex psyche was sustained by religious faith and practice and family

life. He shunned Society. The unintellectuality of Spencer Compton
Cavendish was profound. He was a sportsman and man-about-town,
notoriously waiting for the duke of Manchester to die in order to
legitimise the most enduring of his liaisons. Only a sense of duty held
him to public life. But Salisbury and Hartington shared an inveterate
distrust of Gladstone. To defeat him, after 1885, they would meet and
correspond as often as necessary, but only so often, for they shared a
common ailment – that in public life they were often bored stiff by
people who talked at length and would not, or could not, come to the
point, or whose point they dismissed from the outset as stupid.
Hartington, being somewhat slow-witted, was especially suspicious of
anything indirect; Salisbury, acute of mind, hated prolixity. They
could talk straight and to the point with each other, Hartington not
evoking the tell-tale fidgeting which denoted suppressed exasperation
or the use of the famous paper knife purchased to dig against the leg
to keep Salisbury awake in a tedious interview.

While the Home Rule Bill was before the Commons in 1886 there
*was* cause for Conservative exasperation with the Liberal Unionists. Led
by Salisbury and Churchill, the Conservative party was now particularly
well-equipped to fight a nationwide campaign. The new Chief Whip,
Akers-Douglas, had picked a former naval man named Middleton as
principal agent. It was to be Salisbury's good fortune that 'Captain'
Middleton just outlasted him. Free from the cantankerousness of Gorst
and the pretensions of Bartley (who resigned late in 1884, advertising
his wounded pride in the Radical *Fortnightly*) Middleton brought to his
vital role enthusiasm and unusual organising ability. Gorst had nursed
the unfulfilled vision of a Conservative association in every constituency. Middleton's target, 1885–6, was Conservative propaganda in
every home, delivered, where appropriate, by working men. He had
produced the first of the famous series of Campaign Guides for candidates and speakers. In concert with Akers-Douglas he made the Conservative party a nationwide co-ordinated entity, without attempting an
enslavement of the constituent parts which would have been counter-
productive. In 1886 he was ready to flood the country with petitions
against Home Rule to be adopted at local meetings held on 'non-party'
lines. But the Liberal Unionists would not play. There was a great
demonstration at Her Majesty's Theatre in the Haymarket on 14 April,
where Hartington and Salisbury spoke and from which Rowton sent the
queen, herself emotionally involved, a rapturous report. But Churchill
absented himself and Chamberlain said the meeting was 'perfect mad-

ness'. Even Goschen had to admit a great disinclination to work with the Tories among Liberals (i.e. Liberal Unionists) of 'standing and fairmindedness'. This was not due merely to party habit, but to electoral prudence. Outside Chamberlain's Birmingham bailiwick the Liberal caucus, organised by Schnadhorst (till lately Chamberlain's man) brought the strongest pressure to bear on the constituency associations (such as Hartington's at Rossendale) to press their M.P.s to assist Home Rule in order to get Ireland, and Irish obstruction at Westminster, out of Liberalism's road. Salisbury recognised the reluctance of Liberal Unionists to tarnish their Liberal credentials by appearing on platforms with Tories as a fact, but was baffled by their coyness. If, he said, he were to leave the Conservative party on a point of principle, he would turn his back on the Carlton without a moment's regret (a way of putting it which vastly amused those who knew how difficult it was to induce him ever to enter a club at all!). After all, these Unionists would depend for their seats at the next election on Tory tolerance, promised in principle by Salisbury to Goschen in February. On 28 May Hartington, having moved the rejection of the Home Rule Bill, was able to read his followers an undertaking that any who voted with him would meet no official Conservative opposition at the polls. Three days later Churchill similarly assured the Chamberlainites.

Salisbury, giving the queen favourable reports of Unionist prospects, begged her to make no difficulty about giving Gladstone a dissolution if he asked for it. She complied, and so it fell to Akers-Douglas and Middleton, proficient practitioners of dual control through the Whips' Office and Central Office, to protect the Liberal Unionist M.P.s in their constituencies. That only six of them met Conservative opposition, which was disavowed by headquarters, was a tribute not only to their managerial skill but to the authoritative use of Salisbury's pledged word and an occasional personal intervention.

The result of Gladstone's appeal from the Commons to the country in 1886 was a Unionist – though not a Conservative – majority. Following Disraeli's precedent of 1868, which he had condemned as unconstitutional, Gladstone resigned forthwith and Salisbury was summoned from his convalescence in the Auvergne by a delighted monarch. Not only had the Conservatives recovered ground in the counties; they had done well in the great cities. Who would have expected to find London the real base of Tory principles? Salisbury asked Cranbrook. Salisbury found leading colleagues arguing that 'any sacrifice on the part of the Conservative party should be made in order to induce [the

Liberal Unionists] to coalesce', while Akers-Douglas and Middleton told him in the strongest terms that Conservatives at every other level wanted him to be Prime Minister and, indeed, wanted 'a pure Conservative government'. On his way to the queen at Osborne he asked Hartington (24 June) to allow him to put the Whig's name to Her Majesty for the premiership, but made Hartington's agreement impossible by saying that the inclusion of Chamberlain would be 'too sharp a curve'. This has been thought disingenuous. Probably Salisbury would have been quite happy to take the Foreign Office under Hartington. The latter hated the idea of office, and especially of the premiership or leadership of the Commons. The Liberal Unionists preferred a Conservative Government, Chamberlain informing Salisbury via Balfour that he should form one 'with a definite and complete understanding with Hartington and an adequate though less complete understanding with me'. That was the solution adopted.

Salisbury formed a wholly Conservative administration which was to receive from Liberal Unionists what Akers-Douglas called 'a support such as we gave Palmerston from '59 to '65'. The analogy proved apt. The contingency in which Palmerston had been given to understand that he could rely on his Tory opponents was the resignation of a Chancellor of the Exchequer (Gladstone) whose desire for stringent economy led to bitter disputes about service estimates and made him the hero of Little England Radicals. When he went out of office in January 1886 Salisbury had concluded that, next time, the position of Chancellor, with the leadership of the Commons, ought to go not to Hicks Beach but to Churchill and in June Hicks Beach himself (perhaps hoping to be overruled) advised this. Lord Randolph therefore thought himself overwhelmingly strong. He determined to restore to the Conservative party that reputation for economy and fiscal reform which had given Peel the edge over the Whigs, which the Peelite Gladstone had carried over to the Liberal party and which the Peelite Northcote under Disraeli had been unable to retrieve because of wars and rumours of wars and the Great Depression, which diminished revenue. Now Churchill became the darling of 'a knot of damned Gladstonians' at the Treasury and railed at 'the wild men at the Foreign Office'. He pressed a policy pacific and economical to a point which, the un-Palmerstonian Premier told him early in October, was 'not wise in a patriotic or party sense'. Adept at stealing bathers' clothes, Churchill took up not only the old Liberal policy of peace and retrenchment but Chamberlain's 'unauthorised programme' to boot, made sweeping proposals to a vast crowd at Dartford and complained bitterly when they were eroded in Cabinet. For his first Budget he meditated tax adjustments to appeal to villa Tories (income tax relief) and working-class people (a lower tea tax). These required both reduced expenditure and the taxation of affluence. By December Churchill was locked in combat with W. H. Smith, the least extravagant of ministers, on the army estimates, and Balfour had thought it necessary to write to his uncle to be firm on death duties and owner's rights – 'We cannot turn Radical even to preserve the Tory Party', he said.

Balfour (who was Secretary for Scotland) welcomed an invitation to join the Cabinet because he thought it was flabby in the face of Churchill's demands. In fact, by November, most ministers had found Churchill an impossible colleague, and complained of Salisbury's 'self-renunciation', only to receive the reply: 'The time is not yet.' When he felt the time had come, Salisbury acted surely and swiftly. He took as a resignation a letter sent by Churchill from Windsor which, though peremptory, was by no means unique and left Churchill to tell *The Times* about it. Though Chamberlain at once declared at Birmingham that the reactionary elements in the Tory party had triumphed over the democratic and that he would discuss Liberal reunion, Balfour wrote admiringly that on no question and at no time could Randolph have left more conveniently. It was the Christmas season, with public men dispersed, and Salisbury misled Hicks Beach into staying in Ireland until Churchill's departure was a *fait accompli*. The issue was economy, but the fact that Churchill was succeeded as Commons leader by W. H. Smith and as Chancellor by Goschen (a solitary Liberal Unionist more right-wing than most leading Tories), both prototypes of middle-class respectability, disarmed fears of financial profligacy. Nevertheless Salisbury and his colleagues, and the Conservative press (whose lack of confidence in the Conservative party was, as Middleton complained, 'a grave source of weakness'), thought that in dispensing with Churchill Salisbury had taken a great risk. They did not understand, as Akers-Douglas did, that Churchill's parliamentary position (unless he had the confidence of his colleagues) had depended on the particular circumstances of the 1880–5 House of Commons. Undoubtedly in the future a few M.P.s, many active party workers and even more urban voters found the Tory bill of fare lacking in the spiciness which Churchill had provided. But in treating his colleagues with unendurable contempt, Lord Randolph had relied too much on the ovations of party conferences and audiences like the 14,000 at Dartford. With an election five or six years away he was entirely dispensable. Not yet forty years old at his resignation, he was to succumb gradually and tragically to general paralysis of the insane, oscillating between support for and often sagacious criticism of the Government, his uncertain temper occasionally sweetened by hints that he might be asked to return to office. These were never authorised by Salisbury; who remarked that no man wants to put a boil back on his neck.

V

By January 1887 Salisbury had disposed both of Churchill and Northcote. When he returned to office in mid-1886 criticism of his preoccupation in 1885 with foreign affairs and a sense that he was thought to have treated Northcote shabbily had induced Salisbury to make Iddesleigh Foreign Secretary. He soon regretted this appointment. He missed the only work really congenial to him. And he agreed with the queen that, partly because of Iddesleigh's deficiencies and partly because Churchill, having failed to bounce the Cabinet into alliance with Germany, insisted on extreme isolation and inactivity, Britain spoke abroad with muffled voice. On Churchill's departure, Salisbury dispensed with Iddesleigh on grounds so flimsy and in a manner so slipshod (Iddesleigh read of his dismissal in a newspaper) that the old man's family were incensed, especially when he fell dead in a waiting-room at 10 Downing St.

Salisbury was about to abandon the Prime Minister's offices at 10 Downing St. for ever, leaving them to W. H. Smith and then Balfour, who held the style of First Lord of the Treasury normally attached to the premiership, and concerted parliamentary and party matters to the Whips, including such patronage as Salisbury, who governed from Hatfield and the Foreign Office, could devolve. The party leadership, not the premiership, was the prize he had fought for and won and to which he would cling. In January 1887, when Hartington came home from abroad, Salisbury would willingly have yielded him the premiership except on the only terms on which Hartington would take it – a declaration that the Conservatives could not carry on, which would have been both humiliating and untrue. It was with reluctance that Salisbury at last accepted, as his cross, the position he was told had been 'allotted to him by the voice of the people at the late election' and by overwhelming party opinion. He felt that he had, in addition to the normal prerogatives of a Tory leader, a special right to determine the tone of the party because he had been 'drafted'.

If Salisbury's reluctance to keep the premiership was due to his absorption in diplomacy and a consciousness of lack of aptitude for, as well as interest in, the chores of premiership – deficiencies compounded by his absence from the Commons and the lobbies and his stubborn avoidance of smoking-rooms and clubs and social occasions for political talk – his instinct was sound. Though his prestige and authority were high, his ineffectual leadership threw an unfair burden on others, especially upon W. H. Smith.

The difficulties of managing the House of Commons of 1886–92, when the obstructionism of the Irish was taken up by the whole Opposition, were extreme. The 'closure' had to be used to terminate the debate on the Address in February 1887 and then to get the second reading of a permanent Crimes Bill for Ireland (inherited by Balfour from Hicks Beach) in Holy Week. On 22 January Conservative M.P.s had been summoned to the Foreign Office to hear the party leader, who was a stranger to most of them, stress the importance of new rules of procedure to facilitate legislation. Only the first of these passed, but it was a milestone in British parliamentary history. Under it, with a week's notice, the 'guillotine' fell on the committee stage of the Crimes Bill on Mr Smith's motion at 10 p.m. on 17 June 1887. This meant that all undiscussed clauses and amendments were taken with no debate. The same means terminated the report stage and the 'closure' procured the third reading on 8 July. But there was no relief for Unionist M.P.s, for there then came down from the Lords a Land Bill which constituted the Government's belated admission that the rents fixed under Gladstone's 1881 Act were in some cases oppressive and must be reviewed. On 19 August they were circularised with a reminder that day to day majorities must be maintained and that two hundred of them must be available at forty-eight hours notice for closure motions. They did not get away from Westminster for another month.

Matters were not much easier in 1888, though Smith carried resolutions that the House should normally adjourn at midnight (meeting at 3 p.m. instead of 4 p.m.) and that the closure could be carried with only one hundred, not two hundred, in the majority. In 1890 even stiffer rules were agreed by the Cabinet, as the M.P.s would decline to stay until September a second time. But in July the ministers in the Commons said these proposals must be abandoned and with them virtually all the

Government's legislation. Salisbury was so angry that he told the queen the Cabinet ought really not to stay in office 'when so grave a difference of opinion exists between the Prime Minister and his colleagues'. Of course the failure to pass bills declared important at their introduction was bad for the prestige of the ministry, but it seems that Salisbury's unwonted indignation was due to the fact that one of the victims in 1890 was a tithes bill about which he personally cared deeply.

At the end of 1890 temporary relief was afforded M.P.s for a bizarre reason. The Cabinet had decided, from the outset, to be tough with Ireland and Balfour, as Chief Secretary, came to personify that toughness. It also decided, in March 1888, to press on with the material development of Ireland ('killing Home Rule with kindness') and so a Light Railways Bill in 1889 was to be followed by a Land Purchase Bill drafted by Balfour and described by Gladstone as bold and not a proper subject for partisan warfare, by a Congested Districts Board spending public money (which met for the first time in November 1891) and, finally, a Local Government Bill. But ministers also decided, when a libel action seemed to justify certain allegations made in *The Times*, notably those headed 'Parnellism and Crime', to set up a Judicial Commission with wide terms of reference. The proceedings were rendered suspect by the role of the Attorney-General, who, while in office, had represented *The Times* 'in his private capacity', and by an untimely meeting between the owner of the newspaper and 'his old friend', Smith, who described the proceedings of the Commission as 'a great state trial'. Ministers patently believed the evidence strong enough to discredit their opponents at a quasi-judicial hearing where there would be no question of a party majority openly operating as in privilege proceedings or in a Select Committee such as that on the Marconi scandal a quarter of a century later. When things went wrong, Balfour warned Salisbury that his reputation as head of government was involved, and Balfour's subsequent surprise at 'the absurd demoralisation . . . of our side of the House' is very unconvincing. Things had indeed gone dreadfully wrong. The chief witness against Parnell, Pigott, was at the end of February 1889 exposed before the Commission not merely as a double agent working simultaneously for the Nationalists and the authorities but as a seedy forger. He fled to Madrid and there committed suicide.

Technically, Smith was justified in saying that the Commission's report by no means gave the Nationalists a clean bill of health and that the Gladstonians were tainted by association with anarchical doctrines.

But the report, and the debate in which the House of Commons adopted it, hardly constituted a famous victory, except for Churchill. He had said at the outset that 'prudent politicians would hesitate to go out of their way to play such high stakes as these'. He now declared the proceedings, and Smith's motion, 'without precedent, and of evil omen to the rights of minorities and political opponents for the future'. The debate was not a good augury for the legislation of the session, which was abandoned. But just before Parliament met in November 1890 Captain O'Shea, the former Parnellite M.P., whose relations with Chamberlain had always been very close and whose latest initiative may well have been inspired by Unionist circles, secured an uncontested divorce on the ground of his wife Kitty's long-standing adultery with Parnell. While the Irish Party was engaged first in expressing its confidence in its leader and then in deposing him at the behest of Gladstone, Government business for the first time proceeded with almost embarrassing ease.

Since 1887 the Opposition had been making four or five gains a year in by-elections, and they made five in 1891, thus confirming Salisbury's view that the Parnell divorce and the Irish split would not reverse at a stroke the movement of opinion against his ministry. He thought that Gladstone's action would strengthen the Opposition with Dissenters and moderates alike. Dissenters, moreover, were enraged by a 'Tory trick'. Goschen's proposal to allocate beer and spirits duties to local authorities to be used to buy out the holders of drink licences deemed superfluous to requirements would have established possession of a licence as a property right not to be removed without compensation. There was agitation, and Liberal Unionist and even some Tory M.P.s made trouble. The proposal failed, and 'the whisky money' was appropriated to technical education.

Salisbury's electoral pessimism was strengthened by his belief that the democratic and 'socialist' legislation of his second administration had fatally alienated old-fashioned supporters. Their assent, or acquiescence, was a matter of honour to him as party leader. He strove, most earnestly, in 1888 to persuade them that democratic county government was, if not desirable, inevitable; that the gentry would have only themselves to blame if, in most countries, they did not control the new county councils; that he had drawn the sting from the measure by withholding from these bodies, elected by the labourers, responsibility for poor relief. Similarly, he explained in 1891 that the subsidies to the education authorities which would make elementary schooling in most cases free was simply the corollary of its having been made, years ago, compulsory. In effect, his government enacted the Dartford Programme and more.

In the last resort the issue between Churchill and Salisbury had been whether such things were to be done in one fell swoop, as a big political production, or spread over one Parliament or more – a question not only of pace, but momentum; not only of tempo but of tone. The chronicler who at the end of the day remarked that Salisbury 'had been able to move far in social reform since 1886 but he . . . could not move in the spirit of the rights of democracy' hit the nail on the head. Salisbury displayed *noblesse oblige* and a Tory paternalism hedged by a deep concern for individual liberty and property rights and a preference for local as against central power. The Working Class Dwellings Act of 1885 and the Housing of the Working Classes Act and Public Health Act, both of 1890; the Allotments Acts; the Technical Instruction Act and the Intermediate Education Act, both of 1889; the Factory and Workshops Act of 1890 (*not* merely a consolidating measure) and the Shop Hours Act of 1892 were all significant and some were of great utility. Taken together with democratic local government and free education they constituted an achievement unparalleled, Chamberlain boasted, by any government and far superior to that of the Gladstone administration of 1880–5 (when Chamberlain himself had been President of the Board of Trade) which, at Sunderland on 21 October 1891, he described as 'incompetent, if not unsympathetic, in the treatment of social questions'.

Salisbury was anxious that his legislative performance should not be made the predominant Tory theme, the basis of a bid for the continuing allegiance of a large part of the working-class electorate. He seemed positively unwilling to claim credit where it was due – for allowing a local authority to do this, or compelling all local authorities to do that; for instituting the first inspections of factories employing adult males only or forbidding 'rooms over privies, cesspits, middens or ashpits [to be used] as dwellings, sleeping places or workrooms'; for subsidised workmen's trains. These were the sort of thing, he felt, which one approved in the course of duty, when a clear case was made out, preferring, where possible, to decentralise authority but accepting that recalcitrant or negligent local bodies might have to be coerced. But Salisbury thought it both dishonest and electorally unwise on the strength of such acts to describe oneself as a collectivist, even if Balfour sometimes considered it a good idea. He preferred to go on telling the public that public interference with private right might be dangerous and unjust. The Kaiser must be informed, in the acceptance of an invitation to an international labour conference, that it was 'contrary to all our principles to prevent a man who wished to work nine hours from working more than eight hours', even if this imperilled Balfour's majority in his Manchester seat. Salisbury disliked Chamberlain boasting of the social reform achievements of the Salisbury government. He disliked even more the suggestion that they were due to Liberal Unionist pressure. For that implied that the detailed arguments for the measures were *not* all that convincing and even seemed to justify Gladstone's complaint that Radicalism was rampant because, under the impulse first of Churchill and then of Chamberlain, the Conservatives had ceased to be genuinely Conservative. No doubt Salisbury appreciated that Gladstone himself had procured a very wide working-class following without any significant genuflections to the 'socialism' which he abhorred as much as Salisbury. The Tory leader would offer the masses little except approval in principle of Chamberlain's idea of a contributory scheme of old-age pensions to which the State would contribute only machinery and incentive. He kept as far as possible free of these 'doctrinaire' issues to fight, in 1892 as in 1886, on the issue of Home Rule.

In the absence of electoral bribes, a government hopes to be able to fight an election on a record of all-round competence. This, in 1892, Salisbury's ministers could hardly claim. Even Balfour, who had shone as Irish secretary, was a failure, owing to lack of *gravitas*, when his uncle, very reluctantly (because of the risk to the family reputation), named him successor to Smith (who died of exhaustion) as Leader of the House. Salisbury himself was deemed a competent, even a great, Foreign Secretary. Goschen as Chancellor of the Exchequer had been successful if irritating. But those who judge a Prime Minister by how good a butcher he is may well decide to put Salisbury at the bottom of the list. What other head of government would have kept Henry Matthews as Secretary of State at the Home Office for six years? Few would have appointed him in the first place, at a time when the Home Office was especially important, Gladstone having written to the queen that the riots in the West End during his third administration in 1886 had 'stained the reputation of this country in the eyes of the civilised world'.

The torrid introduction of Sir Stafford Northcote, by Churchill, to Birmingham politics at Aston Park in 1884 had led to court proceedings in connection with which Churchill encountered Matthews, and found in him a Roman Catholic who was a Tory and had been M.P. for an Irish seat. This encounter resulted in Mr Matthews becoming the only Conservative M.P. for a Birmingham constituency, a cabinet minister and in due course Viscount Llandaff, with a reputed descent from 'Gwaethvoed, a chieftain of Gwent'. After one session's experience of Mr Matthews, W. H. Smith begged that he be made a judge, because of his lack of tact, suppleness and quickness in the House. Salisbury confessed that he showed 'an innocence of the ways of the world which no one could have expected in a criminal lawyer of sixty'.

Matthews was not only inept; he was also accident-prone. The fracas in Trafalgar Square on 'Bloody Sunday', 13 November 1887, when the Socialists and unemployed tangled with cavalry and life guards with fixed bayonets and live ammunition, was at least partly due to neglect of the Prime Minister's warnings. It looked like more than 'hard luck' that after the commissioner of metropolitan police had been dismissed for insubordination and his successor required to resign the third should come to the Prime Minister to say that there was no relying on the force as long as Matthews was Home Secretary (July 1890). But Matthews remained. For this latest commissioner, by banning combination, had precipitated the despatch by 'delegates' of a telegram to Matthews threatening strike action by the police. This threat was a symptom of the spread of 'the new unionism' and of an associated spirit of dissatisfaction or disaffection in the public service extending even to guards' regiments. Salisbury admitted that he ought not in the previous autumn have kept Matthews for fear of losing the Birmingham seat, and now he promised the queen that Matthews should go. But in October he told her that there was 'no instance of dismissal and it would require some open and palpable error to justify it'. Victoria was suitably scornful of this application to a political minister of known ineptitude of the rule of civil service tenure. But in December Salisbury shrank from creating a vacancy in Birmingham, and probably in Chatham as well, at a time when the result of the Bassetlaw by-election was in doubt. With Bassetlaw held, Salisbury seemed in January 1891 willing to make Matthews a lord of appeal. However, at this juncture Smith, Goschen and Balfour all agreed that it would be better to bear 'whatever indiscretions Mr Matthews may commit in the House of Commons'. This testimony was persuasive, but the queen was horrified to find Salisbury, on his return to office in 1895, again considering Matthews for office. She ensured that he was paid off with a viscountcy as compensation for his sacrifice of his legal practice to serve the Conservative party. In all the discussions of Matthews's future the question of his suitability for the Bench seems never to have been considered. The Conservative party was to incur odium in the eyes of trade unionists for some of the promotions of political lawyers which Salisbury approved on the recommendation of his very right-wing Lord Chancellor Halsbury, because, as judges they (like some former Liberal M.P.s) eroded, by their judgements, legislative privileges thought to have been conferred not least by Mr Secretary Cross as Salisbury's colleague under Disraeli.

The problems of patronage Salisbury dreaded and disliked, and most of all when they involved the claims of politicians from outside the traditional governing class. Of the 'outsiders' whom he inherited from Beaconsfield he found Smith admirable and Cross tolerable. Upon the merits of C. T. Ritchie he stumbled by accident when Henry Chaplin, the prototype squire-politician, refused the presidency of the local government board in 1886 because, without Cabinet office, it was beneath his dignity. A London merchant and banker raised in the Dundee jute trade, Ritchie had sat for Tower Hamlets and in 1881 advocated the cause of 'Fair Trade'. He entered the Cabinet in 1887 and, because of Salisbury's loyalty, survived the odium of passing the Local Government Act and creating the L.C.C. – and was subsequently to tangle dramatically with Chamberlain in 1903 when their 1881 roles on tariffs were reversed.

Another middle-class paragon, W. L. Jackson, from Leeds, did not climb so high, but Balfour thought him, in 1891, Gorst's only rival for the postmaster-generalship if this was to be regarded as a stepping-stone to the Cabinet. Mr Jackson, he told his uncle, had 'great tact and judgement – *middle-class tact and judgement I admit, but good of their kind*. He justly inspires great confidence in businessmen: he is that rara avis, a successful manufacturer who is fit for something besides manufacturing.' Jackson carried his tact and judgement to the point of refusing the Post Office, because Goschen did not wish to lose him from the Treasury and Balfour wished him to be available for Ireland should Balfour, and not Goschen, succeed Smith as Leader of the House. For the unpopular appointment to the Post Office of Sir James Fergusson, Salisbury's Foreign Office underling, the Private Secretary to the Prime Minister apologised to the Chief Whip. Salisbury, he explained, 'dreads much offending the extreme Right in the declining years of a Parliament'.

The Right would have been offended if the Post Office had been given to Gorst or if, on Jackson taking it, the Liverpool shipowner Forwood had been made Financial Secretary to the Treasury. Fortunately, from the Cecil point of view, 'Forward', as Balfour mis-spelt him, was said to be unpopular and unconciliatory in the House. Both Gorst and Forwood took 'Tory Democracy' seriously, Gorst to the point, as Balfour complained, of showing 'disloyalty to the party' in public speeches as a junior minister. Gorst's claims to promotion and, indeed, to cabinet office, were outstanding. According to Smith he stood next after Balfour and Goschen as a ministerial debater. But Salisbury and Balfour rejoiced that his seat at Chatham was unsafe, so that it was inexpedient to give him an office which entailed re-election, while it was imprudent to make Postmaster-General at a time when government servants were mutinous, and postmen especially, one who was 'rather deeply pledged to take the side of the wage-earners on every possible occasion'. When, on Smith's death, Balfour succeeded him, and Jackson succeeded Balfour, Goschen, who had refused to accept Forwood, was saddled with Gorst. But the latter had had his position spelled out to him in brutal correspondence by Salisbury, too shy to heed Smith's advice to send for him and talk to him like a father. The Prime Minister informed Gorst that in order to secure the general support of a political party something more was necessary than ability – 'the general confidence that the party can rely upon you to stand by them at a pinch'. When Salisbury returned to office in 1895 he made his nephew Gerald Balfour Chief Secretary for Ireland and gave the Post Office to the duke of Norfolk. Gorst became the Commons spokesman for Education of the duke of Devonshire (Hartington) and was pensioned off by Balfour in 1902. No doubt Gorst was his own worst enemy, but Balfour was a close second. The Cecils could be very unforgiving.

As to the conduct of their departments by ministers enjoying, as the case of Matthews shows, an unusual prospect of security of tenure there was the minimum possible interference or co-ordination from above, by Prime Minister or Cabinet, though for this departmentalism Salisbury (to Balfour) criticised Beaconsfield scathingly, citing it as proof that Disraeli had no political principle except that the party must on no account be broken up. Conscious as Foreign Secretary of how little his colleagues appreciated his difficulties and his insights, he had a fellow-feeling for them as departmental heads, was without any experience of a home department and had not the temperament of an administrative reformer. He does not come well out of Hamer's study

*The British Army – Civil and Military Relations 1885-1905*, for from
the outset he adopted a posture of fatalism. It was the duty of British
ministers, he told the queen on 29 August 1886, 'to be always making
bricks without straw, without money, without any strong land force,
with an insecure tenure of power, and with an ineffective agency'. His
confession in the Lords under the impact of the South African disasters
(30 January 1900) that though the British Constitution was unparalleled
for producing happiness, prosperity and liberty in time of peace, it was
'not a good fighting machine' and that it became them to think whether
they should not in some degree modify their arrangements, was
distinctly belated. On 4 March 1888 Churchill had declared: 'I am
certain that if Lord Salisbury really knew how utterly rotten is the
condition of the War Office and Admiralty and how certain a smash
would be in the event of war he would devote all his energies and great
authority to constituting an Army and a Navy in preference to any
other subject, foreign or domestic.' But it was not Salisbury's way to
ask questions to which the answer would be inconvenient, such as
'What are the military requirements of the Empire?' That was an inconvenient question because 'the British public wanted an Empire but
were unwilling to pay for its defence'.

The most important proposal of the Hartington Commission on the
Civil and Professional Departments of the Army and its Relation to
the Treasury etc. (1889-90), for a high-powered cabinet committee
attended by soldiers and sailors as well as ministers, was not given true
effect until Balfour was Premier. On the purely military side the Report
was watered down before publication (and the evidence withheld) when
the Secretary of State, Stanhope, said that both he and the Commander-
in-Chief, the duke of Cambridge, would have to resign because of its
censures. It nevertheless proposed that on an Army Council correspond-
ing to the Board of Admiralty the chief military man should be a Chief
of Staff. Salisbury probably agreed with the Liberal Campbell-
Bannerman that 'a great thinking department' like those of continental
armies (especially the German) would be 'absolutely mischievous and
dangerous to the State'. As Foreign Secretary he had some sympathy
with the view proclaimed, improperly, in public, by Lord Wolseley that
'party government was the curse of modern England'. But he upheld
'civilian control' and when the alleged vulnerability of London and the
ports and coaling stations was canvassed in 1888, he told the Lords that
the experts were always differing among themselves and the public
should put more confidence in the laymen of the front bench. The War

Office ministers declared that the military already had all the threads in their hands and any deficiencies were due to them.

The vehement disputes between Cambridge, representing 'the old guard' and Wolseley, representing the modernisers, enabled the civilians to take all recommendations from professionals with a strong pinch of salt. Salisbury practised the technique of 'divide and rule' to avoid coming to terms with the younger generation of soldiers' demands for less civilian interference and more money. The attachment of the queen, her cousin Cambridge, and also Wolseley, to the office of Commander-in-Chief (which the queen hoped would pass to her son Connaught when Cambridge retired or died) was strong, and Salisbury evaded confrontation with the monarch both over the abolition of the post (advocated by the Hartington Commission) and the succession of Connaught. So the War Office Council established in 1890 with Cambridge, still Commander-in-Chief, overshadowing the other military members, and with the agenda and decisions wholly in the hands of the minister who presided, was but a very incomplete imitation of the Admiralty Board. But when the queen complained (December 1898) that the military hospitals scandal in the Sudan indicated 'a state of confusion and want of proper efficiency' at the War Department, Salisbury replied that Lord Lansdowne was not to be blamed, as similar complaints had been justly levelled at the three previous Tory Secretaries of State. There must be some special defect in the machinery, he said, but it was difficult to find where the neglect or faulty action lay. 'Lord Salisbury will do all he can to remedy these defects, though he is not sanguine of succeeding where so many men have failed.' The South African War showed that the defects persisted, and even Balfour's closest admirers were astonished that he tried to pretend otherwise. It is all too reminiscent of Lord Aberdeen and the Crimea – and no one thought to consult Florence Nightingale!

One of the attractions to Salisbury of losing the 1892 election was that the whole War Office problem, and especially the problem of getting rid of the duke of Cambridge, passed into other hands. Convinced that the Liberals could not carry Home Rule into law against the wishes of Lords, backed by a majority of the British constituencies, he was almost enthusiastic at the prospect of losing. The decision to dissolve in June rather than October was taken at a meeting of Conservative and Liberal Unionist leaders and Whips at Devonshire House on 27 May. Salisbury and Chamberlain were overruled, for, as Salisbury told the queen, 'the decision practically lay with the Conservative and

Unionist Members of the House of Commons' and they would not attend through the summer with an election in sight. The queen was not to worry. Gladstone's 'revolutionary appeal to the jealousy of the poor [would] do much harm' but the return of the Liberals would 'bring to the test many promises which are really hollow'.

It was not in Salisbury's nature to give Victoria the adulation which endeared the romantic (and low-born) Disraeli to her. But before he ever became Prime Minister she accorded him a confidence which Peel won only in his later years. The queen and Salisbury were joint patrons of the anti-Radical cause (though not seeing eye to eye over Cambridge or Connaught or the choice of bishops) and, with Hartington, of the Unionist cause. Protected by the camouflage unwittingly provided by Bagehot, who had assured the nation of royal neutrality, Victoria and Robert Cecil achieved a relationship not greatly different from that of Elizabeth I and William Cecil. They congratulated each other on ensuring that the Foreign Office, under Gladstone in 1886 and 1892, went to Rosebery, who stood for continuity, and, when Gladstone at last resigned in 1894, his successor as Premier was this same Rosebery, the common choice of the monarch and the leader of the Opposition. The queen, indeed, apologised for not being able to send for Salisbury because 'it should be remembered that the present Government have still a majority in the House of Commons'. Rosebery represented himself to the queen almost as a locum tenens until Salisbury could return, and one who would 'take care that the interests of Your Majesty's Empire are maintained abroad' which, as he said, 'some other Liberal Ministers conceivably might not'. Meanwhile – Salisbury's second administration having been turned out by a majority of only forty when the new House of Commons met in 1892 – the Lords, who existed 'to be a check on hasty legislation', were mustered by Salisbury to defeat Home Rule (by ten to one), Welsh Church disestablishment and a local option solution to the drink licenses question; to reduce parish councils (of which Salisbury spoke publicly in contemptuous terms) to a form that 'would do no harm'; to mutilate the Employers' Liability Bill (thus leaving it open to the Unionists to enact in 1897, under Chamberlain's inspiration, the superior, and more socialist, principle of 'workmen's compensation'.)

The queen was anxious for an election as soon as possible, provided a Unionist majority was assured. On the eve of the Lords' defeat of the Home Rule Bill in August 1893 Salisbury told her the Opposition would not address the Crown for a dissolution because this would come better the following summer when the errors reproached against the Salisbury Government had been forgotten. Because the queen did not ask from him neutral constitutional advice but electoral predictions, she corresponded with the leader of the Opposition in cypher. When Rosebery said that the Commons could not be prevented from censuring the Lords for crippling ministerial legislation, Salisbury reported (November 1894) that Unionist electoral prospects were good but that any intervention by the Crown to procure a general election would be counter-productive. In this last phase of Victoria's reign the Opposition, so far from urging on the monarch the use of prerogative in its interest, had to restrain the queen's eagerness to do anything legal (however unwise) to get the existing incumbents out of office.

VI

In June 1895 Rosebery bolted from office after a casual defeat in the House of Commons. Salisbury appealed to the electorate as head of a Unionist coalition, with Devonshire, Chamberlain, James and Lansdowne in the Cabinet. The voters returned not merely a large Unionist majority (411 against 259 Home Rulers) but a small Conservative one.

A crucial decision was Chamberlain's choice of the Colonial Office. This made it certain that Salisbury's third administration would display a more truculent Imperialism than the 'reluctant' brand preferred by the leader who said at Guildhall in November 1897 that 'Africa was created to be the plague of the Foreign Office'. Chamberlain's refusal of the War Office meant that the country drifted into a war in South Africa for which officers and men were ill-trained and ill-equipped without that settlement of national defence questions which Chamberlain, to Devonshire on 23 July 1895, had named as the priority for the new administration. This letter, which might equally have been addressed to Salisbury, said: '. . . We have a chance of doing something which will make this Government memorable. *Do not be alarmed. I do not mean sensational legislation.* . . .' Although in the election Chamberlain declared: 'We are pledged on the one hand to maintain the greatness and integrity of the Empire, and equally pledged to a policy of constructive social reform,' his choice of office, and the words which the present writer had italicised in a letter which reduced the legislative programme to a matter of 'settling . . . some pending English and Irish questions', indicate a shift of interest decisive for his career and of grave import to the Conservative party. For once, Salisbury was almost positive. He told the new Parliament, on 15 August 1895, that though constant revolution was not the political food upon which the English people desire to be fed, 'changes there must be. . . . We may be successful or we may fail in our efforts to ameliorate the conditions of the people by the social legislation we shall propose. We can only do our best and trust to a candid judgement.' It was unlike him to say that he hoped that henceforth all governments would deem it their highest and exclusive duty to secure 'the improvement of the daily life of struggling millions . . . the blessed task that Parliaments are called into existence to perform . . .'.

Perhaps Salisbury was only distinguishing between changes such as Radicals proposed – 'constant revolution' – and bread and butter questions on which the Liberals could be denied any superiority and the Disraelian tradition invoked to claim the support of all men of good will for what government chose to do. But he seemed to establish a test by which, in 1900 – even if it were argued that but for war something would have been done about provision for old age – his ministry could hardly be said to have vindicated itself. Apart from the Workmen's Compensation Act, 1897, the harvest of social legislation was meagre. The limited character of educational reform was not, indeed, wholly ministers' fault, for they tried to do in 1896 most of what Balfour achieved in 1902. But a measure which combined help to the voluntary and the board schools, giving responsibility and surveillance for both elementary and secondary education to committees of county and county borough councils under the general supervision of a government department to be separated formally from the Privy Council, was too comprehensive and ambitious in view of the controversial matters involved. On 22 April 1896 the Cabinet decided to take the whole time of the Commons for the Education Bill, the Agricultural Rating Bill and the Irish Land Bill, which dealt both with statutory rents and with purchase. But a month later it decided to abandon the whole programme for the year. Salisbury expressed in the strongest terms the great danger of this 'unexampled triumph to obstruction'. But even the queen's insistence that her endorsement of the Premier's view be read to the Cabinet could not shift its ten House of Commons members. They conceded only that Balfour should warn the House that it might hereafter be dealt the 'heavy blow to [its] prestige' of 'closure by compartments' as a means of getting complex and contentious bills through committee and report. The Education Act of 1897 merely increased the state subsidy to voluntary schools (mainly Church of England and Roman Catholic), thus reflecting the prime minister's main interest in the field of education. Salisbury welcomed the partial derating of farmers and parsons and the provision (unimportant in practice) of public assistance to workmen wishing to buy houses (1899). He was perhaps decisively responsible, in his dislike of the powerful and collectivist L.C.C., for the establishment in the county of London of second-tier authorities, the metropolitan boroughs.

The Cabinet formed in 1895 was increasingly concerned with Britain's position in the world. It became aware that in face of the conscript armies of the Continent and the technological and economic advances of the United States and Germany, both armed with tariffs and other trading weapons, this position was declining. And the feeling grew that Salisbury, who had returned to the Foreign Office when Devonshire (predictably) refused it, was complacent, too satisfied with his habitual diplomatic techniques and insights. There had been doubts in 1887–92 of the capacity of any man running British foreign relations with as little delegation as Salisbury did, to do anything like justice to the office of Prime Minister. Now, as a consciousness of national insecurity grew, the hope arose that Salisbury would give up the Foreign Office. His health was never robust, and twice in 1898 he was quite seriously ill at times of diplomatic crisis. Thereafter he seemed older than his years. Balfour, who had to take over the Foreign Office during his uncle's illnesses and convalescences abroad, thought him incapable of handling a crisis. It seems possible that these physical collapses were induced by a recurrence, when difficulties came, of the mental tensions which had afflicted his teens and early manhood, and that Salisbury combined a conscious conviction of mastery of diplomacy – which itself seemed to some colleagues a national danger – with an unacknowledged fear of being found wanting. Relatives who knew what vehement and complex emotions had always lurked behind a demeanour of authority and even of placidity, were increasingly concerned to secure his release from the Foreign Office without provoking traumatic effects on his personality. Their success was delayed by Lady Salisbury's seizure, deterioration and death in 1899. Nothing could be done while she languished, and thereafter the wretched widower had to be allowed to compensate for his massive bereavement by immersion in the despatches; these were a necessary supplement to the devoted attentions of his daughter Lady Gwendolen, later his biographer.

The peril which frightened his colleagues was that of diplomatic isolation. Salisbury had always been aware that isolation was unacceptable, because it would tempt the rival groups on the Continent to 'treat the English Empire as divisible booty, by which their differences might be adjusted'. In condemning, as journalist and M.P., Palmerston's bluster over Schleswig–Holstein in 1864, Salisbury had been not a Little Englander but an admirer of (and essayist on) Castlereagh, the exponent of the Concert of Europe. He attacked the 'policy of scold' but insisted (as, indeed, did Gladstone when in office) that 'we are part of the community of Europe and must do our duty as such'. He always stressed, however, that a British Foreign Secretary had to act within strict limits which deprived diplomacy of all simplicity and made it a fascinating art. His victories would be confined to 'a series of microscopic advantages; . . . a judicious suggestion here, . . . an opportune civility there; . . . a wise concession at one moment, and a far-sighted persistence at another; . . . sleepless tact, immovable calmness, and patience that no folly, no provocation, no blunders can shake'. The prime constriction was the knowledge that 'the English people would never consent to go to war for a cause in which England was not manifestly interested' and that it was neither useful nor honourable to promise 'what cannot be done'. His First Mediterranean Agreement of 1887 Salisbury described as being 'as close an alliance as the Parliamentary character of our institutions will permit'. It committed Britain to no more than consultation. It was not really an alliance at all, but merely part of a general friendliness towards the Triple Alliance of Germany, Austria–Hungary and Italy, dictated by the recognition that it was only France or Russia that Britain might have to fight. That friendliness perhaps reached its apogee in the last months of Bismarck's power, when Salisbury managed to sell to the public and the queen the cession of Heligoland as part of the greatest of all his colonial agreements with European Powers, the Anglo-German Treaty of 1890. But he would seek similar agreements with France.

Among inherited commitments, wise or otherwise, was the duty to keep the Russians out of Constantinople, restated by the great State Paper of 1878, the foundation of Salisbury's reputation as a Foreign Secretary. He was incensed when the naval experts said that the Mediterranean fleet ought to be removed to Gibraltar and when in 1892 Intelligence produced a paper, described by Balfour as 'somewhat disquieting', which declared that Britain's only Mediterranean interest worth defending was indefensible. In 1889 Salisbury had assured the queen, when adopting the 'two-power' naval standard, that her fleets would be placed, by appropriate expenditure, in a completely commanding position. Now he left, 'for the early attention' of Rosebery, a memorandum to the effect that the Foreign Office and the service departments had been 'proceeding on lines as far divergent as it is possible for lines of policy to diverge' so that 'the most serious danger threatens'. This is surely a crushing indictment of a Foreign Secretary who was also Prime Minister and therefore had a particular duty to prevent such divergence. Of course, Salisbury was convinced both that the Admiralty was wrong and also that it would not change its mind. So, in 1895 as before 1892, he behaved as though the Admiralty view did not exist, or could be ignored, and had to be compelled by his colleagues to turn to a policy in which he 'entirely misbelieved' – and even to prepare the public mind for the disintegration of the Turkish Empire which, with characteristic pessimism, he deemed imminent (as he told the Tsar in 1896). He became fatalistic even about India, finding it painful to see 'the dominant race deliberately going over into the Abyss' from incorrigible colour-prejudice; about the Persian Gulf, because neither the House of Commons nor the Indian Treasury would pay for railway extension through Afghanistan; about China, where Russia's pressure increased as her communications network made her immune from attack via the Black Sea. But he was resolute over the Nile, once his policy of evacuating Egypt with a right of re-entry had failed; there must be British predominance at Suez and over the whole length of the Nile from Alexandria to Uganda, and the French must be denied any territorial concessions on the river.

Early in 1898 Russian progress in China provoked strong public words from his colleague Hicks Beach, directed less to the public than to Salisbury, who explained, wearily, that it was wise to avoid having too much heather on fire at one and the same time. When, towards the end of the year, Hicks Beach again spoke fiercely over the Nile, Salisbury had to make his words good. He did so regretfully. He did not, of course, like diplomatic rebuffs, but he was almost as afraid of diplomatic triumphs, for these implied a loser who would harbour resentment. Salisbury regretted that, through no fault of his, the French colonel Marchand reached Fashoda on the Upper Nile to be confronted by Kitchener on the morrow of the latter's victory over the dervishes at Omdurman and the reoccupation of Khartoum, so that British interests could be maintained only by the patent humiliation of the French. On 4 November 1898, when Kitchener received the freedom of the City of London, Salisbury announced a French climb-down. It gave his ailing reputation a much-needed boost, but it was dust and ashes to him. He would rather suffer the allegations of Sir Charles Dilke (taken up by Sir Henry Campbell-Bannerman in his new role as leader of the Opposition in 1899) that he was a weak and yielding Foreign Secretary than have ostentatious triumphs of this kind. He did not think an objective observer would deem him careless of material British interests or national honour. His disputes with the Cabinet in 1895-6 over Constantinople and Venezuela had shown that he could be tough and think his colleagues pusillanimous. 'If we are to yield unconditionally to American threats another Prime Minister would have to be found,' he, allegedly, said over Venezuela. But he resigned himself to the fact that 'as the Cabinet declined any step that might lead to war, if the worst comes to the worst we should be forced to enter into unrestricted arbitration'. And later he resigned himself also to American predominance in the Caribbean.

Salisbury's insights were, certainly from 1895 onwards, a matter of controversy at the highest level. Early in 1896 the queen was unconvinced by Salisbury's argument that any alliance involved the danger of being dragged into wars 'that do not concern us'; 'isolation [*was*] dangerous', she insisted. In September 1900 Goschen, First Lord of the Admiralty, wrote to Chamberlain: 'Absolute isolation is playing the devil.' Now, while it is literally accurate to cite Salisbury as author of the phrase 'splendid isolation', the attribution is misleading. He used the adjective sardonically at Guildhall in November 1896 – to describe an attitude of mind not his own. But on the lips of Joseph Chamberlain 'splendid isolation' became a jibe. On 4 May 1898 Salisbury addressed the Primrose League, and analysed with clinical detachment the dangers that arose from the pressure on dying empires (the Turkish, Chinese, Spanish and Portuguese) of rising states. He affirmed: 'We know that we shall maintain against all comers that which we possess, and we know, in spite of the jargon about isolation, that we are competent to do so.' This was a tilt at disquieted colleagues. And to the Premier–Foreign Secretary Joseph Chamberlain, Colonial Secretary, speaking at his Birmingham power-base, gave the lie direct. The British Empire, he declared, was in very great danger, and could get out of it only by alliance with Germany and friendship with the United States. Commons ministers sat squirming as their dominant colleague defended his thesis in Parliament against Asquith's taunt about 'touting for allies in the highways and byways of Europe'. Some of them knew that earlier, while Salisbury was convalescing abroad,

Chamberlain had privately approached the Germans. On the issue of a general alliance with Germany Salisbury remained uncompromising, sure that the German price would be too high and resentful of 'blackmail'. But Chamberlain got his way as regards agreements over China and Portuguese Africa and his admirers could point out that the Anglo-French agreement on West Africa, which stood with Omdurman and Fashoda to Salisbury's credit on the public record, owed almost everything to the vigorous forward policy which Chamberlain had pressed in Nigeria. Even before it was leaked that the Prime Minister referred to the war with the Boers as 'Joe's War', the Opposition had ground for claiming that Chamberlain dominated the Government.

Ministers knew – and opponents such as Haldane knew also – that the war in South Africa was Milner's, rather than Chamberlain's; there was a spirit in the High Commissioner which they did not wholly share and which was likely to lead to consequences from which they, and sometimes Chamberlain himself, shrank. The story is a complex one. Milner received *from the head of the government*, albeit through Chamberlain, encouragement where only active discountenance could have prevented a war of which the *Nineteenth Century* said: 'Surely we never before went to war when there was so much uncertainty as to the casus belli.' In July 1899 Chamberlain expressed joy at Kruger's concessions. Salisbury wrote to him: 'There are other things you still want and above all it is necessary to guard against backsliding.' Later, Salisbury admitted that a vital telegram of mid-August ought to have been submitted to the Cabinet, some of whose members 'with longer memories of South African affairs . . . would have preferred an attitude of more patient forbearance'.

The Boers struck before the British were ready, the Government later explaining that military advice as to reinforcements had been ignored because it would have divided the nation and provoked the Boers. That, on the eve of war, the mobilisation and despatch over a great distance of the largest force ever sent out of Britain did constitute a considerable achievement was obscured by the disasters of the 'black week' in December before those troops arrived. That Balfour, temporarily in charge, treated the news with appropriate solemnity and, on hearing of Buller's bungling at the Tugela River, at once arranged for the despatch of Roberts (Salisbury insisting that he be accompanied by the younger Kitchener), was obscured by the ineptitude of Balfour's speeches in Lancashire in January 1900. In these he played down the reverses and refused to blame Lansdowne – *or accept blame on behalf of the Government.* Sure in his own mind that the fault lay partly with the military planners and partly with the military commanders, but unable, for a host of obvious reasons, to say so, he actually blamed *the public.* So Parliament met with the country, to quote St John Brodrick (Lansdowne's Under-Secretary) 'on fire and flame against the Government' and with all but the most committed partisans agreeing with *The Times* that there was 'need of apology on the part of the Cabinet for serious errors, both in policy and warlike preparations'. Ministers were appalled at the incompetence of Buller and Warren, and later of Gatacre and other officers, and ordered or secured their supersession. But the publication, owing to a misunderstanding by Lansdowne of a Cabinet decision, of Roberts's strictures on commanders, in the Spion Kop despatches, was almost as embarrassing as the ugly talk about War Office contracts and the quality of supplies which had already forced ministers to grant an inquiry and the adverse publicity about medical and sanitary arrangements which soon caused them to grant another. There would obviously follow, in due course, a more general inquiry into the preparations for, and early conduct of, the war. It could hardly redound to the credit of the Government, or of Salisbury as its head. It would show, for instance, that the Defence Committee of the Cabinet, at last set up in 1895, had rarely met and still more rarely decided anything. It had not operated in the spirit of Salisbury's 1895 minute, which represented the aspirations of Hartington, its chairman. Effective action awaited Balfour's premiership.

Here then, in 1900, was an administration which had to anticipate damaging criticism from sundry inquiries, some specific, some general in their terms of reference, criticism which, culminatively, produced a demand for 'national efficiency' which in its turn implied almost criminal negligence on the part of ministers. Yet this government received what only Palmerston's Government in 1865 had received since the 1832 Reform – a renewal of the confidence of the electorate after a long term of office. For within the period 16 February to 13 March 1900 came news of the occupation of Kimberley, the surrender of Cronje after Paardeberg, the relief of Ladysmith and the occupation of Bloemfontein. In May the defenders of Ladysmith, with the naval guns which had enabled them to hold out, were received home with enthusiasm, and the news, on the eighteenth, of the relief of Baden-Powell in Mafeking was hailed throughout the country with hysterical rejoicing. Soon Roberts was in Johannesburg and Pretoria and the South African War seemed over, except for mopping-up operations. In September the

Government, in a general election, held on to its large majority. The Unionists prospered in London and the great cities. In Scotland, for the first time since 1832, the Liberals failed to secure a majority of seats. The timing of the 'khaki election' was attributed to Chamberlain. He was certainly the most strident of the Government's champions in the campaign. He labelled its enemies pro-Boer and was apparently sublimely unaware that those who snatch victory from a transient popular mood are apt to find defeat, when it comes, compounded. Of Salisbury himself it is known that he was with difficulty persuaded to issue an address (having nothing in particular to say) and that he expressed surprise at the result. There is no sign here of compunction at exploiting such an occasion for a party triumph. The Liberals were so obliging as to add to their personal conflicts and basic split on Imperialism a three-way division on the war. The theme of the election was, officially, the future settlement of South Africa but, in fact, the justice of the war and the necessity for British paramountcy in southern Africa. It was an appropriate theme with which to smite the political enemy at home. Keeping the Radicals and Home Rulers from power was what Salisbury, and the Conservative party and the Unionist alliance were in politics for. Salisbury, of course, had no idea how long the Boer commandos would persist nor how large a force, how great a treasure and what stringent measures (including those to be condemned by Campbell-Bannerman as 'methods of barbarism') would be required to master them.

Like Palmerston when he took over from Aberdeen in the Crimean War, Salisbury faced demands for 'administrative reform' coupled with sharp criticism of aristocratic incompetence. Like Palmerston, Salisbury, in reforming his administration, defied the critics. Himself prised from the Foreign Office at last by a conspiracy of colleagues, headed by Balfour and Akers-Douglas, in company with the queen, he named Lansdowne as his successor with his own heir, Cranborne, as Commons' spokesman. Lansdowne's successor at the War Office was another Liberal Unionist, Salisbury's son-in-law Selborne. Gerald Balfour got the Board of Trade. Sir Henry Lucy, in *Punch*, recorded Unionist discontent at these appointments and Bartley, who two years earlier had complained that 'all honours, emoluments and places are reserved for the friends and relations of the favoured few', moved, from the Government side, a critical amendment to the Address. Whether or not Salisbury defended the appointment of relatives by explaining that 'he knew them better than anyone else' Professor Cornford has concluded that 'with every additional member of the family accommodated, the Hotel Cecil came nearer to collapse'.

Like Aberdeen, Asquith and Neville Chamberlain, Salisbury told himself that it was his duty to stay in office until the end of the war into which he had taken the country, the cost of which was estimated in May 1902 at £223 million. After he exchanged the Foreign Office for the Privy Seal he mattered less and less. He could render fruitless Chamberlain's last effort for a German alliance, and deprecate, like almost everyone, the intemperate outburst of Chamberlain against the Germans once he had abandoned the notion. But Salisbury could not dissuade his colleagues from the Japanese alliance of 1902, which marks a repudiation of his style and method which Balfour and Lansdowne would take further to the *entente* with France, and Grey, privily, to that virtual commitment to war which Salisbury always deemed both illicit and unwise. In December 1901 he helped a bare majority of his Cabinet confine the Education Bill to the secondary field, to avoid the perilous question of rate aid to voluntary schools – only to be overruled when Balfour, backed by the Whips, insisted on facing it, with results which Chamberlain told all and sundry would be fatal to the Unionists.

When the coronation was delayed by the illness of Edward VII Salisbury resigned, on 11 July 1902, while Chamberlain was incapacitated after an accident. Probably Chamberlain's assertions that he did not aspire to be the head of a Unionist administration were sincere, though Devonshire appears to have been rueful that he was not given another opportunity to refuse the premiership. Salisbury had been, as Chamberlain's biographer Julian Amery says, the most implacable opponent of Chamberlain's ambitions. His last speech, to the Primrose League on 7 May, was, in effect, a warning against him. Its theme was the 'serious danger' that would arise from an attempt to 'anticipate events or foreclose . . . the precious results' which the Empire held in store if statesmen exercised patience and care. In his Tariff Reform campaign of 1903 Chamberlain made just such an attempt, to the peril less of the Empire than the Unionists. Salisbury had suggested to the National Union in 1892 that there was a case for retaliation against hostile tariffs. But he would never have strained the precarious popularity of Empire by suggesting a tax on food. Consciously a defender of doomed causes, he had never been able to understand how in his youth the party could have been so foolish as to 'erect a mere matter of fiscal detail like Protection into a vital question'. He lived to read his son Hugh (a chip off the block, indeed) defending in a speech of 28 May

1903 the principle of Free Trade and to know of his heir's warning Chamberlain that Imperial Preference might lose 20 per cent of the party.

Salisbury shone no light forward into a future which looked dark – as to him the future always had. But he could hope that a hard Cecil logic, able and persistent, if too often negative and defensive, would play upon the public scene through his politician sons. *They* were Salisbury's principal legacy to British Conservatism.

# 4 Balfour 1902-1911

## ALFRED M. GOLLIN

ARTHUR JAMES BALFOUR became leader of the Conservative Party in July 1902. He seemed in every way qualified for the position. He was a patrician of exquisite sensibility and a politician of genuine skill. As a statesman he had already achieved much for his country. Nevertheless, his course as party leader cannot be looked upon as a success. Despite his comfortable opinion of himself and his capacities Balfour was not without his limitations in the post. Moreover, during the course of his leadership from 1902 to 1911 it was his professional misfortune to be confronted by challenges of a kind that might have threatened or destroyed the unity of any party however adroitly it was led, directed or managed.

In 1902 Balfour was satisfied that his advancement to the premiership and the leadership of his party was a development in the natural order of things, a fitting and proper culmination of his services up to that time. This easy confidence was characteristic of his attitude. He was one of those born to high estate and had long been marked out by the success which often follows from such early good fortune.

His father, James Maitland Balfour of Whittingehame, was a wealthy country gentleman, chairman of the North British Railway and sometime member of Parliament for the Haddington district. However he had made little mark in the world and the most significant influence upon Arthur Balfour's early years was that exercised by his mother, the aristocrat, Lady Blanche Gascoyne Cecil, a sister of the third marquess of Salisbury. Though he suffered from indifferent health as a boy and failed to perform brilliantly at Eton or Cambridge, Balfour in time revealed that keen subtlety of mind and independence of character which became distinguishing features of his maturity. A youthful interest in philosophy remained with him throughout his life and resulted in the publication of a number of philosophical works including *A Defence of Philosophic Doubt*, which appeared in 1879. This taste for speculative and philosophical subjects was used by political critics to suggest that he was unfit to pursue a parliamentary career. His concern with philosophy and his general weakness of health, it was sometimes

For Further Reading relevant to this chapter, see page 250.

said, equipped him more for a life or reflection and study than for one involved in the hard give and take of a British public man. 'Pretty Fanny' or 'Miss Balfour' were names applied to him in order to suggest that he was too delicate and too unbusinesslike to be a success in Parliament.

This was never the opinion of his uncle, the marquess of Salisbury. It was Lord Salisbury who suggested that Balfour stand for the Cecil 'family borough' of Hertford in the Conservative interest in 1874. Victory in the election enabled Balfour to enter Parliament as a supporter of Disraeli's last administration. In 1878 when Salisbury became Foreign Secretary he selected Balfour as his private secretary; and in that capacity the younger man accompanied his uncle to the Congress of Berlin. Although his career in politics was thus firmly launched it developed only slowly. At first Balfour felt diffident and unambitious. Moreover, as time passed he created the impression that he was merely attempting to fulfil, perhaps half-heartedly, the traditional governing duties of one of his class. Even after several years of service in Parliament men doubted the seriousness of his purpose. His great social position and the elegance of the circles in which he moved seemed to be more attractive to him than his public career. His cynical and superior manner in the House suggested he was merely amusing himself with politics, and with his fellow politicians. A contemporary diarist wrote of him: 'As he sprawled on the bench . . . he was taken at best for a Parliamentary *flaneur*, a trifler with debate, anxious chiefly in some leisure moments to practice the paces learned in . . . the Union at Cambridge. . . .'

Even after Lord Salisbury became Prime Minister and appointed his nephew to a number of ministerial posts the true calibre and quality of the younger man were not revealed. A decisive change came, however, in March 1887 when Salisbury offered him the post of Chief Secretary for Ireland. After a moment of hesitation Balfour plucked up his courage and accepted the position. The challenge was a very real one. In those days the problem of Ireland was a matter of vital consequence in British politics; the fate of governments sometimes turned upon it, and Irish Secretaries regularly saw their careers interrupted and their lives ruined by it. At the time of his appointment Balfour remarked to a friend: 'I shall have to lose either life or reputation.' He lost neither. As time passed the country saw that the Irish Secretary was capable of mastering the situation, in the House and also in Ireland. By degrees the astonishment created by Lord Salisbury's selection gave way to feelings of respect and approbation upon the one hand and hatred, anger and grudging admiration upon the other. Balfour's Irish policy of 'coercion' coupled later with remedial measures was forced through with cool skill and ruthless unbending firmness. In the House he dominated the Irish Nationalists and the Home Rulers. He returned their argument and invective with an aloof superiority and an obstinacy of will that marked him out as a master in debate and in the discharge of parliamentary business. In Ireland itself, as one contemporary put it, 'the fair-faced languid youth, too indolent to stand bolt upright' had developed 'into a civil Cromwell, the most unbending thorough adminstrator of iron rule Ireland has known since '98'. It was clear enough that a new star had risen in the Conservative firmament. If 'Pretty Fanny' had not yet entirely disappeared from the political scene, men were now certain that Balfour was a politician to be reckoned with in the future government of the country, and the Empire.

The further progress of his career plainly marked him out as his uncle's successor in the leadership of their party. In 1891 he became First Lord of the Treasury and Leader of the House of Commons, posts he also adorned in 1895 when Lord Salisbury was returned to power after a brief period in opposition. These were significant developments in Balfour's course since he had decided, by this time, that politics were to be the central feature of his existence, and that the study of philosophy and the pleasures to be enjoyed in the salons and country houses of his friends were to be merely appendages to a political life.

Balfour's performance as Conservative leader in the Commons in the years between 1891 and 1902 was sometimes criticised severely. He showed, from the first, a strong disinclination to weary himself in the drudgery of parliamentary management; several of his associates believed that he was not prepared to work very hard in their interest. Nor did he cultivate his followers in the traditional way. At times it seemed to some of them that his indolence was matched only by his 'strong contempt for popularity'. His style of address upon the public platform was also found, upon occasion, to be wanting in those touches which mark out a strong, effective and popular political leader. During the early and anxious days of the Boer War he failed to catch the public mood. His speeches created an impression of nonchalance and even flippancy at a time when the nation had suffered a series of severe and unexpected defeats. At the famous 'khaki' election of 1900, which returned the Salisbury Government to power, much of the result hung upon the popular oratory of Balfour's colleague, Joseph Chamberlain, the powerful Unionist Secretary of State for the Colonies. It has been well said that it was a 'one-man election'; that 'Lord Salisbury's manifesto was an anxious document'; that 'Arthur Balfour's speeches were not trumpet calls'; that 'for all fighting purposes in the constituencies the real leader, and the only leader of the Unionist masses' was Joseph Chamberlain.

It was in Cabinet, however, that Balfour during these years steadily developed his position as his uncle's chief lieutenant and by degrees fixed his grip upon the succession to the leadership. As the 'hinge of the unionist combination' he maintained the partnership between Lord Salisbury and Joseph Chamberlain, a principal leader of those Liberal Unionists who had broken away from the Liberal party in 1886 as a result of their hostility to Home Rule and had accepted office with the Conservatives in 1895. When Lord Salisbury became ill in 1898 and at other times when he journeyed abroad it was Balfour who took charge of the Foreign Office in his uncle's room. During the early and difficult days of the Boer War Balfour demonstrated a steadiness in council and a power of decision in the hour of crisis and danger that contributed significantly to the British recovery of the initiative. Indeed, as Lord Salisbury grew old and tired during the last eighteen months of his premiership, he tended to relax his hold upon policy while his nephew developed his own power, authority and influence in the deliberations of their colleagues and in the work of the Government.

At last in July 1902, worn out with his exertions and his years, Lord Salisbury resigned; and on the same day the king sent for Balfour to form a new ministry. When these developments were made public shortly afterward, Balfour at once summoned the Unionist Members of Parliament to a conference at the Foreign Office. There, his acceptance of the premiership was unanimously endorsed. The duke of Devonshire, who might have entertained some slight claims upon the prize, gave a special pledge of loyalty on behalf of the Liberal Unionists while Austen Chamberlain read out a message from his father, who was indisposed as the result of an accident, to 'welcome Mr Balfour to the leadership'. Balfour's succession had been expected for so long a time that it was accepted by the political world almost as a matter of course. The cordial public approval of Conservatives and Liberal Unionists alike was a feature of his triumph of July 1902.

It should be noted, however, that Balfour did not accept the king's commission until a number of delicate but necessary preliminaries had been completed. On 11 July, the day of Lord Salisbury's resignation,

he saw Chamberlain in his sick room and received from him firm assur-
ances of loyalty and support in his new course. He also told the duke of
Devonshire, titular leader of the Liberal Unionist party, of the king's
invitation. Only after these interviews had been concluded did Balfour
kiss hands. Public announcement was made two days later and it was
then, on 14 July, that the party meeting was summoned and held at
the Foreign Office.

Balfour's relationship with Joseph Chamberlain was a factor of vital
significance in these high developments. The great Colonial Secretary
was a colleague of immense authority, perhaps the most dynamic statesman in the Empire, a man who had to be reckoned with if the new
arrangement was to enjoy any chance or hope of success.

In the opinion of many, Chamberlain, for his own part, had valid
claims upon the premiership in 1902. He enjoyed a tremendous popularity in the constituencies. He possessed the ability to arouse intense
enthusiasm in a way that Balfour could not. He had organised the
electoral victories of 1895 and 1900. He was everywhere recognised as
the first champion of British Imperialism, a movement that still played
a significant role in the minds of contemporaries. Despite these qualifications, however, there was a terrible flaw in Chamberlain's political
armoury and no one recognised it more clearly than he did. In 1886 he
had resigned from Gladstone's Liberal Government because of his
opposition to Home Rule. This act, and his subsequent course, had
smashed the Liberal party to pieces. This was a legacy he could never
throw off in all the years that followed. When he and a number of other
Liberal Unionists agreed to join Salisbury's Conservative Government
in 1895 his marvellous powers and his dynamic driving force were
readily acknowledged as genuine assets in the new ministerial combination. In fact, some of his followers felt that he was now in a position to
determine the policy and direction of the Conservative Government.
The most ardent of them began to regard him as a future Conservative
or Unionist Prime Minister. We must be clear, however, that when he
joined the Conservative Government in 1895 he became its prisoner,
and not its master. Lord Salisbury, brooding upon these developments, had always looked upon him 'as a force to be used'. He was the
implacable enemy of Chamberlain's ambition. It was not his intention
to deliver the Conservative party and all that it represented into the
hands of a Radical and Nonconformist like Chamberlain. Salisbury and
Balfour were prepared to allow him power and initiative in their Government but they remained as the unchallengeable Conservative leaders

while he performed as their ally and subordinate. Even in 1902, after years of service to the alliance, Chamberlain was an outsider with no real claim to the supreme office. He was not even a member of the Conservative party since the Liberal Unionists still maintained a separate organisation with their own Whips, funds, and party structure. Years later when one of his followers spoke of the party leadership to Chamberlain he explained that 'he could not go against Balfour; that Conservatives who agreed with him would not follow him, because their party loyalty would be too strong'. This was exactly his condition in July 1902.

The first loyalty of the Conservatives was to Balfour. His triumph was a reflection of their own continuing ascendancy in the Unionist combination and in all that it represented in the political and social life of the country. Nevertheless, the position of the new Prime Minister was not an easy one. He took up the reins of his authority at a singularly difficult moment in the history of his party and in the history of the country. Moreover, his majority was an inherited one, bequeathed to him with much else by his uncle, and not one he had gained for himself in open contest at a general election. Despite these handicaps, serious as they were, the Prime Minister was a man who could be relied upon to face and meet almost any challenge, and any challenger. By 1902 Balfour had developed into a mature, determined and resourceful political leader, one who meant to lead as he saw fit, and in no other way. Everyone recognised the iron determination he chose to conceal behind a courteous manner and that air of flaccid indolence he presented to the world. As Winston Churchill once wrote of him: 'Neither on the big line nor on the small line . . . could anyone overcome his central will or rupture his sense of duty'.

Arthur Balfour's duty, as he saw it, was to preserve and protect the nation and the Empire. Although he was engaged in politics for these national and patriotic reasons he was also, in his public life, Lord Salisbury's legitimate political heir. In this capacity he looked upon himself as the representative of his own class and order in British political society while he entertained at the same time the comfortable conviction that the nation would prosper best only if it were led by men of his own select calibre. As a result of this attitude, and despite a genuine breadth of vision which marked him out from his fellows, he was often dominated by a partisan and even narrow Tory outlook in his political reflections and in his conclusions about politics. Balfour, the aristocratic 'bachelor of breeding,' represented the old order at a time when new challenges to it were about to make themselves felt with crushing effect upon the further development of British public life.

A chief quality that distinguished him as he entered upon his premiership was his supreme and superior aloofness in politics, and this Olympian attitude was marred only by the distaste he felt for Irish Nationalism, and for Irishmen. Above all else the new Prime Minister could be expected to act with a composed determination and an un-ruffled hardness in carrying out the business of his party and his Government. He would not be turned easily from any political goal he had fixed upon. Winston Churchill, after a friendship lasting through thirty years, emphasised that beneath Balfour's polished courtesies lay a 'cool ruthlessness' where public affairs were concerned. Neville Chamberlain, who knew Balfour in later years, once said of him 'he always seemed to me to have a heart like a stone'. And Lord Beaver-brook, another observer of Balfour's political career at a later period, came to the conclusion that he was 'charming and ruthless'. Despite the awful complexities of the time and the various burdens of his position Balfour, serene, lucid in thought, experienced in the workings of government and composed in his outlook, was well equipped to dis-charge the task he took up in July 1902.

Adequate solution of the problems that confronted Britain's political leaders in 1902 was a matter of vital consequence for the entire destiny of the nation. All recognised that the high summer of the Victorian era was over. It was necessary for the Government to embark upon positive courses of action in order to secure and render safe the position of Great Britain in the difficult circumstances of the new century. The complacent attitude of earlier years could not be allowed to continue if Britain were to deal adequately with the economic, social, military, strategic and diplomatic issues that confronted her. Several of the required policies had already been put in train in Lord Salisbury's time, but the Boer War and the inefficiencies it revealed had made obvious the need to work out a number of essential changes, and to work them out with all possible despatch. This was the goal Balfour set for himself as Prime Minister. Unfortunately for his purpose, however, Joseph Chamberlain fixed upon a revolutionary plan of his own in order to retrieve the situation. Both were strong men and although their objects were largely the same they relied upon different methods in order to secure them. As time passed each felt more and more certain that his own way was best. As a result of this general and particular situation there now fell upon Balfour's ministry a series of disasters that determined, in large measure, his entire course as Prime Minister and party leader. Chamberlain, the Imperialist, looked to the Empire in order to find new sources of strength to bolster up the position of the United Kingdom. Since the 1880s he had recognised a steady decline in the condition of his country compared with that of the other major powers. It seemed to him that Britain was neglecting her Imperial resources in her struggles with the great nation-states of the day. As Secretary of State for the Colonies he had enjoyed a long association with the various leaders of the so-called 'Great Colonies' and felt that he combined a clear understanding of British requirements with a grasp of Colonial needs, aspirations, and desires. A more closely knit imperial organisation of some kind seemed to be needed in order to exploit the vast resources of the Empire with more efficiency than had been achieved under existing institutions of imperial government. Since the 1870s the idea of Imperial Federation had been discussed regularly, but with no result. When the 'Great Colonies' rallied to Britain's side in the crisis of the Boer War Chamberlain, the enthusiast, was fortified in his resolve to work out an imperial arrangement that would permit British and colonial statesmen to direct the forces of a united Empire in the most efficient manner possible. He felt that a new political institution, a Council of Empire, should be created so that the mother country and the 'Great Colonies' could co-ordinate their diplomatic, military and naval programmes instead of pursuing separate and even conflicting policies in the conduct of their affairs. If such a council could harness the energies and resources of the whole Empire it would control a unified Imperial power that no nation on earth would dare to defy. This was Chamberlain's dream.

His problem was to determine how he could begin upon such a grandiose scheme in the face of that developing colonial nationalism which desired, above all else, independence from the authority of the Government in London. In time he decided that a start could be made only if a community of economic interests within the Empire could be created. Upon this solid base Chamberlain felt that he could go forward and achieve those imperial arrangements which were his objects in the first place. On 15 May 1903, after much jockeying in the Cabinet, the Colonial Secretary spoke out at Birmingham so dramatically that all his contemporaries were astonished at his audacity. In this famous speech he demanded a 'new definition' of Free Trade, including preferential tariffs for the colonies in the United Kingdom market, so that the task of creating a 'federal union that will make the British Empire powerful' might be begun. By 28 May, after prodding by Lloyd George, Chamberlain announced in the House of Commons that '. . . if you are to give a preference to the colonies . . . you must put a tax on food . . .'.

Arthur Balfour appreciated the terrific quality of the challenge that now confronted his ministry. The Free Trade system, for half a century past, had been looked upon in Britain as the source of the country's commercial greatness and affluence. Tariffs upon foodstuffs, or 'food taxes' as they were sometimes called, were traditionally regarded as the cruel device of particular interest groups only, levied for their own profit at the expense of the entire national community. In 1846 the Conservative party had been seared by this issue of protective tariffs and had broken into quarrelling factions as a result of it. Balfour at a very early stage came to the conclusion that the British electorate would never vote for tariffs upon imported articles of foreign food and a consequent increase in the cost of living even to achieve the more closely unified Empire of Chamberlain's aspiration. The Prime Minister understood that all the Liberals and many Conservatives and Unionists entertained an unquestioning belief in the validity of Free Trade as the only fiscal system for their country. If Chamberlain's dramatic proposals destroyed the unity of his party Balfour's majority in Parliament would be lost and when a general election came the fate of Britain would be delivered into the hands of the Liberals, men he believed to be unfit for high office.

Balfour realised that in the Conservative party he had inherited from his uncle a magnificent instrument for the exercise of power and he determined from the first to use it for his own purposes. Even before he became Prime Minister he had begun a series of educational, naval, military and diplomatic reforms – all designed to bolster up the national position. In order to achieve his objects he had to rely upon the party to provide him with the political power required to carry his proposals into effect. He was convinced that the changes he contemplated would produce more genuine results for the country than Chamberlain's highflown design. Moreover, his unemotional nature could place no faith in a single scheme or plan as the solution to all the problems of the nation. He felt that his own policies and plans were more valid than Chamberlain's and he determined from the first to work his own will upon the future course of events, despite Chamberlain's challenge or that of anyone else.

The Prime Minister's object, in the face of Chamberlain's remarkable conduct, was to preserve the unity of his party. Inside the Government the Colonial Secretary's proposals proved attractive to some ministers while they aroused hostility in others. In the House of Commons and

c.l.—6*

in the country many Conservatives were suspicious of Chamberlain and his plan while others began to look upon him as a national saviour. Balfour hoped at first to stave off a crisis by delaying any decision upon the matter. In consequence, he urged his colleagues in the Cabinet to treat the question of Imperial Preference as an 'open one'. All were entitled to their own opinions upon the subject, he explained, but these opinions need not bind the Cabinet as a whole. He also proposed a lengthy governmental enquiry into the entire subject; and he asked his colleagues to refrain from discussing it in Parliament. Despite this 'truce' between ministers their disagreements could not be concealed from the public. By July 1903 a Unionist Free Food League, composed of those who opposed Chamberlain, and a Tariff Reform League of his supporters had been formed. It was obvious, in these circumstances, that Balfour had to demonstrate decisive qualities as a party leader or the Unionist factions would destroy each other and thus achieve for the Liberals a result they were powerless to secure by their own efforts.

The ministerial truce was employed by Balfour as a kind of breathing space, and he put it to good use. The task he set himself in the period from June to August 1903 was to solve the political problem caused by the disagreement between Unionist Free traders and Tariff Reformers, and this could be done if he devised a fiscal programme that each faction of the party might accept as a valid compromise. After much study and many secret consultations with official and unofficial economists the Prime Minister was at last ready to lay his solutions before his colleagues at a cabinet meeting fixed for 13 August 1903. At this meeting he invited ministers to discuss two papers he had circulated to them. One of these documents, later published as *Economic Notes on Insular Free Trade*, argued that Free Trade was impossible in 1903 owing to the activity of other nations. Balfour's solution to the problem was so to change the law that the British Government could approach Free Trade by *retaliating* against any nation that imposed protective duties. By means of this weapon of *retaliation* the Government could force foreign states to comply with the rules of Free Trade or suffer the burden of British tariffs when they sought entry for their goods into British ports. Balfour hoped that this policy of *retaliation* might prove acceptable to the great mass of the Tory party as a compromise between the arguments of the Free Trade extremists upon the one hand and those of the Tariff Reformers upon the other.

A second document prepared by the Prime Minister and known since as the 'Blue Paper' was also discussed at the cabinet meeting of

13 August. In this memorandum Balfour proposed acceptance of a programme that included, with safeguards, the adoption by Britain of preferential tariffs and food taxes. After discussion ministers began to quarrel among themselves towards the end of the Cabinet meeting and in the face of this confusion Balfour would not allow any decisions to be taken. It was agreed by ministers that a further meeting of the Cabinet should take place on 14 September when definite conclusions about the policy of the Government would be worked out. By this stage of the crisis four cabinet ministers clearly resented their Prime Minister's attitude since he seemed to be 'leaning' to Chamberlain's side while Balfour felt, as he put it in a message to the king, that as a result of his careful strategy the majority of the Cabinet would 'support him in the moderate, yet important, suggestions which he . . . is prepared to recommend'.

The fate of the Balfourian ministry now turned upon the Prime Minister's tactical skill. In the period after 13 August the Unionist Free Trade ministers, led by C. T. Ritchie, the Chancellor of the Exchequer, became very active. They concentrated their attention upon the duke of Devonshire and sought to convince him that he should oppose Balfour's proposals. Devonshire, Lord President of the Council, and a lifelong Free Trader, was so trusted in the country and at Westminster that he might be accepted as a compromise leader of the Unionists in their difficult situation. Beyond this, even if the duke refused to challenge Balfour for the leadership he could deal the ministry a crippling blow if he emerged as the formal leader of its Free Trade faction. In order to meet these dangers Balfour made a number of changes in his own policies, though he carefully refrained from explaining all of them to any colleague. His first object was to detach the duke from the Unionist Free Trade ministers so that his Government would not be shaken too severely if they were all forced to resign. He hoped that this could be done if he abandoned the extreme proposals contained in his 'Blue Paper'. In the second place Balfour decided that his ministry would be committed to a change of principle, that the fiscal issue could no longer be looked upon as an 'open question' but that the Government must commit itself to a policy of fiscal change of some kind, and that no one could serve with him who did not accept this vital alteration. By these secret designs the Prime Minister proposed to break his Unionist Free Trade colleagues when the crisis came on 14 September. They had intrigued against his leadership and would be required to pay for their opposition, at his convenience.

There now took place what has been called by a modern authority, and with reason, one of the 'most drastic series of expulsions, resignations and reshuffles engineered by any Prime Minister in the twentieth century'. Balfour acted without mercy and with icy calculation. He dealt first with Joseph Chamberlain. For reasons already touched upon Chamberlain could not offer open defiance to the Prime Minister, despite his genuine enthusiasm to achieve his grand design of Empire. Therefore, on 9 September, he wrote to Balfour in order to suggest that he should be allowed to resign from the Government so that he could carry on a great campaign of propaganda and education that might convince the electorate of the validity of his proposals. In subsequent exchanges the two men resolved that if Chamberlain left the ministry and eventually succeeded in winning popular approval for his plan Balfour would consolidate his gains and see to it that they were passed into law.

This 'offer of resignation' put the initiative in the Prime Minister's hands. When the Cabinet met on 14 September Balfour did not reveal the existence of Chamberlain's letter to his colleagues. Moreover, he allowed the Unionist Free Trade ministers to believe that his 'Blue Paper', including proposals for food taxes and preferences, was still under consideration. When Ritchie and Lord Balfour of Burleigh criticised these views they were instantly dismissed from their offices. They were pushed out because, in their arguments, they violated Balfour's new principle that his Government was now to be a ministry of fiscal change.

By Balfour's design the Unionist Free Trade ministers prepared their letters of resignation under the impression that Chamberlain would remain in the Government and that his policy might be accepted as the official programme of the Ministry. This was not Balfour's intention. He decided to accept Chamberlain's offer to resign and to abandon his 'Blue Paper'. By these devices he felt that he could separate the duke of Devonshire from his friends and win his support for the Government. As a consequence, the plague of fiscal enthusiasts that had poisoned his life would disappear. As a result of his arrangement with Chamberlain the Prime Minister knew that he and his Government were protected from any attack by the most savage political fighter of the day. When the Unionist Free Trade ministers removed themselves, they would no longer be in a position to tamper with the deliberations of the Government. Balfour would thus be able to go forward, supported by a Cabinet of moderates, and achieve those goals he had fixed upon as the most important requirements of the nation and the Empire.

Devonshire remained as the key to the ultimate success of these manoeuvres. After the cabinet meeting of the fourteenth the Prime Minister hinted to him that Chamberlain might resign and on the next day told him that Chamberlain was almost certain to resign. This information was conveyed to the duke with the clear request that he should 'not mention this to anyone'. On the day after, 16 September, the Prime Minister received letters of resignation from Ritchie and from Lord George Hamilton, the leading Free Traders, and he knew that Lord Balfour of Burleigh was preparing to follow their course. In these circumstances he wrote to Chamberlain and accepted his suggestion that he should be allowed to leave the Government. On the evening of that day he called upon Devonshire and told him Chamberlain had resigned. He invited the duke to withdraw his own resignation and to remain as a minister. In response to Devonshire's request Balfour firmly refused to extend a similar invitation to the Free Trade ministers. When the duke consented to stay on as Balfour's colleague the Prime Minister felt he could congratulate himself upon a triumphant solution of all his problems. It is small wonder that the *Annual Register* referred to a 'widespread impression that the Free Trade element in the Cabinet had been reduced to conditions hardly compatible with that mutual confidence which was assumed to characterise the relations between ministerial colleagues'.

On 1 October 1903 Balfour spoke to the annual meeting of the National Union of Conservative Associations at Sheffield, where he took the opportunity to explain to the party the moderate fiscal policy of his Government, after the resignations. The Duke of Devonshire, smarting under attack by his Free Trade friends, seized his chance and informed Balfour that the arguments of the Sheffield speech did not permit him to remain in the ministry. The Prime Minister was outraged. His plan to reassert his position as party leader and his plan for a massive Balfour–Devonshire administration, with its appeal to moderate men in every walk of life, lay in ruins. He was so annoyed with the duke that he wrote him an angry reply 'before', as he put it, 'I had even had my bath'.

In a short time the great Unionist party dissolved into three separate factions. One group consisted of the Unionist Free Traders; a second supported the Prime Minister, who based his fiscal policy upon the idea of retaliation and the generally moderate programme contained in his *Economic Notes on Insular Free Trade*; the third and most active faction was made up of those who gave their allegiance to Chamberlain. In Parliament it became impossible for the Prime Minister to rely upon his party whenever a vote on the fiscal question took place. The long-drawn death agony of his administration had begun. Balfour, for his part, rallied manfully to the challenge. His cunning, adroitness and dexterity in keeping the party together and avoiding a formal split became the wonder of the time. Although contemporaries and later critics condemned him for remaining in office too long, in the face of these terrible party divisions, it is only just to emphasise that he held on to the premiership for valid reasons which could not be explained fully to the public at the time. As a statesman he felt it his duty to oversee the reorganisation of the country's military and naval forces and to complete those vital diplomatic arrangements with Japan and France upon which so much of significance turned, before the Liberals, whom he did not respect or trust, won office and power for themselves. His long struggle with a bickering party in a hostile Parliament, so often criticised at the time and later, won the admiration of one whose opinion must find a place in any considered judgement upon Balfour as Prime Minister and party leader. Winston Churchill, in the evening of his days, once remarked that 'he thought the greatest political achievement he had known in his long parliamentary life was the silence of Arthur Balfour in the years between 1903–5 during the battle between Free Trade and Tariff Reform'.

Despite the marvellous skill of the Prime Minister his reconstructed Government staggered from one parliamentary crisis to another until he decided to resign, at the end of 1905. He chose the course of resignation, instead of dissolving Parliament, in the vain hope that the Liberals, themselves divided into squabbling factions, would have difficulty in forming a ministry when they did not enjoy a majority in the Commons. This tactical stroke was unsuccessful. A Liberal Government was formed and at the general election of January 1906, which followed, the Conservatives crashed to defeat in one of the worst electoral disasters of modern British political history. Balfour must bear his full share of the blame for the crushing reverse suffered by his party. The selfishness and shortsightedness of the Unionist leaders aroused their traditional opponents to new heights of vigour and energy in the 1906 election. Nonconformists were irritated by the Government's Education and Licensing Acts. Labour politicians, their hopes largely ignored by the Tories, felt that the only promising course for them was co-operation with the Liberals. Pride in the Empire, and the Imperial idea itself, which had served the Unionists so well in past elections, were looked upon by the public in a completely different light in the aftermath of the Boer War, marred by scandals like that of 'Chinese Slavery on the

Rand', and the illegal flogging of Chinamen in South Africa. The Chamberlain campaign and the divisions within the party resulting from it made it certain that the extent of the defeat suffered in 1906 was to be without precedent in the recent history of the party. All was compounded by the dissatisfaction caused by Balfour's delaying tactics in Parliament in the years between 1903 and 1906.

Balfour himself was included in the tale of defeated Conservative candidates in the 1906 election. The humiliation was made worse by the fact that in the new House the Tariff Reformers dominated the Unionist ranks while only a handful of Unionist Tree Traders and followers of the policy of retaliation were returned. In these circumstances Chamberlain resolved to force his will upon the Conservative party. He disclaimed any desire for the leadership but he now demanded that Balfour accept his fiscal policy as the official programme of the party: he insisted upon the repudiation of the Unionist Free Traders; and he suggested a reorganisation of the Conservative party on a more democratic basis and a formal union between it and the Liberal Unionist party. Balfour resisted stubbornly for some time but found that he had to give way. On 15 February 1906 an exchange of letters between the two men was published, the so-called Valentine Compact, in which Balfour agreed to the principle of a general tariff on manufactures and the imposition of a small duty on foreign corn. Chamberlain's friends were jubilant at his victory. Henry Chaplin, the 'Squire', remarked that it was 'the greatest political triumph since the days when Disraeli captured the Conservative party'. At a meeting of the party at Lansdowne House the triumph was made complete. Although Balfour presided and received a vote of confidence Chamberlain was the hero of the gathering. He took care to point out that the Valentine Compact was 'not a compromise but a definition'. From this time contemporaries ridiculed what many of them regarded as Balfour's surrender of his independence as a party leader. And Chamberlain, the victor, remarked after the Lansdowne House meeting: 'I do not like the look of Arthur Balfour. He is more tired than I have ever known him and I am really afraid of a nervous breakdown in his case. . . .'

Chamberlain's assault upon the party leadership was not confined to definitions of policy. He also proposed major reforms in party organisation. At the time of the Valentine Compact Balfour was forced to agree to set up a committee to examine the entire issue of organisation, but he and his friends of the Old Guard did all they could to fend off significant changes. Balfour's problems as leader at this time were made more complicated because in the new House of Commons he had lost, for the moment, that easy mastery in debate which had always distinguished his parliamentary performances. This difficult situation in the directing circles of the party was changed with terrible and dramatic suddenness. During their pre-Valentine tussles Chamberlain once said of the party leader: 'He believes in the Balfourian policy of delay... and perhaps at the bottom of his heart hopes to tire out his opponents'. In July 1906 Chamberlain was prostrated by a crippling stroke and instantly removed from the political scene. As he struggled for life and health Arthur Balfour calmly began to reassert his authority over the party, an authority he had almost lost in the months following the election.

After 1906 Balfour led his followers into an era of classical antagonism and rivalry with the Liberals. He and Lord Lansdowne, the Unionist leader in the Lords, employed their majority in the Upper House to throw out one government bill after another even though they had been passed by large majorities in the Commons. By 1908, as a result of this shortsighted, partisan and provocative tactic, the situation at Westminster was becoming critical for the Liberal ministry. In the country also the Liberals had reason for anxiety. There, the Tariff Reformers had gained the initiative and were steadily winning by-elections. At a time of unemployment and trade depression Chamberlain's idea of industrial protection, with its promise of full employment, had become very appealing to large numbers of voters. It was Lloyd George who turned this difficult situation into one of splendid opportunity for the Government. He and his colleagues chose to counter-attack the Tories upon the issue of finance. His budget of 1909, and the campaign that accompanied it, were designed to revive the Liberal party in the constituencies, and by the same series of strokes, to overcome the legislative deadlock at Westminster. It was Balfour's misfortune, and he deserves some sympathy for it, that having survived Chamberlain's terrible onslaughts he was now to suffer under the hammer blows of yet another popular leader of genius, those of Lloyd George, the Radical Chancellor.

The problem for Balfour as leader was to select the most advantageous course for the Unionists as the clash between parties developed. Several factors were involved. In the first place if the Lords threw out a Finance Bill they would lay themselves open to very serious criticism. Secondly, the proposals in the Bill, contemporaries believed, would make Tariff Reform unnecessary because they would enable the Government to rake in the sums needed for national defence and social reform by taxing the rich, without recourse to tariffs. Some experienced Unionists, for constitutional and political reasons, felt that the Budget should be allowed to pass. The Tariff Reformers, fearful for the fate of their cause, demanded rejection. They argued that their policy was the only one popular enough to win votes for the Tories, in the face of Lloyd George's Radical appeal. In August 1909 Balfour decided to use the Conservative majority in the Lords to reject the Budget. A recent scholar has condemned the decision as 'insane'. It was certainly a blunder, but it was made after careful thought, and for cogent reasons. The electoral defeat of 1906 convinced Balfour that his cardinal task was to preserve the unity of his party. As leader he could do so only if he acquiesced in the demands of the Tariff Reformers, the largest and most active group in the Conservative ranks. He gave way to their pressure after calculation and was not hurried by them into his choice. As a result, and unlike his unpleasant experience of 1906, he led a united party to the polls at the general election of January 1910.

The failure of the Unionists to win the election meant that the position of the House of Lords in the legislative process was forced to the front as the issue for 1910. As early as January 1906, in the very hour of the great Liberal victory, Balfour had made the cavalier statement that it was the duty of everyone to ensure that the 'great Unionist party should still control, whether in power or whether in opposition, the destinies of this great Empire'; and from that time he had employed the Conservative majority in the Lords to tamper with the legislative programme of the Liberal Government. A supreme moment in this clash of interests came in 1909 with the rejection of the Finance Bill by the House of Lords. Now, in the contemporary phrase, the 'cup was full' and the Radicals determined to strike back. They decided, after their return to power in 1910, to take up in earnest the constitutional position of the House of Lords.

Behind this issue, grave as it was, lurked the question of Ireland. The Liberal ministry, as a result of the general election of January 1910, depended for its majority in the new House of Commons upon the votes of the Irish Nationalist party. For their part the Irishmen entertained only one goal, Home Rule for Ireland, and they believed that the Government's parliamentary weakness furnished them with the power to demand from it all that they desired.

Much of the further course of events in 1910 was decided by the subtle combination of Arthur Balfour's Irish prejudices and his adherence to party principles.

In April the Government introduced their Parliament Bill designed to curb the legislative powers of the House of Lords. If this measure was secured the Lords would be unable to halt the passage of a Home Rule Bill and the Union with Ireland, in the course of time, would be destroyed. In these circumstances Balfour and the Tories were convinced that owing to a temporary and peculiar parliamentary alliance between the Liberals and Irish Nationalists they were faced with a constitutional revolution for which there was no popular mandate. The sovereign himself was involved in this crisis of the constitution since it was strongly held by the Government parties that if the Lords attempted to resist passage of the Parliament Bill he should overcome their defiance by creating enough new peers to swallow up the Conservative majority in their House.

Exactly at this juncture King Edward died and the leading politicians took the opportunity to call a truce in their struggles in order to attempt a settlement. A constitutional conference composed of the Liberal and Conservative leaders met, but they were unable to agree upon the subject of Home Rule and the conference ended in failure. In his concern about the situation Lloyd George presented a tremendous compromise plan of his own to Balfour, in October. His startling proposal was the formation of a National Government made up of the leading men in each of the great parties to deal with the serious domestic and international issues that confronted the nation. Included in this scheme of national regeneration was the suggestion of a compromise solution of the Irish problem. It was Balfour's duty as Conservative leader to decide whether or not his party should entertain these dramatic ideas.

In discussion Balfour was charmed by the skill of Lloyd George's advocacy, but in the end he refused to accept the plan. Ireland remained as the chief obstacle to any agreement. Earlier in the year when one of Balfour's followers suggested that the Unionists might seek an arrangement of their own with the Irish Nationalists he had dismissed such ideas as 'Eating Dirt'. Upon this occasion when he refused to accept Lloyd George's entire scheme he declared to the Chancellor: 'I cannot become another Robert Peel in my party!' Years later he explained this remark by saying: 'Peel twice committed what seems to me the unforgivable sin. He gave away a principle on which he had come into power. . . . He simply betrayed his Party.'

These failures to compromise meant another general election. The Conservatives realised they could not win it simply by defending the House of Lords so they decided to fight on the issue of Home Rule. Some of their number including several prominent Tariff Reformers, eager for a victory at almost any cost, suddenly urged Balfour to promise that he would submit Tariff Reform to a referendum if their party were returned to power. After a brief interval of coyness and hesitation, which he probably enjoyed, he agreed to the suggestion and in a public speech in November permitted himself to remark: 'I have not the least the least objection to submitting the principles of Tariff Reform to a Referendum.' The general election of December 1910 produced a House of Commons in which the balance of parties remained practically unchanged. Having secured a victory the Government reintroduced the Parliament Bill and Balfour's last major campaign as leader of the Conservative party began.

Balfour's leadership of the party during the Parliament Bill crisis divided it into bitterly quarrelling factions and finally ended with his own resignation as leader. It seemed to him that when the Liberals won a general election for the second time in 1910 they had fought their way to a position from which they could at last decide the future relationship of the two Houses of the legislature. As he reflected upon the matter he decided that constitutional propriety and tactical prudence permitted only one course for his party – to allow the Parliament Bill to pass unamended through the House of Lords. If the Bill were rejected the Conservatives might at once lose their majority in the Lords in a flood of newly created Liberal peers. If it were allowed to pass the Conservatives in the Lords would still enjoy, under its provisions, 'two years' grace', to deal with Home Rule and other measures of significance to them. For these reasons, in the phrase of those days, he eventually counselled 'surrender' to the Parliament Bill. This was not the view taken by significant numbers of Unionists in 1911. These men resolved to resist passage of the Bill to the limit of their ability and preferred to defy their leaders rather than submit. As a result of the difference the party split into sullen and angry groups who squabbled with each other as fiercely as they opposed the Liberals. All the Unionists accepted Balfour's opinion that 'we are the victims of a revolution', but they were unable to agree upon a method of meeting it. In August 1911 the Bill was passed, but the problem of the party leadership now became a matter of urgent moment since Balfour himself had suffered as the particular target of the Unionist rebels.

Ever since 1903 the Tariff Reformers had been savage critics of Balfour as leader. His referendum pledge of 1910 rekindled the hostility of many of them while his leadership during the battle for the Parliament Bill swelled the volume of discontent through other sections of the party.

It was widely held that his unfitness to lead in such turbulent times was proven by the fact that he had led the party in three general elections, which they had lost. In the autumn of 1911 the Halsbury Club was formed by a number of Unionists as a 'spearhead' for their party. Several members of this group wished to pull Balfour down from his place as leader but it is important to remember, because it is often forgotten, that not all those who joined the Halsbury Club did so because they wished to see Balfour replaced.

A key factor in the situation was the attitude of Balfour himself. Harried by dissent he had lost that serenity of outlook which had been a distinguishing characteristic of his public life. In August he confessed to a friend that 'Politics have been . . . quite unusually odious'. When some of his senior colleagues publicly rejected his advice he admitted 'to a feeling that I have been badly treated. I have no wish to lead a Party under these humiliating conditions.' By October he had made up his mind to resign. He had been leader of his party in the Commons for twenty years and as he put it, 'whatever ambitions I have had were satisfied years ago'. He had fought diligently to preserve the unity of the party and had carried it through some of the bitterest episodes in its history. 'I know', he observed to a colleague, 'I cannot be evicted from the leadership,' but now the business of struggling on against his divided enemies in the party was becoming too painful and too tedious. In November 1911 he resigned.

A remarkable phase of Arthur Balfour's political career began only after he was relieved of the burden of the party leadership. He developed, with the passage of time, into one of those elder statesmen who supply so much to the political and intellectual life of the country. His service in peace and in war in several ministries, under a number of different Prime Ministers, added distinction to his name, and contributed significantly to the further progress of nation and Empire. When he died in 1930 he enjoyed that kind of esteem which is seldom offered to a politician in British public life and which comes only with age, and after years of diligent service to the State.

# 5  Between Balfour and Baldwin 1911-1923

## J. H. GRAINGER

LIKE the poet the Conservative party communicates before it is understood. The intelligibility which Conservative politicians achieve is less likely to be found in stated intentions than in their conduct in office. Characteristically their tasks are those of discarding possible worlds, familiarising forgotten virtues, gathering in what has been scattered and selectively renewing worn-out initiatives. Coherence may be impaired by this reluctance to be programmatic, but it is on this diffidence that Conservative claims to integrity will rest and turn.

A party that seeks to be a great governing party is nevertheless at times constrained to expound as well as connect and it was clear that, after the crushing defeat at the election of 1906, the Conservatives with coarse but effective slogans about Chinese Slavery, the Big Loaf and perhaps echoes of Rome on the Rates still ringing in their ears, should, exceptionally, try to make themselves fully intelligible. And it was also obvious that the best way of inducing assent would be to draw upon everything within their tradition that could be conceived of as distinguishing them from the Liberals. There might be assured Conservatives who considered that Liberalism would crumble because of the confusion of its ministerial talents, the brittleness before events and circumstances of its manifold intentions, or simply because of the price it must pay electorally for legislative indulgences to its sectional supports. But as the times became more alarming, the voices of separatists, syndicalists and suffragettes more insistent, Conservatives, in adversity, became programmatic, clarifying a theme which had struggled fitfully and been obscured or lost in both the distant and recent history of the party. Conservatives, or most of them, became possessed with a single organising idea: Tariff Reform, which at once provided them with the prospect of a unified, well-defended Empire and a notable improvement in the human resources of Britain through extended social services together with the means of paying for them. Conservatives need no longer be content with standing on their record and determining what

For Further Reading relevant to this chapter, see page 250; for References, see pages 253-4.

was ripe for determination. Against the random appetites of 'multitudinous' Liberalism, they could now assert a single yet branching purpose.

At the two elections of 1910 the Conservatives recovered ground but not office. Both were lost in the process of resisting, firstly, the major counter-strategy by which the Liberals proposed to finance both increased arms and social services out of taxes on the better-off through a People's Budget, and secondly and consequentially, the reduction of the powers of the House of Lords which had, during the whole of their period in office, as opportunity afforded, obstructed or mangled their legislative programme.

The Conservatives had been led by Balfour, a civilised and skilled politician whose performance as leader of the last Conservative administration had proved that he had a good grasp of the problems of imperial power (Professor W. A. S. Hewins, the intelligence and pedagogue of Tariff Reform from 1903, thought that there was none better).[1] Balfour accepted that the fiscal question had ripened to decision, but declined either to make Tariff Reform the central party doctrine or to commit himself to details. High policy meant fine distinctions, even if those distinctions could not be rendered in the dramaturgy of popular politics. He resigned in November 1911 because he was not prepared to contend with the Liberals in the realm of intention and because he was finding the tribal pressures of his own party, especially on the House of Lords issue, ungrateful.

Balfour departed because politics had become 'unusually odious' to him. His political sensibility was too fine for the party. Conservatives wanted not necessarily coarser but certainly more immediately intelligible leadership, even if it led to their having to choose between the rehearsed statesmanship of Austen Chamberlain and the confused but communicable public spirit of Walter Long. Austen, his father's echo on Tariff Reform and incongruously but acceptably Diehard on the House of Lords, was better qualified ideologically than Long, ancestrally Tory but in favour neither of food taxes nor last ditch resistance in the Lords.

In the event, the Conservatives chose neither as leader in the House of Commons. Bonar Law was elected because the personal antipathy between Chamberlain and Long offered no prospect of the unified support which the Conservative party should give its leader. Neither Chamberlain nor Long, it seems, wanted the leadership strongly enough to secure it at the expense of faction. What was adventitious was later rationalised to prove that it was for the good of the Conservative party and the good of Britain that the arcane rule of the Cecils should have come to an end, that a Glasgow iron dealer, an unmediated business-man, a middle-class *Scotch* Tory, a Presbyterian and a milk-drinker, should have become leader of the Conservative party in the House of Commons and presumptive Prime Minister.

It is not easy to measure the intensity of Bonar Law's drive to office. It seems that he was a man urged and stiffened by Max Aitken, the young *entrepreneur* who, in the vantage of common Canadian roots (less important in Law as it happened than Scottish and Ulster affinities), had grown in his confidence. Of no Prime Minister can it really be said, as Beaverbrook said of Law, that 'ambition was a word in a dictionary he had never opened'.[2] Nor can much credence be given to what J. S. Sandars, Balfour's private secretary, gathered in November 1911 about a 'boundless ambition untempered by any particularly nice feelings'[3] in one who was so often content to play second fiddle. One of the difficul-ties indeed in assessing Bonar Law as a Conservative leader is the lack, in his career, of a too officious striving, his willingness to work within the station his talents deserved and no more. So often one is discussing those who overshadowed him or seemed to be overtaking him, notably Carson from 1912 to 1914 and in 1916, and Lloyd George from 1917. He was not at all like Lord Derby who, said Haig, 'like the feather pillow bears the marks of the last person who has sat on him'. He was resistant, enduring rather than resilient, even if unusually unobtrusive. The ambition, as Asquith said, was meek. Law was a man always making concessions to the superiorities of others, even, for example, when he led the patriotic Opposition in the early days of the war, deferring persistently to the sensibility, knowledge or breeding of Balfour, Curzon or Derby. The story of Bonar Law as leader of the Conservative party may often seem the story of others.

What Bonar Law brought to the task of leading the Opposition was neither presence nor natural talent. He had been a man technically trained for debate in the Glasgow Parliamentary Debating Association. Westminster did not impress him – as a business assembly it was simply past praying for (he was to have similar views about Asquith's Coalition Cabinet). But he had admired and followed Joseph Chamberlain and after the great defeat of 1906 he had become, in the shrunken but markedly Chamberlainite parliamentary party, the most effective Con-servative expositor of Tariff Reform on the floor of the House.

Competence in expounding economic policy was unusual among the

Tories, most of whom wished to know only enough economics to make a few polemical forays. Bonar Law had directed systematic and informed attack upon the 'disturbed ant-hill' of the Liberal administration, contending, in particular, against that radicalism which had sought to meet increased expenditure on arms and social services not by tariffs but by increased taxation. It was this resolution in face of the bland Liberalism of his cultivated opponents that had cheered all those Conservatives who saw themselves not only as dispossessed of rightful political power but also threatened with material ruin by radical will working out its way behind the effortless superiority of an over-civilised front bench.

There was more stridency in Bonar Law, thought L. S. Amery, than was necessary.[4] But stridency is the tone of voice not only of those who are losing authority but also of those who are seeking it. Fortuitously the Conservatives had acquired in 1911 a leader who would not be inhibited by any traditions of civility from hitting the Liberals hard. Hence the expectations of asperity. 'I am afraid', said Bonar Law, as he walked with Asquith from the opening of the parliamentary session in 1912, 'I shall have to show myself very vicious this session.' But the new style which Law developed in response to expectations could not be so easily turned off. The style inhabited the man and the vehemence which he displayed in and out of Parliament in 1912 and 1913, often exceeding that of Carson, was far from being merely histrionic. *We feign a relish till we find a relish come*. . . .

Bonar Law raised hopes both of articulation and resolution. But while he was both lucid and passionate about tariffs he developed no branching idea. Hewins maintained indeed that Law's views were as narrow as those of an eighteenth-century protectionist manufacturer.[5] Joseph Chamberlain too thought that Law had little grasp of the imperial theme. This is perhaps unfair. Law did have the bones of the matter. He was concerned primarily with security, the legitimate defence of Britain and her Empire by tariffs in a world armed with tariffs, the use of tariffs to pay for social services and reduce unemployment. His mercantilism insisted upon increasing production, augmenting the national wealth in terms of men and goods. Tariff Reform was a means of warding off both socialism and revolution. Admittedly, it was often a negative version, some distance from the social-reforming idealism of L. S. Amery and George Wyndham. But there was an imperial argument.

A single unifying idea even when negatively expressed was, however, more than Toryism and the country could bear. For, within Tariff Reform, imperial preference involved the imposition of food taxes as a first obnoxious step and the cry of 'black bread and horseflesh'; it meant, in fact, splitting the party. For not only were the constituency organisations in the north against Bonar Law on this, but also the great houses of Stanley and Cecil. To the chagrin of Austen Chamberlain, Balfour had already taken the immediate electoral burden off Law's shoulders before the second election of 1910 by promising a referendum on the issue of Tariff Reform when the Conservatives were returned to office. This burden was publicly resumed when, in November 1912, Lansdowne (the leader in the Lords) and Law announced at the Albert Hall the long-hardened intention of repudiating the referendum and inferentially making food taxes policy, with reservations about colonial agreement. But in spite of a speech and torchlight procession in the following month in Max Aitken's constituency in Ashton-under-Lyne, braving out his resolution while at the same time making the reservations more explicit, Bonar Law could not hold the party together on the issue. The pressure of Lord Derby through the Lancashire Conservatives (the most effective pressure he ever exerted in politics) and of Lord Northcliffe's newspapers against food taxes proved irresistible.

Bonar Law backed down in January 1913. The newly chosen leader was saved from resignation only by a suitably worded memorial, initiated by Carson among the back-benchers, which enabled him to retain office by resisting a rare and perilous temptation to impose an ideology and programme upon British Conservatism. Thus there was impressed upon Law from the start that the Conservative party could not easily be the instrument of a single transforming idea. But the design for controlling and diverting the course of trade and industry did not die: it went to ground among the Conservative rank-and-file to emerge to run again with vigour in the deliberations of the Unionist Business Committee during the First World War.

Tariff Reform was abandoned because it seemed that the Conservative party, divided on this issue, could not win the next election on it. And the next election had to be won to preserve, if possible, the unity of the kingdom by resisting Home Rule for Ireland. As Bonar Law saw it, the elections fought by the Liberals in 1910 had lost not only the security which the 1906 election had given them; they had deprived the Government of moral authority to legislate on major matters such as Ireland. Yet not only were the Liberals now being propelled towards such legislation by the Irish Nationalist support without which they could not hold office; they also found themselves, through the limitation of the Lords' veto by the Parliament Act of 1911 to a two-year period, in a position to pass a Home Rule Bill to disembarrass themselves of the whole troublesome business of Ireland by a simple majority in the House of Commons.

The Irish were not, however, one people but potentially two and in 1912–13 Ulster established herself as yet another nation 'rightly struggling to be free' with volunteer defenders, arrangements for a provisional government and, in Craig and Carson, articulate leaders. Craig was very much 'the man on the spot' and Carson, although not himself an Ulsterman and prepared at first merely to use Ulster's recalcitrance as a means of making Home Rule for Ireland impossible, was, if any man was, the legislator of Ulster. Amery implies that Bonar Law was only part of the Unionist Greek chorus to Carson but this is clearly belittling.[6] It was not possible for Bonar Law to be the tribune of Ulster as such. As Conservative leader he was at the outset, through his colleagues, Lansdowne, Long and the Cecils, too close to the Protestant ascendancy in the South which denied the existence of *any* independent Irish nation. He was also well aware of that anti-separatist imperialism within the party (perhaps represented most coherently by Amery) which claimed that growing Irish prosperity and contentment, largely brought about by constructive agrarian legislation, was proving that Union, not Home Rule, was Ireland's last best hope. And while it was true that it was for a self-determined Ulster that both Law and Carson were prepared to settle, it was to Carson that Asquith turned in the 1914 negotiations on the status of Ulster, and it was from Carson, with Law acquiescing, that Asquith received on 9 March 1914 the unequivocal demand of Ulster that she would have nothing less than British rule.

Ulster was nevertheless Bonar Law's *patria* and touched the deepest as well as the harshest chords in his Conservatism; not merely because ancestral voices called but because it seemed to him a piece of the main; even today there is a sense in which Ulster is the exceptional obtrusive element in that 'unprovoked allegiance' which constitutes British patriotism. There can be little doubt that from the moment Bonar Law saw the volunteers paraded on the Balmoral showground in Belfast in April 1912 he identified himself with Ulster. It was then that he became aware of 'the soul of a people' whom he saw as a people betrayed. Ulster was resistant, a redoubt not only in and for Ireland but also against the uncomprehending Liberalism of Asquith and his colleagues. Bonar Law became one with the city that had closed its gates. That was always to be an element in his 'hard' Conservatism.

In the Commons the following month he attacked the Home Rule

Bill as 'the high water mark of Radical statesmanship' and, in imagery
akin to but homelier than Burke's, declared that the Liberal Government was about to 'pull down the house in order to improve the ventila-
tion'. Then in the extraordinary, still vibrant speech at the Unionist
rally at Blenheim in July 1912 he saw the Liberal Government as 'a
revolutionary committee which [had] seized upon despotic power by
fraud' and freed the Conservative and Unionist party from the restraints
that would bind it in an ordinary political struggle, reminding his
audience that there were 'things stronger than parliamentary majorities'.

This is Bonar Law on the marble cliffs: the sober administrator, re-
versing Michels' process, has become agitator. The Parliamentarian, the
leader of His Majesty's Opposition, is now fighting a battle outside
Parliament and dramatising it in military terms; moreover, the man
whose secular mind, according to Austen Chamberlain, had no historical
references at call, seems to stake his all upon what happened on the
Foyle and at the Boyne in 1689–90. Or nearly all, because what he was
to say and keep on saying was that there would be no limit to the Conservative commitment if Ulster were coerced *without* any expression of
British will at election or by referendum. Bonar Law appealed to a real
will of the people defined here and now against the automatic parliamentary majorities that would roll on to extinguish his cause. It was a
Tory foray, commoner than is thought, into populist politics. (By April
1914, even Balfour was seen haranguing a mob of peers, Members of
Parliament and working men from a cart in Hyde Park.)

When Asquith refused to be impressed either by 'the reckless rodo-
montade' of Blenheim or the claim that the constitution had been in
suspension since the Parliament Act and that an election was necessary
before any legislation on Ireland was passed, Law with others, including Balfour and Professor Dicey, explored possibilities within the prerogative powers of the Crown, in particular the royal power to dismiss
ministers and appoint others who would ask for a dissolution of Parliament. Blocked by Asquith's firm advice to the king that such power
could only be used at the risk of the destruction of the monarchy, Law
was in February and March 1914 seriously considering depriving the
Government of the military power it might need to enforce the Home
Rule legislation, now nearing the end of its two-year journey through
Parliament, by inducing the House of Lords to reject the annual
Army Bill. But neither a royal change of advisers nor a denial of arms
to the Government was necessary. Ulster's integrity was saved by the
Incident at the Curragh in March 1914. Whatever provoked this,

Churchillian 'pogrom' or military distaste for Liberal politicians, enough was said and done to persuade uninstructed minds that the Government was plotting to arrest the Ulster leaders, Craig and Carson, to precipitate revolt in Ulster and to use the armed forces to crush it. The army in Ireland found itself deep in melodrama, was disturbed and in fact could not be used. Bonar Law had nothing to do with the Curragh Incident but his rhetoric had helped to make the melodrama possible.

Under what conditions and in what shape Ulster would have been accommodated within the United Kingdom was not determined then, and historians have often speculated about how far Bonar Law was prepared to go between 1912 and 1914. He had abandoned the project of having the Army Bill rejected before the Curragh Incident, and after it he did not relentlessly drive Asquith along his line of least resistance to a point where he must use force against Ulster or resign. It was the unpolitical Milner who entertained plans for precipitating the 'tyrann-ous' parliamentary executive in London into action by bringing the Provisional Government in Ulster into being at the instance of the local magistracy.[7] Like Carson, Law sought a political settlement; but that settlement was no less than the permanent exclusion of the province of Ulster from the provisions of the Irish Home Rule Bill. Bonar Law was capable of drawing back, but who can say that he would have done so in this case where his deepest convictions were engaged? It is simply not possible to project the words of Belfast and Blenheim and say that he would have flinched. Had he taken the offensive in 1914 he would not have held his party together so successfully. It was in defending the besieged city against a government that was ceasing to be 'real' to him that he was at strength, and there is nothing to show that he would not have gone as far as *Ulster* would have taken him.

When the First World War began, Law was the custodian of a still occluded Conservatism – three times rejected at general elections, its organising idea in suspension, and Ulster still unchipped from the marble. But about the war itself the Conservatives could claim to be prescient; they had long urged preparedness against Germany and had long sought to concentrate British power in a threatening world. With office out of reach because of continuing Irish and Labour support for the Liberals, they confined themselves in the early days of the war to stealing what they, rightly or wrongly, suspected to be the weakening will of the Asquith Government.

Bonar Law no longer sought an election. From his reflections later it seems that he considered that a Tory government that obtained office through a war-time general election would inevitably provoke a strong anti-war polemic and that the country might be as deeply divided as during the Boer War. With Britain rapidly generating her own unity and creating the largest volunteer army in history the Tories at the outset could do nothing other than act as a loyal and patriotic Opposition. Liberals might better induce the people to accept the hardships of war. The Tories conceded that the Liberals were the governing party; on them was the onus of performance. The issue that arose was whether the Liberal Government could both match and direct the will engendered under it, the will which took the *patria* to Ypres, Loos and the Somme. Could the Asquiths, Greys, Runcimans and Birrells symbolise the common interest and *organise* victory?

Apart from Lloyd George, Liberal ministers were less disposed than Conservatives to believe that only through a single organising will and rigorous control of trade, industry and manpower, could the war be won. Conservatives with their *prior* awareness of Germany as the enemy, their acute sense of beleaguerment heightened by pre-war imperial self-consciousness, were readier to mobilise the war-state. To the Unionist Business Committee, served by Hewins and his Tariff Commission staff, the war was an opportunity for realising imperial self-sufficiency, gathering in and developing resources of the nation and Empire. They were cheered by Lloyd George's intentions of putting industry into a war posture; to Hewins he seemed a man without prejudices.[8] The question was how long it would take for Asquith, the accepted incumbent, to assume responsibility for directing the war.

That Asquith could provide unity was generally agreed. That he could proffer immediate political settlements for problems which remained obdurately those of inspirational leadership and administrative re-orientation was proved by the alacrity with which, as soon as he was aware of dangerous rifts in Parliament and Cabinet, immediately over the personalities and policies of Churchill and Fisher at the Admiralty, but more significantly over the production of munitions of war, he created the first Coalition in May 1915 by taking the Conservative front-benchers into his ministry. But for Asquith it was primarily a matter of preventing *debate*, of precluding a direct attack on his conduct of the war in Parliament; a matter of reconciling place-seekers, rather than remaking policy – and how patriotically tractable Bonar Law and his colleagues were! It was a means of keeping the ministry predominantly Liberal; a means of avoiding the necessity as Law harshly put it, of lying 'thoroughly' or resigning on the munitions issue; a matter of holding the House, rather than winning the war.

Did Bonar Law, who was content to receive the Colonial Office rather than the Exchequer from Asquith and did not press his claim against Lloyd George for the new Ministry of Munitions for which his business experience uniquely fitted him, really think that the war should be conducted differently? A very long fuse was sparked off in May 1915, and there is little to show that at that time the responsible Bonar Law saw what the Unionist Business Committee and the non-responsible Milner and Oliver outside Parliament saw so clearly – that the State must directly command the nation's resources. Bonar Law knew that the Liberals were on the slide. He sought a coalition as a means of avoiding disruptive debate and the obligation to turn the government out.

Before the war Hewins had considered it a gross outrage that the Conservative front bench should come to the back-benchers for their convictions.[9] Within the Asquith ministry Law was seen as a limited, contained man who gave little hope of organising victory. How could such 'meek' ambition ever be harnessed to power? Little wonder that members of the Unionist Business Committee thought of reaching over old party animosities to couple with their own organising ideas the imagination and drive of Lloyd George. Nor was it surprising that the Unionist War Committee, which came into being in January 1916, grew impatient of Bonar Law's studious loyalty to Asquith, his careful assessment of the *political* practicability of conscription, and thought of Carson as Prime Minister and war leader.

Beaverbrook maintained that Law's weakness was that he did not set a value on himself and live up to it.[10] A politician so conscious of his own limitations could develop no style. In wartime, stylish politicians may tend to go in for grand strategy. Bonar Law, who knew nothing, Lansdowne was to say, of European history and politics, was also profoundly unmilitary. Balfour's experience in foreign and military matters was much more valuable both before and during the war to Asquith's Government than anything that Bonar Law could offer. It was only too easy for Asquith to chip away at the currency of Tory leadership by showing preference, for example, for Curzon's gifts and grandeur over Bonar Law's low-pitched moral persistence. And Curzon (with hardly any following) was only too willing to assume that entry into the Coalition had somehow dissolved the Tory hierarchy. Moreover, Asquith himself was in manners and speech a leader not unacceptable to the other Conservative leading politicians.

Slighted at the outset by Asquith by not even being consulted on the composition of a highly important Cabinet committee on conscription, morally outmanoeuvred by Lloyd George on the deputy leadership of the House and thus robbed of his due as Conservative and Unionist leader, Bonar Law seemed to be cast in too small a mould to command attention. True, on the Dardanelles issue in November 1915, after troubled tergiversation, he stood alone in the Cabinet for evacuation and won. But that was a hidden deed; he did not resign dramatically as did Carson over the fate of Serbia. After the Easter Rebellion, he accepted and urged, with Carson and Balfour, Lloyd George's plan for Home Rule in Ireland but was opposed by Long, Lansdowne, Selborne and his own Diehard rank-and-file. He failed to carry the party at the Carlton Club in July 1916 and the plan was subsequently abandoned.

It was Carson who now seemed to many Conservatives the crescent power, the auguring hope. Throughout 1916 Law had been diminished by his former ally with his strong backing from the Unionist War Committee in Parliament and the Press. Carson was the most vigorous advocate of a small War Cabinet and the exclusion of Asquith from the enterprise of war. It was Carson in whom Lloyd George took the keenest interest as the man with a following with whom he might co-operate in a new political alignment, and it was Carson who drew a significant number of supporters away from Bonar Law by taking a mercantilist Tory line in the debate of November 1916 on the disposal of enemy assets in Nigeria. When Bonar Law, his authority in his party seeping away, his stature among his Conservative colleagues shrinking, caballed in good conscience with both Carson and Lloyd George to design a new directing executive for the war and to secure Asquith's acceptance of it, he seemed destined to play the part of the humble factotum, the barren-spirited Lepidus within the new triumvirate.

It is not difficult to see Bonar Law merely as the locus of pressures, the man acted on, as one who had subordinated himself quite willingly to Asquith, who was scrupulously careful not to be disloyal to him and who only moved against him when his own position became precarious. Badgered by Conservative colleagues, depreciated as an 'amateur' in negotiation, his 'character' doubted, propelled into action by Lloyd George and stiffened by the Italianate Aitken who dogged and diminished his autonomy throughout his career – Bonar Law can be reduced to mere tactile political sense. But it is also common sense. Bonar Law is in fact the path-finder and gate-keeper to the Lloyd George Coalition simply because he never lost his grip on reality. He never lost his touch in assessing the pressures around him whether they came from the Conservative rank-and-file, Lloyd George, Carson or his own colleagues. He was aware, as indeed many were, of Asquith's deficiencies and of Lloyd George's unique potency and his growing authority in the nation; and aware also that his own task was not merely to renew his roots in the Conservative party by energising the war executive, but also to link political authority with forces outside the political *élites*, with the back-benchers, the Press and the public at large.

Whether Asquith was induced to take his first fatal step on 3 December 1916, because Bonar Law did not deliver the precise message from his Conservative colleagues on the reconstruction of the government is a question which will doubtless long continue to be debated; but Asquith himself did not charge Bonar Law with less than honourable conduct.[11] It is not enough to say that Asquith had worn out his *imperium*: that he had to go because of both symbolic and operational inadequacy; that he was presiding over a system of government which owed less and less to his propulsions, the war of 'business as usual' having ended with the Ministry of Munitions, the McKenna Tariffs, the reluctant acceptance of conscription and the Paris Conference Resolutions of 1916 which proposed the continuance of war-time tariff policies into the post-war period. There is still a humanising moral world and in the end Bonar Law had to choose between Lloyd George whom he had distrusted all his political life, and not less since he had seen him at closer quarters from May 1915, and Asquith whom he had come to admire. It was not calculation but sense of responsibility that brought down Asquith and placed a 'statesman-organiser' (Milner's 'charlatan') in office to conduct the patriotic, strident war and, at the same time, usher Toryism out of occlusion.

The removal of Asquith was a singularly conclusive act to which Bonar Law made his singular contribution. The Lloyd George War Cabinet, centre of energy and despatch, contained only one Liberal (Lloyd George). Outside it Conservatives held most of the important administrative posts. The Liberal party was potentially if not formally divided between those who manned and supported the administration and those who did not. The only significant threat to the Coalition now came from the Generals, Haig and Robertson, backed by all – the North-cliffe press, Conservative back-benchers and politicians out of favour – who still defended, for one reason or another, their professional auto-nomy and resisted Lloyd George's attempts to take the direction of the war out of their hands. But this was a problem faced primarily by Lloyd

George and not Bonar Law. It was Lloyd George who fought the issue out and in February 1918 succeeded in replacing Robertson by Sir Henry Wilson as C.I.G.S. Bonar Law's veracity might be challenged along with Lloyd George's in the Maurice Debate of May 1918 but it was Lloyd George, briefed by Colonel Hankey, who made a suitable 'great speech' in the House and re-established the political authority of the Government.

Within his own expertise as Chancellor of the Exchequer, although hardly as expert as McKenna, Bonar Law was firm and orderly. The debts rose, but Britain continued to pay the charges out of revenue and to meet more of the cost of the war out of taxation than any other nation. Nothing could have been firmer than Law's conduct in his battle with Lord Cunliffe, the Governor of the Bank of England, over the advice tendered by Sir Robert Chalmers and J. M. Keynes at the Treasury (Cunliffe demanded their dismissal) and over the disposal of British gold reserves in Canada. Thirty years before its nationalisation, Bonar Law insisted that the Bank of England was the servant of the Treasury, demanding and obtaining from the humiliated Cunliffe a written assurance that he would if necessary resign at the Chancellor's request, and securing in fact his replacement by Sir Brian Cockayne – a little bit of hell and high water which brushed off the hovering intervention of Lloyd George. Some antipathies remained: Churchill, for example, continued to be for Law the man without prudence, without character in politics. The dislike went back a long way, to Churchill's desertion of the Tory party over Tariff Reform, to the Ulster 'pogrom' and the campaigns of Antwerp and Gallipoli. His dismissal from the Admiralty had been a condition of the Conservatives entering the Coalition of 1915, and Law was now angered by Churchill's admission to the administration as Minister of Munitions in July 1917. But this was a widely shared, a *characteristic* Tory antipathy. Bonar Law shared it with Curzon, Derby, Long, Sir George Younger, the Unionist Business Committee and the 1900 Club.

Law's main contribution was as the master of House of Commons business, the raiser of war finance, as manager of the party which provided the engine of the Coalition. For Conservatives had half the posts in the Government and most of the important ones. Conservative appointments were made through him, as were dismissals, and sometimes, as in the case of Hayes Fisher, summarily sacked in 1918 for his inefficiency in preparing the electoral register, he tempered the wind to the shorn lamb. And if from now onwards Bonar Law seemed confined within his administrative duties, the mere lieutenant of the politician whom he had so distrusted but who was now, necessarily, the drummer and the gatherer, it is clear that he never lost his objective view of the political situation. He had his own immunity within the contagion of Lloyd George's craft, will and spirit. There had been a time in 1916 when Law had grimly acknowledged that the Tory party might have to be broken. Now he was aware that, with the Liberals in disarray and with Labour bidding against them, the Conservatives were in a position of great strength and that it was his duty to see that they retained their identity.

It was in this mood that he approached the likelihood of a general election in 1918, conceding in a most interesting letter to Balfour that Lloyd George had a right to realise his acknowledged authority as war leader among an electorate greatly increased by the Representation of the People Act of 1918. At the same time Lloyd George would not be allowed to destroy the Conservative party's solidarity. Rather he would be captured by the party as Joseph Chamberlain had been, 'with this difference – that he would be the leader of it'. 'That would,' he continued, 'I am inclined to think, be not a bad thing for our Party, and a good thing for the nation.'

When he admitted that the Conservative party 'on the old lines [would] never have any future in this country' and that the parties must combine to solve the problems of the post-war world, Bonar Law was renouncing the pre-war battle in which he had established himself. He was, indeed, a Conservative who had never greatly cared about the past. He was the trustee for the organisation of the Conservative party, for its acquired position if not for the whole of its spirit. And in the un-determined future, as he told the party at the Connaught Rooms in November 1918, it seemed that 'the flagbearer of the very principles upon which we should appeal to the country' must be Lloyd George. The Conservatives had made him and were therefore entitled to capitalise upon his renown in every constituency in the country. But the party would remain the fixed point in the political situation, giving no hostages to either the symbolism or the policies of Lloyd George.

The opposition offered by the Labour party and Asquith's Liberals consolidated the Coalition electorally, justifying not only the posture of unity with Lloyd George but also the perfectly sensible allocation of government nominations by 'coupon' between the component parties – arrangements which, despite subsequent Liberal mythology, maximised rather than minimised Liberal support within the Coalition. Extensive social reforms to meet war-engendered expectations were promised by the Coalition and the election was in a sense fought on the right of Lloyd George to put his stamp upon what he had earlier characterised as a 'molten' state of society. But neither at home nor abroad was even his statesmanship to be allowed to operate unhampered. For under popular pressures (quickly reinforced by Northcliffe's newspapers) and through the punitive zeal of followers and colleagues, Lloyd George rapidly disencumbered himself of his Liberalism during the campaign and incurred the liability disabling to his future peace-making at Versailles, of having to go through the motions of demanding un-realistically harsh reparations from defeated Germany.[12] Moreover the election results in December 1918 clearly established the Conservatives with 338 members in the Commons as a governing party in their own right. In no sphere could the future have much plasticity for a Prime Minister whose authority in Parliament rested on the brute votes of a party not his own. Bonar Law proved himself not just a man 'on the coat-tails of genius' but also the man on the anchor. His subordination continued after 1918. While Lloyd George travelled about Europe, 'visibly to all men the greatest man in the world',[13] Bonar Law, as Lord Privy Seal and Leader of the House, looked after the parliamentary arrangements in a Commons in which both business and the professions were more comprehensively represented than ever before.

Law was coolly dismissive of demagogic claims for vast reparations, while fully aware that there were times when passion must run its course. He could be firm with strikers and demonstrators, insisting that he would if necessary invoke state power against industrial militants. But there was no new thought. Nor could it be expected. Behind views periodically congealed the politician may obey new injunctions, listen to insistent voices, do good by stealth. But he cannot, if he is to succeed, run counter to expectations which he has raised. Law was a man for defending matured positions. The assured answer which he gave to Asquith's attack upon the Home Rule Bill of 1920 was that of a man who had been so often through the motions before.

When, worn out and ill, Bonar Law resigned in March 1921, Austen Chamberlain was his inevitable successor. Indeed it was at Austen's installation as leader of the Conservative party in the Commons that Captain Pretyman made his famous assertion that a Conservative leader is not elected but 'evolved'. It might have been added that only through evolution could Austen have reached the top. 'I have a great horror', he wrote to J. C. C. Davidson in the month of his elevation, 'of anything that savours of intrigue or pushfulness on the part of a possible candidate.' For although he had been schooled like the younger Pitt for office he had never had, he confessed in 1917, more ambition than was necessary to make a man stick to his work. Ambition had been fired in the year or two before Balfour's resignation in 1911, and he had 'dreamed like others of being some day head of a ministry that should make some history, domestic and Imperial'. Perhaps he had forgotten that even at that time he had wished that 'there was another Balfour, clearly superior to us'.

Austen Chamberlain had not considered Bonar Law in that category, nor was he ever to consider him so, but he had, because of Long, accepted him as the *tertium quid* and even when deeply disappointed over Law's renunciation of food taxes in 1913, concurred in his continuing as leader. Austen had always been both an exemplar and a fastidious critic of political conduct. He had reproached Balfour for his *politique* on the Parliament Act of 1911 and the Liberals, particularly Churchill, for perpetuating party divisions in wartime by putting the Irish Home Rule legislation on the statute book. A firm believer in muted patriotic opposition, he had refrained from embarrassing the Government in the early months of the war. In the first Coalition he had performed dutifully at the India Office and his resignation in 1917, over the mismanagement of the Mesopotamian campaign, had been a model of ministerial correctness. Out of office, he had kept clear of malcontents and until he became Minister without Portfolio in March 1918 he had solicitously performed useful duties and virtuously conducted a parliamentary campaign against over close links between the Government and the Press.

Yet the politician who had been trained to be the architect of power and plenty through Tariff Reform, never got beyond the stage of *looking like* the man to lead a movement. What for Joseph Chamberlain had been a grand design and a new creative idiom in politics became for the son, dutiful, honourable and receptive to received principles, first, a responsibility to be borne and then, an inescapable oppression. More important indeed than the long echoes of Tariff Reform in Austen, was his sense of symbolising the bridge between the Liberal Unionists and the Conservative Unionists. Long ago in 1903 when his father went out to stump the country on tariffs and imperial preference he had been installed in office as Chancellor of the Exchequer as the token and pledge of a continuing alliance. Always highly responsive to dominant influences, he had taken on the manners of a Tory ('an awful Tory', said Lloyd George, when Austen was elected leader in 1921). In 1911 he had become a member of both the Carlton Club and the Halsbury Club. 'Sure only of this am I,' he had written, 'that we are what we are because others before us and around us were what they were.' He saw himself as a man within a tradition, and Bonar Law as a man without one.

The war nevertheless reinforced his sense that the old party boundaries were obsolete. He had agreed to the Coalition fighting the election of 1918 and by 1920 had come to doubt if one party could ever, on its own, see difficult problems through. He had distrusted Lloyd George, but from 1921 he became convinced that only under his leadership could the old parties keep Labour out of power. From now onwards he is once more a pledge, a bridge between the 'brilliance' (Lloyd George, Churchill, Birkenhead) of the Coalition, the intentions and forays of its unmoored statesmanship, and its stolid and irreplaceable Conservative support.

Ideas about fusing the two main parties had gained wide acceptance among the political *élites*. Conservative ministers, knowing that they had not fought a successful election as a single homogeneous party since 1900, unsure now of winning without Lloyd George and conscious of some obligation to him because of his services in 1918, were prepared to accept him as *de facto* leader. In 1920 Balfour is on record as wanting an amalgamation of Conservative and Coalition Liberal organisations. Bonar Law too had been sympathetic to fusion. To him co-operation with Lloyd George and the Liberal Coalitionists was simply another step in the Tory 'gathering in' – an absorption of a minor dissident party by the major party analogous to the fusion of the Conservatives and Liberal Unionists before 1914. Curzon, for whom, as Beaverbrook said, nothing was irrevocable, vacillated on the issue from 1918 to 1922.[14] So too did Derby. Salvidge, the Liverpool political boss, was much closer to Lloyd George (and Austen) in openly urging a union of Conservatives, moderate Liberals and patriotic Labour against Socialists, extreme Radicals and others.

The Liberal Coalitionist ministers, with the exception of Churchill, were chary of losing their identity. They would only run in harness. But the main impediment to a Fusion party lay in the rank-and-file of the Conservative party in the country. The Conservative conference had shown no enthusiasm for fusion in 1920 and both constituencies and the chief officers in the party were making it clear that they wanted neither Lloyd George nor the hegemony which his electoral appeal would secure. In Parliament too there was resistance from a small and vigorous group of Diehards (hard over Ireland but generally without any real policy) and lesser or outmoded men in the administration.

To retain his ascendancy Lloyd George needed not only a *camarilla* and a *claque* (J. M. Robertson's word for his personal 'followers'),[15] but also a vote in the country. But a party vote is not a vote of followers; rather it is the voluntary demonstration of an involuntary allegiance that has been sustained over a period of time in the light or darkness of a partisan self-consciousness. It was just this allegiance, this partisan habit which the Conservative machine slowly wheeled up against the blatant 'policy-mongering' of the Coalition, against the political pea-cockery of Lloyd George, Churchill and Birkenhead, the aristocratic superiority of Balfour and his mannered deprecation of Tory enthusi-asms, against the 'statesmanship' of Austen Chamberlain.

When Lloyd George and his associates including Austen Chamberlain sought a clarifying election in 1922, the Tory organisation, nationally and locally, refused assent until the Conservative party in conference was consulted. The parliamentary party continued to show no 'willing sub-ordination of the heart' to the Coalition. Conservatives rejected the new dimensions of the constitution and party which would allow them to live in pusillanimity under a kind of presidential leadership. The deepest opposition among their leaders came from Baldwin, walking and moralising in the woods at Aix-les-Bains, from Amery and J. C. C. Davidson, from Lord Salisbury, Gretton and the Diehards. The Tory revolt was a Country revolt against a secular Toryism captured by a Court. Ironically Bonar Law, the man chosen to bring down the Court, was himself, to all appearances, not deeply imbued with the spirit and traditions of the party.

Austen Chamberlain, who had more obviously cultivated his Toryism, might seem the likelier choice but, although (unlike Balfour and Birken-head) he was never disdainful of the tribe, he had little sense of it. When the party elected him in 1921, he had disclaimed habitual allegiances, calling for 'a wider outlook and a broader union than any that can be found within the limits of a single party'. Thus he pledged himself to the Coalition at the very time when his stirring party was losing confidence both in the Coalition and in negotiating with Irish nationalism. As early as June 1921, Salisbury made it clear that the Coalition no longer had the confidence of the Conservatives. At the end of October, Austen's Irish policy was fiercely attacked in the Commons and when next month he went to the Conservative Conference in

Orange Liverpool he was aware that he was fighting for his political life. There he renounced the old Conservative policy on Ireland, which had failed 'because the country would not pursue it consistently through good fortune and through bad', because it had not been a national but a party policy. His victory was overwhelming but he owed much to Salvidge's astuteness in insisting (at the cost of that Ulsterism which had sustained Conservatism in Liverpool for so long) that the issue before the Conference was primarily one of leadership. Moreover the victory seems to have instilled even more deeply in Austen that resolution for Coalition Government which was to commit him to defeat with honour in 1922.

For after the Irish Treaty of December 1921 – exactly the sort of measure that only Coalitions could achieve – he came to concur in Lloyd George's move for a general election which would realign the British party system. True, he defended his own party chairman, Sir George Younger, when in January 1922 he publicly declared, on information provided by Sir Malcolm Fraser, the principal agent of the party, that an immediate election under the Coalition would break the Conservative party. But at the same time Austen privately assured Lloyd George that an election was a matter of timing and preparation and that his 'object [had] been to lead the Unionist party to accept merger in a new party under the lead of the present Prime Minister and including the great bulk of the old Unionists and the old Liberals so as to secure the widest and closest possible union of all men and women of constitutional and progressive views'. The party was lost to Austen's senses in a way that it was not for Bonar Law. Lloyd George's talent and charm had worked once more to enlist the fidelities of a man of greater rigour.

Faced in February by a demand from Colonel Gretton and the Die-hards for a clear assertion of the party's identity, Austen would only concede that at a coming election each of the Coalition parties would campaign under its own manifesto; the intention was still fusion. When Lloyd George, realising that, personally, he was an impediment to a fusion government, acceptable to Conservative ministers but not to rank-and-file, offered to resign and assist a government of national unity, Austen, the soul of rectitude, begged him to stay. In March Austen was still talking about Conservatives and National Liberals as 'the two wings of one great constitutional and progressive party'.

By midsummer Diehards, in the country rather than in Parliament, had come out against the whole range of government policies, foreign and domestic and had elected Salisbury leader of a new 'Conservative and Unionist Movement' which claimed to represent 'deep seated Conservative feeling in the country'. Tory decorum was flouted by honours' scandals (the result of Lloyd George's over-systematic sale of political honours to endow his projected Centre party); Tory resentment was nourished by the murder of Sir Henry Wilson by Irish gunmen (seen as a consequence of Lloyd George's detested Irish settlement). The swelling umbrage alarmed junior Conservative ministers, who insisted on meeting their seniors in August to discuss the future of the party. But neither Austen nor Birkenhead would agree to detaching the party from Lloyd George.

After the failure of the Cannes and Genoa conferences earlier in the year, Lloyd George's diplomatic flair was being widely questioned. When in September British troops found themselves standing in the neutral zone at Chanak between the Gallipoli peninsula and eruptive and retaliatory Turkish nationalism, Tory pro-Turkish sensibilities were fully engaged not only against Lloyd George's gratuitous philhellenism but also against Churchill's untoward zeal to assert the military power of the Empire and keep the Turks out of Europe. War, it is true, was averted at Chanak (not by the politicians but by General Harington, the military commander on the spot) and Curzon, the by-passed Foreign Secretary, subsequently obtained a satisfactory armistice. But at all levels of the Conservative party considerable alarm had been aroused by the scrambled, ill-timed and generally ill-received appeal by the British government to the Dominions for help, the reluctance of European allies to co-operate, indeed their inclination to obstruct, and above all by the rash ministerial ultimatum on 29 September to the Turkish forces, which Harington did not deliver. Austen Chamberlain was clearly flying in the face of common sense when, in these circumstances, with Churchillian chauvinism and Georgian audacity so clearly and damagingly exhibited, he decided with leading colleagues to 'play out his hand' (typically it was not *his* hand) and go to the country with Lloyd George and the Coalition as soon as the crisis would allow.

The crisis made Bonar Law fully visible as the alternative leader. Recovered in health, he had returned to politics a year before and *nolens volens* had become a rallying point for Tory dissidents. Resistant to office, he had remained committed only to the exclusion of Ulster from an all-Ireland Parliament and the preservation of Tory unity. When, alarmed by the ministerial ultimatum to the Turks, he wrote the letter to *The Times*, published on 7 October, in which he maintained that Britain on her own could not police the world, he struck the appropriate note of insular, ingathering Tory prudence, and became the man to break up the Coalition.

In an ungenerous moment Austen was to say that Bonar Law tripped him for the second time. But Austen was in fact betrayed by his own uncritical eclecticism. Against Baldwin (the *moral* obstruction in the Cabinet), against the under-secretaries, against Younger, the chairman, Fraser, the principal agent, Sir Leslie Wilson, the Chief Whip, against a 'stampeding' party, he continued to assert the claims of a broadbottom statesmanship and the necessity for an anti-Socialist coalition, to acquiesce in Lloyd George's emphatic iteration, in contempt of his own Foreign Secretary, of anti-French and anti-Turkish sentiments. With the Conservative party conference only a month away Austen declined to consult it. Only under stiff pressure, on the threat of the repudiation of his leadership, did he agree to submit the matter of an election to a meeting of Conservative M.P.s at the Carlton Club on 19 October. Beyond this the only sanction he would acknowledge was that of the electorate. As he was to say on the day of his defeat, he was turning to those who had 'made me what I am'.

The Carlton Club was Austen's chosen ground. Apart from peers who were in the Government only Members of the Commons would be present and they were more favourably disposed to the continuation of the Coalition than the Lords. He was appealing not to an experienced caucus but to the expected, if infrequently rallied, loyalties within an old parliamentary party. He wanted a decision: an endorsement of his 'declaration of faith'. Those who would not subordinate themselves to statesmanship must have the temerity to say so. But as it happened the meeting mobilised rather than dispersed opposition. The junior ministers continued to urge the acceptance of the responsibility of forming a government by the Conservatives if returned as the strongest party; a resolute head of opinion to the same effect was now raised among eighty Members of Parliament by Samuel Hoare. The Executive Council of the National Union empowered Sir George Younger to call an emergency conference of the National Union if the decision went in favour of the Coalition.

With the fundamentalists, the organisation and the emerging cadres refusing to acknowledge Austen's prerogative, attention remained focused on Bonar Law. He had no rival. It was not only Curzon's peerage that made him unsuitable: chagrin had long made him unreliable and inefficiently Machiavellianand he had stayed too long with the Coalition. Derby, often briefly mooted for brief tenure, was always indisposed to make or take opportunities. Salisbury had been continually resistant but had too narrow a base. Baldwin was still too obscure.

In 1918 Law had told Salvidge that 'we must never let the little man go' and he had repudiated nothing that the Coalition had done up to March 1921. He had endorsed the Irish Treaty of December 1921 although deeply disturbed by what happened subsequently. But by February 1922 he had become aware of stirrings in the party and told Lloyd George that it was impossible that things should go on as they were. He was also convinced that Lloyd George was now ill-advised and out of touch: that he too had become an office-holder casting round for policies that would keep him in office and that like other hard-pressed ministers he might possibly go to war to re-establish himself. Before 1914 Bonar Law's moral power had been asserted against complacent incumbents; now he moved against frenetic ones. All his conduct and words indicate that his acute 'political nostril' (that which Lloyd George maintained Milner never had) sensed the instinct of the party towards self-preservation. He knew that at the Conservative Conference in November the leadership would not hold its position and that against tribal power or as R. T. McKenzie would put it, 'internal party democracy', all the brilliance of the Coalition higher command was likely to prove inadequate.

When Law spoke at the Carlton Club on 19 October and turned the turning scale, there is no need to assume that any of his many visitors on the previous day, not even the 'keen-eyed, cunning and audacious political manipulator' Beaverbrook, had made up his mind for him. Those who sought him out, Austen Chamberlain, Curzon, Baldwin, Davidson, Hoare, Gretton, Salvidge and Beaverbrook represented significant varieties of instructed Conservatism. (The 'hardfaced men', those whom in filial loyalty Randolph Churchill called the 'unlettered, base amalgam of self-made self-seekers', were not over-represented).[16] One of the notable things about Bonar Law was the way in which he had learned to work through and with forces more emphatic than anything he could personally muster, and yet go his own way. There was independence even in his irresolution. One may well wonder how a mind so sparsely furnished as that of Bonar Law, so capable of long meditated decision, could ever be usurped by another. It is an illusion of the gossip-raking historian that someone's advice can be proved crucial when there is in fact a long story to be told.

After Baldwin's memorable attack on the destructive dynamism of

Lloyd George, Bonar Law deliberately dismantled the Coalition by declaring that the unity of the party had priority over the business of winning an election. He acknowledged the power of the party and the party voted itself out of the Coalition. Austen's intention had been to tell the parliamentary party bluntly 'that they must either follow our advice or do without us, in which case they must find their own Chief, and form a Government, *at once*. They would be in a d——d fix'. The party refused, in Balfour's words, to treat its Leader as a leader and acknowledged Bonar Law instead. Thirteen Conservative ministers in the Coalition, including Austen Chamberlain, Balfour and Birkenhead, immediately dissociated themselves from any administration that he might construct. In these circumstances it is understandable that before Law was commissioned as prime minister by George V he should insist on being first elected leader of the party. As such he was Edward Heath's only precursor. The party's identity had been recovered by taking what Davidson called 'a slice off the top'. Nothing more clearly underlined the significance of what had happened than the enormity of the vote of Wilson, the Conservative Chief Whip, against the Conservative leader. Thanks to the rigid loyalty of Austen Chamberlain to Lloyd George, the Conservative parliamentary machine had been caught up in a Conservative *movement*.

A function of the leading politician is to simplify politics for others. What Bonar Law did was to restore the old lineaments of British politics. The election of 1922 was won without a programme; the electorate rid themselves of Lloyd George and his bewildering innovations; the people could achieve coherence without the drummer boy. There were times, said Bonar Law, when it was good to sit still. The old threads were resumed; there was an acknowledgement that 'the growing good of the world is partly dependent upon unhistoric acts'. The departments moved back into their grooves; the Garden Suburb died; the deputations were turned away from Downing Street; junior ministers got promotion and there were seven peers in the Cabinet.

The new government strove to exhibit prudence rather than deeds, but no permanent exclusion of the estranged Conservative men of talent was contemplated – Law said he would like to see Austen Chamberlain and even Birkenhead, his most scathing detractor, back at the first possible opportunity. Business in Cabinet and Parliament was conducted with Law's characteristic efficiency but his was a sober and worried administration. The Irish Free State Bill was duly passed and Curzon had his diplomatic triumph in negotiating peace with the Turks at Lausanne, but the French dues-collection of the Ruhr in January 1923 showed how irreconcilable were French and British attitudes on German reparations and how threadbare the *Entente* had become in default of specific British guarantees of French security.

Within the Cabinet Law's brisk authority was surprisingly challenged on the British repayment of the American debt. The American terms seemed harsh but Baldwin, the new Chancellor of the Exchequer, not only accepted them but made it public that he accepted them as the best likely to be offered. Law, who hoped for a wider inter-Allied debt settlement, was prepared to repudiate both debt and Chancellor and threatened resignation to have his way. But his Cabinet colleagues, some of them bridling under his will and persistence, took sides against him. Virtually isolated and highly unwilling to breach the unity of the following which he had so painfully created, Bonar Law capitulated, contenting himself with a letter to *The Times* signed 'A Colonial' in which he expressed his opposition to the deliberated policy of his own Cabinet. Bruised by this major reverse, gloomy though he duly became about the government's prospects – after four months of office, he conceded that he was 'in a fix' – Bonar Law had in the spring of 1923 wrought better than perhaps he knew. The very survival of his government indicated that it might not be necessary to construct a 'Fusion' or 'Centre' administration in order to meet the challenge of Labour. Even without their 'first class brains' the Tories might be able to re-establish their credentials as a governing party of order.

Bonar Law governed for only 200 days but they were sufficient to secure the succession of Baldwin, his major ally at the Carlton Club and his most effective supporter during the election. Baldwin was still inexperienced and had lost ground through his unfortunate conduct of the American debt negotiations. He was not named as successor when illness forced Law's resignation in May 1923. Nor did Law speak for Curzon. For he had accepted Lord Crewe's assurance that he need not proffer advice and the king did not seek it of him.

One must judge a politician, writes Beaverbrook, not by his vagaries but by what is constant in him in great crises.[17] Is there 'a thing inseparate' in Bonar Law? When he was elected leader in 1911 it was to develop the estate, to preserve the unity of the kingdom, to give the Tories some 'mental starch'. The will hardened over Ulster. It may be that in will he fell short of Carson and Milner, but under him the Right was more powerful and fertile in English politics than it has usually been since.[18] The Conservative *patria* was not achieved in peacetime, but the philosophy of preparation and ingathering became a means of survival in wartime. Nationalist, mercantilist Toryism did not arise effortlessly during the war nor was Bonar Law regarded as its chosen instrument. Amery could not find in him his 'single will, expressing the will of the nation; a thinking, foreseeing, planning mind. . . .'[19] Nor was he F. S. Oliver's man to master the 'mechanicians'.[20] In Hamiltonian terms he was not capable of making his passions interesting to mankind. Impulse did not flow into the deed; there was in Bonar Law little of the Tory urge to govern. When his long impeded party became a governing party it sought a surrogate for Joseph Chamberlain in Lloyd George. It was part of Bonar Law's sagacity that he could recognise 'another power'.

From this unctionless, at times bleak, Conservatism it would not be easy to elicit any distinctive interpretation of the Tory cosmology, any notable contribution to the coherence of the Tory mind. There was in Law no play of the Conservative imagination on history and society; he cultivated no cadence. The service that he rendered the Tory intellect was that of ready argument within set or acquired positions. He began as a self-taught attorney for Tory tariffs but was closer to Peel than Disraeli; like Austen Chamberlain he was a late token of Peel's projected alliance with the mercantile classes. He could not match Peel's impressive grasp of the Conservative task within the total political situation; Law was a sagacious man but he did not make the same long-term accommodations to a changing world. His strength lay in his appreciation of immediate situations. He worked within the given political medium, making the best of incoming business, meeting adversity with fortitude rather than with old Tory 'bottom'. His demeanour was acquired not on the hunting field but in the fluctuations of the Glasgow iron market. These are not Conservative endowments as such but they are appropriate to Conservative politics.

He was an undenominational Tory, not obviously conscious of either ordaining hands or forbears. He acknowledged the Tory hierarchy and worked with it and within it. But he did not seek to legitimate himself in the country houses. From his assumption of the leadership in 1911 he had doubts about his ability to symbolise Toryism and this may be why his Conservatism took on its peculiarly indurate quality (the private man was amiable enough). By the end he was accepted; in 1922 Diehards and aristocrats backed him against other more dramatic self-making men of talent.

Late in life he said that he had cared for only two things in politics:

Tariff Reform and Ulster. The rest had only been a game. But it is the rest which gets the praise: the seamanship among the rocks and shoals; the patient leadership of the patriotic Opposition; the solid underpinning of Lloyd George; the labours at his desk and in Parliament; his part in the making, sustaining and breaking of every government between 1915 and 1922.

# 6 Baldwin 1923-1932

## DONALD SOUTHGATE

SINCE Winston Churchill was in 1924 the beneficiary, and from 1931 the victim, of Stanley Baldwin's political skill, it would be surprising if he did not rate him high as a politician, though, because of the events of 1933-7, low as a statesman. The present study extends to 1932 only, and any deficiencies in the Conservative attitude to defence up to that time must be attributed mainly to Churchill's desire, as Chancellor 1924-9, to combine retrenchment with social reform. Baldwin, speaking in the debate on Churchill's first Budget in 1925, rubbed the point in – he said that Churchill had shown himself a true son of his father, 'a staunch Conservative economist and sound financier'. That a man so comparatively mediocre should be in a position to patronise Churchill (while Lloyd George languished in the wilderness for a variety of reasons, not least of which was Baldwin's denunciation of him) tells us a good deal about the inter-war period, or, at least, about the period 1923-37, when circumstances were such that either Baldwin or the Labour party leader Ramsay MacDonald must be Prime Minister. By the end of 1931 they were working in tandem. Churchill writes, in retrospect, that 'nominally the representatives of opposing parties, of contrary doctrines, of antagonistic interests, they proved in fact to be more nearly akin in outlook, temperament, and method than any other two men who had been Prime Ministers. . . . Stanley Baldwin, apart from a manufacturer's ingrained approval of Protection, was by disposition a truer representative of mild Socialism than many to be found in the Labour ranks.'

Nobody was much interested in Baldwin's opinions until the Carlton Club meeting of 1922. He was almost, if not quite, the most insignificant member of Lloyd George's Coalition Cabinet. But within a year his political posture became of immense importance. Haldane, the former Liberal minister who served in the first Labour Government of 1924, would say of him that he was 'out to develop a democratic conservatism and has a great deal of sympathy with the aspirations of Labour'; MacDonald that 'in all essentials his outlook is very close to ours'.

For Further Reading relevant to this chapter, see page 251.

Baldwin in the twenties was, according to the point of view of the observer, a Walpole without the corruption; a middleman; an intermediary; or – his own word – a 'healer'. He succeeded in maintaining this left-of-centre image even after the General Strike and the subsequent Trade Disputes Bill which colleagues and followers were thought to have forced on him. He had a concern for party interest which was represented to the public in such a way as to yield dividends beyond the standard party appeal because there lay behind it a genuine combination of integrity and concern for the *national* interest as he saw it. This is not to say that Baldwin's insights were always intelligent or right, still less that he was 'a simple soul' who did not calculate his party's interest, sometimes rightly, sometimes wrongly. But his mistakes were apt to be attributed to probity and his successes regarded as a due reward for virtue. He tended to receive from the public and even from many of his opponents the benefit of the doubt, of which there was a good deal. Just how much 'cleverness' lay behind the public façade must remain for ever controversial. His mind was slower and less precise than Bonar Law's, though his personality was warmer. But he gained immense advantage from the new medium of the election broadcast, being a natural 'fireside chatter' while MacDonald was, by contrast, a demagogue more effective in the flesh than broadcast by voice only. It is difficult to discount the public image of the iron-manufacturer as a pig-prodder, because one suspects that even if he had not been party leader heavily dependent on rural votes he would still have prodded pigs. If he was not so vague as P. G. Wodehouse's Lord Emsworth, he seems, despite the unhappiness of his school career, to have preserved public school standards, for he described a Balfour note to the United States as saying 'We will pay you if we must, but you will be cads if you ask us to do so'.

Maurice Cowling, in *The Impact of Labour 1920–4*, identifies three long-term decisions made by the Conservative party in these years – to remove Lloyd George, to take up the role of defender of the social order and to make Labour the chief party of Opposition. With each of these decisions Baldwin was closely identified.

The leading Conservative ministers in Lloyd George's Coalition, and especially Austen Chamberlain, did not believe that the Conservative party alone, without the Lloyd George Liberals, could effectively maintain the social order. They thought that the Unionists were as dependent on the 'National Liberals' as, in Austen's youth – the time of his father's eminence – the Conservatives had been dependent on the Liberal

Unionists. Baldwin was the one member of the Cabinet who agreed with most Conservative M.P.s and the party in the country that Tory prospects were rosy only if the party dissociated itself from Lloyd George. The Great Men – Balfour, Birkenhead, Austen Chamberlain, Robert Horne – thought their party could not win without Lloyd George. Baldwin thought it could not win with him. At Unionist meetings on 10 and 12 October 1922, he found only one Cabinet colleague agreeing with him (though Curzon was doubtful). He expected to be overborne and driven from politics, for Bonar Law was not responding to appeals to resume the leadership of the Conservative party, supported though they were by the Chairman and the Chief Whip. But, discounted by the Great Men, Baldwin became the focus of the Conservative junior ministers who would achieve cabinet rank in a Conservative administration, especially if the Great Men stood aloof. At this time the activities of his former P.P.S. Lloyd-Graeme (later known as Cunliffe-Lister and later still as Lord Swinton), of his friend Davidson and of Samuel Hoare on the back benches were crucial. They contrived an ultimatum which Austen Chamberlain was bound to reject, calling instead a meeting of M.P.s at the Carlton to determine on what terms the party would fight the election.

At this meeting, much depended on Bonar Law, who might either absent himself and leave politics or attend and doom the Lloyd George Coalition. Both he and Austen Chamberlain had been informed on 18 October of the opinion of back-benchers, meeting at Hoare's, that there should be 'independent Conservative action, an independent programme, and an independent leader'. The focus then switched to Baldwin's house, where Amery, for the junior ministers, suggested that they fight the election independently and decide their attitude to the Lloyd George Liberals after the result. Baldwin dismissed this proposal as 'not quite straight' and went to Law to urge his attendance at the Carlton meeting. At that meeting perhaps Baldwin rather than Law settled the issue – aided by the news that in Newport in Monmouthshire a Conservative had headed the poll in a by-election, with Labour second and a Lloyd George Liberal third. (The local Conservative agent reported that this victory was won by working-class votes, while 'the residential districts . . . went to the Liberal.'). Law, indeed, spoke like an acknowledged leader. But Baldwin, speaking before Law, was compelling.* Characteristically, he combined an appeal to self-

* This interpretation of the meeting is not accepted by M. Kinnear in *The Fall of Lloyd George* (1973), who argues that since the vote was 'a collective acknow-

interest – Lloyd George, a dynamic force, having split the Liberal party, was now splitting the Conservative party – with an appeal to morality. He did not merely say that a coalitionist stance was unwise, as Law did when he said he would rather lose the election as a Conservative than win it as a Coalitionist. He said that it was wicked, and that upright men should disassociate themselves from it.

Thus Baldwin represented himself to the public as the moral man. By maintaining this posture he was later, in American parlance, to 'run ahead of his party' and carry candidates in 'on his coat-tails'. In 1922 he became Chancellor of the Exchequer, the beneficiary of his own proposition that first-class characters were better than first-class intellects with defective characters. There was about him an ordinariness which the public seemed to like and a conviction that the nation was sound at heart, on which it congratulated itself. For him, moreover, the nation of the sound at heart included very many Labour supporters. He saw it as his duty, and privilege, to reconcile Labour to constitutional methods, to help it see itself as His Majesty's loyal Opposition and alternative government, thereby defusing its revolutionary potential. The General Strike of 1926 merely confirmed his understanding of his duty – and his assurance that it was feasible. No doubt he would have preferred the struggle to be, as it had been before the war, between Conservative and Liberal, except that in such a struggle the Liberal would perhaps have prevailed. But he had seen in 1918–22 the class war translated into political terms, and his own side not very reputably represented, as he remarked, by men who looked as though they had done well out of the war. He understood that though elections were confused by the pertinacious intervention of Liberals of various kinds the real issue was between Conservative and Labour. That the Liberals under Asquith and Lloyd George in a temporary and deteriorating union should put the first Labour Government in and then put it out,

---

ledgement by the Conservative M.P.s of views they had previously expressed [separately]' it is unlikely, 'even on the face of it' (p. 131), that the speeches turned the tide. But he makes much of the fact that the 'rebels' did not expect to win, and it is therefore strange that he should discount last-minute developments, including the speeches and, perhaps even more important, the reception given them. He may be right in placing virtually all the weight on Austen Chamberlain's ineptitude, rather than the speech of Baldwin and the speech (as distinct from the all-important presence) of Law. He certainly does great service in reminding us that many who voted to fight the election independently did not expect the Conservative party to win an independent majority at the election, and that it was this independent majority (rather than the Carlton vote) which transformed party prospects by making coalition unnecessary.

in the same year (1924) and be caned decisively by the electors, some objecting to the one act and some to the other, delimits the extent of Liberal influence. The election of 1924 left Baldwin with a large majority. But one is bound to ask why, in 1923, within months of succeeding Bonar Law, inheriting an ample majority which could have seen him into 1928, he raised the issue of tariffs, uniting Labour and Liberals against him, uniting for the moment even Asquith and Lloyd George and so, in an appeal to the electorate not supported very enthusiastically by many present and future colleagues, forfeited his majority and became dependent for his return to office on Liberal caprice.

There is, however, a prior question to answer. Why did Baldwin rather than Curzon succeed the dying Law? The answer that Curzon was in the House of Lords will not suffice, since Curzon was seriously considered (as was Halifax, as against Churchill, in 1940). The king's decision in 1923 does not prove that a peer could not then be Prime Minister. It only shows that a peer of prickly character, totally lacking the common touch, was not chosen, perhaps in the last resort because Balfour advised against him. Curzon was, if anything, more repugnant to the Conservative leaders who had stood by the Coalition than Baldwin, whom they merely despised. At the critical moment in 1922 Curzon had betrayed them, and so in 1923 he reaped the harvest of their indignation. There is the more detailed question of whether Bonar Law's secretary, Waterhouse, knew the contents of the memorandum which he handed over for the king and indicated that it substantially represented Law's views, for which the king had asked, but did not, constitutionally need, and which Law formally refused to give. The memorandum was written by Baldwin's confidant, Davidson, and *may* have represented in a more positive way Law's reluctant preference for Baldwin – reluctant because the episode of the American loan negotiations (on which Law had considered resignation) had evoked doubts as to Baldwin's diplomatic skill and because, if there were odds against Curzon recovering the Great Men, 'the lost leaders', there were no odds on Baldwin being able to do so. Hence the way Law may have put it privately at home – 'he was afraid' he would have to say – 'Baldwin'.

The discovery of Bonar Law's mortal cancer before he had had time to address himself to the problem of trying to reunite the Conservative leadership, and the king's decision against Curzon, were mighty strokes of luck for Baldwin who had not entered Parliament until he was forty-one (when he succeeded his father in a county seat); who had not got office till he was fifty; who had had only a few months in Lloyd George's Cabinet – but enough to convince him that it was tainted by corruption and that its continuance contained, perhaps, a threat of revolution. No study of Baldwin can pass muster which does not recognise his war-induced belief that there ought to be 'a better world'; that he contri-buted, anonymously, getting on for £¼ million of his war profits to the Exchequer, and was pained that so few followed his example in paying conscience-money; that he believed, despite the industrial turbulence of the late war and post-war years, that a sense of brotherhood might prevail and Britain once again give an example to the world. For this to happen 'a great historic party must capture enough of these new voters to become supreme in the State' and Labour get no majority 'before they had time to gain the experience common to the older parties', so that the Socialist extremists of the rank and file did not cause 'such experiments on an ancient Constitution and an industrial system such as would soon have brought about its ruin'. That his own industrial experience was of an out-of-date paternalistic family firm kind he rather emphasised than disguised, calling for a survival of the old spirit despite the new concentrations of organised capital and labour. 'I want to be a healer', he said; his followers were exhorted to beat off the class war 'by the hardness of your heads and the largeness of your hearts' (Edinburgh, July 1923). Labour had a genuine concern to lift up the masses, and the Conservatives 'though the first to offer a serious contribution to the amelioration of . . . the working classes . . . had lagged behind since Disraeli died'. Both sides in industry ought to think more of their duties than their rights. As Leader of the Opposition he told his party in February 1924 that 'the sordid and miserable experience of the war years had left people peculiarly open to the presentation of ideals; and it is perfectly useless, in any war, to think that you can secure the support of the nation unless your appeal is not only to their head but to their heart'. It was important that he did not belong, like the Cecils and Cavendishes, Balfour and Curzon, to the aristocracy, remote from the problems of industry and trade (though not from the agricultural depression which in 1923 hit Tory strength in county seats), yet, unlike Law, had a deep (and well-advertised) appreciation of the English heritage and countryside. It was important that he had not Birkenhead's kind of cleverness, which provoked mis-trust. It was important that he was an industrialist who sincerely con-demned speculation and exploitation. If some colleagues felt a solidarity with the mine-owners and no common feeling with moderate trade union leaders, Baldwin was not like them. There was an integrity here which the electorate acknowledged quite early. In November 1923 the party organisers, arguing that the return of Birkenhead to the fold before the election was inopportune, told Baldwin that his good name and high reputation were one of the greatest assets with the non-party electorate. It is hardly too much to claim that Baldwin avoided deposition after he lost the 1923 election because Balfour recognised this as an important political fact.

That Baldwin, describing himself as 'not a clever man' and knowing nothing of political tactics (a description heartily endorsed by the Great Men) and an honest man – 'I am not a man to play with a pledge' – should advocate Protection and Imperial Preference at the first party conference rally he addressed as leader (October 1923) is not remarkable. An ironmaster whose firm had been hit by the McKinley tariff in the United States in the 1890s, he had always leaned to Protection. And as foreign competitors heaped tariff on tariff, bounty on bounty, subsidy on subsidy, in the last resort indulging in 'dumping', Protection could seem not an old-fashioned cause politically doomed, but a natural and up-to-date defence against economic aggression. It had handicapped Joseph Chamberlain that his advocacy of 'tariff reform' had been more intended to strengthen imperial connections than to help the British worker. This Baldwin, with Chamberlain's youngest son Neville at the Exchequer and working to reconcile Baldwin with Austen, with Joseph Chamberlain's intellectual and persistent acolyte Leopold Amery in his Cabinet, with the protectionist Lloyd-Graeme at the Board of Trade, all reinforcing the message of Joseph Chamberlain's 'expert', Professor Hewins, could reasonably think no longer the case. The tormented British lion should, because tormented – the torment represented itself in the dole queues – not merely swish its tail but growl. The imperial element in the policy was no longer altruistic, or a bid for long-term benefits; it was realistic, and a bid for short-term benefits. There were also two political points. Protection was likely to recover for the party both Austen Chamberlain and Birkenhead. And if Baldwin did not go for Protection, that dangerous opportunist, Lloyd George, might, on his return from his American tour, do so, thus realigning the Great Men with him and posing for the majority of active Conservatives, who were protectionist, problems of allegiance only less dreadful than those of the minority, represented especially by the Cecils, who were really still Free Traders but most censorious of Lloyd George's style of government and of politics. The prospect of

losing protectionist supporters to Lloyd George and free trade supporters to Asquith or Grey was not one which an insecure Conservative
leader could face with equanimity, especially as he himself believed in
tariffs. And so Baldwin decided that, at the Plymouth rally, he would
ask for an election on tariffs. But at Plymouth he did no such thing. He
declared, indeed, that unemployment was the crucial problem, and that
it could not be fought without Protection, but he said that he had come
to this conclusion 'for himself' and he did not announce an immediate
election. What he had meant to be a brave challenge became a tentative
feeler and it was three weeks before he asked the king for a dissolution.
The explanation is that he knew a great deal about political tactics,
though professing that he did not. He found that, if he gained Austen
Chamberlain and Birkenhead, he might lose the Cecils (Salisbury and
Lord Robert), Devonshire and Derby, whose defection would be fatal
in Lancashire, the Tories' main working-class area. He found also that
there were only four whole-hearted Protectionists in his cabinet, two of
whom, Amery and Lloyd-Graeme, were against a precipitate election.
He therefore agreed, firstly, that there should be no call for an immediate election; that there should be no taxes on meat or wheat, and
even, in effect, that tariffs should be for revenue only. He thus forfeited the advantages, if avoiding some of the disadvantages, of a
protectionist programme. He adopted a policy of 'educating his party',
the majority of whose members did not need any tuition. And yet he
was compelled by the speeches of Neville Chamberlain at the overflow
meeting at Plymouth, and of Austen Chamberlain at Birmingham the
week after, to call an election. On 13 November, the very day Asquith
and Lloyd George agreed to run in double harness as Free Trade
Liberals, the Cabinet was told there would be an immediate election –
by 'the arbitrary fiat of one weak and ignorant man', exclaimed Curzon
angrily. The result was electoral defeat, and it is altogether probable
that the disturbing effect of a programme of industrial protection (on
which various leaders spoke with differing emphasis and confidence),
especially in Lancashire, unaccompanied by any firm prospects of help
for agriculture, caused it. Evidently it was thought so, for, out of office,
the party returned substantially to Bonar Law's position. It would
fight the next election on an assurance to the electorate that it would
not implement the policy in which it professed to believe, and thus save
the country from the party of the capital levy which the defeat of 1923
put in office though not in power.

The first Labour Government was not a necessary result of the 1923 election, for the Conservatives remained the largest party in the House of Commons, and Birkenhead, incurably coalitionist, named four Unionists including Baldwin and two Liberals, not including Lloyd George, under whom a fusionist ministry might be formed to resist fundamental changes ruinous to the industrial, social and economic constitution of the country, and to prevent a Labour Budget which, Derby said, would destroy everybody with anything to lose and attract all with nothing to lose. Regarding Baldwin as discredited, Birkenhead and Austen Chamberlain apparently expected the latter to become Prime Minister, with the goodwill of Asquith, on the recommendation of Balfour. But Balfour saw, and told the king, that Baldwin was more popular with the electorate than any alternative. The Cabinet decided, as the king wished, to meet the new Parliament. The onus for putting Labour in would lie with Asquith and the idea of a Conservative–Liberal coalition, which would certainly have split the Conservative party (and probably also the Liberal party) was laid to rest. Asquith duly opted for a Labour Government, perhaps hoping that office would split the Labour party. He carefully recorded an opinion, much cited by political scientists and constitutional historians, that if a minority government were defeated and advised a dissolution, the king did not have to accept its advice. He did not understand that MacDonald was more eager to sweep the Liberals out of the way than to achieve great reforms with their aid. Essentially Baldwin and MacDonald wanted the same political alignment – competition for power between Tory and Labour. The Prime Minister and the Leader of the Opposition had their way when, following parliamentary defeat by temporary Conservative–Liberal conjunction, an election was fought late in 1924, the king deeming it important to the Crown and Constitution not to seem, by refusing a dissolution, hostile to Labour. Labour lost seats, but increased its vote, as a quite creditable record in office indicated that it should. The Conservatives, led by Baldwin, achieved a majority of a size unrivalled except by Lord Salisbury. The Liberals were reduced to forty. It was still possible that after a future election they would hold the balance, as they did in 1929, but to the relief equally of Baldwin and MacDonald they no longer constituted an alternative government. Thus was consummated a revolution in British politics.

Characteristically, Austen Chamberlain had been proved wrong yet again. Early in 1924 he expected the Conservatives to be in opposition for the rest of his working life. By the end of the year he was Foreign Secretary in the second Baldwin Government. His perennial pessimism about his party's prospects in the new post-war world, unless there was a coalition with some or all the main Liberal leaders, was in itself cause enough for preferring the more optimistic Baldwin as leader. While Austen Chamberlain hankered after a revival of the first wartime Coalition, or the second, and thought in terms of his relations with Asquith, with Grey and with Lloyd George, Baldwin, though bound at times to consider coalition with Asquith, ploughed a straight furrow. He believed his party could win, though perhaps not on the terms it would have preferred, in straight competition with Labour, not the least of its assets being his own image of moderation and conciliation, effective among former Liberal and potential Labour voters. Austen Chamberlain wanted to negotiate with Liberal leaders; Baldwin preferred to attract Liberal voters. Neither operation was very acceptable to Conservatives of strong views, whether Diehard like Salisbury's, or protectionist-imperialist like Amery's. But the Baldwin theme offered party victory and party unity, instead of party schism and party defeat. At the end of 1924 party victory was followed by party unity, with the inclusion in Baldwin's Government of Austen and Birkenhead and the surprising, but astute, inclusion also, at the Exchequer, of Winston Churchill, whose by-election fight for the Abbey division of Westminster, so narrowly unsuccessful, had exposed divisions in the Conservative leadership (March 1924). Churchill's inclusion, in that key office, was an indication that Baldwin would keep his word not to introduce a protectionist system until the electorate had endorsed it. Very soon Churchill and Neville Chamberlain, at the Ministry of Health, were considering how, together, within the existing fiscal system, they could make the second Baldwin Government famous for its social reforms. For Neville had a great programme of reform of the social services and the modernisation of local government, and Churchill was anxious to represent the achievements of the Conservative administration, in which he had so unexpectedly been given a major role, as both an extrapolation of his father's principles and a continuation of the process of building the Welfare State which he with Lloyd George had begun before the war.

Baldwin's capacity to accommodate both these reforming themes under a Conservative umbrella was not the least of his achievements. To start off with the innovation of widows' pensions and end with rating relief for industry was to proclaim a Tory attachment to the interests of the depressed. To keep the essentially Free Trade Liberal Churchill and the essentially Protectionist Tory, Neville Chamberlain, in double harness for nearly five years, was no mean achievement either. It indicated that, as well as the most obscurantist and narrow-minded people, Baldwin had gathered under his banner the most progressive Tories and some of the progressive Liberals of the pre-war era. He had fought the election of 1924 partly in a low key, urging in his election broadcast 'a sane commonsense government' and declaring that 'no gospel founded on hate will ever be the gospel of our people'. He had fought it partly in a shrill key. Even before the release by the Foreign Office of the Zinoviev Letters (now known to be an anti-Bolshevik forgery) inciting the armed forces to mutiny, Baldwin said at Southend that Britain should send a message to the Russians 'Hands off England'. His Cabinet appointments after victory reflected the divergent trends within the party. Churchill, Neville Chamberlain and Amery represented the principle of Tory reform, though the first opposed the others on tariffs. Joynson-Hicks and, for all his coalitionist background, Birkenhead, represented the Diehard tradition. Austen Chamberlain, at the Foreign Office, was pro-French, but was balanced by the Cabinet minister representing Britain at Geneva, Lord Robert Cecil, who was so keenly internationalist that he was bound to oppose French diplomatic hegemony in post-war Europe. These appointments were patently made with the intention of preserving an equilibrium. But the very fact that this was so left the onus on Baldwin, for all his notorious inertia, to contrive on many occasions a final decision which either would or would not produce resignations. His tendency was to avoid or postpone decisions, or, if this was not possible, to dress them up as other than they were. The only minister who resigned, 1924-9, on policy grounds was Lord Robert Cecil. He had tolerated the Treaty of Locarno, 1925, because it was not, in form, as Austen Chamberlain would have approved, simply a guarantee to France against Germany, but warned, March 1926, that he could not continue indefinitely as 'a kind of guarantee to supporters of the League . . . unless I am given some means of delivering the goods'. He resigned in August 1927 in criticism of his colleagues' attitude towards American naval claims at a conference which France and Italy both boycotted. The Cabinet attitude was reasonable, but Cecil stood, as Eden was to stand in the thirties, for an internationalist attitude which required more than Baldwin's rhetoric to convince.

We do not have to judge in objective terms the decision to return to the gold standard at the pre-war parity in 1925. It was, of course, a mistake, equivalent to devaluing all other currencies and making British imports cheaper and British exports more expensive. It was a positively anti-protectionist decision taken by a largely protectionist party. But this was, until Keynes wrote *The Economic Consequences of Mr Churchill*, simply not understood. The objective of a return to 'normality' had been established by the Cunliffe Committee at the end of the war. It was endorsed by Snowden, the Labour Chancellor, in 1924. It was advocated not only by Montagu Norman and the directors of the Bank of England, but by the bank chairmen (only McKenna displaying doubts) and by most economists. And so, after Churchill had posed shrewd questions to Sir Otto Niemeyer, which were parried, the fatal decision became virtually inevitable, and to condemn Baldwin for it is to apply over-exacting standards. *Any* government in Britain in the mid-twenties would have made that decision.

Apart from the return to the gold standard, which was hardly an issue, and Locarno, Baldwin was faced in 1925, and eventually simul-taneously, with the question of how many cruisers to build, whether to impose 'safeguarding' duties to protect the steel industry, and whether to risk a general strike on account of the conflict between colliery owners and miners. On the cruisers Baldwin agreed basically with Churchill, who argued that 'to accept these armament increases is to sterilise and paralyse the whole policy of the Government. There will be nothing for the taxpayer and nothing for social reform' – and nothing but electoral defeat at the end. On the other hand – for the ruminating Baldwin there always seemed to be an 'on the other hand' – his dear friend Bridgeman, already indignant that the fleet was denied its own air arm, must not be driven to resign the Admiralty. So there was com-promise. The steel question was difficult. This industry was undoubtedly of national importance and fairly efficient, yet unable to compete with foreign suppliers. It thus met, on full inquiry by the appropriate body, all requirements to entitle to it, under the Government's election programme of 1924, to 'safeguarding' duties against foreign imports. But it was a basic industry, whose costs, like those of coal, entered into many industrial costs, the raising of which would affect the competitive-ness of British industry in general. Churchill, indeed, argued that to accept the case for the protection of steel was to accept the case for a general tariff, something worse to him than the revenue tariff which had been the programme in 1923 (when he was still a Liberal) but not in 1924. As Churchill put it, 'If Amery . . . is allowed to rush the Con-servative party on to the slippery slope of Protection, then friends will be divided and enemies united and all the vultures will gather for the prey'. Baldwin took the hint and announced in December 1925 that though the steel industry had made its case for safeguarding, it would not get it.

Baldwin's treatment of the coal dispute needs to be read in the light of this political decision about steel, which, of course, affected not only owners and investors but workers liable to be laid off. The steel industry could not compete with its overseas rivals although it was deemed efficient. The coal industry, which required protection not by way of tariff, being a raw material traditionally exported, but by way of subsidy, so that it could continue to export its product, was notoriously inefficient. In 1918 Baldwin, in common with many other Conservatives and Liberals, had gone on record in favour of the nationalisation of this basic industry whose industrial disputes had scarred the immediate pre-war period. But that phase had been forgotten. The brief Labour Government of 1924 had been able to beam benignly upon a wage increase which the collieries could afford because the French occupation of the Ruhr had stopped German production. Within months of Baldwin's return to office he found the owners proclaiming, with a good deal of colour, that they could not remain in business without wage-reductions. The Government, via Baldwin himself at the Board of Trade, had abandoned control of the mines in 1921. But it could not maintain an attitude of disinterest when this basic industry so evidently required a massive injection of capital for modernisation, which there was no incentive for private sources to supply and which even in conditions of optimum planning must have taken many years. The British coal industry was a casualty of capitalist disorganisation. Its proud and militant trade union preferred unemployment for some to wage cuts for all, and showed no sign of being impressed by the argument that the cost of living had fallen since 1921 by more than the proposed wage cuts. It was not likely to listen to the owners' arguments when the owners were so stridently demanding the end of the national minimum wage secured in 1921 and longer hours, which required legislation. And a coal lock-out was likely to spread, via the T.U.C., to the whole of industry and transport.

All this Baldwin knew, or ought to have known, when early in 1925 he secured from the Cabinet a free hand to deal with a private member's bill introduced by the Diehard Macquisten to substitute 'contracting in' for 'contracting out' of the political levy by which the trade unions supported the Labour party. At Birmingham on 5 March he said '. . . I plead for disarmament at home . . . I want a truce of God in this country'. On the following day, opposing Macquisten's bill going any further, he developed a plea that both sides in industry should talk with one another, and try to understand rather than fight one another, to learn the way to partnership. He claimed that the Government had won its large majority by creating the impression that the Conservative party stood for peace between the classes, and he ended by saying 'Give Peace in our time, O Lord'. In political terms this was a brilliant performance, an outstanding example of power withheld in the interests of reconciliation between classes. On some its effect was lasting. Baldwin's most recent biographers quote what the Clydesider, Kirkwood, wrote to Baldwin in 1940, that this was one of the few occasions 'in my experience' in which the word was made flesh – 'you made flesh the feelings of us all, that the antagonism, the bitterness, the class rivalry were unworthy, that understanding and amity were possible'.

In this speech Baldwin set himself too high a standard by which to be judged. He evinced a spirit not at all matched by the mine-owners, and on these he did not exert at crucial moments sufficient pressure to avert a lock-out of miners which, via previously agreed motions of solidarity became, in May 1926, to the alarm of the trade union leadership, a 'general strike' caused, in the Cabinet's view, by the T.U.C. and, in the T.U.C.'s view, caused by the Cabinet.

In July 1925, after the miners had placed themselves in the hands of the General Council of the T.U.C., and had been assured of a complete embargo on the movement of coal if they struck, the Baldwin Government suffered a triple defeat. The miners insisted that the Government become a party to the dispute – and it so became, compelling the owners to accept the principle of a minimum wage. After Baldwin had told them that in the interests of national recovery workers must accept wage cuts and that there could be no government subsidy, a subsidy was granted, up to 1 May 1926, estimated at £10–15 million and actually costing £23 million. The Home Secretary, Sir William Joynson-Hicks, declared in his pompous manner that the issue was 'whether England was to be governed by Parliament and the Cabinet, or by a handful of trade union leaders', but within hours (to the horror of the parliamentary Labour leaders) the Prime Minister capitulated. This was a right decision, because the Government was not equipped to counter a strike of the dimensions threatened, especially when public sympathy was not with the mine-owners. But the preparations for meeting such a strike, or worse, if it occurred, were at once put in hand, under the management of the formidably efficient civil servant, John Anderson, and Baldwin gave plain warning. 'I am convinced', he told the House, 'that, if the time should come when the community has to protect itself [against a minority], with the full strength of the Government behind it . . . the response of the community will astonish the forces of anarchy throughout the world.' This was not idle talk, and it was very unwise of the demagogic miners' secretary, Cook, to go about boasting 'we have already beaten . . . the strongest government in modern times'.

The inquiry into the mining industry, presided over by the Liberal politician Herbert Samuel, with four colleagues of whom none represented labour and none had special knowledge of the mining industry, predictably (in contrast to the Sankey Commission soon after the war) repudiated nationalisation of the mines (though not of royalties). It proposed numerous aids to efficiency and numerous aids to welfare and it upheld the principle of a national minimum and advocated no cut in the pay of the lowest paid workers. It urged that the question of hours be left to the miners themselves. But it insisted that there must be wage cuts. This report of March 1926, later described by the miners as 'part of the moral preparation of the Government' for confrontation, the Government said it would accept if the owners and miners did. But the miners rejected wage cuts and the owners a national minimum. Baldwin's most recent biographers consider that it was at this point that Baldwin lost his last chance of avoiding a general strike. What he did was to inform the T.U.C., late on 30 April, that the owners would accept a national minimum involving a 13·3 per cent pay cut and an eight-hour day, thus taking direct issue with Cook and his slogan 'not a penny off the pay, not a second on the day'. Others may think he had a further opportunity on 1–2 May. Many T.U.C. leaders were more than a little alarmed at the prospect of a general strike on which the miners' leaders, as they dispersed to their constituent branches, were relying. The General Council had no doubt that militant feeling forced them on. But a National Union of Railwaymen representative would say at the January 1927 'inquest' that he did not blame the General Council for calling off the strike, but he did blame 'our people who for years made it impossible for the General Council to resist the general strike'. The top trade unionists entered the struggle reluctantly, not knowing whether it would be better to win or to lose. They tried to avoid the confrontation to which their commitment to the miners bound them. They sought out the Prime Minister. Baldwin was not unfriendly, but he did ask them to negotiate on the basis of the Samuel Report, which the miners had rejected and which the conference of trade union executives had backed them in rejecting. A possible peace formula was, however, being considered, but there came a point when the unions' negotiators found 'that the attitude of the Government representatives had entirely changed'. Downing Street broke off negotiations on the ground of the strike notices which the men's leaders had sent out to the unions and the refusal of compositors to set up the *Daily Mail*. The T.U.C. men were handed a statement that the coal dispute could not be settled except on the lines of sincere acceptance of the Samuel Report and that the Government would not negotiate again until the T.U.C. had withdrawn unconditionally the instructions for a General Strike. It being the middle of the night, Baldwin went to bed and the T.U.C. could only hand in to a dormant 10 Downing St a letter expressing surprise and regret at a 'precipitate and calamitous decision'.

Baldwin told J. H. Thomas, the leading trade unionist who sat on the Labour front bench, that the general stoppage would lead to a noxious Trade Disputes Bill and delay Labour's return to office, and he permitted the drafting of a tough measure. He threw in his lot with Churchill, Joynson-Hicks, Neville Chamberlain and Birkenhead. He warned the public that it, and the Government on its behalf, faced not an industrial dispute but 'a challenge to Parliament, and the way to anarchy and ruin'. The T.U.C. later complained that the Government 'ingeniously obscured their position as a third party in the dispute by raising constitutional issues and treating a sympathetic strike on industrial issues as a political movement' so that there could be only alternative results – the capitulation of the Government or the termination of the strike by a process of attrition. The choice was not really so stark. The Government had for months been preparing measures to avoid the necessity of capitulation, but Baldwin at least must have hoped that the miners, as well as the T.U.C., would read the writing on the wall quickly enough to agree to a basis of discussions within a week or so. He was no Diehard, like Joynson-Hicks. He could not, like Churchill, relish war, even when it was civil war. He could be a calculating man, but in such an affair as this not coldly calculating like Neville Chamberlain. None of these colleagues, nor Birkenhead, could have carried conviction even if he had mouthed the same words as Baldwin in Parliament and on the radio during the General Strike. Any of them would have drawn a bitter laugh from strikers or those who, while not helping them, had sympathy with the strikers, and no one on either side would have regarded those words as other than mere rhetoric. Moving the approval of a State of Emergency, Baldwin told the

Commons that 'before long the angel of peace, with healing in his wings, will be among us again'. There spoke a man 'by temperament strongly opposed to the use of force', who genuinely deplored class war, and is alleged once to have said that the Conservatives could not complain of it because they had started it. The Baldwin who broadcast on the Saturday evening, as the strike took its fullest effect, was Baldwin the healer, the Baldwin of the Macquisten debate, and very beguiling. 'I am a man of peace', he said. 'I am longing and working and praying for peace, but I will not surrender . . . the security of the British Constitution. . . . Cannot you trust me to ensure a square deal, to secure even justice between man and man?'

The General Strike ended (the miners' strike continuing for many months until terminated by attrition) with the T.U.C. negotiating with Sir Herbert Samuel and ordering a return to work on the basis of his memorandum which the miners found too odious to accept. When, late on 12 May, the T.U.C. representatives met Baldwin and some of his colleagues to tell him they were calling off the strike, they paid notable tributes to Baldwin's appeal. Not only Pugh and Thomas, but Ernest Bevin, a militant but a realist, testified that the broadcast had 'helped us to rise to the occasion'. In answer to Pugh, Baldwin thanked God and confirmed 'all I have said in the last two paragraphs of my broadcasted message'. He would do all he could 'to ensure a just and lasting settlement' of the mining dispute. To Bevin he said: 'You know my record. You know the object of my policy, and I think you can trust me to consider what has been said. . . . You will want my co-operation, and I shall want yours to make good the damage done to the trade, and try to make this country a little better and a happier place than it has been in recent years. That will be my steady endeavour. . . .'

The trade union leaders had been looking eagerly for a lifeboat when the good ship *Samuel* hove into view. By 10 May they were regarding Samuel's memorandum as 'an equitable basis for negotiations' (on the mines) and the position as 'too grave to justify their being tied to a mere slogan' (Arthur Cook's). They felt that 'a decision must be reached while the unions remained both strong and disciplined', before they lapsed into bankruptcy and loss or morale. So, according to the irate miners, the General Council provisionally accepted wage reductions for a million miners while the latter and some millions of other workers confidently believed them bound to do no such thing; the General Council replied that, in asking for national sympathetic strikes the miners had put their dispute into the hands of the General Council.

When the General Strike was called off, Baldwin, in a broadcast, stressed that it had failed and that the Government had accepted no conditions. This was literally true. The role played by Samuel, though crucial, had been avowedly 'unofficial', and his memorandum, accepted by the General Council, had been rejected by the miners and was never adopted by the Government. From the Government came an ambivalent message, alternating between triumph and magnanimity. Baldwin provided the note of magnanimity. 'Our business is not to triumph over those who have failed,' he said in a broadcast, and the following day he told the House he would not countenance any attack by employers on wages or hours. But that answer was rendered necessary by an official statement of the previous day that His Majesty's Government had neither power nor obligation to compel employers to take back strikers. Many employers took the opportunity to rub noses in the dirt, and, by so doing, increased the number of Labour voters at the next election.

Baldwin had presided over the administration during a nine days' wonder, which exorcised from the body politic a threat which had haunted it for many years. This was the threat that a democratically elected government would be defeated, and the social fabric which it guaraded torn apart, by the employment of a general strike as a revolutionary weapon. The victory in 1926 proved easy, for the T.U.C., far from harbouring revolutionary intent, did not wish a general strike even for industrial purposes, though some, including Bevin, thought the time had come to challenge capitalism on behalf of the working class. The strike was not even general – the miners officially described it as 'limited . . . both in numbers of workers affected, in the object aimed at, and in the time it lasted'. But it destroyed a myth. The last speeches at the T.U.C. 'inquest' in January 1927 were significant. Cramp, of the Railwaymen, said: 'I never believed in a general strike to achieve something positive . . . but at the time of the Memorial Hall Conference the great bulk of the workers of this country did believe in a general strike. . . .' J. R. Clynes, of the General and Municipal Workers, from 1918 to 1922 chairman of the Parliamentary Labour Party, said that 'the general strike was simply the greatest of all instances of not being able to achieve the impossible'. And J. T. Brownlie, an Engineer, said: 'I am not in favour of a general strike in Trade Union matters. I recognised that a general strike on behalf of the miners or anyone else was doomed to fail from the very beginning. . . . The considered opinion of Trade Union leaders on the Continent, as proclaimed for over a score of years, is that a general strike is generally nonsense. . . . We have to build up a strong, powerful political Labour Party on the recognition of the inefficiency of strikes, believing that by capturing the political machine we can redress all our grievances.' At this admission Baldwin was not more pleased than Ramsay MacDonald, Philip Snowden and J. H. Thomas, all to be his colleagues in a 'national' government in 1931. All agreed that political ends should be sought by political means. In calling off the General Strike, Pugh had recognised Baldwin as 'speaking for the general community of citizens as a whole'. The coal dispute had ceased to be merely an industrial dispute both because the issue was, in effect, lower wages or government subsidies, and because the miners had received guarantees of sympathetic strikes adding up, in effect, to a general strike, a 'strike against the Government'. In the face of it the Government stood firm, but in general avoided provocation. Baldwin's moderating instincts kept the armed forces off the scene, except for one very impressive demonstration at the London docks of the power that was held in reserve. His confidant, Davidson, curbed, when possible, the extravagances of Churchill in the *British Gazette*. The B.B.C. was used, marginally but critically, on the Government side, Reith thereby avoiding Government take-over. The Archbishop of Canterbury was kept off the air. Julian Symons, in his study of the General Strike (1957), awards Baldwin very high marks for political skill.

The failure of this enterprise left the Constitution safer and the economy less prone to disruption by strikes. Indeed, it is possible to argue that the bitterness regarded in the thirties and forties as a residue from the General Strike was more due to post-strike victimisation and the Trade Unions and Trade Disputes Act of 1927. This was repealed in 1946 after debates which refought the General Strike and included a confrontation between Bevin (Foreign Secretary in the Labour Government) and John Anderson (until recently his War Cabinet colleague) – while Churchill, Leader of the Opposition, wintered in the South of France. But the lawyer members of the Labour Government, in minimising the effect of the repeal of the 1927 Act, really made the point that the latter might have been very much more rigorous and vindictive than it was – and than, but for Baldwin himself, it probably would have been. Its declaration that certain kinds of 'sympathetic' strike were illegal if the purpose was to coerce the community, and its restriction of the uses of trade union funds for illegal purposes, simply made explicit what the Liberal lawyer Sir John Simon had said, with great effect, during the General Strike, was already the law of the land. Yet at the time the Chairman of the General Council of the T.U.C., George Hicks, himself a moderate, described the 1927 bill as intended to 'cripple trade unionism, both industrially and politically', and certainly in 1945 its maintenance was as important, if only symbolically, to active Conservatives as its repeal was to active Labour men. In 1927 – although it could hardly be said that in the General Strike the Labour Opposition in Parliament harried the Government on behalf of the strikers – no Conservative leader could have resisted the Macquisten argument that trade unionists who wished to contribute to Labour party funds should have to make the effort of 'contracting in', rather than that those who did not so wish, or were indifferent, should have to 'contract out'. Such a law, however, clashed with the objective of having all seats contested by Conservatives and Labour, with the Liberals squeezed between the millstones. MacDonald, in conversation with C. P. Scott of *The Manchester Guardian*, in July 1927, was very gloomy. He expected an election within fifteen months and reckoned that the new Act would absolutely cripple Labour's resources for a couple of years.

In the event, although by-elections warned him that he was unlikely to control the next House of Commons, Baldwin allowed the 1924 parliament to run almost the whole of its statutory five-year course. The new House would be the first elected by adult suffrage. The matter of equal rights for men and women came to the Cabinet as one virtually decided already (April 1927), for Baldwin had been sitting beside Joynson-Hicks in the House when the latter ('incontinently' as Churchill complained) sold the pass. Birkenhead and Neville Chamberlain, as well as Churchill, were against what was called 'the flapper vote', but the view that it was foolish to give the vote to 'the flappers' – because their view of the puritanical Home Secretary, Joynson-Hicks, was that immortalised by A. P. Herbert – is surely superficial. There were enfranchised in 1928, with them, all women over thirty who were not ratepayers or the wives of ratepayers. All evidence suggests that woman suffrage has, on the whole, assisted the Conservative party, and it is difficult to believe that even in 1929 its effect can have been worse than neutral.

There were matters other than the abolition of sex discrimination in voting which the Cabinet found, in effect, decided before the subject appeared on its agenda. It was so with the partial derating of industry. Baldwin was often inert and seemed nearly always casual. His failure to circularise the Cabinet or to write letters to his colleagues (and to take copies of what he did write) drove his official biographer to bitter lament. But he was accessible to colleagues, in a way that MacDonald, for instance, was not. Outside the hours – usually the afternoon – when he shut himself in the cabinet room to sleep, or read novels, or write non-political letters, he was always ready for a chat. Often, however, the chat was unrewarding. For the colleague who sought him out was apt to want something done, and that something would probably be controversial. And Conservative Chief Whips are apt to prophesy dissidence when anything controversial is contemplated. Baldwin was always not only moderate but proud of the comprehensiveness of his party and hopeful of its capacity to appeal to a new generation. He strove to remain on good terms with impatient young M.P.s at whom the Whips looked askance. He positively rejected certain contentious proposals which would have been widely favoured in the party, such as that of Neville Chamberlain and Cunliffe-Lister to include in the 1927 Trade Union Bill compulsory reference of industrial disputes to arbitration. But he showed also something of Lord Salisbury's proneness to shy away from reforms which might alienate the faithful, simply *because* they might alienate the faithful. He did not always occupy the left of centre ground which many believe the proper stance for a Conservative leader, from which he can appeal with effect to wavering, floating or even presumptively hostile electors and new voters, ignoring the groans of the 'faithful' on the grounds that these have no alternative political home. So, in May 1927, he assented, if reluctantly, to Joynson-Hick's raid on the Communist premises of Arcos, in Moorgate, while Neville Chamberlain, who had recently threatened resignation, waited in vain for approval of his plans for local government reform, which would inevitably disturb the faithful.

The Arcos raid did not yield the police the documents they sought, though it provided enough to explain, and perhaps justify, a breach of official relations with the Soviet Union. It was a concession to the Right which might appropriately have been balanced by approval of the plans of Neville Chamberlain and Winston Churchill to overhaul both the structure of local government and the basis of local government finance. But Baldwin hesitated, until at the end of the year Churchill, in a release of pent-up energy provoked by a natural antipathy to doing nothing and a conscious desire that the Government retain the initiative in the political battle, demanded 'a large new constructive measure'. Let him, by army retrenchment and the taxation of petroleum, find £30 million, and he would demolish 'all the petty interests which have obstructed block grants and rating reform', stimulate industry, reconcile manufacturers to the latest Factory Act, placate agriculture and astonish and gratify all ratepayers. The Chancellor even suggested a departure from the system of rating real property only, which, ludicrously, survives. Baldwin rather liked this grandiose scheme, which Neville Chamberlain, jealous of Churchill's influence, labelled 'fantastic'. Everything was held up until after the bill based on the Blanesborough Report, aimed at maintaining the insurance principle in unemployment relief by segregating it from the dole, emphasised the meaner side of the Conservative coin. But with Baldwin's help Churchill did carry, against Chamberlain, a substantial derating of industry. Here the support of Cunliffe-Lister was important. For Churchill's reforms, which may be described with some meaning as of Asquithian Liberal vintage in their attention to the redistribution of burdens and benefits as the principal form of government intervention in the economy, were meant as an alternative to tariffs. And Baldwin had sometimes to refuse Churchill what *he* wanted because he was at the same time engaged in fighting off what Amery, Joynson-Hicks, Neville Chamberlain and Cunliffe-Lister wanted – namely an appeal to the electorate on tariffs or a sustained campaign of public education as a prelude to such an election. There was, in fact, refought in Baldwin's Cabinet from 1927–9, if only intermittently, the battle that had convulsed the Conservative Government in 1903–5. Baldwin's natural inertia and common prudence combined to ensure that there be no victors and no vanquished – and no resignations on the issue. Baldwin avoided major changes in the Cabinet like the plague, lest the equilibrium among embattled colleagues *seem* to be altered. It was the personal decision of Hogg to go to the Woolsack as Lord Hailsham which made Neville Chamberlain Baldwin's heir-presumptive.

Just as Churchill demanded for 1928 'a large new constructive measure', so Amery, Colonial Secretary and the first Dominions Secretary, who was perhaps more clearly than Austen Chamberlain, or Neville, the executor of Joseph Chamberlain's political testament, urged that the supreme task of government was the reconstruction of the whole basis of the country's industrial and financial system. He meant, of course, unlike Labour, a comprehensive system of tariffs and imperial preference. This Tory intellectual, condemned or disparaged as a one-track mind by people who condemned Churchill for opportunism, had all the gifts that Churchill lacked, and failed to reach a due eminence because he lacked the gifts which Churchill had – the gift of tongues and a romantic imagination. He could be a 'bonny fighter' on a political platform, but not usually effective in the House of Commons – except in the 1940 speech which helped bring down Neville Chamberlain and make Churchill Prime Minister! In the second Baldwin Government he was, so far as the public and Parliament were concerned, muzzled by the offices he held, which made him *ex officio* a special pleader, and in the Cabinet he was restrained by his sense of the need for party unity. Baldwin would have nothing to do with his project for making Churchill responsible for defence, Amery taking the Treasury and Neville Chamberlain the Board of Trade. Was this not a transparent device for converting Churchill into a 'spending' minister coming to Amery for money raised by a tariff?

By his 1924 appointments – of which the crucial one, that of Churchill, seems to have been made on the spur of the moment – Baldwin had, in effect, constituted himself the honest broker between colleagues of widely differing political outlook. And as such he acted. The Protectionists would have tried, by their tariffs, to underpin the traditional Industrial Revolution trades, in which in 1928 employment was still falling off while that in newer forms of industry grew. Himself an ironmaster, Baldwin took the view that the old basic industries must sustain themselves by their own endeavours. He was not being hypocritical when he wrote to the candidate for Howdenshire that 'the coal industry – like other industries – must stand on its own feet'. These industries were helped only by derating. This harsh attitude, a refusal to sustain 'lame ducks', had by 1929 an economically healthy effect; the cotton and steel industries got the message and prepared radical schemes of reorganisation and modification. But the message was not one which made masters and men and shareholders enamoured of the Conservative government. It was a characteristically uninhibited speech by Joynson-Hicks at Broadlands in July 1928 which led to crucial discussions and cautious conclusions based on compromise, or on what Baldwin, answering a sarcastic Labour query as to which minister spoke for the Government on this issue, called 'the many-sidedness of truth'. Even Amery agreed that the party should not stand for food taxes; even Churchill agreed that 'safeguarding' action might be less restricted. So Baldwin was able to write to the Chief Whip that there would be no general tariff or food taxes but that no trade would be excluded from claims for safeguarding.

Here was a team run on loose rein by a man aware that there were many directions in which it could not go without a nasty spill. This negativeness, represented as an honest refusal to turn off the straight and narrow way, led naturally to the election slogan of 1929 'Safety First'. The second Baldwin Government had some real achievements to its credit – in foreign affairs, before Austen Chamberlain's illness; in imperial affairs, with the endorsement by the Imperial Conference of 1926 of Balfour's formula recognising in effect the independence of the Dominions in the same breath as their interdependence with Britain, and their equality of status, though not of function, with Britain; even in Irish affairs, where the abandonment of the Boundary Commission intended to alter the border constituted a *de facto* recognition of Northern Ireland as part of the United Kingdom by the Free State government. Neville Chamberlain at the Ministry of Health earned the reputation of a social reformer as well as a local government reformer and, on the theory that every addition to the housing stock must relieve the badly housed, stimulated impressively private house-building. Baldwin was much taken by the notion of 'a property-owning democracy' as a safeguard against Socialism and in itself healthy, though he wished Neville would not display so monotonously his icy contempt for the Labour party while Baldwin himself, armed with the basic facts from Dod's *Parliamentary Companion* was chatting up trade union M.P.s in the tea room and disarming the wild Clydesiders by a friendliness which he contrived to make unpatronising. Chamberlain's mammoth Local Government Act, which became law in March 1929, was a reform on the scale of Balfour's Education Act. Its passage – which delayed the election beyond what Davidson at Central Office deemed the optimum time – was a masterpiece of parliamentary skill. But it affronted old friends, whose locally prestigious offices were destroyed by the reform of the local government structure, and its financial provisions were distorted by Churchill's insistence on derating as the best contribution to economic revival consonant with his Free Trade views. Farmland and farm buildings were wholly derated at a cost of £4¾ million – no great help to farmers unable despite low wages to make ends meet. The £17 million of rates conceded to the industrialist by the partial derating of premises (a compromise between Churchill who wanted to give more and Chamberlain who wanted to give less), though applauded by young Tories like Harold Macmillan sitting for industrial constituencies, was, to those industrialists who really needed help to maintain investment and employment, a mere drop in the bucket. Churchill also carried the derating of railways, canals and docks, the £4 million saving to be passed on to the farmer (but also the importer) in the form of lower freight charges on foodstuffs. As these concessions were intended to help investment, employment and the consumer, it was perhaps not unreasonable that a mere £3 million should be added to the central grants in aid of rates. It was certainly a measure of social justice, and a notable Tory social reform, to switch a good deal of the Exchequer contribution to local government from percentage grants (whose principle was 'to him that hath shall be given') to block grants which took account of local *need* and also increased the area of local authority discretion as to expenditure. But the effect of the derating provisions and the change in the basis of grants was to increase the rates of shopkeepers and householders – especially in the more prosperous localities – and the fact that the cost of living had fallen, because of cheap food, did not make the new assessments of rateable value, communicated to the occupier on the eve of the election, popular.

Commentators seem agreed that the 1929 result was no crude confrontation between self-interested sections of the population. Some in secure employment were troubled by the failure of the Baldwin Government to reduce unemployment and abate the fear of it. Labour now became the largest party in the House of Commons (though polling fewer votes than the Conservatives) partly because its manifesto, *Labour and the Nation*, retreated from *Socialism in our Time*; partly because it seemed to care about unemployment and poverty; mainly because Lloyd George, as Liberal leader, cut into the Tory vote rather than into the Labour vote with a series of well-publicised manifestoes culminating in *We Can Conquer Unemployment*. It is worth noting that the second Baldwin Government started the national electricity grid, which the first Labour Government had envisaged. But to expansionist proposals of public expenditure, of the Lloyd George kind, Baldwin would reply with the question whether anyone had £100 million lying idle (even when Davidson, whom he had enlisted to win the election for him, asked that sum for an imperial development programme). Churchill recalled how in 1921 Lloyd George at Gairloch had come down against 'big national schemes of artificial employment'; he insisted that the election be fought on 'sound finance'. The civil servants were put to work to examine Lloyd George's proposals in order to compile an official condemnation of almost everything except London transport development. Baldwin's own election address was a meander.

By fighting five-sixths of the seats Lloyd George put the Baldwin Government out, though with small profit to the Liberals in terms of seats. We may see the effects of the Conservative party's lack of positive appeal and of Liberal intervention in Birmingham, where four Cabinet ministers – the two Chamberlains, Amery and Steel-Maitland (who had been Bonar Law's party chairman from 1911–17 and an unimpressive Minister of Labour since 1924) were up for re-election. Such had been the power of the Chamberlain machine that no non-Unionist had been elected for a Birmingham constituency since 1885, except for a Labour gain by 133 in one of the twelve seats in 1924 in a three-cornered contest. This seat was now, in a three-cornered contest, recovered. In Ladywood, where Neville Chamberlain had beaten the brilliant Labour champion Oswald Mosley by only 77 in 1924, the young Tory Geoffrey Lloyd lost a straight fight by only 11 (Neville Chamberlain having transferred to the lush electoral pasture of Edgbaston). It was now Austen Chamberlain's turn to suffer recounts. He held West Birmingham by a mere 43, while in other straight fights Aston and Duddeston fell to Labour, the former won by Mosley's apprentice John Strachey. But Labour also had three gains in seats now contested by Liberals, where there was no Liberal in 1924, and two of them were clearly due to Liberal intervention. Steel-Maitland, elected by over 5000 in 1924, lost Erdington by 133, the Liberal polling over 6000.

To Baldwin the 1929 result was a bitter and, apparently, unexpected blow and he resigned at once, saying that he had asked for the trust of the electorate, and it had been denied. But he was not minded to be driven from the party leadership, in effect by Lloyd George. Nor would he, to get Labour out, accept Lloyd George's contemptuous patronage, still less give him, as the price of it, what Churchill (despite his anti-expansionism) and Austen Chamberlain (despite his Protectionism) urged – an electoral reform which would greatly enhance Liberal prospects. He could rely on Amery to argue that it had been bad enough to have a Conservative Government behaving like 'a Whig Coalition', without actually going back to 1922, and to point out that neither party would tolerate a Tory–Liberal compact arranged by their leaders, even though a keen Protectionist like Cunliffe-Lister could see no other course.

To understand the damaging effect of the raucous appeal for 'Empire Free Trade' launched in their newspapers by the megalomaniac Rothermere and by Beaverbrook, a simple-minded zealot for all his cunning and love of intrigue, upon the Conservative party, it must be realised that Amery was alone in the Shadow Cabinet in arguing that mere anti-Socialism could only advance Socialism, and that the Tories must have a dynamic of their own. This dynamic was Joseph Chamberlain's policy of tariffs and imperial preference, to

which the majority of Conservative M.P.s, by their adherence to Sir
Henry Page Croft's Empire Industries Association, indicated their
loyalty. Neville Chamberlain told them that the party's defeat had
liberated it from all negative pledges made before the election. But in
the Shadow Cabinet, after mild expostulation, he accepted Baldwin's
verdict that all members of it were still bound by his pledge of 'No
Protection' in his letter to the Chief Whip of August 1928. With
Davidson in Central Office, Baldwin was even able to insist that all
official candidates, to be worthy of the customary letter of endorsement
and Central Office aid, adopt the leader's stance. The candidate for
Joynson-Hicks's old seat at Twickenham, an Empire Free Trader,
barely scraped in, in August 1929, in the absence of these assets.

Such a degree of 'centralisation', imposed by a leader and a party
chairman who was his crony, affronted traditions of local autonomy,
already breached before the election by Davidson's method of 'cleaning
an Augean stable'. Much that Davidson did needed doing, but it made
enemies. On taking over from F. S. Jackson, he sacked the principal
agent who made it clear that his principal objective was to get rid of
Baldwin because he was a semi-socialist. But the successor he chose was
not respected and *his* successor, Topping, was too pessimistic. It was
necessary to penetrate and break up the scandalous activity of Maundy
Gregory as an honours broker, but a puritanical attitude to patronage
had for many all the attractiveness of a cold douche, forcibly applied.
Derby's son, Lord Stanley, made vice-chairman to supervise organisation, practised an aristocratic insubordination. He opposed Davidson's
efforts to enhance the status of women in party activity, as a result of
which Marjorie Maxse became deputy chief agent and the Countess of
Iveagh, M.P., vice-chairman of the National Union. 'I was not a good
chairman of the party any more than Baldwin was a good party leader,'
Davidson confessed. 'I was not sufficiently narrow in my outlook. I
took the line that the dyed-in-the-wool Tories, although the Praetorian
Guard of the Party, were a wasting asset, and unless we recruited from
the Left and from the young, the Party was doomed.' This attitude was
not general among active party workers, high and low, and agents tended
to reflect the narrow outlook of those upon whose voluntary contributions and services they must rely. A great deal of Conservative history
is concentrated into Lady Londonderry's complaint when an agent in
the north-east was removed without her opinion being asked – 'If you
treat *me* in this very off-hand fashion, I hardly like to contemplate what
occurs elsewhere.' Her husband's forebear had been accustomed to

instruct Disraeli to oppose mines bills and by her social patronage of Ramsay MacDonald she was to get Lord Londonderry into the 'National' Government as the nominee of MacDonald, not Baldwin.

Davidson's establishment of separate directorships of publicity and information at Central Office, and the recruitment to fill them of the rather sinister Joseph Ball (who successfully 'penetrated' Labour's H.Q. through an agent in Odhams' Press) and the able civil servant Patrick Gower, were important. So was the establishment of Ashridge, in memory of Bonar Law (though 'political education' was to some a novel and disturbing idea) and of a research department to brief Opposition speakers by supplying fact and analysis rather than propaganda. This was not successful under Lord Eustace Percy, the donnish ex-President of the Board of Education, who was sufficiently out of touch to believe that people were not interested in the fiscal question over which the party was tearing itself to pieces before his eyes. But in April 1930, it was given over to Neville Chamberlain, moved out of Central Office to Old Queen Street, and made directly responsible to the party leader. From it in future would come blue-prints for action, notably the plan for a general tariff worked out by a committee under Cunliffe-Lister. Soon after being installed at Old Queen Street, Neville Chamberlain, with all the chill that he could bring to a personal interview, was telling Davidson, most loyal of Baldwinites, that it would be 'a tremendous service to Baldwin' if he gave up the chairmanship, which Neville, as a sacrifice, would take on. This must have seemed to Davidson poor reward for the care which he had taken not to allow Baldwin to plunge into naked confrontation with Beaverbrook, and for bringing Neville Chamberlain as much as possible into all negotiations with Beaverbrook. But even Bridgeman, Baldwin's most selfless supporter (who refused the chairmanship which Neville so clearly wanted), agreed that Davidson must go – to save Baldwin. It is not pleasant to record that Baldwin let him go without a public word of gratitude. Davidson says he was hurt by this omission, but later realised that Baldwin was 'playing a deep game'. This is not convincing. Baldwin was, as usual, doing as little as he could for as long as he could, regardless of whom it hurt. It is barely credible that after this Davidson allowed his astute and vivacious wife Mimi, with whom Baldwin had an avuncular relationship, to holiday abroad with the Leader of the Opposition in order that, while tramping the hills, she might bring him up to scratch for the autumn session 1930 by her usual method of straight talk which, as Baldwin reported to her husband, 'hardly leaves a feather on me to preen. She leaves me always . . . with a sense of feebleness, mainly mental, and of general incapacity. . . .'

Baldwin personalised differences of opinion on policy and tactics. He could disarm an Amery with friendliness when the colleague was fuming because Baldwin had let him down, but he could equally evade a policy decision which he ought to have made by a speech of studied irrelevance to policy in which he portrayed himself as an honest, harassed man beset by the wicked and the crooked, whom he genuinely believed to be wicked and crooked. This was a formidably effective technique for hanging on to the leadership. It was the more effective in that it was with the greatest difficulty that he was induced to make a stand at all, instead of just drifting, or even, at times, just fading away. Such inertia, interspersed with oratorical triumph, kindly people called 'playing a deep game'. It certainly made the way of his critics hard. Provided one was not an Amery passionately and intellectually committed to the adoption of a bold policy or a Churchill romantically attached to a concept of the old Indian Empire, it had merit. For divided though the Conservatives were, they made such steady progress in by-elections that Baldwin as early as 31 October 1930 could say to Tom Jones – 'I suppose I must see the party through the next election, change the country over to a protectionist basis, and then clear out.' But the suggestion that this was the path of duty conceals the fact that this avowed Protectionist had to be coerced and cajoled to adopt a Protectionist policy, resenting both the coercion and the cajolery, yet never moving except under pressure. Even his best friends regarded him as an appallingly bad Leader of Opposition. Thus Bridgeman wrote, 5 October 1930: 'This long holiday has rather emphasised S.B.'s attitude of detachment and superiority to the vulgar turmoil of party strife – and he must get out of that frame of mind. Most Conservatives don't want a man who is above the duty and hard fighting – and dislike anyone's posing as being too high-minded for such things. They like and admire his honesty but they don't like the idea of his being "too proud to fight" like President Wilson. . . .' Bridgeman was here referring to fighting the Government. It is always difficult for an ex-Prime Minister of less than Churchillian ebullience or (Harold) Wilsonian egocentricity to attack consistently, with at least apparent sincerity, an administration which is probably doing very much what he himself would have done if still in office. Ramsay MacDonald's inaugural appeal in 1929 that the House of Commons, in the absence of any party majority, regard itself as a 'Council of State' probably struck a chord in Baldwin.

Baldwin, no doubt, remembered the fate of Balfour. The 'B.M.G.' movement, which wearied Balfour into retirement after losing three elections, dividing the party into Diehards and others so that a new leader was required to draw them together, was paralleled, but also telescoped, in 1929–31, with the difference that Baldwin, when at length he decided to 'go', changed his mind and fought back triumphantly. But for nearly two years he was increasingly under pressure to give up and he provides a case study of the vulnerability of a Conservative leader *out of office*.

The first serious challenge came over India, and Baldwin, setting a pattern, met it with an effective speech on 9 November 1929. Davidson wrote to the Viceroy, Edward Wood, Lord Irwin (later Lord Halifax) two days later as follows:

> About three weeks ago those in our Party who regard S.B. as an ineffective, supine Leader, and whose sympathies are clearly Coalition in character, decided to use the India situation to get rid of him for once and all. . . . It is really a desperate thought . . . that our Party contains so many perfect fools. For days it had been obvious that that arch-tactician, the Goat [Lloyd George], was setting the trap. . . . If there had been a Division . . . it would have meant that S.B. and probably two-thirds of the Party would have been brigaded with the Socialists in the one Lobby, and the 'Goat' and his old colleagues in the Coalition, and the Diehards and all S.B's personal enemies would have trooped into the other. . . . S.B. was superb and delivered, I believe, the finest speech that has been heard for many a long day in the House of Commons. . . .

'Empire Free Trade' as a policy was a nonsense; the Dominions and even British-controlled India (protected against Lancashire cottons) would have none of it. But at least it was a cry, and one consonant with majority Tory belief since 1906. Joseph Ball's blood might boil 'to see our B.F.s' lauding Beaverbrook 'for bringing Empire to the front of the political battle, when I know that the sole object of the United Empire Campaign has been to down S.B. . . .' But Baldwin was in danger only because his feet had to be dragged away from the election posture of no Protection, except perhaps safeguarding. Warned by Central Office that he must say something positive to M.P.s and candidates on 5 February 1930, he said they must look at the Empire as an economic unit, with Empire Free Trade as the (ultimate) objective. When Amery publicly deplored Baldwin's negativism, Linlithgow called for his removal from

the Shadow Cabinet but Amery, unwilling to brand himself Beaverbrook's man, was able to avoid the breach for some months. Baldwin
made it clear in private to Beaverbrook that this indulgence of Amery
was personal and exceptional. The Rothermere press called for Beaverbrook to succeed Baldwin and Beaverbrook hailed Rothermere as 'the
greatest trustee of public opinion that we have ever seen in the history
of journalism'. In mid-February the Press Lords launched the United
Empire Party, with a strident manifesto which, because of its oblivious-
ness of Dominion attitudes, Baldwin called dishonest. Soon it was
announced that the new party would attack fifty Conservative seats in
the south of England. Recruitment then slackened and, as Rothermere
became increasingly wild, Beaverbrook became more moderate in a
speech at Gloucester, after which the local Tory member proposed to
him a compromise which Baldwin (accompanied by Cunliffe-Lister)
accepted in talk with Beaverbrook on 3 March. Baldwin announced it
to the Council of the National Union at the Hotel Cecil the following
day. The party would ask the electorate to give it a free hand to negotiate with the Dominions and, if the Dominions asked for food taxes,
there would be, not a second general election to ask for a mandate for
these (as Baldwin had suggested) but a 'yes' or 'no' referendum. This
was all too reminiscent of the last days of Balfour and the early days of
Bonar Law, except that in those days that tactic had indicated retreat
from Tariff Reform. Now it indicated Baldwinian advance. No one was
more relieved than Davidson, whose tactic of avoiding confrontation
with Beaverbrook (even when the Shadow Cabinet wanted one), in
order that Beaverbrook and Rothermere might fall apart, seemed
justified, but who realised how precarious the condition of the party
had been – 'our great machine both in the House of Commons and outside remained intact, but it was very like a pie crust, for the rank and file
of the Party were seething with uncertainty and unrest underneath.'

The Baldwin–Beaverbrook agreement did not last. Beaverbrook was
angered when it was represented as a Baldwin victory and outraged by a
Central Office circular issued on 12 April glossing it as a Baldwin pledge
that 'there will be no food taxes at the General Election and no food
taxes ever without a direct vote of the people' – the more so as a few
days after the agreement he found Neville Chamberlain (put into contact
with him on the urging of Davidson) concurring in the aim of dispensing
with the referendum. The Free Traders in the party (Churchill,
Salisbury, etc), as Beaverbrook complained when repudiating the
referendum on 19 May, were using the referendum not as a spear

but as a shield. Fortified by the recovery of West Fulham by the former member Sir Cyril Cobb (a victim of Liberal intervention in 1929), which was trumpeted as an Empire Free Trade victory although Cobb acknowledged the endorsement of Baldwin and Central Office aid, Beaverbrook objected strongly to such endorsement and aid being given in Nottingham Central to the brilliant barrister, Terence O'Connor. This former Free Trade Conservative accepted the party leader's policy as propounded by Central Office, though he and other 'young Tories' whom Tom Jones found at the Astor house at Cliveden in October (Ormsby-Gore, Walter Elliot, Robert Boothby, Harold Macmillan, Brendan Bracken) in general did not like the spectacle of the party leader running after Beaverbrook. Outside the highest levels all party workers suffered in morale because they did not know what was really going on, as the principal agent, Topping, reported to Davidson on 2 May. Either the difference between Baldwin and Davidson on the one hand and Beaverbrook on the other was a sophisticated 'theological' dispute, a luxury which the party could not afford, or it was a serious matter of policy, which ought to be decided. That so many should be so baffled was in itself an indictment of Central Office, and Davidson's position became untenable. He had, however, the pleasure of hearing, on the same day that his replacement by Neville Chamberlain was announced, 29 May, that O'Connor had greatly increased the Tory majority in Nottingham Central. He had the even greater pleasure of being able to speak out on the day of his retirement, 25 June, 'now that the challenge of Lords Rothermere and Beaverbrook to dominate and destroy the Unionist Party has been taken up by the leader of the Party . . . yesterday'.

This was a reference to Baldwin's speech at Caxton Hall to M.P.s and candidates after Beaverbrook had repudiated the referendum and, aghast at Baldwin speeches which indicated no hope of protection for agriculture, allied himself again with Rothermere, and asked Conservatives to send their subscriptions to him to run Protectionist candidates. Rothermere delivered himself (and Beaverbrook) into Baldwin's hands by a letter to the Birmingham Protectionist, Sir Patrick Hannon, saying that he must know exactly the party policy, receive guarantees that it would be implemented and know half the next Tory Cabinet. This, Baldwin made clear, was a situation familiar to him – it was a variant of the T.U.C. dictation of 1926. He would not bow. At the last election the Lloyd George candidates had smelt; the Rothermere–Beaverbrook candidates would stink. On this theme he prevailed, though only by two to one, against Colonel Gretton and Brigadier-General Sir Henry Page Croft. A majority of those present undoubtedly wanted a Conservative Government with a free hand to introduce Protection (including food taxes) with imperial preference and Empire development, and many attended the great protest organised by the Empire Industries Association in Hyde Park four days later against Snowden's ditching of safeguarding duties. Stimulated by Snowden's assertion that at the forthcoming Imperial Conference the Labour Government would consider neither Protection nor food taxes, Neville Chamberlain, while Baldwin was at Aix hearing home truths from Mimi Davidson, launched what he called 'my unauthorized programme'. From this the referendum was absent. The party should stand for an emergency tariff, a wheat quota, and a free hand to negotiate preferences with the Dominions. This was astute, for the Federation of British Industries was overwhelmingly for Protection with wide imperial preference; the bankers had abandoned the Free Trade ethic which the London merchants had adopted in 1820; the Chambers of Commerce were all for safeguarding, if not more; the Economic Committee of the T.U.C., with Bevin to the fore, carried through the General Council a motion which, in diplomatic language, endorsed imperial preference (and by implication tariffs) and looked for progress at the forthcoming Imperial Conference, progress which Snowden had vetoed in advance. The unfortunate Jimmy Thomas, like MacDonald now resigned to tariffs, but unable to say so, could only alternate silence with rudeness to the Dominions, thus leaving it to the Conservatives to congratulate Canada's Bennett on his proposals for increased duties on foreign goods entering the Empire, which Snowden labelled 'lunatic'.

Baldwin, in mid-October, accepted Chamberlain's policy of more effective imperial preferences and a wheat quota, but glossed it as a demand for a 'free hand'. This would have pleased the Caxton Hall meeting in June, but would not now suffice. Baldwin called another Caxton Hall meeting for the end of October on the day of polling at Paddington South and, as friends like Bridgeman advised, made the leadership, not the policy, the issue. The leader, having 'rubbed the seat of my breeches with cobbler's wax as a precaution', appeared, was acclaimed, made a speech which Gretton, the leader of 'the troops of Midian', acknowledged to be the best he had ever made, declaring 'our fiscal policy is the policy of the free hand and I ask you to endorse it' and went away, amid loud acclaim. Gretton *then* moved that a change of leadership was necessary in the national interest, and various not very articulate people supported him, while Beaverbrook, descried in the body of the hall, was compelled to speak, to a largely hostile audience, to the effect that it was policy, not leadership, that concerned him. However true that was it was in marked contrast to an attack on Baldwin which he had made on behalf of Vice-Admiral Taylor in Paddington. Hailsham, with forensic skill, hammered home, rather against his personal interest (he and Neville Chamberlain were soon to form an alliance for joint control of the party), the argument that if Gretton won every *future* leader of the party would have to dance to the tune of the press plutocrats. Baldwin was upheld by 462 votes to 116. It was a famous victory. Derby, sent for by Baldwin before the meeting, had told him he ought to retire, but now promised full support. Baldwin himself thought the change in circumstances 'miraculous' and found that Beaverbrook, 'beat fair and square', was trying to climb back.

Within two months Baldwin was again in peril. In October Churchill had tried to prevent the proclamation of 'the free hand' by threatening public dissent. Neville Chamberlain thought this might 'yet save Stanley', but the inveterately coalitionist Austen Chamberlain dissuaded Churchill, who promised Amery (himself dropped from the Opposition's Business Committee) that he would 'stick to you with all the loyalty of a leech'. This determination could not stand the strain of Baldwin's speech on India in the House on 26 January 1931, after the Indian princes' acceptance of the principle of a federal India.

The Indian question was whether it was time for 'a great and risky experiment', whether the risks of generosity were less than those of timidity or repression. As Baldwin remarked in March: 'No Party is so divided as mine . . . it ranges from Imperialists of the Second Jubilee [a clear reference to Churchill, who had 'become once more the subaltern of Hussars of '96'] to young advanced Democrats who are all for Irwin's policy. I am for that policy myself.' And so, in January, despite careful coaching by Hoare, he departed from his script and instead of emphasising the safeguards for British, imperial and sectional Indian interests, emphasised advance and generosity to Indian nationalists. Churchill, who had made what Baldwin described as the speech George III would have made on America if he had possessed the eloquence of Edmund Burke, resigned from the Shadow Cabinet. He was never again a colleague of Baldwin in opposition or in office. He resumed his links with Lloyd George, who was illiberal on India. He was close to Salisbury, Free Trader and Diehard, who in June resigned the Tory leadership in the Lords, telling Baldwin 'You and I do not belong to the same school of Conservatism'. And, though an anti-Protectionist, Churchill provided eloquent cover for Protectionist Diehards like Lord Lloyd and Page Croft, whose gut reaction was one of undiscriminating hostility to the winds of change blowing in India as in Egypt, from which the Labour Government had recalled Lloyd in disgrace, making him a Diehard hero. The Lancashire cotton interest hailed Churchill as a saviour. Taking advantage of the fact that any Conservative M.P. could attend the parliamentary India Committee of the party, the Diehards on 9 March carried a motion subversive of Baldwin, though professing to support him. Baldwin published the resolution and made, in the Commons debate of 12 March, yet another 'speech of his life', hailed by Amery as 'full of breadth of vision and courage'. Amery was restored to the Shadow Cabinet.

This speech, in which Baldwin said that if they were not going to change their leader they should not keep making difficulties for him, coincided with the most serious crisis of Baldwin's career as leader of the Conservative party. Despite the Caxton Hall victory, he had failed to inspire confidence as a Protectionist leader. Vice-Admiral Taylor had won Paddington South, and early in 1931 in Islington East, while the Labour and Liberal vote was more than halved, the seat was won not by the official Conservative but by an Empire Crusader fighting her. What then would happen in St George's Westminster, so safe a Conservative seat that (as in Abbey in 1924) an official and an unofficial candidate could fight to the death without risk of the seat being lost? On 28 February the newspapers announced the withdrawal of the official Conservative, Moore-Brabazon, after the nomination of Beaverbrook's candidate. Two days earlier Neville Chamberlain, as party chairman, had received from principal agent Topping a memorandum to the effect that the party would not win an election under Baldwin's leadership. Chamberlain had to be very careful. He above all was well placed to turn Baldwin out; he above all, as the destined successor, was inhibited from striking. But he thought his hour had come. When he showed the Topping letter to Austen, Hailsham, Hoare, Cunliffe-Lister, Bridgeman and the Chief Whip, all agreed that Baldwin must see it, and all but Bridgeman thought Baldwin must go, but Hailsham insisted that no action be taken till after Baldwin's speech at Newton Abbot on 6 March. Neville Chamberlain felt that the news from St George's altered the situation, and on Sunday 1 March sent Cunliffe-Lister to convey the gist to Baldwin and advise him to yield the lead to Chamberlain. Despite the arrival of Davidson and Gower to disparage Topping

as a perennial pessimist, the Baldwins prepared to retire to Worcester-
shire and at lunch Chamberlain was asked to arrange a farewell meeting
between Baldwin and his colleagues the next day. But in the evening
Davidson mobilised Bridgeman, who went to Baldwin and said 'Farewell
be damned'. Davidson had the sweet revenge of posting a letter to
Neville Chamberlain asking him to call next morning to be told that
Baldwin had decided to fight for his position. The front-benchers still
thought his day was done, but after the Indian debate Baldwin broke
the convention by which a party leader did not speak at by-election
meetings and at the Queen's Hall on 17 March in support of Duff
Cooper, who had come forward for St George's, vanquished the Press
Lords with a phrase.

> The papers conducted by Lord Rothermere and Lord Beaverbrook
> are not newspapers in the ordinary acceptance of the term. They are
> engines of propaganda for the constantly changing policies, desires,
> personal wishes, personal likes and personal dislikes of two men.
> What are their methods? Their methods are direct falsehood, mis-
> representation, half-truths, the alteration of the speaker's meaning by
> putting sentences apart from the context, suppression, and editorial
> criticism of speeches which are not reported in the paper. . . . What
> the proprietorship of these papers is aiming at is power, but *power
> without responsibility – the prerogative of the harlot throughout the ages.*
> This contest is not a contest as to who is to lead the party, but as to
> who is to appoint a leader of the party. It is a challenge to the accepted,
> constitutional parliamentary system, and that is why Liberals and
> Socialists alike resent this interference with the liberty of a political
> party, just as much as we do, because it may be their turn tomorrow
> to suffer for what we have to suffer today. . . .

It was not without pleasure that Baldwin received the reluctant
resignation of Neville Chamberlain from the chairmanship of the party.
This had been offered by Austen as part of the move to overturn
Baldwin, the argument being that Neville must give more time to
Parliament. The necessary concession to party feeling on policy took
the form of an exchange of letters between Neville and Beaverbrook
published on 30 March. The party was committed to protect not only
industry but agriculture by whatever means proved most convenient,
and there would, of course, be imperial preference. From the general
congratulation of Neville Chamberlain Baldwin abstained. But, told
by his colleagues that his leadership against the Government must be

more positive, he obliged with an address to the Unionist Working Men's Association at Liverpool. He described the ministry as a cracked and crumbling ruin held up by Lloyd George and remarked that he would as soon have a building in which he was interested underpinned by a stick of dynamite. He said that the first action of a Conservative government would be to introduce an emergency tariff to allow the rationalisation of industry; quotas, import prohibitions and duties would help agriculture and expand home and Dominion wheat.

Thus the bitter debate on policy, during which Baldwin – and others – learned the rarity of true friendship at the top, ended with the loss of Churchill and Salisbury. Remaining colleagues, who had either given Baldwin up for lost or co-operated in attempts to depose him, had developed a real, if often grudging, respect for his gift for words, which at every crisis saved him. But his had been an odd kind of leadership, devoid of initiatives (except on India) and consisting, with regard to tariffs, of mere, and reluctant, responses to the pressure of colleagues, followers and professional bullies. The *merits* of tariffs he had seemed to consider hardly at all, though unemployment mounted to a hideous official average of over 2,500,000 and public insolvency threatened. Perhaps this does no more than confirm Tom Jones's verdict that 'he had no profound faith in political action as a cure for man's miseries'.

Baldwin was probably not much impressed by Keynes's advocacy in March 1931 of tariffs to the tune of £50–£75 million, against which those mutually antagonistic eminences of the London School of Economics, Beveridge and Robbins, mustered academic opinion. For Keynes urged also not only cuts in unemployment benefit but public works, and the leading politicians who had shown interest in his un-orthodox teachings had been Mosley (now leader of the New Party) and Lloyd George, by temperament an activist. Baldwin would be more impressed by the break from Lloyd George and his deputy Samuel of Liberal M.P.s led by Sir John Simon who in June favoured 'some block in the way of the flow of free imports'. By April the official Conservative policy on imports had been settled and stated. By-elections in Gates-head and Manchester Ardwick in June seemed to confirm that Baldwin had merely to sit back and wait for public disillusionment with Labour, with the uneasy Labour–Liberal alliance and with the alleged blessings of Free Trade to waft him back to 10 Downing St either before or after an election. That he would have to wait four years was hidden from everybody, including those colleagues of Ramsay MacDonald who later professed to have foreseen his intention of leaving a Labour ministry (many of whose members he despised) and 'going over to the enemy'. Their claims are weakened by their 'stupefaction' when on 24 August MacDonald told them he intended to help the Liberals and Tories do the unpleasant duty which they shirked. It is no credit to the majority of scholars – including not only Robert McKenzie, with his historical impercipience, but the usually reliable Mowat – that they have adopted, with an astonishing disregard for known facts, the official post-1931 Labour libel on the conduct of MacDonald, Snowden, Thomas and Lord Sankey. With these Labour ministers Baldwin, to his surprise, found himself and three other Conservatives, with two Liberals, serving in an emergency Cabinet of ten formed by MacDonald on 25 August.

Doctrinaire Protectionists, such as Amery, were inclined to ascribe to Baldwin, before and after the event, a *penchant* for that kind of government, because they mistrusted his attitude to their cure-all. But when Baldwin said at Hull on 17 July that in the national interest he would co-operate with anybody of any party he had in mind neither that sort of government nor the sort of emergency that produced it five weeks later. He said that he could not work with anyone except on the basis of guarding the home and developing the Empire market. No doubt he was informed at the end of July that Snowden, the Labour Chancellor, deeply committed to Free Trade, and Neville Chamberlain, the Protectionist, had agreed that, as Parliament dispersed, the latter should declare confidence in the British economy and the former warn that drastic, shocking, economies would be required. In three weeks or so Baldwin and Samuel (who was leading the Liberals while Lloyd George recovered from a serious prostate operation) would have to confer with MacDonald and Snowden on these economies. For the committee set up, on a Liberal motion in February, under the chairman-ship of May ('the man from the Pru'), had just predicted a deficit in the coming year of £120 million (soon enlarged by Snowden to £170 million) and urged expenditure cuts of nearly £100 million. Baldwin left for a leisurely journey to Aix-les-Bains, as in an ordinary summer, on 8 August, but was contacted at Angers on the twelfth by Davidson and induced to return, because the bankers wished to know the attitude of all parties, none having a majority in the Commons. Davidson put to him talk of 'a ministry of all the talents', but the prospective victor of the next general election displayed his usual reluctance to commit him-self to anything. He wanted his holiday, and he did not want to be 'drawn into something'. It was for the Government to make proposals, and then he would see if he could support them, as Clynes and Snowden in mid-August publicly stated the Opposition parties should (thus making it clear that consultations between Government and Oppositions were sought by Labour, not its opponents). In the absence of Baldwin, Neville Chamberlain (with Hoare) and Samuel told ministers on the twentieth that proposals for cuts of nearly £80 million in expenditure were 'bold and courageous', coming from a Labour government, though, after consulting their colleagues, they thought them inadequate. That day the Labour ministers received peremptory dictation from the T.U.C.'s Economic Committee to abandon almost all the proposals, though Passfield (Sidney Webb) commented at the time 'the General Council are pigs' and later, when committed to libellous denunciation of MacDonald, paid tribute to the Prime Minister's 'great patience and ingenuity' in endeavouring to secure an agreed decision from his cabinet.

On the evening of the twentieth Chamberlain telephoned Baldwin to come home. His reception at Victoria Station on the evening of the twenty-second was that accorded to a prospective Prime Minister summoned in a crisis as the saviour of his country. He still, indeed, expected to receive the commission from George V. MacDonald expected the same, unless more of his colleagues at the twelfth hour joined the small majority willing, if necessary to secure American and French loans or credit to save the pound sterling, to consider recommending to Parliament cuts including reductions in standard unemployment benefit. (Fifteen out of twenty preferred a ten per cent tariff, as advocated by the *Daily Herald* under the influence of Bevin, but that alternative was abandoned because neither Snowden nor the Samuelite Liberals would look at it.) Baldwin was informed that on the twenty-first MacDonald had told the Tories and Liberals that cuts of under £60 million were the Cabinet's 'last word' and been told by them that of course this was inadequate and when Parliament met the Government would be turned out. But that would be too late! The pound would crash in a day or two, if not sooner, unless political arrangements were made which would restore foreign confidence. Therefore the Cabinet on the morning of the twenty-second, without committing itself to cuts of nearly £80 million, involving a 10 per cent cut in unemployment insurance benefit, had agreed that New York be asked whether that would suffice to restore confidence. The Opposition parties had said they thought Parliament would pass such cuts, but the question was whether foreign opinion would think them adequate. The reply from New York was awaited. What, however, disturbed Baldwin was the unwillingness not only of Chamberlain, but of Davidson (who had met him at the Paris Ritz on the night of the twenty-first to brief him), to see Baldwin become Prime Minister, dependent on Liberal support to pass the unpopular measures (which it was likely that the Labour Government as a whole would refuse to endorse) and then dissolve. He wholly agreed that the best solution, from the Tory as from the Liberal point of view, would be for MacDonald's Labour Government, either as constituted or after resignations and replacements, to propose cuts and carry them with the support of the Opposition parties; Chamberlain had told MacDonald on the twenty-first that it was his duty to contrive this. But Baldwin's second preference was a Conservative government, committed to balance the budget and then dissolve. The Liberals could not oppose it and nor, since the balancing proposals would be those of MacDonald, Snowden, etc., could most of the principal Labour ministers, perhaps even a majority of them.

It was not easy to understand why Neville Chamberlain was so determined to prefer to Baldwin's solution the MacDonald Government which in fact emerged. Chamberlain was most anxious to split Labour, but the 'National Government' of which he has been described as 'the constructive engineer', split Labour *less* than would otherwise have been the case. It was attractive to MacDonald not only because (as his critics always stress) his vanity made him wish to remain Prime Minister and the saviour of his country from sectional interests, but because it would *minimise* Labour party divisions. Despite his disgust at its irresponsibility, MacDonald was concerned to maintain the prestige of Labour as one of the two great parties in the state. And here was Neville Chamberlain, whose antipathy to Labour was far greater than Baldwin's, and based on an intellectual arrogance which Baldwin had often deplored, urging, instead of a Conservative government under Baldwin, which the majority of Tory organisers, workers and voters certainly wanted, an interim government under MacDonald including Labour, Liberal and Tory people. One must wonder whether Chamberlain would have taken the same view if *he* had become Conservative leader in March. It seems evident that his anti-Socialism took precedence over his Protectionism, Baldwin being a moderate by both tests. Chamberlain therefore urged upon both MacDonald and Baldwin a MacDonald-Baldwin-Samuel coalition to balance the Budget before an election. Baldwin was sceptical – he had destroyed one coalition, he said, and did not wish to *form* another (still less did he wish to serve in another). But in mid-afternoon on the twenty-third, after persuasion by

Geoffrey Dawson of *The Times*, and finding that while he was incommunicado Samuel had proposed a National government under MacDonald (and convinced the king, though not yet MacDonald), Baldwin, while making it clear that he was willing to form a Conservative government with Liberal support, told the king he would serve under MacDonald. The terms of service, as annotated by Samuel in conference at the Palace the next day, were strict. The Coalition was not a coalition in the ordinary sense (because MacDonald could not carry his party). It was to be a government of individuals, of leading personalities in the three political parties, formed by MacDonald in co-operation with Baldwin and Samuel, and, according to a later official statement, Snowden. Its remit was simply to balance the Budget and so save the pound. This done, it was announced, the parties would 'resume their respective positions'. 'It is not a Coalition Government,' said the Prime Minister in his explanatory broadcast; 'it is not a Government which compels any party to it to change its principles.'

In view of these authoritative statements, sceptics like Amery, who remarked that coalitions had a way of continuing, were overwhelmed. When the Conservatives met on the twenty-eighth, Hailsham's motion of support for Baldwin and the National Government was seconded by Page Croft and supported by Gretton and carried without a vote. Hailsham, indeed, said that he hoped the election would occur in a couple of months or so. Baldwin said that at the Palace on the twenty-third he had had no choice but to concur with Samuel. But once the Budget was balanced 'our agreement ends and we part company'. The balance-of-payments problem could be dealt with only by a tariff. 'When this Parliament dissolves, you will then have a straight fight on tariffs, and against the Socialist party.' What could be fairer than that? – taking into account that the Snowden Budget and the MacDonald National Economy Bill coming up when Parliament reassembled in September would be the measures considered, though not endorsed, by the Labour Government and could not be regarded as typically Tory proposals. Then, the Tories were told, they would have an election on the basis which the majority of them had wanted since 1929 – and, indeed, before.

Such an election, however, never took place. On the same day that the Tories and Liberals unanimously backed their leaders the Labour ex-ministers and M.P.s capitulated to the T.U.C. The ex-ministers, with the temporary exception of Henderson (elected leader of the Labour party on the twenty-eighth) and Greenwood (who admitted on

6 September that they had been 'trembling on the very verge of national ruin') began to say, blindly and recklessly, to quote *The Manchester Guardian*, an organ of Free Trade Radicalism, that the national credit had *not* been at stake. There had been 'a sinister manoeuvre by British and foreign bankers to destroy a Labour Government and reduce the British standard of living. . . .' If true, this meant that in the Labour Cabinet's committee of five appointed to consider the May Report, Henderson and Graham had been duped by MacDonald, Snowden and Thomas (now members of the National Government) who had wilfully misled them. Ex-ministers were perfectly prepared to say that they had been fools, duped by rogues who now supported the National Government, while insisting that their foolishness had been purely provisional; at the end of the day they had fled from the 10 per cent tariff and then from most of the economies. Some demanded an election, to capitalise their ultimate resistance to cuts in unemployment benefit and the salaries of teachers and others. The Deputy Leader Willie Graham, was even more inept. He said, on the last day of August, that Labour was at last in sight of a clear majority, because by 1932 its record in office would be forgotten. The Liberals as an independent force were ruined, and the Conservatives would be loaded with unpopular measures while denied freedom to advocate the major items in their programme. Talk of this kind invited Conservative demands for an early election, on a partisan basis, lest delay help Labour. Not only Amery but Churchill – both of them excluded from office – took up the challenge when Parliament met. Churchill announced his conversion to an industrial tariff and, like Amery, demanded an election, as Labour's attitude made the designation 'National Government' inappropriate.

In the early debates, which showed a 'National Government' majority of sixty, Mosley compounded his unpopularity with Labour by remarking that if the change of government was due to a bankers' ramp, all was now well. But others felt, with justice, that the violence of Opposition Labour imperilled the pound. It was, said Amery, under suspended sentence. Churchill declared that there would be 'no restoration of confidence at home or abroad until the Socialist party has been again decisively defeated at the poll'. Winding up as Lord President of the Council Baldwin remarked with characteristic moderation (nobody was currently threatening his party leadership) that 'if foreigners feel that there is a large section of the community . . . which does not recognise the gravity of the issue . . . , that mere fact itself will tend to render nugatory a great deal of what we may do. . . .' This was true enough.

With ratings at Invergordon refusing to muster after hearing of their pay cuts by wireless and Sunday newspaper, a reaction publicised throughout the world as 'mutiny' by the Royal Navy, and the official Opposition spokesman (the egregious Dalton) demanding a general election which foreigners thought Labour might win, the run on the pound gathered impetus. On Sunday 20 September the Government formed to save the pound accepted the Bank of England's advice to 'go off gold'.

This departure from the gold standard and acceptance of a managed currency was no bad thing. It rectified the error of 1925. But it was the opposite to what the 'National Government' had been formed for. It was a major defeat and it invalidated the basis on which the leading ministers had come together. They were to have balanced the budget to save the pound and then go their separate ways, the Conservative party being freed from all obligations to MacDonald, Snowden, Samuel and Maclean. There was to have been an election, on a party basis, and Baldwin was to have become Prime Minister, committed to tariffs, though the apparent confidence of the Opposition Labour onslaught on proposals, most of which their ministers had at least provisionally accepted (though preferring a tariff), had produced doubt as to the result of such a contest. The inability of the 'National Government' to save the pound produced a new situation. The circumstances under which there was to be 'no coupon' no longer obtained. There could be, without any dishonour, a 'coupon election' on the issue of the balance of payments, provided the ministers could agree on a programme. The attitude of Labour, which, if not simply muddle-headed, was irresponsible, positively invited the smashing defeat which would be visited upon it if the belief in political democracy which MacDonald and Baldwin shared was to be vindicated. But the balance of trade and of payments, and the related issue of the international value of a pound no longer tied to gold, raised in an acute form the issue of Protection as against Free Trade. This had ceased to be a matter of dogma to MacDonald and Thomas, and to Simon and Runciman, who were very eager to replace Samuel and Maclean in the cabinet. It had not been a matter of dogma to the majority of the Labour ex-ministers, or to the General Council of the T.U.C. But both of the latter were now willing, for electoral purposes, to cling to the Old Religion, as was Lloyd George, with his misbegotten funds, if the election was held before he was fully fit, though it was understood that if it were delayed he would consider tariffs. The crucial question was whether the intransigent Free Trader, Snowden, who was to remain Chancellor only until a new parliament met, and the Samuelite ministers could be got to agree to an election and an appeal which would permit the imposition of tariffs.

The presence in the administration of the Samuelites and Snowden gave a validity to the designation 'National' which their replacement by Simonites would not preserve. Willing though he was to consider tariffs, MacDonald did not wish to appear the prisoner of the Tories. In the Government which he had formed in the August crisis the Conservatives had only four cabinet offices out of ten (held by Baldwin, Neville Chamberlain, Hoare and Cunliffe-Lister) and, taking the administration as a whole, but excluding Whips and Household officers, they had only twenty-one out of forty-six. This was a gross under-representation of the party which provided nearly 80 per cent of the Government's supporters in the House of Commons, and a patent under-representation in terms of its electoral strength. It is hardly surprising that the Tories were anxious for an election held under conditions which would allow their policy of tariffs and imperial preference to prevail, and that Baldwin, as the custodian of their fortunes, who had promised them a speedy election on tariffs and anti-Socialism, was put, probably not unwillingly, under pressure. He was considerate towards MacDonald, and liked the earthy Thomas, but he had obligations to his followers (and, indeed, to the electorate). Few people liked Samuel, and Baldwin abominated Lloyd George as much as ever. So the Tory leader had to insist that MacDonald make up his mind. Either he must dissolve the Government, which could be represented as a dereliction of duty in view of the trade problem, and would deny him a public endorsement of his putting country before party, or he must contrive some method by which his new Government could appeal to the electorate without depriving the Conservatives of their long-awaited opportunity to get a mandate for the policies of Joseph Chamberlain.

Neville Chamberlain produced a formula, mentioning tariffs as an option open to the Government, which would ask the electorate for a free hand. It was intended to force Samuel's departure, but Samuel withdrew his threat to leave the Government rather than assent to an election, and MacDonald refused the Tory terms, although he knew from 23 September that a majority of Liberal back-benchers were now Simonite. Ironically, *until* Chamberlain produced his formula on the thirtieth, MacDonald, though leaning to an election, was resisting the Tories, whose business committee on the twenty-fourth (Amery alone dissenting) decided to seek one under his aegis. The statement issued on his behalf on the twenty-eighth to the effect that he wanted to seek 'a doctor's mandate', that he 'would not lend himself to the plans of any one party' and that he would have to resign if all his colleagues would not join in a national appeal was surely directed as much against the Tories as against the Samuelites, who were hoping to avoid an election. It is likely that before going to the Palace on the twenty-ninth he warned Baldwin that the latter might be on the receiving end of a royal appeal that 'party differences should be sunk' and that 'all decent-minded politicians' should unite to 'save the country' (the words are the king's to MacDonald). Baldwin had just been told by his friend Montagu Norman, the Governor of the Bank of England, that there must be an immediate election as foreigners regarded the Government as a makeshift one without a strong majority. When on 3 October Macdonald appeared at the Palace despondent, and had to be urged by the king to 'brace himself up', it was because *Samuel* was now being very difficult.

According to Samuel himself, the deadlock in Cabinet was broken, just before midnight on 5 October, by a Tory capitulation of which he wrote that 'it preserves the individuality of the Liberal party and frees us from any concession in the form of words to be used with regard to tariffs'. The Tories had got the election they wanted, but not on the terms on which they wanted it. They had, however, done very well for themselves – because they were well placed so to do. Lloyd George (who withdrew his son and son-in-law from the Government and persuaded the principal Liberal manager to go with the Lloyd George money-bags) and *The Manchester Guardian* were enraged, agreeing with the General Council of the T.U.C. that 'in this strange combination the Conservative party is master, the Prime Minister its docile servant'. For what had in fact been decided was that MacDonald, as well as Baldwin (and Simon) would say to the nation what Samuel and Snowden were not willing to say. Each party would issue its own election appeal, but with the Prime Minister's covering note. And MacDonald's *Appeal to the Nation* declared that 'the Government must . . . be free to consider every proposal to help [recovery and readjustment], such as tariffs, expansion of exports and contraction of imports, commercial treaties and mutual economic arrangements with the Dominions. . . .' Baldwin simply endorsed as essential policies what MacDonald said should be considered with an open mind, and did so with confidence because, in the very nature of things, the great majority of National Government candidates with a chance of election were Conservatives and Liberal

Nationals. Samuel's appeal, though necessarily professing an open mind as to emergency measures, insisted on Free Trade as a permanent policy and regretted that controversial issues should have been introduced into the contest. Liberal complaints that not every Tory candidate withdrew in a Liberal-held seat, though understandable, are difficult to defend in the light of Samuel's failure to accept, until *after* nomination day, Baldwin's invitations to repudiate the advice of the official Liberal organiser, Ramsay Muir, that Liberals 'fight every Protectionist candidate (*sic*, not 'member') whom we can hope to unseat without letting Labour in'.

Baldwin himself endorsed sincerely the further points made in MacDonald's *Appeal*. There were, basically, three. 'The Government', wrote the Prime Minister, 'is to be comprehensively national, and not sectional, in the obligations which it is to keep before it. . . .' This is only a variant of Tom Jones's verdict on Baldwin – 'For fourteen years he sought to lead party, nation and commonwealth . . . through industrial conflict into the ways of unity and peace.' National unity, wrote the Prime Minister, through the co-operation of parties (and Baldwin endorsed the addendum 'all the parties, by preference, if that were possible') was as necessary now as in August. And yet Baldwin's party's interests were safeguarded. 'Our present conditions', wrote the Prime Minister, 'must not involve a loss of political identity, because the immediate tasks are temporary. . . .' Yes, indeed! *The Times* said that MacDonald's appeal to the nation was also an appeal to his colleagues, to 'unite not only in name but also in fact . . .' because 'the dogmatisms of former party politics are now completely obsolete. . . .' Yes, indeed – but in raw political reality the Liberal dogmatisms were more obsolete than others.

Baldwin shared Snowden's contempt for Labour as 'the party that ran away' and had since made 'a disgraceful surrender to the trade union caucus' and indulged in a purely class appeal, against which all men of good will would of course rally, though Snowden's expression 'political depravity without parallel in party warfare' may have struck him as a bit harsh when directed against nice men like Arthur Henderson and Willie Graham instead of real villains like Lloyd George and Beaverbrook. But Snowden's description of the hastily-contrived Labour programme of nationalisation and physical controls of trade and finance (a riotous extravaganza of the Mosley programme Labour had so recently rejected) as 'Bolshevism run mad' cannot have seemed to Baldwin immoderate. He quite agreed with the Chancellor that a

Labour victory on that basis would 'destroy every vestige of confidence and plunge the country into irretrievable ruin'. And was it not quaint that Labour could not see that theirs was 'the most extreme form of Protection'? – to be fought for under the banner of Free Trade! There was a cutting edge of venom in Snowden's devastating attacks on his former colleagues which Baldwin made no attempt to rival. The waving of worthless German marks was left to Ramsay MacDonald and the scare about the savings banks under Labour rule was contributed by the Liberal Runciman and worked up by Snowden. But they were all making, in their characteristic ways, contributions to Conservative victories which Baldwin must have thought the more pleasing in that they enabled him personally (and he took both the broadcasts allocated to the Conservative party) to fight a clean and calm campaign with God on his side.

The result, once it was known, seemed pre-ordained. Only by adding two Independents, likely in general to support the Government, to the Opposition could one bring the Government's majority below 500 in a House of just over 600. Against 556, Labour and I.L.P. could muster only 52, to which might be added Lloyd George, his son, his daughter and his son-in-law. Of a total of 568 Conservative candidates no less than 471 were returned, giving Baldwin a majority of well over 300 over all others, including his avowed allies (35 Simonites, 33 Samuelites, 13 MacDonaldites, 2 'Nationals', 2 'Independents'). It was a victory beyond the dreams of avarice, unparalleled in the past and unlikely ever to be repeated. It was, of course, distorted by the electoral system. In terms of votes the National Government was endorsed by not much more than two to one, something over 14 million to rather under 7 million, though these figures underestimate the victory (owing to unopposed contests) and are in any case astonishing. The Tories polled 12 million of the 21·5 million cast, and had 49 of the 67 M.P.s returned unopposed. No one pretended they could have done so well on their own. Snowden said afterwards that MacDonald, whom he did not like, was obviously more popular than he had thought, and Snowden's own propaganda had been devastating. It was evidently not the attraction of Baldwin and Neville Chamberlain, plus tariffs, which saw MacDonald to a majority of nearly 6000 in Seaham Harbour, in County Durham (where in 1929 the Labour and Communist votes had totalled 37,000 against 12,000 for the Liberal and Conservative) and his son Malcolm to a 7000 majority (compared with Labour's 14,000 in 1929) in the mining constituency of Bassetlaw in Nottinghamshire and caused

Ernest Bevin in Gateshead to lose by 13,000 a seat with an overall Labour majority of 3000 in 1929. 'But for Mr. MacDonald and Mr. Snowden,' declared *The Manchester Guardian*, which had ended up by urging most of its readers to vote Labour (to save Free Trade) 'there would probably have been no Tory majority.' Baldwin reacted appropriately. 'This is no party victory,' he said. It was a declaration in favour of 'national co-operation' to 'restore the fortunes of our country' and a lesson to the parties that 'the common sense of the people is proof against the propaganda of the demagogue', a repudiation of 'the insidious doctrines of class warfare. . . .' The electorate, and the working class electors too, had justified Baldwin's confidence in them. Mary Agnes Hamilton, defeated Labour Member for Blackburn, who was to be the biographer of Arthur Henderson, agreed. She thought the 1931 election showed that democracy was real, that men and women vote *as citizens* (rather than as members of a class) and even that 'a passion for abstract justice . . . bore Labour down'. Such behaviour imposed on ministers obligations towards the working class, and these Baldwin acknowledged.

It was, however, naïve to suppose that, with a vast majority in both Houses of Parliament, the Conservatives would not have recourse to tariffs. Neville Chamberlain was technically entitled to tell his eve-of-poll audience at Dudley that they did not have to decide whether to have a tariff or free trade (25 October), but his general message was 'It is essential to establish a system of mutual preference between the Dominions and the Motherland, and this can only be brought about by putting a duty on goods which come from outside the Empire'. If any of Snowden's listeners on 17 October were impressed by his assertion that he did not 'believe that the Conservative leaders would regard a majority obtained in the circumstances of this election as giving them a mandate to carry a general system of protection', they should have noted the press statement issued on Baldwin's behalf a week later to the effect that the Conservative party was 'convinced of the supreme value of the policy of tariffs in the present trade crisis'. However 'objective' the inquiry into proposed measures promised by MacDonald and assented to by Snowden and Samuel, it must have been evident to all instructed people that the odds were now against Free Trade. Labour and its press said so; *The Manchester Guardian*, reduced by the threat to the Old Religion to a mood of hysteria, warned the electors (9 October) that the alliance against Labour was one of (Tory) tigers with (Liberal) sheep and that 'for the Conservative Party the "National" Government means tariffs first and foremost. . . .' There was therefore nothing surprising in the aftermath of the election. A reconstitution of the ministry produced a cabinet of twenty instead of ten. 'National Labour' and the Samuelites held respectively four and three places, but the Simonites acquired two (Simon at the Foreign Office and Runciman at Trade) and the Conservatives now had eleven out of twenty places, instead of four out of ten. The incomers to the Cabinet included Hailsham and the former Chief Whip Eyres-Monsell (Austen Chamberlain resigning to make way), Londonderry and the able young Ormsby-Gore. There was no room for Amery, as the transfer of Neville Chamberlain to the Exchequer created problems of the distribution of 'sensitive' offices between parties. The inclusion of Churchill was not considered. Emergency measures to defend British products were rushed through Parliament and the Cabinet then gingerly approached the question of a general 10 per cent tariff, with some exceptions on a free list. As befitted an architect of the National Government Chamberlain proposed the strange device – a suspension of a basic rule of the British Constitution, collective ministerial responsibility – whereby ministers, assured of an enormous majority in Parliament, could propose a measure and Samuelite ministers in the Commons and Snowden in the Lords could oppose it and align themselves on it with the pitifully weak Opposition. This strange device could, however, be used only once. The agreements reached with the Dominions and colonies at Ottawa in the autumn of 1932 led to the resignation of Snowden and the Samuelite ministers.

Macdonald had already written to the king that the Government was now more clearly than ever a Conservative one and his own position anomalous and degrading. It would have been appropriate if Baldwin had taken his place. But, once he had been convinced that it was right for the ministers to go to the country under MacDonald's leadership, Baldwin declined to do anything to displace him. Indeed, at Aix in the summer of 1932, he told the Davidsons and Tom Jones that if the Conservatives tried to hound MacDonald from the premiership he, Baldwin, would have to resign too. One may feel that he shrank from the captaincy when the assumption of it would merely formalise his responsibility and expose him to pressures which he could, in the existing circumstances, divert. But he felt that he, with MacDonald and Simon, had achieved what he had never expected – a *reputable* coalition. The fact that posterity judges it *disreputable* – because of MacDonald's increasing senility and the ignominious performance of Simon at the Foreign Office – should not blind us to that opinion. Baldwin thought that, as Bassett indicates in the introduction to his enlightening book *Nineteen Thirty-One*, recent events had, despite the form of a coalition, clarified the political situation 'by promoting an alignment into two main parties' (with half the Liberal M.P.s for him and the other half not for years clearly against him, and hating one another much more than him) and enabled the Conservative party which he led to broaden its base and transform its policy. And as Bassett says in his conclusion, describing the policy of the National Government as 'empirical, moderate, progressive', its existence 'represented a most important further stage in the broadening and modernisation of British Conservatism. . . .' To anyone considering, late in 1932, the past record (or, indeed, the current appeal) of MacDonald and Thomas, Simon and Runciman, with perception unscarred by knowledge of the catastrophes that awaited their reputations, it could indeed seem that Baldwin's willingness to remain merely Lord President of the Council (though for most practical purposes Leader of the House, because leader of the vast majority of the House), rather than grasping at the premiership, was a wise reticence. But in eschewing formal power he also failed to act with a due awareness of his immense reponsibility.

# Further Reading

Unless otherwise stated, the place of original publication is London.

## 1  WELLINGTON AND PEEL 1831–1846

Elizabeth Longford, *Wellington*, 2 vols (1969; 1972).
H. Maxwell, *Life of Wellington*, 2 vols (1899).
G. S. R. Kitson Clark, *Peel and the Conservative Party* (1929).
R. L. Hill, *Toryism and the People 1832–1846* (1929).
N. Gash, *Politics in the Age of Peel* (1953).
———, *Reaction and Reconstruction in English Politics 1832–52* (1965).
———, *Mr Secretary Peel* (1961).
———, *Sir Robert Peel* (1972).

## 2  DERBY AND DISRAELI

The 14th Earl of Derby has attracted few biographers. George Saintsbury's *The Earl of Derby* (1892) was written from the point of view of a Tory 'who would, at the respective times and in the respective circumstances, have opposed Catholic Emancipation, Reform, the Repeal of the Corn Laws, and the whole Irish Legislation of Mr Gladstone'. T. E. Kebbel's *Life of the Earl of Derby* (1890) shared much the same attitude. *Lord Derby and Victorian Conservatism* (Oxford, 1956) by Wilbur Devereux Jones added much information but continued to rely on papers other than Derby's. A new biography, using Derby's papers, is promised by Lord Blake. Robert Stewart's *The Politics of Protection* (Cambridge, 1971), dealing with the period up to 1852, is largely based on the Derby MSS.

Disraelian literature is vast, and it is impossible here to mention more than a personal selection of volumes. However, Robert Blake's *Disraeli* (1966; 1969) contains a useful list of Disraeli's own publications and a select bibliography. Lord Blake's sympathetic study, based on modern research, is invaluable. But it does not replace the monumental 'official' biography by W. F. Monypenny and G. E. Buckle, *The Life of Benjamin Disraeli, Earl of Beaconsfield*, 6 vols (1910–20); this, despite selective (and sometimes sensitive) omissions, gives the best series of extracts from Disraeli's correspondence, now preserved by the National Trust at Hughenden Manor.

Contemporaries' biographies of Disraeli still deserve consideration, not least because they indicate the variety of views held about their subject. *The Times*'s cautious evaluation (on 20 April 1881) of 'one of the most extraordinary careers recorded in our political annals' is reprinted in *Eminent Persons*, Vol. II (1893). T. P. O'Connor's vicious *Lord Beaconsfield, A Biography* originally preceded Disraeli's death and reached an eighth edition (1905). J. A. Froude's works, *The Earl of Beaconsfield, K.G.* (1890; 1906) and *The Life of the Earl of Beaconsfield* (Everyman edn, 1914) were more perceptive in some respects than might have been expected from an academic anti-semite. Sir William Fraser's *Disraeli and His Day* (1891) is the product of an occasional M.P. and, as Buckle noted, 'enshrines, if it sometimes mangles, many of the best stories about its hero'. T. E. Kebbel's *Life of Lord Beaconsfield* (1888) and *Lord Beaconsfield and other Tory Memories* (1907) are also informative books by a committed Tory who knew Disraeli. A. C. Ewing's *The Right Hon. Benjamin Disraeli, Earl of Beaconsfield, K.G., and his Times* 2 vols (1882) was a fulsome hagiography, issued in five blue and gold covered parts to adorn Primrose Leaguers' libraries.

Georg Brandes's, *Lord Beaconsfield: A Study*, trans. Mrs George Sturge (1880) was an interesting attempt by a foreigner 'to apply a literary-critical method' by studying 'the statesman Lord Beaconsfield through the novelist Benjamin Disraeli'; at Berlin in 1878 'almost against his will, a feeling of sympathy took possession of [Brandes's] mind'. Inevitably, his own writings are essential reading in any study of Disraeli. The novels have been issued quite often and commentaries on them have regularly appeared. Arguably the most important novels, *Coningsby, or The New Generation* and *Sybil, or The Two Nations*, have been republished with sympathetic introductions respectively by Walter Allen (1948) and Walter Sichel (1950). Walter Sichel also wrote the still fascinating *Disraeli, a Study in Personality and Ideas* (1904). Collections of the novels have been published in 1881 (Longmans, 11 vols.), 1904–5 (M. W. Dunne, 20 vols.), 1905–6 (John Lane, The Bodley Head, 9 vols.), 1926–7 (Peter Davies, 12 vols.) and 1927–8 (John Lane, The Bodley Head, 11 vols.). Critical evaluations include M. E. Speare, *The Political Novel: Its Development in England and in America* (New York, 1924); R. E. G. George, 'The Novels of Disraeli', *Nineteenth Century*, XCVI (1924); M. Masefield, *Peacocks and Primroses* (1953); Lord David Cecil, *Early Victorian Novelists* (1934); S. M. Smith, 'Willenhall and Woodgate: Disraeli's Use of Blue Book Evidence', *Review of English Studies*, n.s. XIII (1962); Raymond Williams, *Culture and Society, 1780–1950* (1958; paperback 1961); Boris Ford (ed.) *From Dickens to Hardy* (1958) and Robert Blake, 'Disraeli's Political Novels', *History Today*, XVI (1966).

Disraeli's letters to various ladies have been published and constitute an important part of his autobiographical evidence. Correspondence with his devoted sister Sarah has been issued several times and is most conveniently collected in *Home Letters by Lord Beaconsfield, 1830–1852*, with an introduction by Augustine Birrell (1928). Equally fascinating are the collections in the Marquess of Zetland (ed.) *The Letters of Disraeli to Lady Bradford and Lady Chesterfield*, 2 vols (1929) and the Marchioness of Londonderry (ed.) *Letters from Benjamin Disraeli to Frances Anne, Marchioness of Londonderry, 1837–1861* (1938), which illustrate Disraeli's curious relationships with titled ladies, in additon to providing insights on his political attitudes. Some of Disraeli's major political writings and various journalistic pieces (not all provably by Disraeli) are included in Walter Hutcheon (ed.) *Whigs and Whiggism: Political Writings by Benjamin Disraeli* (1913). The major collection of speeches is T. E. Kebbel (ed.) *Selected Speeches of the late Earl of Beaconsfield*, 2 vols (1882).

Many 'popular' biographies have been published, including E. T. Raymond's gossipy *Disraeli: The Alien Patriot* (1925); D. C. Somervell's *Disraeli and Gladstone* (1925); and André Maurois' *Disraeli* (John Lanc, The Bodley Head, 1927; Penguin 1937; Blackie, 1947). Wilfrid Meynell's *The Man Disraeli* (1927 edn), R. W. Setson-Watson's *Disraeli, Gladstone and the Eastern Question* (1935) and Sir Harold Beeley's *Disraeli* (1936) remain useful. Disraeli's continuing appeal to the Right is illustrated in many publications of and about the Conservative Party. H. W. J. Edwards's *The Radical Tory*, with an introduction by G. M. Young (1937) consists mainly of a useful collection of Disraelian extracts and an editorial clarion call for Tory-Radical reaction to modern 'Whiggism'. A champion of British agriculture, Sir R. George Stapledon, developed a Disraelian interest 'but of yesterday' before writing *Disraeli and the New Age* (1943). Sir Edward Boyle (ed.) *Tory Democrat* (1950) reprints the great speeches of 1872 and includes Walter Elliot's assertion that Disraeli's 'approach is his own. His problems are ours'. This was published by the Conservative Political Centre. A similar attitude pervades another C.P.C. publication, *Tradition and Change* (1954), a collection of essays by such distinguished Tories as Lord Butler, T. E. Utley, Enoch Powell, Iain Macleod and Angus Maude.

New insights are provided in Cecil Roth's *Benjamin Disraeli, Earl of Beaconsfield* (New York, 1952) on Disraeli's Judaic Christianity, and in B. R. Jerman's *The Young Disraeli* (Princeton, 1960) on youthful embarrassments. The later hostility to Disraeli's leadership and his interest in party organisation are treated from different viewpoints in E. J. Feuchtwanger's *Disraeli, Democracy and the Tory Party* (Oxford, 1968) and 'The Conservative Party under the Impact of the Second Reform Act', *Victorian Studies*, II (1959), in James Cornford's, 'The Transformation of Conservatism in the Late Nineteenth Century', ibid. VII (1963), and in Paul Smith's *Disraelian Conservatism and Social Reform* (London and Toronto, 1967) – which is less sympathetic.

There is an extensive and controversial literature on the 1867 Reform Act. Asa Briggs's *The Age of Improvement* (1969 impr.) provides a balanced, general survey. F. H. Herrick's 'The Reform Bill of 1867 and the British Party System', *Pacific Historical Review*, III (1934) and 'The Second Reform Movement in Britain, 1850–1865' *Journal of the History of Ideas*, IX (1948) provide sensible antidotes to partisan accounts. Royden Harrison's 'The 10th April of Spencer Walpole', *International Review of Social History*, VII (1963), reprinted in R. Harrison, *Before the Socialists* (1965), is a less convincing survey, written from a socialist viewpoint. F. B. Smith's '"Democracy" in the Second Reform Debates', *Historical Studies, Australia and New Zealand*, XI (1964) and *The Making of the Second Reform Bill* (Cambridge, 1966) are valuable on details, but should be balanced by Maurice Cowling's *1867: Disraeli, Gladstone and Revolution* (Cambridge, 1967) – a vital Tory analysis – and Gertrude Himmelfarb's 'The Politics of Democracy: The English Reform Act of 1867', *Journal of British Studies*, VI (1966) largely reprinted in G. Himmelfarb, *Victorian Minds* (1968). A subsequent discussion between Mr Smith and Miss Himmelfarb was published in *Journal of British Studies*, IX (1969). Robert Blake's *The Conservative Party from Peel to Churchill* (1970) draws many modern parallels with past events.

## 3 THE SALISBURY ERA 1881–1902

A. L. Kennedy's *Salisbury: Portrait of a Statesman* (1953) remains the only rounded biography. Algernon Cecil's study of his uncle in *Queen Victoria and Her Prime Ministers* (1953) is a model essay. Lady Gwendolen Cecil's privately printed *Biographical Studies of the Life and Political Character of Robert, 3rd Marquess of Salisbury* is the acknowledged basis of the valuable sketch in the early pages of J. A. S. Grenville's *Lord Salisbury and Foreign Policy* (1964).

Salisbury's early career is well covered in the first two volumes of Lady Gwendolen's *Life*. His writings and speeches as an M.P. are the subject of Michael Pinto-Duschinsky's *The Political Thought of Lord Salisbury 1854–68* (1967). Lady Gwendolen's fourth, and last, volume reaches only to 1892 and of its fourteen chapters only two are given over to 'the Prime Minister's Department'.

Such has been the concentration on Salisbury as foreign secretary (the office which was his great love) that the student of Salisbury as party leader and prime minister (occupations which he regarded as distinctly part-time) has to rely on those studies of his principal aides which are well-documented, and especially:

Balfour, *Chapters of Autobiography* (1930)
Dugdale, Blanche E. C., *A. J. Balfour* (1936)
Lord Chilston, *W. H. Smith* (1965)
——, *Chief Whip* (1961), re Akers-Douglas
R. Rhodes James, *Lord Randolph Churchill* (1959).

James Cornford reveals pertinent insights into the Conservative Party in Salisbury's time in two articles: 'The Transformation of Conservatism in the Late Nineteenth Century', *Victorian Studies*, VII (September 1963); and 'The Parliamentary Foundations of the Hotel Cecil', in *Ideas and Institutions of Victorian Britain: Essays in Honour of George Kitson Clark*, ed. Robert Robson (1967). Lord Blake has clearly made much use of these in *The Conservative Party from Peel to Churchill* (1970).

Since this volume went to press, Lady Milner's glimpses of Salisbury 'at home' in her *My Picture Gallery, 1886–1901* (1951) have been supplemented by Lord David Cecil in *The Cecils of Hatfield House* (1973).

## 4   BALFOUR 1902–1911

Blanche E. C. Dugdale, *Arthur James Balfour*, 2 vols (1936); Kenneth Young, *Arthur James Balfour* (1963); E. T. Raymond, *Mr Balfour* (1920); J. L. Garvin, *The Life of Joseph Chamberlain*, vol. II (1933), vol. III (1934); Julian Amery, *The Life of Joseph Chamberlain*, vol. IV (1951), vols V and VI (1969); Winston Churchill, 'Arthur James Balfour', in *Great Contemporaries* (1937); A. G. Gardiner, 'Arthur James Balfour', in *Prophets, Priests and Kings* (1908); Austen Chamberlain, *Politics From Inside* (1936); Lord Newton, *Lord Lansdowne* (1929); Bernard Holland, *Life of Spencer Compton, Eighth Duke of Devonshire* 2 vols (1911); Robert Blake, *The Unknown Prime Minister* (1955); Robert Blake, *The Conservative Party From Peel to Churchill* (1970); Alfred Gollin, *The Observer and J. L. Garvin 1908–1914* (1960); Alfred Gollin, *Balfour's Burden* (1965); Richard A. Rempel, *Unionists Divided* (1972); Sydney Zebel, *Balfour: A Political Biography* (Cambridge, 1973).

## 5   BETWEEN BALFOUR AND BALDWIN 1911–1923

Robert Blake, *The Unknown Prime Minister: the Life and Times of Andrew Bonar Law 1858–1923* (1955)*; Sir Charles Petrie, *The Life and Letters of The Right Hon. Sir Austen Chamberlain*, 2 vols (1939–40)†; Sir Austen Chamberlain, *Politics from the Inside* (1936); W. A. S. Hewins, *The Apologia of an Imperialist*, 2 vols (1929); Lord Beaverbrook, *Politicians and the War 1914–16*, 2 vols

* Lord Blake's is a well-worked biography, notable not only for the delayed justice done to Bonar Law but also for the unobtrusive but effective part it has played in 'Tory' criticism of the widely accepted historiography of the period 1909–22.
† An uncomplicated and articulate politician, Sir Austen Chamberlain presents few problems to a biographer. Sir Charles Petrie's biography is a careful well-proportioned work in which Sir Austen is allowed to speak for himself.

(1928–32), *Men and Power 1917–18* (1956), *The Decline and Fall of Lloyd George* (1963); L. S. Amery, *My Political Life*. vols I and II (1953).

Randolph S. Churchill, *Lord Derby: 'King of Lancashire'* (1959); Roy Jenkins, *Asquith* (1964); A. M. Gollin, *Proconsul in Politics: A Study of Lord Milner in Opposition and in Power* (1964); R. R. James, *Memoirs of a Conservative: J. C. C. Davidson's Memoirs and Papers 1910–1937* (1969); Keith Middlemass and John Barnes, *Baldwin: A Biography* (1969); Keith Middlemass (ed.), *Thomas Jones: Whitehall Diary*, vol I *1916–1925* (1969).

R. T. McKenzie, *British Political Parties* (1955); Ivor Bulmer-Thomas, *The Growth of the British Party System*, vol. I *1640–1923* (1965); A. J. P. Taylor, *Politics in Wartime* (1964); Trevor Wilson, *The Downfall of the Liberal Party 1914–1935* (1966).


# 6  BALDWIN 1923–1932

To the unsatisfactory official *Stanley Baldwin*, by G. M. Young (1952) A. W. Baldwin replied with *My Father: The True Story* (1955). A vast biography, *Baldwin*, by K. Middlemas and John Barnes, appeared in 1969.

On the rise of Baldwin, Robert Blake, *The Unknown Prime Minister: The Life and Times of Bonar Law 1858–1923* (1955), Sir Charles Petrie, *Life and Letters of Austen Chamberlain*, 2 vols (1939–40), Lord Beaverbrook, *The Decline and Fall of Lloyd George* (1963) and Maurice Cowling, *The Impact of Labour 1920–4: The Beginning of Modern British Politics* (1971) provide context.

For Baldwin's leadership 1923–32 Robert Rhodes James, *Memoirs of a Conservative* [J. C. C. Davidson] (1969) is crucial and *Thomas Jones: Whitehall Diary 1926–30*, ed. Middlemas (1969) and *A Diary With Letters* (1954) are important. Of Baldwin's colleagues, only L. S. Amery left commentary in depth: *My Political Life*, vols II and III (1953). The period 1923–32 is the only part of Churchill's political life up to 1945 on which he never wrote at length. The *Neville Chamberlain* of Keith Feiling (1946) and that of Iain Macleod (1961) are useful.

For the formation of the National Government, and the subsequent election, Richard Bassett's *Nineteen Thirty-One; Political Crisis* (1958) is indispensable.

A study of Baldwin by Montgomery Hyde was announced while the present volume was in the press.

# References

## 2  DERBY AND DISRAELI
### *J. T. Ward*

1. Paul Smith, *Disraelian Conservatism and Social Reform* (1967) p. 11; F. B. Smith, *The Making of the Second Reform Bill* (Cambridge, 1966) p. 28.

2. John Bateman, *The Great Landowners of Great Britain and Ireland* (1879 edn) p. 123 (1883 edn, intro. D. Spring, Leicester, 1971) p. 127; cf. Bateman's less accurate *Acreocracy of England* (1876) p. 56 and comments thereon in W. D. Jones, *Lord Derby and Victorian Conservatism* (Oxford 1956) p. 3n. For details of the Derby estates see R. S. Churchill, *Lord Derby: 'King of Lancashire'* (1959). On Disraeli's property see W. F. Monypenny and G. E. Buckle, *The Life of Benjamin Disraeli, Earl of Beaconsfield*, III (1914) pp. 147, 151; 'Return of Owners of Land, 1873', *P.P.* LXXII (1874) Bucks. section, p. 6.

3. D. H. Elletson, *Maryannery* (1959) passim; Georgina Battiscombe, *Mrs Gladstone* (1956) p. 158; Jones, *Lord Derby* p. 151; Robert Blake, *Disraeli* (1969 edn.) pp. 421, 357.

4. J. T. Ward, *Sir James Graham* (1967) pp. 79f; John Gore, *Creevey* (1949 edn) p. 321; D. G. Southgate, *The Passing of the Whigs, 1832–1886* (1962) ch. 2 *et passim*.

5. See Robert Stewart, *The Politics of Protection* (Cambridge, 1971) *passim*; Blake, *Disraeli*, pp. 313–14 and *The Conservative Party from Peel to Churchill* (1970) pp. 60–82; C. C. F. Greville, *A Journal of the Reign of Queen Victoria from 1837 to 1852*, III (1885) pp. 447–8.

6. Earl of Malmesbury, *Memoirs of an ex-Minister* (1884) p. 44; Marchioness of Londonderry (ed.) *Letters of Benjamin Disraeli to Frances Anne, Marchioness of Londonderry* (1938) p. 130.

7. R. J. White, *The Conservative Tradition* (1950) p. 29; Lord Hugh Cecil, *Conservatism* (1912) p. 116; F. J. C. Hearnshaw, *Conservatism in England* (1933) p. 38; Arthur Bryant, *The Spirit of Conservatism* (1932 edn) p. 61; Lord Eustace Percy, 'The Conservative Attitude and Conservative Social Policy', in *Conservatism and the Future*, ed. E. T. Cook (1935) p. 23; Kenneth Pickthorn, *Principles and Prejudices* (1943) *passim*; Quintin Hogg, *The Case for Conservatism* (1947) pp. 10–11.

8. F. Eyck, *The Prince Consort* (1959) p. 197.

9. John Morley, *The Life of William Ewart Gladstone*, I (1903) p. 579; Blake, *Disraeli*, p. 408; Mrs Hardcastle, *Life of John, Lord Campbell*, II (1881) p. 430; *Quarterly Review* (April 1860); Sir Edwin Hodder, *The Life and Work of the Seventh Earl of Shaftesbury, K.G.*, III (1886) p. 68.

10. See Gertrude Himmelfarb, 'The Politics of Democracy: the English Reform Act of 1867', *Journal of British Studies*, VI (1966), largely reprinted in G. Himmelfarb, *Victorian Minds* (1968) ch. 13; Blake, *Disraeli*, p. 451; Jones, *Lord Derby*, p. 297.

11. *Quarterly Review*, CXIX (1866); Lady Gwendolen Cecil, *Life of Robert, Marquis of Salisbury*, I (1921) pp. 224–5; Charles Whibley, *Lord John Manners and his Friends*, II (1925) p. 126.

12. Asa Briggs, *The Age of Improvement, 1783–1867* (1969 impr.) p. 505; Blake, *Disraeli*, p. 463.

13. H. J. Hanham, *Elections and Party Management: Politics in the Time of Disraeli and Gladstone* (1959) pp. 284–322, 26; Jones, *Lord Derby*, pp. 274–5.

14. See Blake, *Disraeli*, ch. 1–3; Cecil Roth, *Benjamin Disraeli, Earl of Beaconsfield* (New York, 1952); Wilfrid Meynell, *The Man Disraeli* (1927 edn); B. R. Jerman, *The Young Disraeli* (Princeton, 1960); C. L. Cline, 'Disraeli and Peel's 1841 Cabinet', *Journal of Modern History*, XI (1939).

15. L. J. Jennings, *Memoirs . . . of John Wilson Croker*, III (1884) p. 9. See Lord Lamington, *In the Days of the Dandies* (1890); Monypenny, *Life of Disraeli*, II (1912) ch. 6; Whibley, *Lord John Manners*, I, ch. 4; Percy Craddock, *Recollections of the Cambridge Union* (Cambridge 1953); J. T. Ward, 'Young England', *History Today*, XVI (1966).

16. *Quarterly Review*, CVII (1860); Lady G. Cecil, *Salisbury*, I, pp. 89–97; Lord Hugh Cecil, *Conservatism*, pp. 70–1; [Monypenny and] Buckle, *Life of Disraeli*, IV (1916) pp. 289–91.

17. Lady G. Cecil, *Salisbury*, I, pp. 291–5; Blake, *Disraeli*, p. 499.

18. T. E. Kebbel (ed.) *Selected Speeches of the Late Earl of Beaconsfield* (1882); Sir Edward Boyle (ed.) *Tory Democrat* (1950); Donald Southgate in C. J. Bartlett (ed.), *Britain Pre-eminent* (1969), p. 162.

19. Viscount Cross, *A Political History* (1903) p. 25; Monypenny and Buckle, *Life of Disraeli*, III, p. 125; *Glasgow Herald*, 21 November 1873; Balme MSS. (Bradford City Library); Boyle, *Tory Democrat*, pp. 46–7; Sir A. H. Hardinge, *Life of Henry Fourth Earl of Carnarvon*, II (1925), p. 78.

20. T. P. O'Connor, *The Life of Lord Beaconsfield* (1905 edn) p. 672; Blake, *Disraeli*, p. 211; Norman Gash, 'The Founder of Modern Conservatism', *Solon*, I (1970). See Robert Blake, *A Century of Achievement* (1967); R. L. Hill, *Toryism and the People* (1929); J. T. Ward, *The Factory Movement, 1830–1855* (1962); W. J. Wilkinson, *Tory Democracy* (New York 1925).

21. Sir Winston Churchill, *Lord Randolph Churchill* (1951 edn) pp. 130–1; R. R. James, *Lord Randolph Churchill* (1959) pp. 85–6, 97–9; cf. Blake, *Disraeli*, pp. 729–32.

22. O'Connor, *Beaconsfield*, pp. xi–xii, xv; Sir Philip Magnus, *Gladstone: A Biography* (1954) p. 201, Lytton Strachey and Roger Fulford (ed.) *The Greville Memoirs*, VI (1938) p. 343; Lord Stanmore, *Sidney Herbert*, II (1906) pp. 173, 177.

23. Hanham, *Elections and Party Management*, pp. 356–68; H. E. Gorst, *The Earl of Beaconsfield* (1900) pp. 126–7; Blake, *Disraeli*, pp. 536–7, and *A Century of Achievement* pp. 17–21.

24. G. M. Young in H. W. J. Edwards, *The Radical Tory* (1937) pp. 11–12; Walter Elliot in Boyle, *Tory Democrat*, pp. 10–11; *The Scotsman*, 31 October 1867; Sir Edward Boyle in *Great Conservatives* (1953) p. 29; R. A. Butler in *Tradition and Change* (1954) p. 10.

25. Lady Londonderry, *Frances Anne* (1958) p. 295.

## 5 BETWEEN BALFOUR AND BALDWIN

### J. H. Grainger

1. W. A. S. Hewins, *The Apologia of an Imperialist*, I (1929) p. 10.

2. Lord Beaverbrook, *The Decline and Fall of Lloyd George*, (1963) p. 234.

3. See Kenneth Young, *Arthur James Balfour* (1936) p. 316, and R. Blake, *The Unknown Prime Minister* (1955) p. 90.

4. L. S. Amery, *My Political Life*, I (1953) p. 387.

5. Hewins, *Apologia*, I, p. 11.

6. Amery, *Life*, I, p. 460.

7. A. M. Gollin, *Proconsul in Politics*, (1964) p. 214ff.

8. Hewins, *Apologia*, II, p. 21.

9. Hewins, *Apologia*, I, p. 296.

10. Beaverbrook, *Politicians and the War 1914–1916*, II (1932), p. 15.

11. See correspondence in *The Times* 22 November to 17 December 1969 between Lord Coleraine and Roy Jenkins, with Lord Blake, A. J. P. Taylor and A. J. L. Barnes intervening.

12. See Bentley B. Gilbert, *British Social Policy* (1970) pp. 13–25.

13. See Sir Arthur Salter, *Personality in Politics* (1947) p. 52.

14. Beaverbrook, *Men and Power 1917–18*, (1956) p. 314.

15. J. M. Robertson, *Mr Lloyd George and Liberalism* (1923), ch. 2, *passim*.

16. Randolph S. Churchill, *Lord Derby*, (1959) p. 439.

17. Beaverbrook, *Politicians and the War*, II, pp. 96–7.

18. J. R. Jones, 'England' in *The European Right*, ed. Hans Rogger and Eugen Webber (1965), p. 35.

19. Amery, *Life*, II, p. 73.

20. F. S. Oliver, *Ordeal by Battle* (1915) p. 434.

# Notes on Contributors

NORMAN GASH, Professor of History, University of St Andrews; author of *Politics in the Age of Peel*; *Reaction and Reconstruction in English Politics 1832–52*; *Mr Secretary Peel*; *Sir Robert Peel*, etc.

ALFRED M. GOLLIN, Professor, University of California, Santa Barbara; author of *The Observer and J. L. Garvin 1908–14*; *Balfour's Burden*; *Proconsul in Politics: A Study of Lord Milner* . . . etc.

J. H. GRAINGER, Reader in the Department of Political Science, the Australian National University, author of *Character and Style in English Politics*, etc.

DONALD SOUTHGATE, Reader in Modern Political and Constitutional History, University of Dundee; author of *The Passing of the Whigs 1832–86*; '. . . The Most English Minister . . .': *The Policies and Politics of Palmerston*; various Scottish electoral studies, etc.

J. T. WARD, Senior Lecturer in History, University of Strathclyde; author of *The Factory Movement 1830–1855*; *Sir James Graham*, etc. Editor, *Popular Movements c. 1830–50* in the 'Problems in Focus Series'.

# Index of Persons

EXPLANATION

1. Except where otherwise stated, the politicians listed are Conservatives.
2. The names of official leaders of the Conservative Party up to 1937 are given in CAPITALS.
3. Where a person is listed by his peerage, the surname (if different from that of the title) is given in *italics*.
4. An asterisk indicates the date of first entry to cabinet.

ABBREVIATIONS

| | |
|---|---|
| Admy | Admiralty |
| Ady | First Lord of the Admiralty |
| A.-G. | Attorney-General |
| a/s | assistant secretary |
| B. | Baron |
| Ch.D. | Chancellor of the Duchy of Lancaster |
| Ch.Exr | Chancellor of the Exchequer |
| Ch.S. | Chief Secretary for Ireland (office abolished 1922) |
| D. | duke of |
| e. | earl |
| Ed. P. | President of the Board of Education (office existed 1900–44) |
| Ed. V.-P. | Vice-President of the Privy Council, Education Dept. (to 1902) |
| F.S.T. | Financial Secretary to the Treasury |
| G. | Governor of |
| G.-G. | Governor-General of |
| H/O | Household official (Whip) |
| (I) | Ireland |
| Ind.P. | President of Board of Control for India (office replaced by S.S. 1858) |
| jr | junior minister |
| L.C. | Lord Chancellor |
| Ld | Lord |
| Ldr | Leader |
| Ldr C. | Leader of the House of Commons |
| Ldr L. | Leader of the House of Lords |
| L.L.I. | Lord Lieutenant of Ireland (office lapsed December 1922) |
| L.P.C. | Lord President of the Council |
| L.P.S. | Lord Privy Seal |
| M. | Minister of |
| Msp | Minister without Portfolio |
| mss | marquess |
| M.W.C. | member of the small war cabinet of Lloyd George 1916–19 or Churchill 1940–5 |
| P.B.A. | President of the Board of Agriculture |

P.B.T.    President of the Board of Trade
P.C.      Privy Councillor. This honour, conveying the style 'Rt Hon', is noted only where conferred without membership of the cabinet; all cabinet ministers are made privy councillors in order to be bound by the oath of secrecy.
P.L.G.    President of the Local Government Board (1871–1919)
P.M.      Prime Minister. Except during most of the premiership of Lord Salisbury, the Prime Minister was First Lord of the Treasury
P.M.G.    Postmaster-General
P.P.L.    President of the Poor Law Board (1847–71, predecessor of Local Government Board)
P.P.S.    Parliamentary Private Secretary
p/s       private secretary
Pyr-G.    Paymaster-General
R.P. (I.)   Representative Peer of Ireland
R.P. (Sc.)  Representative Peer of Scotland
S.-G.     Solicitor-General
S.S.      Secretary of State
S.Sc.     Secretary for Scotland (1885–1926 when the office was elevated to a secretaryship of state)
U.-S.S.   Under-Secretary of State
V.        Viscount
V.P.B.T.  Vice-President of Board of Trade
Wks       First Commissioner of Works
x         defeated candidate

Aberdeen, Geo. Hamilton *Gordon* (1784–1860), 4th e. of 1801; S.S. Foreign 1828–30, 1841–6, War & Cols 1834–5; P.M. (Peelite) Dec 1852–Jan 1855    61, 63, 66, 138, 148, 149
(Fuller-) Acland-Hood, Capt. Sir Alexander (1853–1917), 4th Bt 1892, 1st B. St Audries 1911; M.P. Somerset W. 1892–1911; Whip 1900–2, Conservative Chief Whip 1902–11; P.C. 1904    27–8, 31
*Aitken* – see Beaverbrook
Akers-Douglas, Aretas (1851–1926), 1st V. Chilston 1911; M.P. Kent E. 1880–1911; Conservative Chief Whip 1885–95; P.C. 1891; Wks *1895–1902, S.S. Home 1902–5    26, 28, 114, 124–7, 148
Albert, Prince of Saxe-Coburg-Gotha (1819–61), consort (1840) of Queen Victoria    84, 122
Althorp, Viscount, John Charles *Spencer* (1782–1845), 3rd E. Spencer 1834; Pittite M.P. 1804–7, Whig (Northants) 1807–34; Ch. Exr & Ldr C. 1830–4    60
Amery, H. Julian (b. 1919), son of L. S. Amery; M.P. 1950–66 & since 1969; ministerial offices 1957–64 & since 1970; biographer of Joseph Chamberlain    149, 250
Amery, Leopold C. M. S. (1873–1955), Fellow of All Souls', journalist, historian, Tariff Reform crusader; Birmingham M.P. 1911–45; a/s War Cabinet 1917–18; jr 1918–22; Ady *1922–4; S.S.Cols 1924–9, Dominions 1925–9, India 1940–5    174, 176, 188, 195, 199, 203–4, 206–8, 218–19, 222, 225–7, 230–1, 234, 237–8, 240, 245, 251, 254
Anderson, Sir (1919) John (1882–1958), 1st V. Waverley 1952; civil servant to 1932; G. Bengal 1932–7; M.P. (National) Scottish Universities 1938–50; cabinet minister 1938–45 (M.W.C. 1940–5)    209, 215

Argyll, Geo. Douglas *Campbell* (1823–1900), 8th d. of 1847; Peelite cabinet minister 1852–8, Whig cabinet minister 1859–66, 1868–74, 1880–1 resigned; Unionist 76
Ashbourne, Edward *Gibson* (1837–1913), 1st B. 1885; M.P. Dublin University 1875–85; A.-G. (I.) 1877–80; L.C. (I.) *1885–6, 1886–92, 1895–1905  118
*Ashley  see* Shaftesbury
Asquith, Herbert Henry (1852–1928), 1st e. of Oxford & Asquith 1925; Liberal M.P. 1886–1918, 1920–4; S.S. Home *1892–5; Ch.Exr 1905–8; P.M. 1908–16  14, 21, 34, 121, 145, 149, 173, 176–82, 184–5, 200–1, 204–6, 218

Bagehot, Walter (1826–77), of *The Economist*, political biographer & writer on British Constitution  15, 66, 139
Baillie, Henry Jas (1803–85), M.P. Inverness Co. 1840–68, jr 1852, 1858–9  81
Baillie-Cochrane (Cochrane-Wishart-Baillie), Alexander D. R. (1816–90), 1st B. Lamington 1880; M.P. 1841–80 except 1852–7, 1857–8, 1868–70  81
BALDWIN, STANLEY (1867–1947), 1st e. Baldwin of Bewdley 1937; Harrow & Trinity, Cambridge (University Chancellor from 1930); ironmaster; M.P Bewdley 1908–37; F.S.T. 1917–21; P.C. 1920; P.B.T. *1921–2; Ch.Exr 1922–3; Ldr Conservative & Unionist party May 1923–37; P.M. 1923–4, 1924–9, 1935–7; Ldr H.M.'s Opposition 1924, 1929–31; L.P.C. 1931–5  197–246. Also 3–6, 9, 11–12, 14, 16–18, 20, 24, 29, 32–4, 188, 191–2, 194, 251
Balfour of Burleigh, Alexander Hugh *Bruce* (1849–1921), 6th B.; R.P. (Sc.); jr 1888–92; S.Sc. *1895–1903 resigned (Unionist Free Trader)  162–3
BALFOUR, ARTHUR JAMES (1848–1930), 1st e. of Balfour 1922; Eton & Trinity Cambridge (University Chancellor from 1919); p/s uncle Salisbury 1878–80; M.P. Hertford 1880–5, Manchester E. 1885–1906, City of London 1906–22; member of 'Fourth Party' 1880–2; P.C. 1885 & P.L.G. 1885–6; S.Sc. 1886–7; *Nov 1886; Ch.S. 1887–91; 1st Ld of Treasury & Ldr C. 1891–2, 1895–1905 & also P.M. 1902–5; Ldr Conservative & Unionist party 1902–11; Ldr Opposition in Commons 1892–5; Ldr H.M.'s Opposition 1905–11; Ady in Asquith Coalition 1915–16; S.S. Foreign 1916–19 & L.P.C. 1919–22 in Lloyd George Coalitions; L.P.C. under Baldwin 1925–9  151–70. Also 2–4, 6–8, 10–12, 20–2, 24–32, 95, 101–3, 106–7, 112–18, 123, 126–30, 132–7, 141–3, 146, 149, 172–3, 175, 177, 181, 186 8, 193, 198–9, 201–3, 205, 220, 226–7, 250
Balfour, Gerald William (1853–1945), 2nd e. of Balfour 1930, brother of above; M.P. Leeds C. 1885–1906; Ch.S. 1895–1900; P.B.T. *1900–5, P.L.G. 1905  136, 148
Ball, Major Sir (1936) G. Joseph (1885–1961); intelligence officer; Director, Conservative Research Dept 1930–9; Deputy Chairman Security Executive 1940–2; director of companies engaged in S. Africa  224, 226
Bartley, Sir (1902) George Christopher Trout (1842–1910); civil servant to 1880; Principal Agent Conservative party 1882–4 resigned; disgruntled M.P. Islington N. 1885–1905  124, 148
Bassett, Reginald, of the London School of Economics, author of *Nineteen Thirty-One – Political Crisis* (1958)  245–6, 251
Bath, John A. *Thynne* (1831–96), 4th mss of 1837; independent-minded Conservative peer  72
Baxter, (Robert) Dudley (1827–75) parliamentary agent and electoral expert  73, 98
Beach, Sir Michael Edward Hicks (1837–1916), 9th Bt 1854, 1st V. St Aldwyn 1906, 1st e. 1915; M.P. Glos E. 1864–85, Bristol W. 1885–1906; jr 1868; Ch.S. 1874–8, 1886–7; P.C. 1874; S.S. Cols *1878–80; Ch.Exr & Ldr C. 1885–6; Msp 1887–8; P.B.T. 1888–92; Ch.Exr 1895–1902  114–16, 120, 126–7, 129, 144

Beaverbrook, Sir (1916, 1st Bt) W. Maxwell *Aitken* (1879–1964), 1st B. 1917; Canadian-born presslord, friend of Bonar Law; M.P. Ashton-under-Lyme 1910–16; P.C. 1918, Ch.D. & M. Information; strong critic of Baldwin 1929–31; minister under Churchill 1940–2 (M.W.C.), 1943–5   157, 173, 175, 180, 187, 192, 194, 222–32, 242, 250, 251, 253, 254

Bennett, Richard Bedford (1870–1947), 1st V. 1941; Ldr Conservative Party of Canada 1927–38 & P.M. thereof 1930–5   229

Bentinck, Lord (William) George Fredk Cavendish (1802–48), p/s to uncle Canning 1822–5, M.P. Lynn 1828–48; Ldr Protectionist M.P.s 1846–Dec 1847   54–5, 62, 82–4

Beresford, Major William (1797–1883), M.P. Essex N. 1847–65; Derbyite Chief Whip; Sec. at War 1852   62, 83, 98

Bevin, Ernest (1884–1950), gen. sec. Transport & Genl Workers; Labour M.P. 1940–50; M.W.C. 1940–5; S.S. Foreign (Labour) 1945–50   213–16, 229, 235, 244

Birkenhead, Fredk Edwin *Smith* (1872–1930), 1st Bt 1918, 1st B. 1919, V. 1921, e. of 1922; M.P. Liverpool Walton 1906–18; P.C. 1911; S.-G. 1915; A.-G. *1915–19; L.C. 1919–22; S.S. India 1924–8   187, 188, 190, 199, 202–7, 212, 216

Birrell, Augustine (1850–1933), law professor, Lib. M.P. 1889–1918 except 1900–6 & cabinet minister 1905–16   179, 248

Blake, Robt N. W. (b. 1916), Ld 1971 (life peer); Oxford don; author of *The Unknown Prime Minister* (Bonar Law) (1955); *Disraeli* (1966); *The Conservative Party from Peel to Churchill* (1970), etc.   3, 63, 75, 87, 91, 98, 247, 248, 249, 250, 251, 252, 253, 254

Bonham, Francis R. (1785–1863), M.P. Rye 1830–ix, Harwich 1835–7; Peel's party organiser   10, 25, 45, 98

Boothby, Robert J. G. (b. 1900), Ld 1958 (life peer); M.P. Aberdeenshire E. 1924–58; P.P.S. to Churchill at Exr 1926–9; jr 1940   228

Borthwick, Sir (1880) Algernon (1830–1908), 1st Bt 1887, 1st B. Glenesk 1895; editor *Morning Post* 1852–72, owner 1876; candidate Evesham 1880; Fair Trader; an instigator of Primrose League 1883; M.P. Kensington S. 1885–95   6

Boyle, Sir Edwd C. G. (b. 1923), 3rd Bt, Ld B. of Handsworth 1970 (life peer); editor *Tory Democrat* 1950; M.P. 1950–70, minister 1954–64   99, 249, 253

Bracken, Brendan (1901–58), 1st V. 1952; M.P. Paddington N. 1929–45, Bournemouth 1945–51; Churchill's P.P.S. 1939–41, M. Information 1941–5, Ady *1945   228

Bradford, Selina (d. 1894) *née* Weld-Forester, wife (1844) of 3rd e. of (1819–98); correspondent of Disraeli   95, 248

Bridgeman, William Clive (1864–1935), 1st V. 1929; M.P. Salop W. 1906–29; jr 1915–22; S.S. Home *1922–4; Ady 1924–9   208, 224–5, 229, 231–2

Briggs, Asa (b. 1921), historian   75, 249, 253

Bright, John (1811–89), Radical M.P. from 1843; Unionist 1886; minister *1868–70 resigned, 1873–4, 1880–2 resigned   30, 69–70 73, 76

Brodrick, Hon. Wm St John (1856–1947), 9th V. Midleton 1907, 1st e. of Midleton 1920; M.P. Surrey W. 1880–5 & Guildford 1885–1905; jr 1886–92, 1895–1900; P.C. 1897; S.S. War *1900–3, India 1903–5   104, 117

Brougham, Henry (1778–1868), 1st B. 1830; a founder of the *Edinburgh Review*; Whig M.P. 1810–12, 1815–30; supported Canning 1827; L.C. *1830–4   59

Buckingham & Chandos, Richard Plantagenet Temple-Nugent-Brydges-Chandos-*Grenville* (1797–1861), 2nd d. of 1839; as Ld Chandos M.P. Bucks 1818–39; *L.P.S. 1841–Feb 1842 resigned; fervent protectionist   54

Buckingham & Chandos, Richard (1823–89), 3rd d. of 1861, son of above; as mss of Chandos M.P. Buckingham 1846–57; a jr Whip 1852; chairman, L.N.W. Railway 1852–61; L.P.C. *1866–7, S.S. Cols 1867–8; G. Madras 1875–80  86

Burke, Edmund (1729–97), Whig politician and writer much quoted by Tories 177, 230

Butler, Richard Austen (b. 1902), Ld 1965 (life peer); M.P. Saffron Walden 1929–65; jr 1932–41; P.C. 1939; Ed.P. 1941–4, M. Education 1944–5; M. Labour *1945; Chairman Conservative Research Dept from 1945; Chairman National Union of Conservative & Unionist Associations 1945–56; Chairman Conservative Party Organisation 1959–61; Ch.Exr 1951–5; Ldr C. 1955–61 as L.P.S. 1955–9 & S.S. Home 1957–62; 1st S.S. & Deputy-P.M. 1962–3; S.S. Foreign 1963–4; candidate for premiership 1957, 1963; Master, Trinity College Cambridge 1965  99, 249, 253

Cairns, Hugh McCalmont (1819–85), 1st B. 1867, 1st e. 1878; M.P. Belfast 1852–66; S.-G. 1858–9; A.-G. 1866; judge 1866–8; L.C. *1868, 1874–80  86, 90, 103, 108

Cambridge, Field-Marshal H. R. H. George (1819–1904) 2nd d. of 1850, Commander-in-Chief 1852–95  137–8

Campbell, John (1779–1861), 1st B. 1841; Whig M.P. & Law officer 1830–41; L.C. (I.) 1841; Ch.D. *1846–50; judge 1850–9; L.C. 1859–61  70

Campbell-Bannerman, Sir (1895) Henry (1835–1908), Liberal M.P. 1868–1908, jr 1871–4, 1880–4; Ch.S. 1884–5; P.C. 1884; S.S. War *1886, 1892–5; Ldr Opposition in Commons 1899–1905; P.M. Dec 1905–1908  6, 137, 145, 148

Canning, George (1770–1827), leader of the more liberal disciples of Pitt; M.P. from 1794; jr 1796–1801, 1804–6; S.S. *Foreign 1807–9, 1822–7; Ind.P. 1816–21; Ldr C. 1822–7; P.M. & Ch.Exr Apr–Aug 1827  36–8, 59, 62, 64

Canningites, 1827–30  37–8, 59

Cardwell, Edwd (1813–86), 1st V. 1874; M.P. Clitheroe 1842–7, (Peelite) Liverpool 1847–52x, Oxford 1853–7x, (Liberal) Oxford 1857–74; jr 1845–6; P.B.T. 1852–5 resigned; P.C. 1852; cabinet minister 1859–66, 1868–74  10, 47

Carlisle, Geo Howard (1773–1848), 6th e. of 1825; as V. Morpeth anti-Foxite Whig M.P. 1795–1825; jr 1806–7; minister under Canning 1827; *L.P.S. July 1827–Jan 1828; Msp under Grey 1830–4; L.P.S. 1834  60

Carnarvon, Henry Howard Molyneux (1831–90), 4th e. of 1849; S.S. Cols *1866–7 resigned; 1874–8 resigned; L.L.I. 1885  74, 75, 90–1, 94, 116, 118–19

Carson, Sir (1900) Edwd Henry (1854–1935), Ld 1921 (life peer); M.P. Dublin University 1892–1918 & Belfast, Duncairn 1918–21; Law Officer (I) 1892; S.-G. 1900–5; P.C. 1905; Irish Unionist & Ulster champion 1911–14; A.-G. *1915 resigned; Admy Dec 1916–July 1917; M.W.C. July 1917–Jan 1918; judge 1921–9  15, 173, 175–6, 178, 180–2, 194

Castlereagh  see Londonderry

Cecil, Jas Brownlow Wm (after 1821 Gascoyne) (1791–1868), 2nd mss of Salisbury 1823; L.P.S. *1852; L.P.C. 1858–9  63, 85

CECIL, ROBERT ARTHUR TALBOT GASCOYNE (1830–1903), 3rd MSS OF SALISBURY 1868; Eton & Christ Church, Oxford (University Chancellor 1869–1903), Fellow of All Souls' 1853; as Ld Rbt Cecil & (1865–8) V. Cranborne, M.P. Stamford 1853–68; working journalist; S.S. India *1866–Feb 1867 resigned, & 1874–8; S.S. Foreign 1878–80, 1885–6, 1887–92, 1895–1900; Ldr Lords Opposition 1881–5; P.M. June 1885–Jan 1886, June 1886–Aug 1892, June 1895–July 1902 but not 1st Ld Treasury except June 1886–Jan 1887; L.P.S.

1900–2; Ldr Conservative party 1885–1902; Ldr H.M.'s Opposition 1886, 1892–5 **101–150**. Also 2–11, 13, 18–22, 25–6, 28, 31, 70, 74–7, 84–8, 90, 94, 151–7, 205, 217, 249–50

Cecil, Georgiana (1827–99), wife of above from 1857, da of the judge Sir Edwd Hall Anderson, Baron of Exchequer 101, 114, 115, 142

Cecil, Lady Gwendolen (1864–1945), daughter of above and biographer of her father 5, 142, 249, 252, 253

Cecil, Jas Edwd Hubert Gascoyne (1861–1947), 4th mss of Salisbury 1903; as V. Cranborne M.P. Darwen 1885–92, Rochester 1893–1903; U.-S.S. Foreign 1900–3; L.P.S. *Oct 1903–5 & P.B.T. 1905; L.P.C. Oct 1922–Jan 1924 & Ch.D. Oct 1922–May 1923; L.P.S. 1924–9; Ldr L. 1925–9; Ldr Opposition Lords 1929–31 resigned; important elder statesman role 1940 120, 148, 150, 188, 190, 203–4, 206, 227, 230, 233

Cecil, Lord E. A. Robert G. (1864–1958), 1st V. of Chelwood 1923; M.P. Marylebone E. 1906–10* & Hitchin 1911–23; P.C. 1915, U.-S.S. Foreign 1915–18, M. Blockade 1916–18; Assistant S.S. Foreign 1918–19; L.P.S.* 1923–4; Ch.D. (M. League of Nations Affairs) 1924–Aug 1927 resigned; Pres., League of Nations Union 1923–45; Nobel Peace Prize 1937; staunch High Churchman 150, 203–4, 207, 253

Cecil, Lord Hugh R. H. G. (1869–1956), 1st B. Quickswood 1941; M.P. Greenwich 1895–1906, Oxford University 1910–37; Unionist Free Trader and staunch High Churchman; P.C. 1918; Provost of Eton 1936–44; author of *Conservatism* (1912) 3, 85, 104, 149–50

Cecil, Algernon (1879–1953), cousin of above three brothers; author 249

Chadwick, Sir (1889) Edwin (1800–90); Poor Law Commissioner 1832–6; Board of Health 1846–54 19

Chamberlain, Joseph (1836–1914), Birmingham M.P. 1876–1914 (Radical 1876–86, then Unionist); Liberal P.B.T. *1880–5, P.L.G. 1886; Ldr Lib. Unionist M.P.s 1891–1906; S.S. Cols 1895–1903 resigned 3, 11, 14, 18, 19, 21, 22, 26, 27, 111–12, 114–17, 122–7, 131–3, 135, 138–40, 145–6, 148–9, 153–63, 165–6, 173–4, 184, 186, 195, 198, 203, 222, 240

CHAMBERLAIN, SIR (JOSEPH) AUSTEN (1863–1937); M.P. Worcs. E. 1892–1914 & Birmingham W. 1914–37; jr Whip 1892 (Lib. Unionist); jr Admy 1895–1900, F.S.T. 1900–2; P.M.G. *1902–3, Ch.Exr 1903–5; Ldr Lib. Unionist M.P.s 1906; candidate for Unionist leadership in Commons 1911 (withdrew); S.S. India May 1915–July 1917 resigned; M.W.C. Apr 1918–19; Ch.Exr Jan 1919–Mar 1921; L.P.S. Mar 1921–Oct 1922 & Ldr Cons. & Unionist M.P.s (deposed); S.S. Foreign 1924–9; K.G. 1925; Ady 1931 **185–93**. Also 4–6, 9, 12, 14, 24, 154, 172, 175, 177, 195, 198–9, 203–7, 218–20, 222, 230–2, 245, 250

Chamberlain, (Arthur) Neville (1869–1940), half-bro. of above; Ld Mayor Birmingham 1915–16; Director-Gen. Natl Service 1916–17; M.P. Birmingham Ladywood 1918–29, Edgbaston 1929–40; P.M.G. *1922–3; Pyr-G. 1923; M. Health 1923, 1924–9; Ch. Exr 1923–4, 1931–7; Chairman Conservative Research Dept 1929–40; Chairman Conservative Party Organisation June 1930–Apr 1931; P.M. 1937–May 1940; L.P.C. & M.W.C. May–Sep 1940; Ldr Conservative & Unionist party May 1937–Oct 1940 3, 5, 6, 12, 17, 20, 149, 157, 203–7, 212, 216–20, 222–4, 227–32, 234–6, 240, 243–5, 251

Chaplin, Henry (1840–1923), 1st V. 1916; M.P. Mid-Lincs. 1868–1906x, Wimbledon 1907–16; agricultural protectionist; Ch.D. 1885–6; *P.B.A. 1889–92; P.L.G. 1895–1900 135, 165

Churchill, John Winston Spencer (1822–83), 7th d. of Marlborough 1857; as mss of Blandford M.P. Woodstock 1844–5 resigned & 1847–57 (initially

Peelite); P.C. and H/O 1866–7, *L.P.C. Mar 1867–8; L.L.I. Nov 1876–80 75, 86

Churchill, Lord Randolph Henry Spencer (1849–94), son of above; M.P. Woodstock 1874–85, Paddington S. 1885–94; founder of 'Fourth Party', 'Tory Democrat', instigator of Primrose League; S.S. India *1885–6; Ch. Exr & Ldr C. June–Dec 1886 resigned    3–4, 6–7, 9, 10, 14, 16, 19, 25–7, 29, 30, 95–6, 99, 101, 106–9, 111–14, 116–18, 120–8, 131–4, 137, 197, 206

Churchill, Sir (1953, K.G.) Winston Leonard Spencer (1874–1965), son of above; M.P. Oldham 1900–5 (from 1904 Liberal); Lib. M.P. 1906–22 & unsuccessful candidate 1922, 1923; Liberal jr 1905–8; P.C. 1907; Liberal cabinet minister *1908–15 resigned; M. Munitions July 1917–Jan 1919; S.S. War 1919–Feb 1921 & S.S. Air 1919–Apr 1921, S.S. Cols Feb 1921–Oct 1922; Constitutional & (1925) Conservative M.P. Epping 1924–45, Woodford 1945–64; Ch.Exr 1924–9; resigned Shadow Cabinet 1931; Ady & M.W.C. Sep 1939–May 1940; P.M. (head of coalition) May 1940–May 1945, May–July 1945 (head of caretaker govt), Oct 1951–Apr 1955 (Conservative govt); Ldr Conservative & Unionist party Oct 1940–Apr 1955; Ldr H.M.'s Opposition 1945–51    29, 88, 156–7, 164, 178, 179, 183, 186–8, 190, 197, 201, 206–8, 212, 215–22, 225–7, 230–1, 233, 238, 245, 250, 251, 253

Churchill, Randolph F. E. S. (1911–68), son of above, journalist & political commentator; M.P. Preston 1940–5x    192, 251, 252, 254

Clarendon, Geo. W. F. *Villiers* (1800–70), 4th e. of 1838; diplomat; Whig cabinet minister 1839–41, 1846–52, 1853–8, 1864–6, 1868–70    71

Clarke, Sir (1886) Edward Geo. (1841–1931), M.P. Southwark 1880x, Plymouth 1880–1900, City of London 1906; S.-G. 1886–92; P.C. 1908; writer on legal & ecclesiastical subjects    94

Clarke, P. F., historian, author of *Lancashire and the New Liberalism* (1971) 30, 32

Clerk, Sir George (1787–1867), 6th Bt 1798; M.P. Midlothian 1811–32x, 1835–7x, Stamford 1838–47, Dover (Peelite) 1847–52x; jr 1819–30; Chief Whip 1834–5, 1841–5; P.C. Feb 1845; V.P.B.T. 1845–6    45

Clynes, John Robert (1869–1949), Lancs. trade unionist & Labour M.P. (1906–31x); jr 1917; P.C. 1918; Food Controller 1918–19; Ldr Lab. M.P.s 1912–22; cabinet minister 1924, 1929–31    214, 235

Cobb, Sir (1918) Cyril Stephen (1861–1938), barrister, chairman L.C.C. 1913, M.P. Fulham W. 1918–29x, 1930–8    228

Cobden, Richard (1804–65), leader (with Bright) of Anti-Corn Law League and champion of Peace, Retrenchment, Reform; Radical M.P. 1841–65    29, 110

Collings, Jesse (1831–1920), shop assistant, commercial traveller, Birmingham merchant, councillor from 1868, mayor 1878; colleague of Joseph Chamberlain in National Education League and of Joseph Arch in 'land for labourers' movement ('three acres & a cow'); M.P. Ipswich (Radical) 1880–5, Birmingham; Bordesley (Unionist) 1885–1918; jr (Lib) 1886, resigned, & 1895–1902 (Unionist) at Home Office; P.C. 1892    114, 117, 122

Connaught, H.R.H. Arthur (1850–1942), 1st d. of 1874, third son of Queen Victoria; Field-Marshal 1902    138

Cooper, Alfred Duff (1890–1954), 1st B. Norwich 1952; M.P. Oldham 1924–9*; Westminster St George's 1931–45; jr 1928–9, 1931–4, F.S.T. 1934–5; S.S. War *1935–7; Ady 1937–8 resigned; M. Information 1940–1, Ch.D. 1941–3; ambassador to French 1943–7    232

Coppock, James (1798–1857), Liberal electoral organiser    45

Cornford, Jas Peters (b. 1935), professor of politics Edinburgh from 1968    11, 32, 148–9, 249, 250

Corry, Hon. Henry Thos Lowry (1803–73), M.P. Co. Tyrone 1825–73; Whip

1834–5; P.C. 1835; jr 1841–6 & 1858–9; Ed. V.-P. 1866–7, *Ady 1867–8 75, 86

Corry, Montagu William Lowry (1838–1903), 1st B. Rowton 1880; son of above; p/s to Disraeli 1866–8 & 1874–80; philanthropist (nephew of Shaftesbury) 95

Cowling, Maurice John (b. 1926), Cambridge don; candidate 1959; author of illuminating books on party history 198, 249, 251

Craig, Capt. Sir James (1871–1940), 1st Bt 1918, 1st V. Craigavon 1927; M.P. Down E. 1906–18 & Mid 1918–21; champion with Carson of Union and of Ulster Protestants; Whip 1916–18, jr 1919–21; P.C. 1921; P.M. Northern Ireland 1921–40   176, 178

Cranbrook   see Hardy

Crewe, Robert O. A. Crewe-*Milnes* (1858–1945), 1st e. of 1895 & mss of 1911 (2nd B. Houghton 1885); Liberal politician; jr 1886; L.L.I. 1892–5 & P.C.; cabinet minister 1905–16; Ldr L. 1908–16; ambassador Paris 1922–8; S.S. War in National Govt Aug–Nov 1931; Ldr Lib. peers 1936–44   194

Croft, Brig.-Gen. Sir Henry Page (1881–1947), 1st Bt 1924, 1st B. 1940; M.P. Christchurch 1910–18 & Bournemouth 1918–40; ardent tariff reformer, imperialist & diehard; U.-S.S. War 1940–5   223, 229, 231, 237

Cross, Richard Assheton (1823–1914), 1st V. 1886; M.P. Preston 1857–62, Lancs. S.W. (defeating Gladstone) 1868–85, Newton 1885–6; S.S.* Home 1874–80, 1885–6; S.S. India 1886–92; Ch.D. 1895 & L.P.S. 1895–1900   19, 30, 90, 93, 113, 135, 253

Cunliffe, Walter (1855–1920), 1st B. 1914; G. Bank of England 1913–18   183, 208

Cunliffe-Lister, Major Sir (1920) Philip, M.C. (1884–1972), 1st V. Swinton 1935, 1st e. of Swinton 1955; name (till 1924) Lloyd-Greame; M.P. Hendon 1918–35; jr 1917–18 & Aug 1920–2; P.B.T. *1922–4, 1924–9, Aug–Nov 1931; S.S. Cols Nov 1931–5; S.S. Air June 1935–May 1938; minister in Churchill coalition June 1942–5; Ch.D. & M. Materials Oct 1951–Nov 1952, S.S. Commonwealth Relations 1952–5   199, 203–5, 217–18, 222, 224, 227, 231, 240

Curzon, Hon Geo Nathaniel (1859–1925), 1st B. (I.) 1898, 1st e. 1911, 1st Mss C. of Kedleston 1921; Fellow of All Souls' 1883; M.P. Southport 1886–98; jr (India) 1891–2; U.-S.S. Foreign 1895–8; P.C. 1898; G.-G. India 1898–1905; active as R.P. (I.) 1906–11; L.P.S. *1915–16; K.G. 1916; L.P.C. & M.W.C. Dec. 1916–Oct 1919; S.S. Foreign 1919–24; passed over for premiership 1923; L.P.C. 1924–5; Ldr L. Dec 1916–Jan 1924, Nov 1924–5; Ldr Cons. peers 1916–25   9, 173, 180, 183, 187, 190, 192–4, 199, 201–2, 204

Dalton, Hugh (1887–1962), Ld 1960 (life peer ; Labour M.P. 1924–31x, 1935–59; jr 1929–41; minister in Churchill coalition 1940–5; Labour Ch.Exr 1945–7 & Cabinet 1948–51   239

Davidson, John Colin Campbell (1889–1970), 1st V. 1937; p/s to Lib. S.S. Cols 1910–15 & to Bonar Law 1915–20; M.P. Hemel Hempstead 1920–3, 1924–37; P.P.S. Bonar Law 1920–1, 1922–3, Baldwin 1921–2; Ch.D. 1923–4, 1931–7; jr (Admy) 1924–6; Chairman Conservative Party Organisation Nov 1926–May 1930; P.C. 1928   25, 28–9, 188, 192, 193, 199, 201, 215, 220, 221, 223–8, 231–2, 234, 236, 251

Davidson, Frances Joan ['Mimi'] (b. 1894), wife of above from 1919; life peer (Bss Northchurch) 1963; *née* Dickinson (da of Lib. M.P. who became Lab. & Nat. Lib. peer); M.P. Hemel Hempstead 1937–59   224–5, 229

Dawson, (Geo.) Geoffrey (1874–1944), *né* Robinson; Fellow of All Souls' 1898; civil servant; member of 'Milner's Kindergarten' in S. Africa 1901–10; Editor *The Times* 1911–19, 1923–41   237

Derby, Earls of  *see Stanley*
Devonshire, Spencer Compton *Cavendish* (1833–1908), 8th d. of 1891; as mss of Hartington M.P. (Whig) Lancs. N. 1857–68x, Radnor Boros 1869–80, Lancs. N.E. 1880–5, Rossendale 1885–91 (Unionist from 1886); jr 1863–6; Liberal cabinet minister *1866, 1868–74, 1880–5; Ldr Liberal M.P.s 1875–80, Lib. Unionist M.P.s 1886–91; Ldr Lib. Unionist party 1886–1906; L.P.C. 1895–Oct 1903 resigned (Unionist Free Trader); Ed. P. 1900–2; Ldr L. 1902–3   19, 26, 93, 107, 113, 118, 122–6, 128, 136–40, 142, 147, 149, 154–5, 161–3
Devonshire, Victor Christian William *Cavendish* (1868–1938), 9th d. of 1908, nephew of above; M.P. Derbyshire W. (Lib. Unionist) 1891–1908; Deputy Chief Whip 1900–3, F.S.T. 1903–5; Unionist Chief Whip Lords 1911–16; jr (Admy) 1915–16; G.-G. Canada 1916–21; S.S. Cols *1922–4   204
Dilke, Sir Chas Wentworth (1843–1911), 2nd Bt; M.P. (Radical) Chelsea 1868–86, Forest of Dean 1892–1910; U.-S.S. Foreign 1880–2, P.L.G. *1882–5; ministerial career blighted by divorce action 1886   115, 145
DISRAELI, BENJAMIN (1804–81), 1st E. OF BEACONSFIELD 1876; journalist and novelist; M.P. Maidstone 1837–41, Shrewsbury 1841–7, Bucks 1847–76; Ldr Protectionist M.P.s 1849; Ch.Exr & Ldr C. Feb–Dec 1852, Mar 1858–June 1859, July 1866–Feb 1868; Ldr Opposition M.P.s 1849–52, 1852–8, 1859–66; P.M. Feb.–Dec 1868, Mar 1874–Apr 1880; Ldr H.M.'s Opposition 1868–74, 1880–1; Ldr Conservative party 1868–81   78–100. Also 2, 5, 7–11, 13–14, 16, 18, 21, 23–5, 30, 42, 51, 55, 58–9, 63, 64, 66–76, 101–3, 113–15, 118, 125, 126, 135, 136, 139, 141, 165, 195, 223, 247–9, 252
Disraeli, Mary-Anne (1792–1871) *née* Evans, wife of above from 1839 (widow of Wyndham Lewis); Vss Beaconsfield, 1868   10, 58, 81, 87–9, 97
Drummond, Henry (1786–1860), banker, M.P. 1810–13 & Surrey W. 1847–60; High Tory; Founder of Oxford chair of political economy and of Irvingite 'catholic apostolic' church   70

Ecroyd, William Farrer (1827–1915), candidate 1874, 1880, 1885, M.P. Preston May 1881–5; champion of 'Fair Trade'   31
Eden, Sir (K.G. 1954) (Robert) Anthony (b. 1897), 1st e. of Avon 1961; M.P. Warwick & Leamington 1923–57; P.P.S. Austen Chamberlain (S.S. Foreign) 1926–9; U.-S.S. Foreign 1931–3; L.P.S. 1933–5; M. League of Nations Affairs *June–Dec 1935; S.S. Foreign Dec 1935–Feb 1938 resigned, Dec 1940–5 (M.W.C.), Oct 1951–Apr 1955; S.S. Dominions Sep 1939–May 1940; S.S. War May–Dec 1940; Ldr C. 1942–5; P.M. & Ldr Conservative party Apr 1955–Jan 1957   207
Edward VII (1841–1910) reigned 1901–10   20, 88, 149, 154, 168
Elliot, Col Walter (1888–1958) M.C.; M.P. Lanark 1918–23, Glasgow Kelvingrove 1924–45, 1950–8, Scottish Universities 1946–50; jr (Scotland) 1923–4, 1924–9; F.S.T. Sep 1931–2; M. Ag. & Fish. *1932–6, S.S. Scotland 1936–8, M. Health 1938–40   99, 228, 253
Eyres-Monsell, Commander Sir (1929) Bolton Meredith (1881–1969), 1st V. Monsell 1935; M.P. S. Worcs. & later Evesham 1910–35; Opposition Whip 1911–14; Deputy Chief Whip Feb 1919–21, jr (Admy) Apr 1921–May 1923; P.C. 1923; Conservative Chief Whip 1923–31; *Ady 1931–June 1936   219, 223, 231, 245

Fergusson, Col. Sir Jas (1832–1907) 6th Bt 1849; M.P. Ayrshire Dec 1854–7x, Oct 1859–68; jr 1866–8; P.C. 1868; colonial governor 1868–75, 1880–5; defeated candidate 1876, 1878; M.P. Manchester N.E. 1885–1906x; U.-S.S. Foreign 1886–91, P.M.G. 1891–2   135
Ferrand, William Busfeild (1809–89) *né* Busfeild; M.P. Knaresbro' 1841–7,

Devonport Feb 1863–6; defeated candidate Aylesbury 1851, Devonport 1859, Coventry 1867; social reformer 61–3, 81–2

Forwood, Sir Arthur Bower (1836–98) 1st Bt. 1895; shipowner; Liverpool mayor 1878–9, candidate 1882; M.P. Ormskirk 1885–98; jr (Admy) 1886–92 136

Fraser, Capt. (R.N.) Sir (1919) (John) Malcolm (1878–1949) 1st Bt. 1921; newspaper editor; press adviser Cons. Central Office 1910; Principal Agent 1920–3; editor, *British Gazette* in genl strike 1926; Vice-Chairman Cons & Unionist Orgn 1937–9 189

Fremantle, Sir Thos Francis (1798–1890), 1st Bt. 1821, 1st B. Cottesloe 1874; M.P. Buckingham 1827–46; Conservative Chief Whip 1833–44 (in office 1834–5, 1841–4); Sec. at War May 1844–5; Ch.S. 1845–6; Chairman Customs Bd 1846–74 45

Gash, Norman (b. 1912), historian 5, 9, 17, 92, 247, 253

Geddes, Sir (1916) Eric Campbell (1875–1937), railway management expert; M.P. Cambridge July 1917–22; *Ady & P.C. Sep 1917; M.W.C. 1919, M. Transport 1919–21; Chairman Ctee on Natl Expenditure 1921 23

George IV (1762–1830), regent 1811–20, reigned 1820–30 37

George V (1865–1936), reigned 1910–36 193, 201, 205, 237

George, David Lloyd (1863–1945), 1st E. Lloyd-George 1945; Liberal M.P. Carnarvon Boros 1890–1945; P.B.T. *1905–8, Ch.Exr 1908–15, M. Munitions 1915–16, S.S. War 1916; P.M. (coalition governments) Dec 1916–Oct 1922 when Conservatives revolted; Ldr Lib. M.P.s Oct 1926–31 8, 13, 21, 29, 34, 158, 166–8, 173, 179–83, 187–93, 195–206, 221–2, 226, 228, 230, 233–4, 239–40, 242–3

George, Henry (1839–97), American radical tax reform advocate 110

Gladstone, William Ewart (1809–98). As Conservative (member of Carlton Club till 1860), M.P. Newark 1832–45 resigned, Oxford University from 1847; jr Whip 1834, jr (War & Cols) 1835, P.C. 1841, V.P.B.T. 1841–3, *P.B.T. May 1843–Jan 1845, S.S. War & Cols Dec 1845–June 1846. As Peelite, Ch.Exr Dec 1852–5 resigned. As Liberal, M.P. 1859–95; Ch.Exr 1859–66 & Ldr C. 1865–6; P.M. 1868–74, 1880–5, 1886, 1892–4 resigned; Ldr Commons Opposition 1866–8; Ldr H.M.'s Opposition 1874–5 resigned, 1885–6, 1886–92; Ldr, Liberal party 1868–75, 1880–94 7, 8, 10, 11, 14, 19, 26, 42, 47, 52, 61, 67–9, 71, 73, 75–8, 87–9, 92–7, 101, 105, 107–110, 115–26, 129–33, 139, 143

Gladstone, Herbert John (1854–1930), 1st V. 1930, son of above; Lib. M.P. Leeds 1880–1910, jr 1881–5, 1886, 1892–4; P.C. 1894; Wks 1894–5; Opposition Chief Whip 1899–1905; S.S. *Home 1905–10; G.-G. S. Africa 1910–14 21, 27

Goderich see Ripon

Gorst, Sir (1885) John Eldon (1835–1916); candidate Hastings 1865; M.P. Cambridge 1866–8x, Chatham Feb 1875–92, Cambridge University 1892–1906x; Principal Agent, Conservative Central Office 1868–74 resigned & 1881–2 resigned; Vice-Chairman National Union of Conservative & Constitutional Associations 1881–4, resigned; a founder of the 'Fourth Party' and the Primrose League; Q.C. 1875; S.-G. 1885–6; jr (India) 1886–91, F.S.T. 1891–2; Ed. V.-P. 1895–1902; Unionist Free Trader 1903; Liberal candidate for Preston 1910 10, 25–7, 30, 45, 89, 95, 96, 98, 112–14, 124, 135–6

Goschen, Geo. Joachim (1831–1907), 1st V. 1900; banker; Liberal M.P. 1863–86, jr 1865 & cabinet minister 1866, 1868–74; Lib. Unionist M.P. St George's Hanover Square 1887–1900; Ch.Exr 1887–92; Ady 1895–1900; Chancellor Oxford University 1903–7 20, 125, 127, 131, 133–6, 145

Goulding, Sir Edwd Alfred (1862–1936) 1st Bt 1915, 1st B. Wargrave 1922; candidate 1906; M.P. Wilts. E. 1895–1906x, Worcester 1908–22; P.C. 1918; tariff reformer; eminent businessman 23, 28

Gower, Sir (1924) (Robert) Patrick (Malcolm) (1887–1964); civil servant; a/s Law & Austen Chamberlain 1917–22 & to Law & Baldwin as P.M.s 1922–4; deputy director 1928 and director 1929–39, publicity, Conservative Central Office 224, 231

Graham, Sir James Rbt Geo. (1792–1861), 2nd Bt; Whig M.P. 1818–37, *Ady 1830–4 resigned; Cons. M.P. Pembroke Dist. 1838–41, Dorchester 1841–7, S.S. Home 1841–6; Peelite M.P. Ripon 1847–52, Carlisle 1852–61 (latterly a Liberal); Ady 1852–55 resigned 45, 59, 60, 65, 69, 81, 97

Graham, William (1887–1932), journalist; Edinburgh Labour M.P. 1918–31x, F.S.T. 1924; *P.B.T. 1929–31 238, 242

Granby see Rutland

Granville, Granville Geo. Leveson-Gower (1815–91), 2nd e. 1846; Whig M.P. 1837–46, jr 1840–1, 1846–51; cabinet minister 1851–2, 1852–8, 1859–66, 1868–74, 1880–5, 1886; Ldr Liberal peers 1855–65, 1868–86 95

Greenwood, Arthur (1880–1954); Labour Party economic & social researcher; M.P. Nelson & Colne 1922–31x, Wakefield 1932–54; jr (Health) 1924; M. Health *1929–31; Deputy Ldr Labour Party (acting leader 1939); M.W.C. 1940–2; in Labour cabinet 1945–7 237

Gretton, Col. John (1867–1947), 1st B. 1944; brewer; M.P. Derbyshire S. 1895–1906; Rutland 1907–18, Burton 1918–43; P.C. 1926; diehard critic first of Lloyd George & then of Baldwin 188–9, 192, 229, 237

Greville, Chas Cavendish Fulke (1794–1865), Clerk to Privy Council, famous as diarist 57, 63–4, 68, 97, 252

Grey, Charles (1764–1845), 2nd e. 1807; Whig M.P. 1786–1807; as V. Howick *Admy 1806, S.S. Foreign 1806–7; P.M. 1830–4 resigned 35, 38, 40–1, 43, 60, 65

Grey, Sir Edward (1862–1933), 3rd Bt, 1st V. of Falloden 1916; Liberal M.P. 1885–1916; U.-S.S. Foreign 1892–5; P.C. 1902; S.S. Foreign *1905–16; K.G. 1912; Ldr Liberal peers 1916–24 149, 179, 206

Hailsham see Hogg

Haldane, Richard Burdon (1856–1928), 1st V. of Cloan 1911; Liberal M.P. 1885–1911; P.C. 1902; *S.S. War 1905–12, L.C. 1912–15, 1924 (under Labour); K.T. 1913; O.M. 1915 146, 197

Halifax see Irwin

Halsbury, Sir Hardinge S. Giffard (1825–1921), 1st B. 1885, 1st e. of 1898; M.P. Launceston 1877–85; S.-G. 1875–80; L.C. *1885–6, 1886–92, 1895–1905; Ldr Lords diehards 1910–11 135, 170, 187

Hamilton, Lord George Francis (1845–1927); M.P. Middlesex 1868–85, Ealing 1885–1906; jr (India) 1874–8, *Ed. V.-P. 1878–80, Ady 1885–8, 1886–92; S.S. India 1895–1903 resigned (Unionist Free Trader) 163

Hamilton, Mary Agnes (1883–1966), novelist & biographer, Labour M.P. Blackburn 1929–31 244

Hankey, Col. Sir (1919) Maurice P. A. (1877–1963), 1st B. 1939; a/s Ctee of Imperial Defence 1908–12, sec. 1912–16, 1919–38; sec. M.W.C. 1916–19; sec., cabinet 1919–38; Msp *1939–40; Ch.D. May 1940–July 1941, Pyr G. 1941–Mar 1942 183

Hannon, Sir Patrick J. H. (1874–1963); candidate 1910; M.P. Birmingham Moseley 1921–50; active for agricultural reform Ireland 1896–1904, S. Africa 1905–9 & with Tariff Reform League 1910–14, National Service League 1911–15, Navy League 1911–18, British Commonwealth Union

1918–25; Hon.Sec. H. of Commons Industrial Group 1921–9 & Empire Industries Association 1925; President Nat. Assoc. of British Manufacturers 1935–53   228

Harcourt, Sir William Geo. Granville Vernon (1827–1904); Liberal M.P. 1868–1904; S.-G. 1873–4; S.S. Home *1880–5; Ch.Exr 1886, 1892–5; Ldr C. 1894–5; Ldr Commons Opposition 1895–9 resigned   19, 110

Hardwicke, Chas P. Yorke (1799–1873), 4th e. of; *P.M.G. 1852, L.P.S. 1858–9   63

Hardy, Gathorne (1814–1906), 1st V. Cranbrook 1878, e. of Cranbrook 1892; M.P. Leominster 1856–65, Oxford University 1865–78; jr (Home) 1858–9; P.P.L. *1866–7, S.S. Home May 1867–8; S.S. War 1874–8, India 1878–80; L.P.C. 1885–6, 1886–92   9, 16, 86, 90, 93, 102

Hartington   see Devonshire

Henderson, Arthur (1863–1935), Labour M.P. at intervals 1903–31 and leader of such 1908–9, 1914–18, 1931; *Ed. P. 1915–16, Pyr G. 1916; M.W.C. Dec 1916–Aug 1917 resigned; S.S. Home 1924; S.S. Foreign 1929–31; Ldr H.M.'s Opposition 1931   237–8, 242, 244

Henley, Joseph Warner (1793–1884), squire (son of London merchant); M.P. Oxon 1841–78; *P.B.T. 1852, 1858–Feb 1859 resigned   63, 84

Herbert, Hon. Sidney (1810–61), 1st Ld of Lea 1861, father of 13th & 14th e.s of Pembroke; M.P. Wilts. S. 1832–61; jr (India) 1834–5 (Admy) 1841–5; S. at War *Feb 1845–6 & (Peelite) Jan 1853–Jan 1855, S.S. Cols Jan–Feb 1855 resigned; S.S. War (Liberal) 1859–61   61, 97

Herries, John Charles (1778–1855), London merchant family; financial civil servant 1807–22; M.P. Harwich 1823–41, Stamford 1847–53, defeated Ipswich 1841; F.S.T. 1823–7, Ch.Exr *1827–8, Master of Mint 1828–30, P.B.T. 1830; Sec. at War 1834–5; Ind. P. 1852   63, 83–4

Hewins, William A. S. (1865–1931), director, London School of Economics 1895–1903; secretary, Tariff Commission 1903–17; M.P. Hereford 1912–18; jr (Cols) Sep 1917–Jan 1919   172, 174, 179, 180, 203, 250, 253, 254

Hoare, Lt-Col. Sir Samuel John Gurney (1880–1959), 2nd Bt 1915, 1st V. Templewood 1944; M.P. Chelsea 1910–44; S.S. Air 1922–4 (P.C. 1922, cabinet May 1923) & 1924–9; Treasurer Cons. Party Orgn 1929–30; S.S. India 1931–5, S.S. Foreign June–Dec 1935 resigned; Ady June 1936–May 1937; S.S. Home 1937–9; L.P.S. Sep 1939–Apr 1940, S.S. Air Apr–May 1940; ambassador Madrid 1940–4   192, 199, 230, 231, 235, 240

Hogg, Capt. Sir (1922) Douglas McGarel (1872–1950), 1st B. Hailsham 1928, 1st V. 1929; M.P. Marylebone 1922–8; A.-G. 1922–4 & *1924–8; L.C. Mar 1928–9 & June 1935–Mar 1938; Ldr Lords Opposition 1930–1; Ldr L. & S.S. War Nov 1931–5; L.P.C. Mar–Oct 1938   218, 230, 231, 237, 245

Hogg, Hon Quintin McG. (b. 1907), 2nd V. Hailsham 1950–63 (disclaimed peerage), B. Hailsham of St Marylebone 1970 (life peer); M.P. Oxford 1938–50, Marylebone 1963–70; jr (Air) 1945; Q.C. 1953; Admy Sep 1956–Jan 1957; M. Education *Jan–Sep 1957; L.P.C. Sep 1957–Oct 1959 & Chairman Cons. Party Organisation; M. Science 1959–64 & L.P.S. 1959–60 & L.P.C. 1960–4; Ldr L. 1960–4; candidate for premiership 1963; L.C. from 1970   3, 66, 252

Horne, Sir (1919) Robert Stevenson (1871–1940), 1st V. 1937; philosophy don & K.C.; M.P. Glasgow Hillhead 1918–37; jr (Admy) 1918–19; M. Labour *Jan 1919–20; P.B.T. Mar 1920–21, Ch.Exr Apr 1921–Oct 1922; subsequently business magnate   199

Hughes, Percival, Principal Agent Conservative Central Office Dec 1906–Jan 1912   28

Hunt, George War (1825–77), squire; M.P. Northants N. 1857–77; F.S.T. 1867–8, *Ch. Exr 1868; Ady 1874–7 86, 90, 94

Huskisson, William (1770–1830), M.P. 1796–1830, for Liverpool from 1823; jr 1795–1801, F.S.T. 1804–6, 1807–9; P.M.G. 1814–23; P.B.T. *1823–7, S.S. Cols 1827–8 resigned; Ldr C. Scp 1827–Jan 1828; Canningite 37, 60

Hylton see Jolliffe


Iddesleigh see Northcote

Irwin, Hon. Fdk Lindley (1881–1959), 1st B. 1925, 3rd V. Halifax 1934, 1st e. of Halifax 1944; Fellow of All Souls' (University Chancellor 1933–59); M.P. Ripon 1910–25; U.-S.S. Cols 1921–2; Ed. P. *1922–4 & 1932–5; M. Agriculture 1924–5; G.-G. India 1926–31; S.S. War 1935, Foreign 1938–40; L.P.S. 1935–7, L.P.C. 1938–8; Ldr L. 1935–8, Apr–Dec 1940; ambassador Washington 1940–6 201, 226, 230

Iveagh, Gwendolen (1881–1966), Ctss of, née Onslow, wife (1903) of Rupert Guiness whom she succeeded as M.P. Southend 1927–35; Chairman Conservative Women's Orgn 1924 223


Jackson, William Lawies (1840–1917), 1st B. Allerton 1902; Leeds M.P. 1880–1902; F.S.T. 1886, 1886–91; Ch.S. 1891–2; P.C. 1890; Chairman Gt Northern Rlwy Co. 135–6

Jackson, Hon. Sir (1927) F. Stanley (1870–1947), son of above; M.P. Howdenshire 1915–26; jr (War) 1922–3; Chairman Conservative Party Organisation 1923–6; P.C. 1926; G. Bengal 1926–32; England cricketer 223

James, Sir Henry (1828–1911), 1st B. James of Hereford 1895; Liberal M.P. Taunton 1869–85 & S.-G. 1873, A.-G. 1873–4, 1880–5; P.C. 1885; M.P. Bury 1885–95 (Unionist 1886); Ch.D. *1895–1902 140

James, Robert Vidal Rhodes (b. 1933), Fellow of All Souls 1965, prolific biographer & historian 25, 250, 251, 253

Jenkins, Roy H. (b. 1920), Labour M.P. from 1948 & minister 1964–70; economist & historian 22, 251, 254

Jolliffe, Capt. Sir William G. Hylton (1800–76), 1st Bt 1821, 1st B. Hylton 1866; M.P. Petersfield 1830–2x, 1833–5x, 1838, 1841–66; U.-S.S. Home 1852; Conservative Chief Whip (in office 1858–9); P.C. 1859 78, 98

Jones, Thomas (1870–1955), a/s cabinet; C.II. 1929; important diarist 228, 233, 242, 251

Joynson-Hicks, Sir William (1865–1932), né Hicks, 1st Bt 1919, 1st V. Brentford 1929; solicitor; M.P. Manchester N.W. 1908–10x, Brentford 1911–18, Twickenham 1918–29; jr 1922–3; Pyr-G. & P.M.G. 1923; F.S.T. *1923, M. Health 1923–4, S.S. Home 1924–9; Evangelical and puritanical churchman 207, 210, 212, 216–19, 223


Keith-Falconer, Maj. Hon. Chas Jas (1832–89) 89, 98

Kennedy, Aubrey Leo (1885–1965), of The Times foreign dept; author 109, 249

Keynes, John Maynard (1883–1946), 1st B. 1942; civil servant 1906–8 & during world wars; creative Cambridge economist; Liberal party adviser 23, 183, 208, 233

Kirkwood, David (1872–1955), 1st B. 1951; Labour M.P. Dumbarton Burghs 1922–50, Dunbartonshire E. 1950–1; trade unionist (Scottish engineers); P.C. 1948 210


Lansdowne, Henry Petty-Fitzmaurice (1780–1863) 3rd mss of 1809; Whig minister 1806–7; *S.S. Home July 1827–Jan 1828; Whig minister 1830–4, 1835–41, 1846–52, 1852–8 59, 60

Lansdowne, Henry Chas Keith *Petty-Fitzmaurice* (1845–1927), 5th mss of 1866; Whig jr 1869–74, 1880 resigned; G.-G. Canada 1883–8, India 1888–94; Unionist S.S. War *1895–1900, Foreign 1900–5; Ldr Unionist peers 1903–16; Msp 1915   8, 15, 138, 140, 146–9, 165–6, 175–6, 180, 181

Lascelles, Hon. Wm S.S. (1798–1851); M.P. 1837–41x, 1842–51; Peelite jr in Whig govt   62

LAW, ANDREW BONAR (1858–1923); Glasgow High School; M.P. Glasgow Blackfriars 1900–6x, Dulwich May 1906–Dec 1910; candidate Manchr N.W. Dec 1910; M.P. Bootle Mar 1911–18, Glasgow Central 1918–23; jr Trade Aug 1902–5; Ldr Conservative & Unionist M.P.s Nov 1911–Mar 1921 resigned; S.S. Cols *1915–16, Ch.Exr 1916–19, L.P.S. 1919–21, being deputy-Ldr C. under Lloyd George; Leader of Conservative & Unionist party Oct 1922–May 1923 (resigned) as P.M.   171–202. Also 5–9, 11–15, 23–4, 28, 29, 31, 32, 204, 222, 224, 227

Lincoln, Henry *Pelham-Clinton* (1811–64), Lord, 5th d. of Newcastle 1851; M.P. Notts. S. 1832–46x, Falkirk (Peelite) 1846–51; jr whip 1834–5; minister 1841–6, *Ch.S. 1846; S.S. War & Cols 1853–4, War 1854–5, Cols 1859–64   61

Linlithgow, Maj. Victor J. A. *Hope* (1887–1952), 2nd mss of 1908; jr Admy 1922–4; Dep-Chairman Cons. Party Orgn 1924–6; G.-G. India 1936–42   226

Liverpool, Robert Banks *Jenkinson* (1770–1828), 2nd e. of 1808; M.P. 1790–1803 when B. Hawkesbury; jr 1794–1801; S.S. Foreign 1801–4, 1809, Home 1804–6, 1807–9, War & Cols 1809–12; Ldr L. 1804–6, 1807–27; P.M. 1812–27   36–7

Lloyd, Geoffrey Wm (b. 1902); p/s Hoare 1926–9, Baldwin 1929–31; P.P.S. to Baldwin 1931–5; M.P. Birmingham Ladywood 1931–45, King's Norton 1950–5, Sutton Coldfield since 1955; jr 1935–45; deptl minr 1945, 1951–5; cabinet 1957–9   222

Lloyd, Capt. George Ambrose (1879–1941), 1st B. of Dolobran 1925; M.P. Staffs. W. 1910–18, Eastbourne 1924–5; G. Bombay 1918–23; P.C. 1924; High Commr Egypt 1925–9 (dismissed); S.S. Cols & Ldr L. 1940–1; ardent imperialist   231

Londonderry, Robert *Stewart* (1769–1822) 2nd mss of 1821 (Irish peerage); famous as V. Castlereagh, M.P. from 1794; as Ch.S. 1798–1801 contrived the Union; Ind.P. *1802–6; S.S. War & Cols 1805–6, 1807–9; S.S. Foreign & Ldr C. 1812–22; K.G. 1814   36, 143

Londonderry, Frances Anne (1800–65) wife (1819) of Chas Wm, 3rd mss of (1778–1854); *née* Vane Tempest; correspondent of Disraeli   64, 223, 248, 252

Londonderry, Fredk W. R. *Stewart* (1805–72) 4th mss of 1854; stepson of above; M.P. Down 1826–52; temporary a Peelite   99–100, 223

Londonderry, Chas (1878–1949), 7th mss of 1915; son of above; M.P. Maidstone 1906–15; jr Air 1820–1; M. in Govt of N. Ireland 1921–6; P.C. 1925; Wks 1928–9 & 1931; S.S. Air *1931–5; L.P.S. & Ldr L. 1935   223–4, 245

Londonderry, Edith Helen (1879–1959), Lady, wife (1899) of above; da of Henry Chaplin   223–4, 248, 252, 253

Long, Walter Hume (1854–1924), 1st V. of Wraxall 1921; M.P. Wilts. N. 1880–5, Devizes 1885–92, Liverpool West Derby 1893–1900, Bristol S. 1900–6, Dublin S. 1906–10, Strand 1910–18, Westmr St George's 1918–21; jr 1886–92; P.B.A. *1895–1900, P.L.G. 1900–5, 1915–16; Ch.S. 1905; candidate for party leadership 1911 (withdrew); S.S. Cols 1916–19, Ady 1919–21   5, 172, 176, 181, 183, 186

Lonsdale, William *Lowther* (1787–1872), 2nd e. of 1844; as V. Lowther, M.P. 1808–41, mainly Westmld; jr 1809–27; P.B.T. *1834–5; P.M.G. 1841–5; L.P.C. 1852   63

Lowe, Robert (1811–92), 1st V. Sherbrooke 1880; legislator in Australia 1843–50; Lib. M.P. 1852–80; jr 1853–8; P.C. 1855; Ed. V.-P. 1859–64; led Adullamite revolt 1866; Ch.Exr 1868–73, S.S. Home 1873–4   71–2, 76, 104

Lucy, Sir (1909) Henry Wm (1845–1924); parly correspondent *Daily News* 1873; 'Toby M.P.' in Punch 1881–1916   148

MacDonald, James Ramsay (1866–1937); sec. Labour Repn Ctee & then of Labour party 1900–12, Treasurer 1912–24; Labour M.P. 1906–18; 1922–31, 'National Labour' Seaham Harbour 1931–5x, Scottish Universities 1936–7; Chairman, I.L.P. 1906–9 & Labour party 1909–14 resigned; Ldr H.M.'s Opposition 1922–4, 1924–9; P.M. 1924, 1929–35; S.S. Foreign 1924; L.P.C. 1935–7   21, 197, 198, 205, 215–17, 224–5, 229, 233–46

MacDonald, Malcolm J. (b. 1901), son of above; Lab. M.P. Bassetlaw 1929–31, Nat. Labour 1931–5x, Ross & Cromarty 1936–45; jr Dominions 1931–5, S.S. Dominions &/or Cols *1935–40, M. Health 1940–1, after which long service overseas   243

McKenna, Reginald (1863–1943); Lib. M.P. Monmouthshire N. 1895–1918; F.S.T. 1905–7; cabinet 1907–16; Chairman Midland Bank 1919–43; offered Exchequer by Law 1922, Baldwin 1923   182–3, 208

McKenzie, Robert T. (b. 1917), of London School of Economics; author & publicist   192, 234, 251

Maclean, Sir (1917) Donald (1864–1932), solicitor; Lib. M.P. Bath 1906–10x, Peebles & Selkirk 1910–22x, Cornwall N. 1929–32; Ldr Lib. M.P.s 1918–22 (Asquithian); Ed. P. *1931–2   239

Macmillan, Capt. (Maurice) Harold (b. 1894), publisher & writer; M.P. Stockton 1924–9x, 1931–45x Bromley 1946–64; M. in Churchill coalition 1940–5; S.S. Air *1945; successively M. Housing & Local Government, M. Defence, S.S. Foreign & Ch.Exr 1951–7; P.M. & Ldr Conservative party 1957–63   24, 220, 228

Macquisten, Fredk Arthur (1870–1940), K.C. M.P. Glasgow Springburn 1918–22x, Argyll 1924–40   209–10, 216

Malmesbury, John Edward *Harris* (1807–89), 3rd e. of, 1841; S.S. Foreign 1852, 1858–9; L.P.S. 1866–8, 1874–6   63, 86, 90, 252

*Manners   see* Rutland

*Marlborough   see* Churchill

Matthews, Sir Henry (1826–1913), 1st V. Llandaff 1895; Q.C. 1868; Conservative Home Rule M.P. Dungarvan 1868–74x; Conservative candidate Birmingham N. 1885; Cons. & Unionist M.P. Birmingham E. 1886–95; S.S. Home 1886–92   133–5

Mawdsley, James (1848–1902), Lancs. cotton spinner; member T.U.C. Parly Cttee 1882–97; Conservative candidate Oldham 1899   29

Maxse, Dame (1952) S. A. Marjorie (b. 1891); Chief Organisation Officer Cons Central Office 1921–39; Vice-Chairman Cons. Party Orgn 1944–51   223

May, Sir (1918) George Ernest (1871–1946), 1st Bt 1931, 1st B. 1935; Chairman, Economy Committee 1931, Import Duties Advisory Ctee from 1932   234, 238

Mayo, Richard Southwell *Bourke* (1822–72), 6th e. of 1867; as V. Nass M.P. Kildare 1847–52, Coleraine 1852–7, Cockermouth 1857–67; Ch.S. 1852, 1858–9, 1866–8; G.-G. India 1868–72 assassinated   86

Melbourne, William *Lamb* (1779–1848), 2nd V. 1829; Whig M.P. 1806–12; Tory (Canningite) 1816–29; Ch.S. 1827; resigned with Huskisson 1828; Whig S.S. Home 1830–4; P.M. July–Nov 1834 & 1835–41   41, 48, 60

Middleton, Lieutenant (R.N.) Richard C. E. (1846–1905); Conservative agent W. Kent 1883–4; Principal Agent Conservative Central Office Mar 1885–July 1903   6, 25–8, 124–7

Miles, Sir William (1797–1878), 1st Bt, 1858; M.P. before Reform Bill & for Somerset E. 1834–65   85
Milner, Sir (1895) Alfred (1854–1925), 1st B. 1901, V. 1902; Oxford don, barrister, financial civil servant 1887–97; High Commr S. Africa 1897–1905; P.C. 1901; M.W.C. 1916–18, S.S. War Apr 1918–Jan 1919, Cols 1919–Feb 1921; K.G. 1921   146, 178, 180, 182, 192, 194
Montagu, Lord Robert (1825–1902), M.P. Huntingdonshire 1859–74, West-meath (Cons. Home Ruler) 1874–80; Ed. V.-P. 1867–8; a Roman Catholic 1870–82, then passionately anti-papist & Unionist   74
Moore-Brabazon, Lt-Col. John Theodore Cuthbert (1884–1964), M.C. 1st B. Brabazon of Tara 1942; Britain's first aviator; M.P. Chatham 1918–29x, Wallasey 1931–42; jr Transport 1923–4, 1924–Jan 1927 resigned; M. Transport Oct 1940–May 1941, M. Aircraft Production 1941–Feb 1942   231
Mosley, Sir Oswald Ernald (b. 1896), 6th Bt, son-in-law (1920) of Curzon; M.P. Harrow (Cons. 1918–22, Ind. 1922–4), Smethwick (Lab. 1926–31, New Party 1931x); Ch.D. 1929–30 resigned; leader, British Union of Fascists 1932–40, Union Movement from 1948; interned 1940   222, 233, 238, 242
Muir, Ramsay (1872–1941), history professor, Manchester 1913–21; Lib. M.P. Rochdale 1923–4x, Chairman Liberal Party Organisation Committee 1930–1, National Liberal Federation 1931–3   242

Nevill, William Nevil (1826–1915), 5th e. 1868, 1st mss of Abergavenny 1876; a principal superintendent of Cons. orgn in Kent & nationally, especially 1867–74   98
Newdegate, Chas Newdigate (1816–87), M.P. Warwickshire 1843–85; P.C. 1886; a Tory Whip   83
Niemeyer, Sir (1924) Otto Ernst (1883–1972), Treasury official   208
Norfolk, Lt-Col. Henry Fitzalan-Howard (1847–1917), 15th d. of, 1860; P.M.G. 1895–1900   136
Norman, Montagu Collet (1871–1950), D.S.O., 1st B., 1944; Dep.-Govr 1918–20 & G. Bank of England 1920–44; P.C. 1923   208, 241
Northcliffe, Sir Alfred C. W. Harmsworth (1865–1922), 1st Bt 1904, 1st B. 1905, 1st V. 1918; owner of newspapers including (1908) The Times; Director of Propaganda to Enemy Countries 1918   175, 182, 185
Northcote, Sir Stafford Henry (1818–87), 8th Bt 1851, 1st e. of Iddesleigh 1885; p/s to Gladstone; historian of budgets; M.P. (Peelite) Dudley 1855–7, (Cons) Stamford 1858–66, Devon N. 1866–85; P.B.T. *1866–7; S.S. India 1867–8; Ch.Exr 1874–80; Ldr C 1876–80; Ldr Commons Opposition 1880–5; peer & 1st Ld Treasury June 1885–Feb 1886; S.S. Foreign 1886–7   7, 8, 10, 25–6, 72, 86, 90, 93, 95–6, 101–6, 108, 112, 114, 116, 126, 128, 133
Northumberland, Adm. Lord Algernon Percy (1792–1865), 4th d. of 1847 (1st B. Prudhoe 1816); Ady *1852   63
Northumberland, Algernon (1810–99), 6th d. of 1867; as Ld Lovaine M.P. Beeralston 1831–2, Northumberland N. 1832–65; jr Admy 1858; V.P.B.T. 1859; L.P.S. *1878–80   78

Oastler, Richard (1789–1861) Tory radical, factory reformer, candidate for Huddersfield 1837   61, 63, 74
O'Connell, Daniel (1775–1847) 'the Liberator', Irish Roman Catholic leader, M.P. 1829–47   37, 42, 44, 51, 60, 65
O'Connor, Sir (1936) Terence James (1891–1940), M.P. Luton 1924–9x, Nottingham C. 1930–40; S.-G. 1936–40   228
O'Connor, Thos Power (1848–1929); newspaper editor; Home Rule M.P.

Scotland division of Liverpool 1885–1929; P.C. 1924; highly partisan biographer of Disraeli, Parnell, Campbell-Bannerman etc. 91, 97, 247, 253

Oliver, Fredk Scott (1864–1934), one of Milner 'kindergarten' in S. Africa, author of *The Endless Adventure*, 3 vols (1930–5), *Politics and Politicians* (1934) 180, 195, 254

Ormsby-Gore, Capt. Hon. Wm Geo. Arthur (1885–1964), 4th B. Harlech, 1938; son-in-law (1913) of 4th mss of Salisbury; M.P. Denbigh Dist. 1910–18, Stratford 1918–38; a/s War Cabinet 1917; jr Cols 1922–4, 1924–9; P.M.G. 1931; *Wks 1931–6; S.S. Cols 1936–8  228, 245

O'Shea, Capt Wm Henry (1840–1905), Lib. M.P. Clare 1880–5, candidate Liverpool Exchange 1885, M.P. Galway 1886  131

O'Shea, Katherine ('Kitty'), (d. 1912), wife of above 1867–90 (divorced) and, 1891, of C. S. Parnell; sister of Field-Marshall Sir Evelyn Wood  131

Pakington, Sir John Somerset (1799–1880), Bt 1846 (*né* Russell); 1st B. Hampton 1874; country gentleman; candidate 1832, 1833, 1835; M.P. Droitwich 1837–74x; S.S. Cols *1852; Ady 1858–9, 1866–7; S.S. War 1867–8; 1st Civil Service Commissioner  63, 86

Palmerston, Henry John *Temple* (1784–1865), 3rd V. (I.); M.P. 1807–65; Tory minister 1807–28 (in cabinet 1827–8, resigned with Huskisson); Whig S.S. Foreign 1830–4, 1835–41, 1846–51 dismissed; S.S. Home 1852–5; P.M. 1855–8, 1859–65  8, 10, 19, 29, 37, 63, 66–8, 71, 73, 126, 143, 147, 148

Parkes, Joseph (1796–1865), of Birmingham; parliamentary solicitor & Liberal organiser  45

Parnell, Chas Stewart (1846–91), Home Rule M.P. Co. Meath 1875–80, Cork 1880–91; Ldr Irish Nationalist M.P.s 1879–90 when ousted over O'Shea divorce  107, 117–18, 123, 130–1

Passfield, Sidney Jas *Webb* (1859–1947), 1st B. 1929; civil servant 1878–91; a founder Fabian Society 1885; L.C.C. member 1892–1910; historian; M.P. (Labour) Seaham Harbour 1922–9; P.B.T. *1924; S.S. Dominions & Cols 1929–30, Cols 1930–1  19, 235

PEEL, SIR ROBERT (1788–1850), 2nd Bt 1830, Harrow & Christ Church, Oxford (University M.P. 1817–29x); 'double first' in classics & mathematics 1808; M.P. Cashel 1809–12, Chippenham 1812–17, Westbury 1829–30, Tamworth 1830–50; jr War & Cols 1810–12; Ch.S. 1812–18 ('Orange Peel'); S.S. Home 1822–7, 1828–30; Ldr C. 1828–30; Leader of Commons Opposition 1830–4, 1835–41; P.M. 1841–6; founder of Conservative Party and its official leader 1834–46  37–57. Also 1, 6, 7, 10–14, 16–18, 20–1, 25, 29–30, 60–2, 65, 69, 81–2, 84, 92, 98, 103, 118, 126, 139, 168, 195, 247

Peel, Gen. (1854) Jonathan (1799–1879), brother of above; M.P. Norwich 1826–31, Huntingdon 1831–68; a minister 1841–6; S.S. War 1858–9, 1866–7 resigned  74, 75, 86

Peelites  61–3, 67, 70–1, 84, 97–8, 102, 122, 126 (See also Aberdeen, Argyll, Gladstone, Graham, Herbert, Lincoln.)

Pelling, Henry Matheson (b. 1920), Cambridge don, Labour historian  32

Percy, Lord Eustace Sutherland Campbell (1887–1958), 1st B. Percy of Newcastle 1953 (where Rector of King's College 1937–52); diplomatic service; M.P. Hastings 1921–37; jr Education 1923, Health 1923–4; Ed. P. *1924–9; Msp 1935–6  224, 252

Pitt, William (1759–1806), Ch.Exr 1782–3; P.M. 1784–1801, 1804–6; his competing 'Tory' heirs were Castlereagh & Canning  21, 36, 186

Praed, Winthrop Mackworth (1802–39), poet and promising politician; M.P. St Germans 1830–ix, Yarmouth 1835–7, Aylesbury 1837–9; jr India 1834–5 47

Pretyman, Capt. Ernest Geo. (1860–1931), M.P. Woodbridge 1895–1906, Chelmsford Dec 1908–23; jr Admy 1900–5 & 1916–Jan 1919, Bd Trade 1915–16; P.C. 1917   185

Richmond and Lennox, Chas Gordon *Lennox* (1791–1860), 4th d. of 1818; ultra-Tory P.M.G. *1830–4 (resigned) under the Whig Grey; President, Agricultural Protection Society 1845   54, 60

Richmond and Lennox, Chas Henry (1818–1903), 6th d. of 1860 (& 1st d. of Gordon 1876); as e. of March M.P. Sussex W. 1841–60; P.P.L. *1859, P.B.T. 1867–8, 1885, L.P.C. 1874–80, S.Sc 1885–6; Ldr Conservative Opposition in Lords 1870–4, Ldr L. 1874–6   75, 86, 90

Ripon, Hon. Fredk John Robinson (1782–1859), 1st e. of 1833 (V. Goderich 1827); M.P. 1806–27; jr 1809, 1810–12; P.C. 1812, P.B.T. *1818, Ch.Exr 1823–7, S.S. War & Cols 1827 and Ldr C., P.M. Sep 1827–Jan 1828; resigned from Wellington's govt as a Canningite 1828 & from Grey's (S.S. War & Cols 1830–3, L.P.S. 1833–4) as a Stanleyite; P.B.T. 1841–3, Ind. P. 1843–6 59, 60

Ritchie, Chas Thomson (1838–1906), 1st B. of Dundee 1905; M.P. Tower Hamlets 1874–85 & St George's division thereof 1885–92x, Croydon 1895–1905; jr Admy 1885–6; P.L.G. 1886–92, P.B.T. 1895–1900, S.S. Home 1900–2, Ch.Exr 1902–3 resigned (Unionist Free Trader)   135, 161–3

Robbins, Lionel Chas (b. 1898), B. 1959 (life peer); professor of economics London 1929–61, economic section War Cabinet 1941–5   233

Roberts, F.-Marshal Sir Fdk Sleigh (1832–1914) V.C., 1st Bt 1881, 1st B. 1892, 1st e. 1901; C.-in-C., S. Africa 1899–1900, & of H.M.'s Forces 1901–4; champion of national service and friend of Ulster Protestants   146–7

Rose, Sir Philip (1816–83), 1st Bt 1874; treasurer of county courts 1858–83 98

Rosebery, Archibald Philip *Primrose* (1847–1929), 5th e. of 1868; Lib. jr 1881, first S. Sc 1884, *L.P.S. 1885; S.S. Foreign 1886, 1892–4; P.M. 1894–5; first chairman L.C.C. 1889; Ldr Liberal Party 1894–9; Liberal Imperialist 139–40, 144

Rothermere, Harold Sidney *Harmsworth* (1868–1940), 1st Bt 1910, 1st B. 1914, 1st V. 1919; newspaper owner, bro. of Ld Northcliffe; President, Air Council Nov 1917–Apr 1918   222, 227–8, 232

Rothschild, Lionel Nathan de (1808–79), Baron of Austrian Empire, elected Lib. M.P. City of London from 1847 & sat 1858–74   83

Rowton   *see* Corry

Runciman, Sir Walter (1870–1949), 1st Bt 1906, 2nd B. 1933, 1st V. 1937; Lib M.P. 1899–1900, 1902–18x, 1924–9, St Ives 1929–37 (Lib. Nat. from 1931); jr 1905–8, cabinet 1908–16; shipowner, rail director, banker; P.B.T. Nov 1931–May 1937, L.P.C. Oct 1938–Sep 1939   179, 239, 243, 245–6

Russell, Lord John (1792–1878), 1st e. 1861; prominent Whig; minister 1830, cabinet 1831–4, Ldr C. 1835–41; Ldr Opposition 1841–6, 1852; P.M 1846–52; Ldr C. 1852–5 (under Aberdeen) resigned; S.S. Cols 1855 resigned; S.S. Foreign 1859–65; P.M. 1865–6   41, 53–5, 60, 63, 65, 67, 68, 70, 71, 77, 79, 83

Rutland, Chas C. J. *Manners* (1815–88), 6th d. of 1857; as mss of Granby M.P. Stamford 1837–52, Leics. N. 1852–7; titular Ldr Protectionist M.P.s 1848 83–4

Rutland, Lord John J. R. *Manners* (1818–1906), 7th d. of 1888; bro. of above; M.P. Newark 1841–7 ('Young England'), Colchester 1850–7, Leics. N. 1857–85, Melton 1885–8; Wks *1852, 1858–9, 1866–8, P.M.G. 1874–80, 1885–6, Ch.D. 1886–92   63, 81, 83, 86, 90

Sadler, Michael Thomas (1780–1835), M.P. Newark & Aldeboro 1829–32; defeated Leeds 1832 (by Macaulay), Huddersfield 1834; Tory humanitarian 61

St Leonards, Sir Edwd B. *Sugden* (1781–1875), 1st B. 1852; M.P. 1826–32x, 1837–41; S.-G. 1829–30; L.C. (I.) 1835, 1841–6; L.C. *1852 63

Salisbury *see* Cecil

Salvidge, Sir (1916) Archibald T. J. (1863–1928), Liverpool brewer, councillor and party organiser; P.C. 1920 28–9, 187, 189, 192

Samuel, Sir (1920) Herbert Louis (1870–1963), 1st V. 1937; Lib. M.P. 1920–18x & 1929–35x (Darwen); jr 1905–9; P.C. 1908; cabinet 1909–16; High Comr Palestine 1920–5; Chairman Lib. Party Orgn 1927–9; Deputy-Ldr Lib. M.P.s 1929–31 (acting leader 1931 crisis); S.S. Home 1931–2 resigned; Ldr Parly Lib. Pty 1931–5; Ldr Lib. peers 1944–55 211–14, 233–7, 239–45

Sandars, John Satterfield (1853–1934), p/s to Matthews 1886–92 & Balfour 1892–1905; P.C. 1905 173

Sandon, Dudley F. S. *Ryder* (1831–1900), V., 3rd e. of Harrowby 1882; Lib. M.P. Lichfield 1856–9, Cons M.P. Liverpool 1868–82; Ed. V.-P. 1874–8, P.B.T. *1878–80, L.P.S. 1885–6 92

Sankey, John (1866–1948), 1st B. 1929, 1st V. 1932; judge 1914–29; L.C. *1929–35 (Lab. & then Nat. Lab.) 211, 234

Selborne, William Waldegrave *Palmer* (1859–1942), 2nd e. of 1895; son of Lib. L.C. (Unionist 1886) & son-in-law (1883) of 3rd mss of Salisbury; as Ld Wolmer M.P. Hants E. 1885–92 (Lib. & then Unionist), Edinburgh C. 1892–5; jr Cols 1895–1900; Ady *Nov 1900–Dec 1905; High Comr S. Africa 1905–10; P.B.A. May 1915–July 1916 resigned 148, 181

Shaftesbury, Anthony *Ashley Cooper* (1801–85), 7th e. of 1851; as V. Ashley M.P. Woodstock 1826–30, Dorchester 1830–1x, Dorset 1831–46 resigned (Free Trader), Bath 1846–51; leading Evangelical, philanthropist and Tory social reformer 16, 70

Sibthorp, Col. Chas de Laet Waldo- (1783–1855), M.P. Lincoln 1835–55; squire and diehard Protectionist 61

Simon, Sir (1910) John Allsebrook (1873–1954), 1st V. 1940; Lib. M.P. 1906–18x & 1922–40 (Spen Valley; from 1931 Lib. Nat.); S.-G. 1910–13, A.-G. *1913 15, S.S. Home 1915 16 resigned; Chairman, Lib. Nat. M.P.s 1931–45; S.S. Foreign 1931–5, Home 1935–7; Ch.Exr 1937–40; L.C. 1940–5 233, 239–41, 243, 245–6

Smith, William Henry (1825–91), newsagent; M.P. Westminster 1868–85, Strand 1885–91; F.S.T. 1874–7, Ady *1877–80 ('ruler of the Queen's navee'); S.S. War 1885 6, 1886 7, Ch.S. Jan 1886; 1st Lord of Treasury & Ldr C. 1887–91 6, 94, 102, 110, 112–13, 122, 127–31, 133–6

Smythe, Hon. George A.F.P.S. (1818–57), 7th V. Strangford, 1855; M.P. Canterbury 1841–52 ('Young England' and later Peelite); jr Foreign Jan 1845–6; writer for *Morning Chronicle*; fought last English duel 1852 63, 81, 82

Snowden, Philip (1864–1937), 1st V. 1931; Lab. M.P. Blackburn 1906–18x, Colne Valley 1922–31; Ch.Exr *1924, 1929–31 (when Nat. Lab.), L.P.S. 1931–2 resigned (Free Trader) 208, 215, 229, 234–45

Somerset, Lord Granville C.H. (1792–1848), M.P. Monmouthshire 1818–48; jr Whip in office 1819–30 & party supervisor in opposition from 1830; minister & P.C. 1834; Ch.D. *1841–6 45

Spofforth, Markham (1825–1907), for twenty years Conservative principal agent; senior taxing master, Chancery, from 1876 45, 98

Stanhope, Hon Edward (1840–93), M.P. Mid-Lincs. 1874–85, Horncastle 1885–93; jr India 1878–80; chairman party organisation committee 1882; Ed. V.-P. 1885, P.B.T. *1885–6, S.S. Cols 1886–7, S.S. War 1887–92 113

STANLEY, EDWD GEO. GEOFFREY SMITH (1799–1869), 14th EARL OF DERBY 1851;
Eton & Christ Church, Oxford (University Chancellor 1852–69), as Mr
Stanley & (from 1834) Lord Stanley, M.P. 1820–44 (when peer as B.
Stanley) successively for Stockbridge, Preston, Windsor & Lancs. N.; jr Whip under
Canning 1827, jr War & Cols under Goderich 1827–8; under Grey Ch.S.
1830–3 (*1831) & S.S. War & Cols Apr 1833–May 1834 resigned. Moved via
independence ('The Derby Dilly') to Conservative Party. S.S. Cols 1841–Dec
1845; Ldr Protectionist peers 1846. Failed to form govt 1851. P.M. Feb–Dec
1852, Mar 1858–June 1859, July 1866–Feb 1868   58–80. Also 2, 4, 6, 8–11,
13, 14, 23, 24, 41, 42, 45, 53, 82–4, 87, 90, 118, 247, 252
Stanley, Edward Henry (1826–93), 15th e. of Derby, son of above; M.P. Lynn
1848–69; jr Foreign 1852; S.S. Cols *Feb–May 1858, last Ind. P. & first S.S.
India 1858–9; S.S. Foreign 1866–8, 1874–8 resigned. Moved via independence to Lib. Party. S.S. Cols 1882–5. Unionist 1886   8, 10, 29, 59, 64, 71–2,
85–7, 90–6
Stanley, Col. Hon. Fredk Arthur (1841–1908), 16th e. of Derby; brother of
above; cr. B. Stanley 1886; M.P. Preston 1865–8, Lancs. N. 1868–85,
Blackpool 1885–6; jr Admy 1868, War 1874–7, F.S.T. 1877–8, S.S. War
*1878–80; Ed. V.-P. 1885; S.S. Cols 1885–6; P.B.T. 1886–8; G.-G. Canada
1888–93; Chancellor, Oxford University 1907   95
Stanley, Edwd Geo. Villiers (1865–1948), 17th e. of Derby, son of above; M.P.
Westhoughton 1892–1906x; jr Whip 1895–1900, jr War 1900–3, P.M.G.
*1903–5; U.-S.S. War 1915; S.S. War 1916–18, 1922–4; ambassador Paris
1918–20   29, 173, 175, 183, 187, 204, 230
Stanley, Capt Edwd Montagu Cavendish (1894–1938), heir of above & elder
bro. of Oliver Stanley (1896–1950). Lord Stanley was M.P. Liverpool
Abercromby 1917–18 & Fylde 1922–38; jr Whip 1924–7; deputy-chairman
Conservative Party Organisation 1927–9 and Chairman Junior Imperial
League 1927–38; jr Admy 1931–5 & 1935–7 & Dominions June–Nov 1935
& India–Burma May 1937–May 1938; S.S. Dominions *May–Oct 1938
223
Steel-Maitland, Sir Arthur Herbert Drummond Ramsey (1876–1935), 1st Bt
1917, né Steel; Fellow of All Souls'; Birmingham M.P. 1910–29, Tamworth
1929–35; first Chairman Conservative Party Organisation 1911–16; U.-S.S.
Cols May 1915–17, jr Foreign Trade Sep 1917–Apr 1919; M. Labour *1924–9
28, 222
Stewart, Robert, historian, author of The Politics of Protection (1971)   62, 247,
252
Strachey, E. John St Loe (1901–63), M.P. 1929–31x (Labour & then Mosley's
'New Party'), 1945–63 (Lab.); Marxist writer in 1930s; minister 1945–51   222
Swinton   see Cunliffe-Lister
Symons, Julian Gustave (b. 1912), author, inter alia, of The General Strike
(1957)   215

Taylor, Vice-Adm. Sir (1952) Ernest Augustus (1876–1972), M.P. (Empire
Crusader & later Conservative) Paddington S. 1930–50   230
Thomas, James Henry (1874–1949); National Union of Railwaymen; M.P.
Derby 1910–36 (Labour to 1931 when Nat. Lab.); P.C. 1917; S.S. Cols *1924,
Aug–Nov 1931, Nov 1935–May 1936; L.P.S. 1929–30; S.S. Dominions June
1930–Nov 1935   212–13 215, 229, 234, 238–40, 246
Topping, Sir (1934) H. Robert (1877–1952), party organiser Dublin 1904–11,
S. Wales 1911–23, Lancs & Cheshire 1924–8; Principal Agent Feb 1928–
Feb 1931 & then General Director 1931–45 at Conservative Central Office
223, 228, 231

Trevelyan, Sir George Otto (1838–1938), 2nd Bt, 1886; Lib. M.P. 1865–97 (briefly Lib. Unionist 1866–7); jr 1869–70, 1880–3, Ch.S. 1882–4, Ch.D. *1884–5; S.Sc. 1886 resigned & 1892–5; O.M. 1911    123

Victoria (1819–1901) reigned 1837–1901    20, 45, 69, 73–4, 78, 85, 87, 89, 92, 97, 106, 108, 115–16, 122, 125, 128, 134–5, 139–41, 145, 148

Walpole, Sir Robert (1676–1745), Whig politician, P.M. 1722–42    198
Walpole, Spencer Horatio (1806–98), M.P. Midhurst 1846 (Protectionist) 1856, Cambridge University 1856–82; S.S. Home *1852, 1858–9 resigned, 1866–7 resigned    63, 84
Walter, John (1776–1847), chief proprietor (manager-editor 1803–16) of *The Times*; independent-minded and humanitarian M.P. Berkshire 1832–7, Nottingham 1841–2; defeated Southwark 1840    81
Waterhouse, Lt-Col. Sir (1923) Ronald D. (1878–1942); p/s to Law 1920–1, A. Chamberlain 1921, H.R.H. d. of York 1921–2; principal p/s to premiers 1922–8    201
WELLINGTON, HON. ARTHUR RICHARD *Wellesley* (1769–1852), 1st DUKE OF, 1814 (Maj.Gen 1802, K.C.B. 1804, Lt-Gen. 1808, 1st V. 1809, 1st e. 1812, 1st mss 1812, Field-Marshal 1813); M.P. (Irish) 1790–5, (U.K.) 1806–9; P.C. & Ch. S. 1807–9; Master-Gen. Ordinance *1818–27 resigned, C.-in-C. 1827 resigned Apr, Aug 1827–Feb 1828, 1842–52; P.M. Jan 1828–Nov 1830, acting P.M. Nov–Dec 1834; S.S. Foreign 1834–5; Msp & Ldr L. 1841–6; Chancellor, Oxford University 1834–52    35–42. Also 13, 43, 45, 48, 61, 65, 247
Wemyss & March, Francis *Wemyss-Charteris* (1818–1914), 10th e. of 1883; as Mr Charteris & from 1853 as Ld Elcho M.P. Glos. E. 1841–Feb 1846 resigned (Peelite), Haddingtonshire 1847–83; jr Whip 1853–55; extreme opponent of state intervention, author of *Socialism at St. Stephens* 1869–85 etc    20
William IV (1765–1837) reigned 1830–7    38, 41
Wilson, F.-Marshal (1919) Sir Henry Hughes (1864–1922), Chief of Impl Genl Staff Feb 1918–Feb 1922; Ulster Unionist M.P. 1922, assassinated    183, 190
Wilson, Lt-Col. Sir (1923) Leslie Orme (1876–1955), M.P. Reading 1913–22, Portsmouth S. 1922–3; jr Shipping 1919–21; Chief Whip Apr 1921 July 1923; P.C. 1922; G. Bombay 1923 8    193, 199
Wolff, Sir (1878) Henry Drummond (1830–1908), M.P. Christchurch 1874–80, Portsmouth 1880–5x, after diplomatic service; member of 'Fourth Party' 1880; re-entered diplomacy 1885    95–6, 114
Wolseley, Field-Marshal Sir Garnet Joseph (1833–1913), 1st B. 1882, 1st V. 1885; commanded Egypt 1882, Souday 1884–5; C.-in-C. 1895–1900    137–8
Wyndham, Lt-Col. Hon. George (1863–1913), M.P. Dover 1889–1913; p/s & then P.P.S. to Balfour as Ch.S. 1887–91; jr War 1898–1900; Ch.S. 1900 (*Aug 1902)–Mar 1905 resigned    121, 174

Young, Geo. Fredk, Protectionist organiser, M.P. Tynemouth 1851–2x    63
Young, Geo. Malcolm (1882–1959) Oxford historian, biographer of Baldwin 98–9, 248, 251, 253
Younger, Sir George (1851–1929) 1st Bt 1911, 1st B. of Leckie 1923; brewer, banker, rail director; M.P. Ayr Burghs 1906–23; Chairman Conservative & Unionist Orgn 1916–23, treasurer thereof 1923–9    25, 183, 189, 199